April 27TH 2002

To Charles W. Johnson,
My mentor and friend

Contents

Acknowledgments

Although writing is a solitary enterprise, an author rarely produces anything without the assistance of others. Such is the case with this book.

I am grateful for the resourceful assistance of the respective staffs of three excellent archives. The Mighty Eighth Air Force Library and Archives in Savannah, Georgia, is a treasure trove of veteran's memoirs, letters, and diaries.

The World War II letters housed in the Western Historical Manuscript Collection at the University of Missouri constitute one of the single best sources for anyone wishing to gain insight into the mindset of those Americans who fought the war. I sincerely appreciate all of the guidance and support provided by the staffs of the Columbia and St. Louis Branches of the WHMC.

The Special Collections Library at the University of Tennessee, home to an extensive archive of World War II material, may be the best single source in existence on individual Americans in World War II. The collection is the product of years of work by the staff at the university's Center for the Study of War and Society.

I would like to thank E. J. McCarthy, Presidio's patient and amiable executive editor, not only for his expertise, from which this book has greatly benefited, but also for his friendship.

Russell Buhite provided valuable advice on how best to research a book like this. His guidance has made me a better author and a better person. The same goes for Charles Johnson, who helped inspire in me a deep and abiding curiosity about Americans in World War II.

My mother-in-law and father-in-law, Ruth and Nelson Woody, have never ceased to be understanding in welcoming a World War II obsessed son-in-law into their family. I am also grateful to my own family—my brother Mike, my sister Nancy, and especially my parents Mike and Mary Jane. Without their love and support, this book could not have been written. They have my enduring thanks and often make me realize how lucky I am. Special gratitude goes to my indulgent wife Nancy. Her patience with a husband who is sometimes absorbed in other worlds, and her constant sense of humor are but two of her many great qualities. She is the best thing that has ever happened to me.

Perhaps my greatest debt of gratitude should go to the veterans themselves, the young men of yesteryear who jumped into their planes and flew the missions that ensured freedom for untold generations. At heart this book is theirs. They have welcomed me and treated me as one of their own. There is no greater honor.

Introduction

Once I was part of world history in the making. My presence and participation in this epic event was definitely microscopic. But, with so many others like me, all such microscopic bits were forged into an over-all effort which, in retrospect, appears to be all but unbelievable today.

—J. Fred Baumann, fighter pilot, 52d Fighter Group

Engines roared in the misty, predawn air at an American airbase. One by one, young Americans maneuvered their lethal flying machines into position for takeoff. As the sun emerged over the eastern horizon, burning away layers of mist and fog, the first plane careened down the runway and lifted into the air. Another plane followed, quickly followed by one after the other until every plane had left the safety of the ground—heading, ultimately, for the horror and danger of enemy airspace. In a few minutes their shapes grew increasingly faint until they became mere specks in the sky dancing and blending with clouds and rays of sunlight. In another moment they were gone, off to face the day's unknown peril, some to return unscathed, others to return bloodied and damaged, still others never to return. This drama was repeated thousands upon thousands of times during World War II among American combat airmen all over the world. It occurred from places as familiar as Norwich (England), Paris (France), and Foggia (Italy) to such exotic locales as Henderson Field (Guadalcanal), Piardoba (India), or Saipan in the Mariana Islands.

For the young American men aboard those planes, the war—life, really—consisted of flying their missions until they were either shot down or had finished enough missions or combat hours to complete a tour of duty. Some had a better chance of surviving than others but, when flying their first combat mission, none of them really knew for certain if they would ever complete their tours and go home again. This was true for every American combat airman in World War II, no matter whether he negotiated the dangerous daytime skies over Germany, the eerie and perilous nighttime skies of Japan, or the comparatively tranquil skies of the Central and South Pacific. The same uncertainty held true for everyone. Would today's mission be the day that luck ran out? Or would it be tomorrow? Or would the luck ever run out? Could the verdict be influenced by bravery, competence, or some kind of personal talisman? Every combat airman lived with these questions and, either consciously or unconsciously, struggled to answer them.

The potential for disaster was real and terrifying. Planes often collided in midair, plunging to the earth in flames, in the process incinerating their occupants. Some, burdened with heavy loads of bombs and fuel, malfunctioned and crashed on takeoff and were consumed by fire. Enemy fighters or antiaircraft shot down thousands of American planes, often killing airmen in the process. The best an American airman could hope for upon being shot down was to escape and evade the enemy, a process that usually took months or even years of endured privation. The more likely outcome was capture—an unwelcome and unpleasant prospect in the European theater and a dreaded, almost unthinkable prospect in the Pacific, where the Japanese routinely tortured and starved prisoners.

In spite of these dangers, hundreds of thousands of young Americans volunteered to be combat airmen. In fact, almost all combat airmen were volunteers. Indeed, most of those who ended up flying in combat were eager to do so and had worked extremely hard to achieve that status. Upon entering combat, the vast majority endured to the end of their missions or until they were shot down. It was quite rare for a combat airman to turn in his wings and refuse to fly in combat. Why did they so readily endure such horror and life-threatening danger? Pride and comradeship. American combat airmen in World War II had a pride in their training (most had successfully negotiated at least one year of intense training) and their ability to do the job. These traits made them competent in combat and often brought them comfort in the midst of mortal danger. More important, though, they endured all of this for each other. The intense danger of aerial combat in World War II and the teamwork required to survive forged a bond of deep and abiding brotherhood among American combat airmen.

Their story has never been adequately told. Tales of the Eighth Air Force abound, but what of those who flew in other theaters, most notably the Fifth Air Force in New Guinea or the various fighter and bomb groups in the China-Burma-India theater? It is important that the story of America's combat airmen—whether Navy or Marine pilots, Army Air Force bomber crews or fighter pilots—be told collectively.

Each and every one of them experienced the war differently. Correspondingly, they carried their own unique views and descriptions of those experiences. Wesley Wells, a ball turret gunner in the 379th Bomb Group, certainly found this to be true in talking to his buddies after missions: "Everyone on a crew may see the same mission . . . in a whole other light and possibly each member of a crew . . . might perfectly honestly give you a different story according to their perspective."

Although they understood their daily purpose far better than their ground-combat comrades, American combat airmen cared little for the big-picture, grand-strategy view of the generals. Like all combat men, theirs was a war of individual survival or death. Everything else was secondary. Most of the history of World War II has been written from the perspective of those at the top, so it is of overwhelming importance to hear the stories of those who carried out the orders. Only then can we understand what the war was really like and what kind of effect it had on those who had to fight it.

Elmer Bendiner, a pilot in the 379th Bomb Group, explained this fact very well: "I am driven to the conclusion that generals do not necessarily share the same war with lieutenants and sergeants. To expect otherwise, I suppose, is to imagine that horse and rider experience the same sensations during the gallop. An ordinary soldier judges whether an engagement has been tough by the effects on himself and on the men he knows. He fights in a narrow space barely big enough for his own terrors and triumphs. That other

larger battle of gains and losses, victories and defeats, is something
he reads about."

Robert Ramer, a 20th Air Force pilot who flew bombing missions
over Japan, underscored this point: "I don't think anybody was
thinking about the overall picture of what we were accomplishing at
our level. In the movies you see somebody like Gregory Peck lec-
turing a crew about the significance of what they are doing. Keeping the world free, part of the big picture, that sort of thing. I don't
remember any of that at all. At our level we were into pranks and
jokes. Things that to this day I'm ashamed of."

Radioman Merle Perkins of the 483d Bomb Group recalled that,
upon learning that he was keeping a journal of his war experiences,
one of his buddies urged him to write about the truth of what he saw
and not the glory-filled skies and grand causes of generals and
politicians: "Go for the realism. Tell it like it is or not at all! Give
your readers lots of blood and guts. Show us bleeding, body, mind,
and soul! Stress the emotions. Make the truth read like a novel!"

Historians are often just as guilty as generals and correspon-
dents in speaking of battles and casualties in detached terms. In
some World War II books, "grand victories" are won at an "acceptable cost" or with "light casualties." To those who did the fighting,
victories were important but usually not as important as survival;
casualties were never light or acceptable because they meant the
death, wounding, and captivity of friends. As Perkins put it,
"These were not just men. They were friends or acquaintances;
players on squadron football, baseball, and softball teams; drinking buddies; participants in dialogues at mess . . . and worry warts
between missions."

Jule Berndt, a navigator in the 490th Bomb Group, was moved
enough by the death of a buddy to sit down and write about the human cost of war in his diary: "Tonight they are removing his personal effects from our hut. A few days ago he was like you and I are,
filled with life, now he is no more. His name will appear eventually
on a list with a lot of other fellows just like him. Probably thousands
of people will read it, but what will it mean to them—probably nothing more than another name. Do they realize the story that lies behind that simple announcement? Can they visualize his wife when

she receives the telegram bearing that simple but most tragic message: 'The army regrets to inform you that your husband has been killed in action.' So few words but so meaningful. It means that another wife must start life anew without the presence of the man with whom she promised to go through life. It means another son or daughter will never see their father. It means another young man will never be able to do the many things you and I do everyday."

Not surprisingly, combat airmen often grew incensed at the trivialization of tragedy. Willis Marshall, a top turret gunner in the 389th Bomb Group, recalled one such instance in which a plane close to his took a direct flak hit: "It folded like a book with the left wing wrapping up around the doomed aircraft and it plunged to earth in a blaze. The next day this . . . picture . . . appeared in the *Stars and Stripes* and was labeled 'Blaze of Glory.' What glory, there were 11 young men in that blaze." Gerald Rose, a pilot in the 384th Bomb Group, underscored the often-forgotten point that, "Even if you lose one plane out of a hundred, to the guys in that one it may as well have been a hundred." Reading the official account of his squadron's battle experiences fifty-three years later, he bristled at a description of a mission to Merseburg as "uneventful." He and his crew endured intense flak over the target and were hit repeatedly. One burst flipped the plane on its side and Rose was not able to get it under control until it had plunged several thousand feet. They fell out of formation and limped home, fortunate no German fighters found them. Perhaps the mission was only uneventful for those who were not there. Wesley Wells also noticed this tendency of official history toward detachment: "When I read the Official Mission Reports, the missions don't seem as dangerous as they looked from my vantage point in the ball turret."

Truthfully, the war Wells and his comrades describe is far closer to reality than the war of official histories. Combat airmen, who experienced the life-and-death drama of war every day, knew that many of the descriptions of war they read at the time or later were, at best, hyperbole, and at worst, fabrications. John Marshall, a fighter pilot in the 404th Fighter Group, wrote to his father and expressed his opinions of wartime newspaper accounts: "We here merely chuckle at half of what we read. What comes out of a printing machine as a 'smashing advance supported by great air superiority' is something which is never as complete and easy as it sounds." Only those Americans who experienced it can truly tell the story of air combat in World War II.

Tom Prior, a pilot in the 457th Bomb Group, wrote to his brother and tried, through a sports analogy, to express something of the realities of air combat from his perspective: "The referee over here is the greatest referee of all—He is God. In our game we can't even lose one game, there's no such thing as a tie score, no such thing as a sub, you play each game to the finish. You either win or else! Their [the Germans'] job is to get you out of the game, fair means or foul—usually the latter . . . not for five minutes, five days . . . they aren't satisfied till you're out of the game forever."

Combat airmen understood that war in the air meant killing or being killed every bit as much as it did for their ground-combat counterparts. Even so, the war in the air had a somewhat detached quality to it. Kenneth Jones, a pilot in the 389th Bomb Group, expressed this sentiment in a memoir he wrote long after the war: "Our aerial view of World War II was almost devoid of mud and the sight of blood. It was a clean war in one respect, we saw only one returning aircraft unloading dead and wounded [the majority of casualties went down over the target, never returning to base]. Mostly we saw a lot of flak aimed at us, bombers on fire—trailing smoke or going down in flames—or simply blowing up in small pieces. You returned from a mission to fly another day or you just didn't come back."

Combat in the air usually meant leaving the security and relative comfort of the base and sallying forth into danger. This struck some, like Terrence McArron, a pilot in the 401st Bomb Group, as an odd sort of war: "I often thought of the strangeness of our existence; up early, face the danger for a few hours, back to a secure and comfortable base with club facilities where you might enjoy a cocktail, music, a card game or a movie, then off for a few hours' sleep and start the cycle again. It was for the most part, a totally impersonal war where you seldom saw the enemy, or the destruction you delivered, unless you were unlucky enough to engage in close air-to-air combat, or be shot down."

Ray Zuker, a pilot in the 486th Bomb Group, pointed out that, in spite of their luxuries back at base, combat airmen dealt with their own brand of hell in battle: "Our field of battle was in the thin cold air of 25,000 feet. There we did not contend with land mines and barbed wire. Our misery was German anti-aircraft fire, including the terrible and infamous German 88M cannon. Along with the cold and flak, [an] Me-109 fighter would appear, boring in from 12:00 with cannon firing. When one of our bombers was mortally wounded she would fall to earth leaving a plume of smoke marking her path."

Still, most combat airmen knew they had a good existence compared to those fighting the war on the ground. Vince Cahill, a bombardier in the 491st Bomb Group, expressed this sentiment in a letter to his family: "We've got a good deal here. After a hard day's work one can come back to warm barracks, get good hot food, and get a good warm bed. The towns are nearby and there is enough to keep us busy."

Many American veterans of the air war in World War II have marveled at how young and how different they were in those days. To them, the war seems like another lifetime ago. Robert Bieck of the 453d Bomb Group described himself as "adventurous and a true believer in the war and terribly naive. I had absolutely no difficulty equating my obvious role with what was expected of me—none whatsoever." James Goodson, a fighter pilot who flew with the U.S. 4th Fighter Group, had also served for two years as an American volunteer in the Royal Air Force prior to American entry into the war. "I'd describe myself as serious, enthusiastic, committed, with no doubts about the justice of our cause. Today I would possibly be called naive." Ask a combat veteran to describe himself during his days in the service and you will often hear the word "naive" enter the description. It is a word elderly veterans often associate with youth and, in the 1940s, those who flew combat missions on behalf of the United States usually were very young. This was certainly true for Wayne Rothgeb, a fighter pilot who flew with the 35th Fighter Group in New Guinea: "We were 20 to 24 years old and the love of flying was our common bond. The fact that death could be minutes away never seemed to bother anyone. Flying, fighting, and living together . . . welded us into a comradeship that is still strong over fifty years later." Charles Brown, a pilot in the 379th Bomb Group, wrote of the overwhelming need to grow up quickly in the deadly skies he encountered over Europe as part of the famous Eighth Air Force: "As boys, we were quickly and rudely thrust into manhood in a most dramatic, although unwelcome manner. Before our missions were completed, we learned that during our combat period, valor was a way of life. We also learned that our two primary objectives were to do our job well and survive. Unfortunately, they had to be pursued in that precise order of priority."

R. H. Tays, also a pilot, flew with the 392d Bomb Group. He encapsulated very well what he and his comrades were like and the task they faced: "I was 23 years old with five of my crew only 18. We were young, inexperienced, and had volunteered for this duty and were anxious to destroy the enemy or his will to fight. Uncle Sam had spent hundreds of thousands of dollars to train us and had enough confidence in us to give us an airplane to do the job. This was pretty heddy [sic] stuff to live with, but it . . . reinforced our confidence to be able to bomb assigned targets with accuracy, fight off the fighters, flak, and weather and return to base to fly again the following day. So long as I live the mental attitude of flight crew members, all of whom had volunteered, is one of the most profound and awesome forces I have ever witnessed."

Indeed, most American World War II combat veterans saw the war, terrible as it was, as a special and defining time, but one that could never and should never be repeated. Robert Bieck summed up the feelings of many in relation to the war: "We could never do that again. Society as a whole would rebel against it. Today I am appalled at the enormous cost to our nation, yet we accepted it almost without a murmur. It was the thing to do."

The world these men fought to preserve changed greatly over the many decades following America's victory in 1945. As 31st Fighter Group pilot Robert Goebel explained, the awesome destruction of the war and the onset of nuclear weapons made his generation's total war a thing of the past: "We are a dying breed . . . and soon we will all be gone. I suppose there are those who will say,

'Good riddance,' not referring to us as individuals but to us as symbols of a barbaric and destructive way of settling disputes."

The one element that will remain among America's World War II combat airmen is their memories of their experiences. That will never change. For most of them, the war was the single most important and formative experience of their lives and, like it or not, their memories could never really be expunged. Ray Zuker knew that his days piloting a B-17 over Germany had changed him forever: "There are younger-day experiences that leave no impression on us, and there are experiences that reach our inner cores, marking us and changing us for the rest of our lives. War experiences usually mark us deep and permanently change our attitudes and outlooks on life." J. Fred Baumann, a fighter pilot in the 52d Fighter Group, was amazed at the level and clarity of detail he could conjure up when he sat down to write his wartime memoirs: "The most surprising facet of these attempts at recalling and composing this personal memoir was the manner in which so many of the incidents reappeared with such clarity of image, a seemingly never ending series of chain reactions in which one name, one photograph, one event, or one date would summon forth such all-but-forgotten memories, many of which were accompanied by fragments of their originally experienced emotions."

For most veterans, it was impossible to recollect the war without some degree of emotion, but as Quentin Aanenson, a fighter pilot in the 366th Fighter Group, explained, the excercise of remembering also sometimes served as a healing process: "It has been a traumatic experience for me to go back through all this. But perhaps . . . it has helped purge some of the devastating memories that have haunted me for almost 50 years." As difficult as it sometimes could be to write about his experiences as a navigator in the 381st Bomb Group, David McCarthy still found motivation to tell his story because he knew there was something special about his youthful days as a member of a bomber crew: "Those were the most exhilarating, frightening, gratifying, and downright *proud* [italics in original] days of my life. They were shared with some of the finest men ever assembled." John Crowe, a pilot in the 491st Bomb

Group, shared McCarthy's sense of comradeship as well as the feeling that what he did over the skies of Europe mattered in the grand scheme of things: "I am . . . deeply grateful for the bonds of friendship of the uncommon men who flew beside me in a common cause. We lifted up on silver wings through endless corridors of clouds, breaking out on top into a vast, silent, cold blue sky filled only with blinding sunlight and miles of snow-white contrails behind the whirling propellers of a thousand airplanes. We shared a lifetime of living in a few short days and it was one hell of a time while it lasted. For some, time ran out."

Why remember all this? What is the ultimate purpose of knowing and understanding the lives and experiences of America's combat airmen in World War II? Luther Smith, a fighter pilot in the famous 332d Fighter Group (usually referred to as "The Tuskegee Airmen"), hit upon the answer as he wrote about his wartime experiences: "There are thousands of stories just as amazing as mine. Future generations must never forget the unity and sacrifice that preserved our freedom."

1

Who Were These Combat Airmen?

Our Crew was a not so unique composite of young men brought together from scattered areas of the U.S. from Maine to California.
Our Crew represented 7 states and included young men from 19
years to 33 years old. We blended into a team that was concerned
about the well being of each member.
　　　　　　—David Redfern, waist gunner, 491st Bomb Group

They came from nearly every town, city, and state in America.
They were the sons of the elite, the impoverished, and everyone in between in 1940s America. By and large, they had one
thing in common, no matter their background or their region of
origin: They all volunteered to fight the war in the air against America's enemies in World War II. In order to achieve that goal, they
worked like demons and trained diligently to prove themselves and
earn the wings that would be their passport to combat. What did it
mean to be a combat airman in World War II? It meant that you either were part of a bomber crew or were a fighter pilot. That is how
the U.S. military classified its combat air personnel. Undoubtedly
the transport pilots who flew the Hump over the Himalayas in order
to supply China, or those who flew paratroopers into combat zones,
or the others who piloted glider troops to the battlefield resented
their status as noncombatants. After all, they were at times in as
much danger as fighter pilots and bomber crews. But their danger
was the exception rather than the rule. For every C-47 pilot braving
German flak to drop paratroopers into Normandy, there were many
more such pilots ferrying supplies in secure rear areas. For most
transport pilots, the main danger to life and limb was accidents. For
fighter pilots and bomber crews, accidents were but one of many
potential hazards, ranking a distant third behind enemy fighter

planes and antiaircraft fire. The vast majority of the 121,867 casualties, including 40,061 killed, the Army Air Force suffered in World War II was among fighter pilots and bomber crews. (The Air Force was part of the Army in World War II.) In the cases of the Navy and the Marines, almost all of the aviators who became casualties were fighter pilots, torpedo pilots, dive bomber pilots, or their accompanying crewmen. Clearly, airmen from the official combat arms had the most treacherous flying duty in the war.

Most of them were highly motivated, reasonably well-educated young men whose desire for air combat bordered on eagerness. They originated from no particular locale or region in any overwhelming quantities. Instead, they hailed from everywhere. In terms of social class and status, they generally had more advantages than their ground-combat counterparts but still cannot be thought of in any way as strictly products of America's elite classes. For example, when the Army researched the educational backgrounds of its entire population of enlisted men, it found that more than half had not completed high school. In the case of enlisted combat airmen, though, more than two-thirds had completed high school. Some had even attended or graduated from college. These men were better educated than enlisted men in other branches of the service, but most still did not possess that true measure of elite status in mid-twentieth-century America—a college degree.

In the first two years of American involvement in World War II, the Army carried out a deliberate policy to channel the men it thought of as bright, capable, and motivated into the Army Air Force. Later in the war, when the Air Force had far more pilot candidates than it could ever hope to train, and the Army brass realized it would need large numbers of bright, well-trained soldiers to win the war on the ground, such men were then channeled into Army Ground Forces. Still, the Army experienced its greatest growth during the first couple of years of the war and, even late in the war, the Air Force continued to receive more than its fair share of men deemed to be intelligent and motivated and thus essential to the war effort.

The Army's most far-reaching barometer for evaluating the millions of men who entered the service in the war years was the Army

General Classification Test, usually referred to as the AGCT. This test, given to all recruits, was a forty-minute written exam consisting of 150 multiple-choice questions designed to measure intelligence and general aptitude. Most recruits tried hard to score well on the test because they thought that a higher score would lead to a better Army job. In grading the tests, the Army devised five categories according to raw scores. Class I had a score of more than 130; Class II, between 110 and 129; Class III, 90 to 109; Class IV, 70 to 89; and Class V, 69 or lower. Army leaders put great stock in the results of the test and constantly battled one another to acquire as many high-scoring men as possible for their respective branches of the service. Although the AGCT could certainly be thought of as "culturally biased," and sometimes revealed more about a recruit's level of education and experience than his native intelligence, it nonetheless was still a reasonable barometer of the ability level of Army recruits.

Throughout the war, the Army Air Force received a high proportion of men who scored in Class I or Class II (those the Army evaluated as high-quality manpower). This pattern of top scorers ending up in the Air Force was especially true in 1942 and 1943. For example, 44 percent of the Air Force's replacements in 1942 had tested in Class I or II. Another 35 percent came from Class III. The numbers were roughly the same for 1943. The Air Force needed generous numbers of intelligent and skilled men to handle the rigorous challenge of operating high-performance, cutting-edge aircraft in combat. Only men between the ages of eighteen and twenty-seven were admitted for pilot, bombardier, and navigator training, and they had to be in perfect physical condition with especially keen eyesight. After that, they took rigorous physical and mental tests. Many of those who made it past those requirements were later rejected or "washed out" from pilot training. Perhaps most important, only men who had volunteered for air combat were accepted for training. No one was drafted and forced into the role of combat airman. Many of those who ended up in air combat volunteered because of the romance of flying. They had been raised on tales of flying adventures from Eddie Rickenbacker to Charles Lindbergh to Jimmy Doolittle and, if they had to fight, they wanted to join the "glamorous" branch of the service, where they would be treated like gentlemen. All of these factors combined to guarantee that combat airmen would be highly motivated warriors.

The Army confirmed this in a study of enlisted aircrew members. It found that, in relation to men from other branches of the service, combat airmen had higher AGCT scores and higher educational backgrounds. There were a higher proportion of young men (younger than twenty-five years old), a higher proportion of men in good physical condition, and a higher proportion of men who volunteered for the service. They also tended to be more content with their roles as combat airmen than were their ground-combat counterparts. In a survey, the Army asked a representative group from both branches, "How satisfied are you about being in your present Army job?" Seventy-two percent of combat airmen expressed some level of satisfaction with their jobs, while only 21 percent of infantrymen did so.

Needless to say, most of these combat airmen were white. In World War II, the U.S. military, like much of the rest of society, was segregated. In the case of the Army, most of the senior commanders, from George Marshall on down, felt that African-Americans were inferior and thus should serve in segregated units and be withheld from combat. Often poorly educated and hailing from low socioeconomic backgrounds, blacks tended to score low on the AGCT. In 1943, more than 79 percent of black recruits scored in Class IV or V. Such poor test scores only served to confirm previously held assumptions of black inferiority in the minds of senior officers, and they resolved to exclude African-Americans from a significant combat role. However, there were exceptions in the Army Air Force. Small groups of black men began to receive segregated pilot training in Tuskegee, Alabama, early in the war. These men had high AGCT scores and had passed all of the other rigorous Air Force tests. They were trained as fighter pilots and would one day make up the bulk of the 332d Fighter Group, which saw a great deal of combat in Europe and compiled a distinguished record of achievement. The Air Force created and trained one other black unit, the 477th Bomb Group, but never allowed it to go overseas.

Thus, with the exception of the 332d Fighter Group, the vast majority of American combat airmen in World War II were white and products of middle- and upper-middle-class families. By and large, they were intelligent, idealistic, highly motivated young men who yearned to serve their country and strike a blow at America's enemies. In terms of regional background, class status, and education, they were a reasonable cross-section of mainstream, upper-middle-class America.

C. L. Anderson, who flew with the 390th Bomb Group, offered a snapshot of his crew as a microcosm of the America he knew: "I was a farm boy, born and raised near the little town of Patterson, California. Our radio operator was also a farm boy, as was our waist gunner, who came from a Texas farm. The navigator was a percussion musician from New York. The tail gunner—a Golden Gloves boxer—was a nineteen-year-old kid from Pennsylvania. The engineer, also nineteen, was the son of a banker in Iowa. The bombardier was from the outskirts of Chicago. Our pilot grew up on an Oklahoma farm and had moved west with his parents to Stockton, California. I guess we were just a bunch of kids."

Chester Bennett, a U.S. Navy psychologist, had the job of studying combat airmen in his service. He recorded a dispassionate assessment of them and their various backgrounds in a letter home to a former colleague: "I met . . . a couple of ministers' sons and the son of a psychology professor, a country boy from Warrensburg [Missouri] who went to the Teacher's College, a U[niversity] of Missouri law student . . . and a San Jose, California, boy. There's a tall Texan with a Master's Degree in political science who 'comes from a family of teachers' and still plans to teach, working out his Ph.D. if and when he can. There's a 'West Virginia hillbilly' with a degree in agriculture, supporting an invalid mother—who's going back to the farm just as fast as the Navy will let him. There's a Montana forester who's heading straight back to the woods. So there you are. The fact is, they're a cross-section of American youth, as mature and as flippant, as socially sensitive and as selfish as the mythical average, but with more than average abilities."

The last part of Bennett's passage is the most significant. Combat airmen undoubtedly possessed "above-average abilities." Sometimes this was cultivated by advantageous educational opportunities and socioeconomic backgrounds but sometimes not. Samuel

Hynes, a Marine torpedo bomber pilot, felt that in the Marine Corps, ability counted for more than economic background: "Those like myself who felt provincial, or common, or underbred, chose the Marine Corps, where those qualities wouldn't show. The Marines that I knew, both the officers and the enlisted men, seemed to be mainly southerners and midwesterners—country boys, rednecks, and yokels. I don't think I ever met a Marine from New York or San Francisco, or a rich one."

For those who had the necessary test scores and physical requirements to enter the air combat arms, there was a fairly well-defined classification process. Meeting the basic requirements did not guarantee that a young man would end up in the cockpit of a fighter or bomber. In fact, 39 percent of those who entered flight training in the Army Air Force did not end up becoming pilots. Understandably, the Air Force sought to test, classify, and prepare its future airmen as much as possible. Before Pearl Harbor, anyone entering the air cadet program had to have at least two years of college, but this requirement was waived in January 1942. This paved the way for expansion of the Air Force and opened doors for many bright eighteen-to-twenty-one-year-olds who simply did not have the social advantages necessary for a college education. After passing the minimum requirements (AGCT, age, good health), young men were immediately put through the extensive evaluation process known in the service as the "classification battery."

If you were one of these potential air cadets, the classification battery in practical terms meant being subjected to a battery of psychological and motor tests. You would take aptitude tests known as "stanines," designed to determine your proficiency in one of three jobs—pilot, bombardier, navigator. Each test had a scale of one through nine; the higher the score, the better. The various stanine tests measured such abilities as speed and accuracy of perception, ability to read and understand technical information, resourcefulness and judgment in problem-solving, as well as knowledge of math and mechanical principles. Other tests measured motor skills, coordination, finger dexterity, and reflexes. Scoring high in the physical tests might slate you for pilot training, while high scores on math and problem-solving tests might point you toward navigator school.

During the two weeks required for this process, you would also be given a battery of medical and psychological examinations, all designed to determine your mental and physical fitness for air combat. Needless to say, the process was dizzying and required complete mental and physical absorption for the potential air cadets. Robert Goebel, a Wisconsin native who ended up flying fighter planes with the 31st Fighter Group, recalled his experiences at the classification center: "We were a herd of nude, two-legged cattle who followed signs, arrows, lines on the floor, and pointed fingers that directed us from place to place to be struck, stuck, pinched, and peered at. Only two verbal orders were addressed to each of us . . . 'Bend over and spread your cheeks' and 'Turn your head and cough.' To this day when I hear the latter, I rise up on my toes in anticipation of that dreadful stabbing finger in the groin."

Eugene Fletcher, who piloted a B-17 in the 95th Bomb Group, had similar experiences: "Some of the cadets actually fainted at the thought and sight of needles penetrating the flesh of those ahead of them in line. For me I thought both arms would fall off. Then came the psychological, mental awareness . . . and motor skills tests. The motor skills tests were used to measure manual dexterity and reaction time. The mental tests were a little scary. After all, who wants to tell some sinister stranger what he sees in ink blobs. We all wanted to fly and we surely didn't want to lose this opportunity just because an ink blob might look like spilled ink, a naked lady, or some other screwy imagined image or hallucination. We found ourselves giving answers to questions we didn't even understand. No one knew why we had to respond to these strange people."

John Crowe, who became a bomber copilot in the 491st Bomb Group, had a vivid memory of one of his psychological interviews: "The interviewer made a special effort to bring the discussion down to a very informal level with questions related to ethnic background, religion, school, and so forth, and then right into the gut of the issue of sex and sexual preference. He appeared to be somewhat uncomfortable with his role when he asked me how I felt about the opposite sex, but then warmed up to his task when I told him that I really did enjoy the opposite sex. I answered . . . in response to the obvious question that I wasn't queer if that's the question that was being asked."

Robert Fesmire, a pilot in the 492d Bomb Group, was a twenty-year-old native Tennessean at the time of his classification. He never forgot the process, including the bizarre nature of the psychological tests: "We underwent a fantastic number of tests at the Classification Center. We had to be in excellent physical condition and have an excellent mental aptitude. There were several written tests. We were tested in a chamber depressurized to the equivalent of 15,000 to 20,000 feet to see if sinus or ear problems would interfere with high altitude operations. And we were tested in a pitch-black chamber for night vision. I had the highest possible grade in night vision, and later would have vivid memories of this test during my night combat missions. But the most unusual test I had was an examination by a military psychologist. He asked me general questions about my family background ('What was your childhood like?'), education ('Exactly what did you study at Vanderbilt?'), religion ('Do you attend church regularly?'), my social life ('Do you have a girlfriend?'), and so on. I calmly answered each of his questions, no matter how silly or trivial they seemed to me. Then the major turned to the subject of sex. 'Did you ever have sex with your mother or sister?' I was amazed and shocked by the incredulity of the question, nevertheless, I calmly answered, 'No, Sir.'"

If you managed to make it through this process without being rejected for some physical or psychological defect, you were then approved for entry into the air cadet program and assigned as a pilot, navigator, or bombardier trainee. Some of those who washed out during the "classification battery" did end up in air combat, but as gunners on heavy bomber crews. For those who did make it, the Air Force determined whether they would be pilots, bombardiers, or navigators on the basis of three criteria—their job preference, their test results, and the present needs of the Air Force. Early in the war, you were likely to be assigned an aircrew job on the basis of your test scores and preference, but, beginning in 1944, the determining factor was the current need of the service. For example, late in the war, the Air Force found itself with plenty of pilots, so your chances of becoming a pilot decreased, regardless of whether you wanted to be one or whether your test results suggested you should be one. The service channeled men where it most needed them.

Naturally, the vast majority of potential aviation cadets wanted to be pilots. Clyde Bradley, a copilot in the 303d Bomb Group, remembered his excitement at being slated for pilot training at the end of his two weeks of classification tests: "Finishing all of the written and aptitude tests I was categorized . . . for Pilot training. To say that it was a great and exciting moment is an understatement, even tho [sic] there were 14,000 other applicants there, I still considered myself fortunate, a dream come true." But many others did not end up classified as pilot trainees. They were slated to become navigators and bombardiers, and some of them were bitterly disappointed. Philip Ardery, a Kentucky lawyer who ended up as a lead bomber pilot in the 389th Bomb Group, recalled the enduring disappointment of some of those who had to settle for being bombardiers and navigators: "Many of those who were eliminated from my original group survived to do service as bombardiers or navigators. Giving a washed-out pilot a shot at navigating or bombardiering has its faults. I lived to see in the combat zone the frustration of a would-be pilot relegated to a bombsight or a navigator's computer. It was a problem with no adequate answer."

Nevertheless, there were some who wanted to fly but had no special desire to become pilots. Elmer Bendiner, a navigator in the 379th Bomb Group, found himself drawn to the idea of navigating for a crew of comrades in combat: "Why not navigation school? I had not yet learned to drive a car; a plane could wait. The important thing was to fly. And navigation—what with sextants, astrocompasses, and gorgeous maps—struck me as altogether fascinating."

If you were among the lucky ones chosen for pilot training, the process was long and tortuous. The first step was preflight instruction, usually little more than military indoctrination and hazing. Cadets at this stage did not yet get to fly. After preflight, you went to primary flight school. This would be your first exposure to flying. Cadets learned to fly a small, uncomplicated airplane with low horsepower. The cadets negotiated four phases during primary flight training. In the first phase, you learned how to handle the airplane, recover from stalls and spins, and how to land. In the second phase, you learned how to fly patterns. The third phase taught you precision approaches and landing techniques. The fourth phase, usually known as the acrobatic phase, required students to perform difficult maneuvers such as loops or snap rolls. About halfway through the ten-week primary school, you had to prove yourself with a solo flight. By the end of the training, you probably would have made at least 175 landings.

Cadets were liberally washed out of primary flight training for any perceived weakness—from airsickness to rough landings to poor stick-and-rudder techniques. Robert Goebel recalled the daily stress of watching his fellow cadets fall by the wayside: "The attrition began in earnest now, and the long faces and red eyes at chow in the evening told the story of the fledgling pilots who had had their wings clipped permanently that day. Some wanted to be left alone in their misery, others sought companionship, but the talk was always awkward. One fellow spoke loudly about how his father was going to get him reinstated through some congressman friend of the family. But, as far as I could see, it didn't do any good; he shipped out along with the other washouts. Just when it seemed that our class was to be exterminated, the attrition slowed and then stopped."

If you were fortunate enough to make it through primary training, the next step was another ten-week course known as basic flight training. At basic it was understood that primary graduates knew the main rules of piloting. Now the job was to turn them into military pilots. As a student at basic, you learned how to fly a heavier, more complicated airplane. Now you would be expected to master instrument, night, formation, and cross-country flying. Instructors emphasized precision and smoothness and repeatedly drilled students so that flying techniques became instinctive. Because the emphasis was on becoming not just a pilot, but a *military* pilot, washouts sometimes occurred among those who, as they began to grow in confidence and cockiness, had also developed maverick tendencies. Goebel recalled one such instance when a dedicated and competent cadet was washed out for an unauthorized flight: "One look at his face . . . told us that his punishment was a lot worse than anyone expected. He was finished as a cadet. I thought that after a period of appropriate contrition, he would be reinstated. I didn't know the Army. Eric had used up his one and only chance."

Those who made it to the end of basic flight training then entered an important phase. At this point, the Air Force began to think of you not just as a trained military pilot but as one who performed some sort of specialty. Before you graduated and moved on to the twelve-week advanced flight training, the service classified you as either a single-engine pilot or a two-engine pilot. Single-engine training was generally the road to fighters; two-engine training was the road to bombers or transport aircraft. The assignment was based on a combination of factors—everything from your preference to your aptitude to your physical size and, most important after 1943, to the current needs of the Air Force. The vast majority of budding pilots wanted to go to single-engine training in order to become fighter pilots. By 1944, the demand for single-engine training so far exceeded the need that the Air Force routinely disregarded student preference in making advanced flight training assignments.

The elation over getting your preferred assignment—or, conversely, the disappointment over not getting it—could be great. It was relatively rare for a pilot to want two engines and instead be relegated to single engines. Most of the disappointment centered on the opposite problem. Keith Schuyler, a B-24 pilot in the 44th Bomb Group, worked extremely hard during his training to become a fighter pilot. It was all he dreamed of doing. By the end of basic, it looked as though his goal was well within his grasp, because he was initially assigned to single-engine advanced flight training. But then the brass discovered that too many graduates from his class had been assigned to single-engine training, and twenty men had to be cut. Schuyler was one of the twenty. His disappointment bordered on rage, and he confronted his commanding officer: "'From the day I've entered the army I wanted fighters,' I practically screamed. 'I've kept my nose clean, worked my guts out, did everything that was asked of me. I came into flying for one thing: to fly fighters. If I can't have them, send me to the infantry.' It did no good. The CO gave me his sympathy, but he could do nothing toward getting the orders changed. I'd be all right as soon as I got over my disappointment, he said."

Predictably, the training at advanced flight school was more specialized than the two earlier stages. For example, single-engine cadets received more training in armament and gunnery than their two-engine counterparts. Future fighter pilots needed to know how to shoot at a moving target and destroy it. Future bomber pilots did not. Upon graduation from advanced flight training, you received your pilot's wings and, in most cases, a commission as a second lieutenant. For the newly minted pilots, graduation day was a very proud day indeed. It was the culmination of nearly a year of hard work and intensive learning. Those who made it could look back upon each phase of their training and remember many comrades who had washed out or fallen victim to accidents or other. Nearly 40 percent of those accepted for primary flight training never became pilots.

The road to becoming a pilot in the Navy or the Marines was roughly similar, although those services placed greater emphasis on single-engine training, because the majority of their combat aircraft were not equipped with multiple engines. Samuel Hynes found in training that he was not an instinctive or natural pilot, but he mastered the principles of flight all the same. Other cadets were not as fortunate: "I learned to control the plane and myself with it. There were some young men for whom even this was impossible. In some, fear of the air was as deep and as irrational as fear of water or of the dark is in others; it kept them tense and helpless in flight, jerking the plane about with sudden, desperate gestures, skidding into turns, overcorrecting mistakes, bouncing on landings, never making those easy movements that are all she needs."

Such cadets almost always washed out. Robert Nelson, a Navy carrier pilot who flew a torpedo plane in Air Group 10, outlined the process he went through to earn his wings: "They had three different grades: you went from the bi-planes, to a funny looking single-engine plane made by Curtiss . . . and finally, a few old beat up bi-plane dive bombers. They had these checks when you moved from one squad [phase] to another. I did all right the first time, and the second time my ground school grades were good because I had a bit of an education. A lot of guys couldn't understand navigation or anything else. I had two roommates that . . . washed out."

As in the Army Air Force, pilot training in the Navy could be exacting and extremely demanding. This meant plenty of washouts.

Jim Campbell, a fighter pilot in Air Group 5, felt that washouts were a necessary evil: "The Navy didn't want mediocre flyers and nobody wanted an inferior pilot flying with him in combat. Usually if the student desired, and if he qualified, he would be dropped from flying status, but be retained in the Navy, as a potential officer. We had to be very precise[;] a knot or two off on a designated airspeed or a foot or two off on a rate of climb or descent was not tolerated. They were not merely teaching us to fly, but were trying to make us the best pilots in the world. There is no tolerance on a carrier landing in the middle of a dark night in heavy seas and with no lights. They were hard on us, but later on we realized that it was best for us and for those who flew those hazardous missions with us."

Cadets in the Navy, like their Army Air Force counterparts, were constantly evaluated not only on their flying abilities but also on the basis of what sort of flying would best suit them. Karl Smith, a fighter pilot in Air Group 23, recalled this aspect of his training: "All through the training you're taking aptitude tests and they're looking at you and deciding where you'd fit in best, whether you'd be best as an individual on your own or whether you'd be best as a team member." Most preferred to fly on their own as fighter pilots.

As a newly commissioned pilot, you would go through one last phase to the individual training process. Upon earning your wings, you would receive several more weeks of specialized training learning to fly combat aircraft. As a new fighter pilot, you would become acquainted with one or more front-line fighter planes in the American arsenal. Heavy bomber pilots would learn to fly the B-17 or B-24 and medium bomber pilots would learn to handle the B-26 or A-20. Fighter pilots were then sent on to operational units where, ideally at least, they received further tutelage in formation flying or combat tactics. Upon mastering his bomber, the brand-new bomber pilot would be blended with his crew. According to Eugene Fletcher, a significant amount of thought and care went into this process: "People were assigned in a manner designed to avoid personality clashes. One member of the crew must have Type O blood, a universal donor, and no more than two people from the same state could be on one crew." As a group they would receive several more weeks of Stateside training before heading overseas. Even when they reached combat units, most bomber crews endured further training, most of it centering on proper formation flying and coping with radio silence.

What about those airmen who were accepted as air cadets but not as pilots or who had washed out of pilot training? By and large they ended up as bombardiers or navigators attending a training school for their specialty. In the case of the bombardiers, the training could last from as long as twelve weeks (very common early in the war) to twenty-four weeks (common late in the war). Much of the training centered on learning to use the Norden bombsight, one of the most secret and technologically advanced American weapons. Upon graduation, a bombardier received a commission as a second lieutenant and was sent on to a six-week gunnery training course. The overall washout rate for bombardier schools during the war was 12 percent.

Prospective navigators would be sent to a fifteen-to-twenty-week navigation school. The main objective was to teach proficiency in different sorts of navigation, including dead reckoning (navigating by ground features), celestial (navigating by the stars), and radio (navigating by radio signals received from ground stations). Successful completion of the training required excellent mathematical ability, good reading comprehension, and good powers of observation. Navigators acted as the eyes and ears of a bomber crew, pointing the pilot in the proper direction and keeping a log on any observed activity outside the aircraft. In fact, the Air Force could often be more restrictive in choosing its future navigators than it was in choosing future pilots. Only those with extremely high test scores in relevant areas were chosen to go on to navigation school. About 20 percent were washed out during navigation training. Like new bombardiers, graduates of navigation school were commissioned and sent to a gunnery course.

Enlisted combat airmen usually performed one of three duties— gunner, radio operator, or aircraft engineer. Most men who washed out during classification were sent on to gunnery school or perhaps to radio or engineers' school. Many enlisted airmen were washed-out pilot, bombardier, or navigator trainees. Elmer Zeidman, who ended up as a tail gunner in the 487th Bomb Group, washed out of pilot training: "Like most gunners . . . I was a washed out Aviation Cadet. I washed out of Primary Flight Training in Uvalde, Texas. I could say that the civilian instructor didn't like me and that's why I washed out. That may have been partly true, because I thought he was a real jerk. But actually, I just didn't learn fast enough. I got laid up with pneumonia for a week, which dropped me to the bottom of our 5-man group, and I couldn't catch up. I was . . . sent to Harlingen Gunnery School in Harlingen, Texas, with a large group of washed out cadets."

This was an all-too-familiar story for many of those who ended up as enlisted members of bomber crews. The Air Force simply did not have the time or inclination to lighten the load for its prospective pilots. If you were sent to gunnery school, your main goal would be to learn not just how to shoot large-caliber machine guns, but also how to shoot them at moving targets. The best way for students to do this was to go up in a plane and fire at long cloth sleeves towed on the back of another aircraft. Needless to say, pilots did not exactly view flying a target plane as prime duty. Even so, accidents seldom occurred. In addition to gunnery training, future radiomen and aircraft engineers attended training schools in which they learned their respective jobs. Washout rates in gunnery and specialized schools were low.

By the time a combat airman flew his first mission, he had usually received a great deal of training at his job, no matter what it happened to be. It is worth knowing and understanding exactly what jobs these airmen performed and what exactly those jobs entailed.

World War II fighter pilots were modern war's closest equivalent to feudal knights. In theory at least, their role was to fight with the enemy at the most basic level—one on one, to the death. Correspondingly, they enjoyed a glamorous image, since they seemed to stand for the supposedly honorable, gentlemanly ways of pre-industrial wars. In reality, much of this was pure myth, but fighter pilots nonetheless brought a certain degree of personality to an impersonal war. Young pilots often wanted to become fighter pilots not just because of the glamour but also because the job offered independence and the chance to fly the hottest planes of the time. Even so, successful fighter pilots almost always had two qualities—

the ability to work closely with other pilots, and pure aggressiveness. Bruce Holloway was a fighter pilot in the American Volunteer Group, generally known as the "Flying Tigers." After World War II, he would rise to high rank in the newly independent Air Force. In his estimation, fighter pilots had to be team players: "A fighter pilot should never forget that he is part of a team. Every member of his formation is dependent upon every other member. I knew a fellow who had a way of streaking off alone, and he finally was shot down. There is romance in the life of a fighter pilot, of course, and to be successful he must like to fly combat missions. But in the main, it's a pretty grim business. It gets tough."

Larry Klebba, a flight surgeon in the 35th Fighter Group, had a great deal of experience selecting and dealing with fighter pilots. He felt that they possessed not only unique piloting skills but also unique personality traits: "Fighter pilots were a breed of their own. They had to be individualists. They had to be extroverts. They had to believe there was nothing they couldn't do. After all each is his own pilot, copilot, gunner, bombardier, and navigator. A fighter pilot is up there all alone. The world belongs to him. Whatever happens to him is his destiny. They are ready for adventure. We selected fighter pilots on that basis."

As Klebba suggests, fighter pilots tended to be very self-involved, fiercely independent people used to taking care of themselves. Although most of them would routinely risk their lives for their comrades in combat, they were usually not very comfortable accepting *responsibility* for anyone's safety but their own. This was certainly true for Karl Smith: "One reason I liked to fly fighters was because you didn't have to worry about sticking your neck out for the guy in the backseat or looking after somebody else. If I wanted to slip away and buzz a ship . . . it was only my neck. It wasn't anybody else's."

Francis Gabreski, a fighter pilot who flew with the 56th Fighter Group and became one of the top American aces in Europe, stressed the point that being a good fighter pilot came from much more than just being able to fly a plane well: "There were certain individuals who were good pilots but not real good combat fighter pilots. They were too busy flying the plane to get maximum performance out of it. It's a combination: You have to feel, you have to have sight, you have to have perception, and you have to have training. They're all combined into one. You have to have them all working for you."

Dogfighting with the enemy was just one aspect of a fighter pilot's job. In fact, many American fighter pilots flew entire tours of duty without encountering an enemy fighter plane. This was especially true for those who flew in the latter stages of the war in Europe, when Germany found itself critically short of experienced pilots and fuel. The other main fighter-pilot jobs consisted of escorting bombers to and from their targets and, the most dreaded task of all, strafing. Strafing was dangerous because if you were hit by antiaircraft fire, there was little chance of bailing out, because you were at such a low altitude. In addition, most fighter planes did not stand up well to direct hits from flak. It all added up to dangerous and stressful combat. J. Fred Baumann, who saw combat in the latter stages of the war in Europe, half joked that you could always tell what sort of mission pilots were set to fly that day by attendance at the chaplain's final pre-mission prayer. If his group was slated to escort bombers, hardly anyone would be there. If they were expected to encounter German fighter opposition, there would be a few pilots receiving last-minute absolutions. But if a strafing mission was on tap, the room was packed.

Some fighter pilots, such as Roy Simmons of the 111th Combat Recon Squadron, flew dangerous reconnaissance missions over enemy territory in stripped-down fighter planes: "As Tac Recon pilots, we were instructed to not engage the enemy if it could be avoided, to not strafe, but to visually observe and photograph enemy movements, reporting such observations that would enhance the cause of friendly forces. Often while over enemy territory we would give target coordinates to the Army. They would then place artillery fire on these targets, so we could observe and report the results."

Hugh Dow, a fighter pilot in the 350th Fighter Group, summed up the job of the fighter pilot in comparison with that of his bomber-pilot brethren: "The fighter pilots had much more freedom to respond to the events of combat than did the bomber crews. Bomber operations were highly structured and allowed little room for individual initiative, evasion of flak and fighter attacks, or close observation of the results of their work. Theirs was a team activity requiring several individuals to operate a single flying machine effectively. The fighter pilot also functioned as part of a team but also had a great deal of freedom to express his own individuality. In the final analysis, the bomber crew members had much less control over their destiny than did the fighter pilot."

The last sentence of Dow's analysis provides perhaps the most compelling reason why the majority of young pilots wished to become fighter pilots. The limited degree of independence a fighter pilot enjoyed provided him with at least some measure of control over his fate in a war that generally dealt out death in an indiscriminate manner.

Bomber pilots often found themselves powerless to fight back against the twin perils that threatened their lives—fighters and flak. Even so, their greatest burden was probably the responsibility of having other men's lives in their hands. The senior pilot on every bomber was the aircraft commander. As such, he was responsible for nine or ten other men and generally carried out the majority of the piloting duties. American heavy bombers in World War II required strength and skill to maneuver. This meant that two pilots were needed. The "first pilot," or aircraft commander, usually sat in the left seat and handled most of the tough flying such as takeoffs, landings, and formations. Harry Crosby, a navigator in the 100th Bomb Group, vividly recalled the physical and mental strain that formation flying in foggy English weather placed on his pilot: "For 120 minutes he can see nothing. We could hardly see the inboard engines. All he can do is stare at his instruments. He must keep the airspeed at 150 miles per hour. He must keep his turn and bank indicator at a single needle width. His rate of climb indicator must show 150 feet per minute. He must be sure all four engines are exactly synchronized. He is probably watching fifteen instruments."

Eugene Fletcher provided a succinct overview of his job as pilot of a B-17: "I served as first pilot and aircraft commander. In this position I was responsible for everything that happened aboard this aircraft and its relationship to other aircraft in the formation." Robert Ramer, a B-29 pilot in the Twentieth Air Force, flew bombing missions over Japan. He scoffed at the propaganda-induced notion that his job was glamorous. To him, the job meant heavy responsibility and mind-numbing routine: "We were like truck drivers. Take a load from here and drop it over there and come back and get another one. I mean, how glamorous can that really be? We were the truck drivers and the fighter pilots were the racing car drivers." Behind the routine and mechanics of flying into combat was always the specter of responsibility. The pilot knew that his actions could lead to the demise not only of himself but also of his friends. His word was law. He was empowered to make the final decision in any potential crisis. In contrast to fighter pilots, bomber pilots tended to be a little more serious, a little less aggressive, and, in many cases, natural leaders. Psychological tests the Air Force gave during classification and pilot training were designed to identify these qualities, and they largely did an adequate job.

The copilot on a bomber crew acted as an executive officer (second in command) and shared the flying duties. If the pilot was killed or became incapacitated, the copilot took over as aircraft commander. Hank Koenig, a pilot in the Eighth Air Force, outlined the tasks he assigned his copilot: "While copilots had to be thoroughly familiar with first pilot duties, they also had to know and understand the basic tasks of other crew members. In day to day operations, they supervised and integrated the various aircrew efforts. On combat missions, they were the primary contact point for coordinating combat tasks of the aircrew. During the course of their combat tours, copilots often . . . were promoted to first pilot duties."

Eugene Fletcher heaped additional duties on his copilot: "He monitored the VHF radio and served as our voice link with the other aircraft in the formation, and with the base. He would summon fighters for people in trouble. He took his turn at flying. We would alternate this duty, flying either fifteen-minute or half-hour shifts depending upon the stress of the type of flying we were doing and the condition of our airplane. He would also be available for any type of help that was needed in the cockpit or elsewhere in the aircraft."

Keith Lamb, a copilot in the 100th Bomb Group, thought of his job as "similar to an executive officer's job on a Navy ship: he sees that the pilot's orders are carried out. I . . . saw that the plane was gassed, guns oiled and checked again, and that everything else was ready." John Crowe found his copilot job to be mildly frustrating. He described his duties as "a rather dull and thankless job of pulling levers, pushing buttons, and watching dials and instruments. I know how the Vice-President of the country must feel . . . but then somebody has to do it and I was at least flying even if not alone in a fighter aircraft as I had hoped."

Third in a bomber crew's pecking order was usually the navigator. His responsibility was almost as enormous as the pilot's. A navigator had to plot the course to and from the target, know the plane's location at all times, and try to direct the pilot away from known flak concentrations. A good navigator could save lives and a poor one could get a formation of bombers lost over enemy skies— something that could lead to the deaths of many men. David Mc-Carthy, a navigator in the 381st Bomb Group, helped guide his plane on some of the toughest missions of the war, including the October 1943 Schweinfurt-Regensburg raid over Germany. He knew that his was a heavy responsibility: "In flight, the navigator can be the busiest member of the crew. If he continually takes readings, makes his computations, and keeps his log current, he does not have time to scan the skies for enemy fighters. Thus, he avoids the apprehension that waiting for trouble always induces. Besides, I enjoyed celestial navigation and the satisfaction of knowing our position and speed."

Harry Crosby was such an outstanding navigator that he often led not just his group or wing but the entire Eighth Air Force. Charged with breaking in rookie navigators, he found himself troubled by their inexperience, knowing that it could lead to catastrophe: "I saw that most of them were as unskilled as I had been when I arrived. As I looked over their logbooks I realized that on missions, they had little idea where they were. They were content to follow the leader and play gunner." Blindly following the leader was highly risky. If a plane had to drop out of formation or encountered any problem that separated it from the group, the navigator had to point the way home. To do this, he had to know the plane's exact location as well as the best route home. Commanders usually took strong measures to make sure each navigator understood this.

Jule Berndt, a navigator during the latter stages of the war with the 490th Bomb Group, was told in no uncertain terms that he was to constantly plot his plane's course, heading, and speed. In addition, he was to record anything of importance happening outside the plane, such as flak concentrations, enemy aircraft, downed American aircraft, and parachute sightings. Theoretically, the navigator should be perhaps the busiest person on the plane with the possible exception of the pilot. Berndt wrote in his diary: "All navigators must keep flight logs which record a history of the flight. Necessary entries are times and altitudes at control points, IP [initial point, the beginning of the run to the target], and target. They must also keep check on their position in case they must leave the formation and come back alone. The navigator has the responsibility of giving the crew ample time to put on their flak suits before a flak area is reached."

On most bomber crews, the fourth officer was the bombardier, a commissioned officer specially trained to drop the bombs on the target. In fact, one could build a compelling argument that the bombardier's job was the most important because it entailed the main focus of a mission—dropping the bombs on the target. Berndt had nothing but boundless admiration for bombardiers. As a navigator, he saw firsthand what they went through, because he shared a compartment with the bombardier in the plane: "Sitting up in the glass nose of a B-17 with flak popping all around and getting very little moral support from the thin glass around them, they must keep watching the level [lead] plane. It is impossible for them to shut out the view of flak if they wish to attain any accuracy with their bombs. It is the same story as when most people are struck by something. It is a natural impulse for a person to close his eyes on coming danger. I guess this is the same reason as not trying to see the flak helps alleviate the emotion of fear."

Curtis LeMay—a bomb group commander who would one day command the Twentieth Air Force and, after World War II, the United States Air Force Strategic Air Command, plus serve as chief of staff of the United States Air Force—outlined with great clarity the main job of a bombardier: "It took considerable skill for a bombardier to drop a bomb on the target. This is very exacting precision work, requiring a great deal of care even under the best of circumstances, so it is a considerable problem when somebody is shooting at you. Even with the Norden bombsight, the bombardier still had to see the target and identify it. He had to find the aiming point, and he had to do that far enough back so that he could level the bombsight. If the plane made even a little turn, the . . . accuracy would go off. The bombardier also needed to know the ballistic characteristics of the bomb, and to determine how high the plane was, using the barometric pressure and the altimeter. When the plane was finally going straight toward the target at the proper time and the proper drop angle, the bombardier dropped the bombs."

James Campbell, a pilot in the 380th Bomb Group, described the bombardier's role on a mission: "After leaving the IP inbound to the target the bombardier aims at the target with his Norden bombsight that has all kinds of adjustments for wind drift, altitude, bomb weight, trajectory, etc. When he gets the cross hairs in the sights lined up and leveled, then he, the bombardier, flys [sic] the aircraft by the controls of the bomb sight. For a few seconds . . . the aircraft must be straight and level on a constant course at a constant altitude. This is a very dangerous time."

Not all bombardiers made such intricate calculations. Often the lead bombardier would perform this task and others would simply drop their bombs on his cue. Edward Schlesinger of the 379th Bomb Group was one such bombardier: "Normally on a bomb run, I would have my hand on the bomb release mechanism waiting for the lead plane to drop." When not occupied with a bomb run, bombardiers had other important duties, as Eugene Fletcher recalled: "He was responsible for his guns and giving aid to the navigator. During the mission, at altitude, he initiated a crew check at fifteen-minute intervals, making sure everyone was physically okay, for a lack of oxygen could cause severe problems within minutes, while the victim would have a sense of well-being and euphoria."

B-29 crews often had five officers aboard during a mission. The fifth officer was known as a flight engineer. His job was specific to the B-29, making him the eleventh member of that plane's crew. On B-17s and B-24s, an enlisted top turret gunner served as flight engineer. Often the B-29 flight engineer was himself a trained pilot. His job was to sit behind the pilot and copilot and monitor the vital signs of the plane. John Patterson, a flight engineer, flew bombing missions over Japan as part of the Twentieth Air Force. He recalled the learning process necessary to master his complicated job: "There were eleven guys on a B-29 crew, including the Flight Engineer. My position was back-to-back with the copilot. I remember sitting in front of my panel for the first time and thinking, 'There's no way I'm gonna learn to work all this stuff.' There were levers and dials and switches all over the place. But I'd practically memorized the manuals and I started recognizing things pretty quick."

The flight engineer also attended to such seemingly minor details as making sure ground crews topped off the plane's fuel tanks before takeoff. Chuck Castle, a flight engineer in the 39th Bomb Group, did this before every mission. "If the tanks were filled at night, the heat of the next day and the weight of the gas in the rubberized tanks caused the tanks to expand, allowing you to add as much as forty gallons . . . in each wing tank. Little things like that were why some planes never made it back."

On a typical ten-man bomber crew, six of the crewmen were enlisted men, the highest ranking of whom was usually a technical sergeant who functioned as the top turret gunner/engineer. His job was not only to man the top gun turret but also to know every inch of the plane and monitor its vital signs during flight, much as a B-29 flight engineer did. Lloyd Haefs, a bombardier in the 2d Bomb Group, described his crew's engineer: "Directly behind the cockpit was the engineer/top gunner. He manned a powerful turret with two .50 cal. guns that incorporated a self-computing sight. He could also monitor the entire instrument panel in the cockpit to aid the pilots and could, in case of damage to the fuel tanks, transfer fuel to minimize fire and save leaking gasoline to insure getting home. There were many ways he could keep this machine flying as he was intimate with most of its operating parts."

Exceptional mechanical aptitude was the most important attribute for an engineer, even more so than gunnery expertise. Merle Perkins, a radio operator in the 483d Bomb Group, remembered that his crew's engineer liked objects better than people: "He was a naturally gifted mechanic. He knew almost intuitively how things worked. He knew . . . their logic better than people and liked them better. 'Things obey their laws; people are aberrant.'" This is not to say that top turret/engineers were antisocial. Most blended quite well with their crewmates. Keith Schuyler depended heavily on his engineer: "He sweated out every miss in an engine, every needle that trembled between normal and redline, the whine and wheeze of the landing gear and flaps, uncertainty of the gasoline supply. For, if anything went wrong with the airplane, it was him to whom I must turn. He was quietly proud of his job, and I was proud to have him as my engineer."

Eugene Fletcher also remembered his engineer with great affection: "He was our systems specialist . . . and the ranking NCO of the crew. His was a job that could make or break a crew, and he carried his responsibility well. His knowledge of the aircraft saved our necks more than once."

Next in line on the enlisted pecking order was usually the radio operator, another technical sergeant and specialist trained to man the plane's radio and maintain communications with the outside world. In some cases, the radio operator worked closely with the navigator. He would pick up radio signals from beacons on the ground and relay the information to the navigator. Hank Koenig outlined the typical responsibilities of a radio operator: "With few exceptions, the radio operator was on constant radio alert throughout the mission and was required to keep himself fully informed of the progress of the mission at all times. Working with complex radio codes, he could often pick up and report changes in enemy fighter locations . . . affecting the bomber stream. He also worked closely with the . . . navigator to stay abreast of exact route positions and if necessary was in a position to provide radio bearings to selected destinations in the event unforeseen emergencies occurred."

Crawford Weaver, a radio operator with the 40th Bomb Group, flew many raids to Japan. This meant flying over hundreds of miles of Pacific Ocean. It was Weaver's job to plan for an emergency ditching: "As the radio operator, it was my job to try to get help if we had an emergency. Along the strike route to the target we had rescue ships plus a submarine and two airborne planes called super dumbos. I had all their positions and radio frequencies and if we had to bail out, or land in the water, our navigator would determine where we would hit the water and I would try to get some help to that point."

The radioman also reported preliminary bombing results to the base. No sooner had the bombs dropped than crew members reported visual results to the radioman. Earl Benham, a radio operator in the 100th Bomb Group, recalled the procedure: "After the crew members had given me the bombing results, I was to transmit this 'strike report' to our base. A photo reconnaissance airplane would go to the target site and take official photographs of the area." In the European theater, radio operators often had one additional duty. They threw strips of aluminum foil, known as "chaff," out of the plane to jam German radar. Sam Ross, a ball turret gunner in the 384th Bomb Group, remembered that during bomb runs, his radio operator "fed packages of 'chaff' out of a chute in the side of the plane. He had a number of cartons of chaff . . . like the tinsel we hang on the Christmas tree."

One of the most harrowing jobs on a B-17 or B-24 crew was ball turret gunner. Both of those aircraft came equipped with a turret under their bellies. It was electrically powered into place during a mission so that the plane's vulnerable underbelly would be defended. In order for that to happen, a man with courage, small physical stature, and no traces of claustrophobia had to climb into the tiny turret. Ball turret gunners, like the remaining gunners on a bomber crew, were usually staff sergeants. Bill Hefley was a ball turret gunner in the 92d Bomb Group: "I was big (5'8") for a ball turret gunner. I could not wear a parachute when in my position. You were in sort of a seated position, your knees up, one hand on each gun . . . sitting on a cast iron seat looking out the Plexiglas. The turret rotated electrically with a hydraulic system. Your thumbs were on the triggers and your fingers holding two handles with which you rotated the turret."

Wesley Wells of the 379th Bomb Group described some of the many perils to being a ball turret gunner: "The drawback to the Ball Turret was that if we were hit . . . and the airplane went out of control, there was no way I could have gotten out of the turret and if I had, you could not wear either a parachute or a flak suit. You had to wear an oxygen mask, the temperature might be 60 degrees below zero at 30,000 feet altitude. No restrooms. I had a relief tube. If you could get through all the flying suits, heated suits, etc., you could urinate if you dared. I had a computing sight in front of me, two .50 caliber machine guns by my shoulders, and a thousand rounds of .50 caliber in the turret ammunition cans. The most you could move was to cross your hands or lower legs. It really was cramped and you knew that if the plane was hit and went out of control, there was no possible way you would get out. If this sounds like a lousy place to be, it was!"

Knowing how vulnerable he was over enemy territory, Donald Askerman, a ball turret gunner in the 461st Bomb Group, took steps to protect himself: "When going over the target I would roll the ball so the door was inside the waist and would open it so I could get out easily if we were hit. I was much too big to fit easily in that ball, but managed to do my job." So what did it feel like to hang from a moving aircraft thousands of feet above the ground while crammed inside a small steel and Plexiglas turret? Kenneth Drinnon, a ball turret gunner in the 487th Bomb Group, described the sensation: "The eerie, empty, and lonely feeling of being suspended in space each time I climbed into the ball turret made me squeamish as long as I flew there. I would get myself acclimated by gradually moving the turret from the vertical, or looking downward position, to the horizontal position. In a minute or two my mind would get used to the feeling and I could move the turret in any position without thinking about it. I can still recall those feelings."

The tail gunner also occupied a somewhat isolated position on a bomber crew. His job was to man a .50-caliber machine gun in the rear of the plane to protect the aircraft's blind spot from enemy fighters. Because it afforded protection in such a notoriously vulnerable area, this was perhaps the most important gunnery position on a bomber. Jack Novey, a waist gunner in the 96th Bomb Group, freely admitted that his buddy in the tail had the most crucial gunnery spot: "The tail gunner reclined in his narrow Plexiglas compartment somewhat isolated from the rest of the crew. He was probably the most important gunner on the airplane. I'm sure that if you told a pilot he had to fly a mission with just one gunner, he would pick the tail gunner. If a tail gunner was killed or wounded and the enemy pilots saw it, that B-17 was almost a sitting duck. Whenever that happened, another crewman would quickly replace him, even if it meant unceremoniously pulling a wounded man—or a dead body—out of the way and jumping onto the gun."

The sense of isolation endemic to the job made some tail gunners apprehensive. After all, it was only natural to seek companionship in times of stress and danger. Tail gunners had to discipline themselves to remain at their posts, communicating only through the plane's intercom system. This could be especially difficult for B-29 tail gunners. They found themselves almost completely isolated in the rear of the plane in a pressurized compartment during the long flights (some lasting as much as twelve hours) over the Pacific. Kevin Herbert, a B-29 tail gunner in the 498th Bomb Group, recalled that some men cut corners and could not wait to leave the solitary confinement of their tail positions: "Many tail gunners, perhaps most, were in the habit of leaving their station as soon as their plane passed the coastline [of Japan] on the way back to base. In effect, the rear end of the plane was left undefended in a zone of danger that might well extend from the coastline to some 200 or more miles to sea. These gunners could not stand the isolation of their position after being there for some two to three hours . . . and they wanted to go forward to discuss the strike in the company of the men in the central section of the plane. But I set myself a rule that I would not leave the tail until we were at least 200 miles to sea, and usually I stayed much longer."

If the tail and ball turret gunners had to deal with isolation, the waist gunners on a heavy bomber at least had each other's company. Most bombers had two gunners stationed in the midsection of the plane. Their main job, of course, was to ward off any attacking fighters who flew into their radius of fire. Since fighters often chose that section of the bomber to attack, the waist gunners had to be alert at all times. If they got distracted even for a moment, it could mean disaster. Jack Novey understood the grave nature of his job: "It was deadly serious work. If I relaxed and missed a target, I put myself, my crewmates, and the whole formation in danger." Bill Winchell was a waist gunner on the famous *Memphis Belle* in the 91st Bomb

Group: "I was the left waist gunner, which means my job was to protect the plane on the left side, upper, lower, from maybe about 7 o'clock to 10 o'clock." Before and after the plane reached enemy territory, waist gunners often had other responsibilities. William Binnebose, a waist gunner in the 95th Bomb Group, helped arm the bombload: "It was my job to arm the bombs so they would explode when they hit the ground, and see that all of the guns were in the best working condition, and to see that there was enough ammo for the mission, but not too much to overload us for takeoff." Sometimes waist gunners were even trained to handle radio duties. This was true of Eugene Fletcher's crew: "The right waist gunner . . . was also a trained radio operator, and served as the . . . back-up in case anything happened to Hinman [the regular radio operator]."

Not all Navy or Marine pilots were fighter pilots. Many of them piloted dive bombers or torpedo bombers and flew with two enlisted men under their command as part of a three-man crew. One such pilot was Samuel Hynes. He described the duties of his two other crewmen: "He [the radioman] rode in the belly of the plane, aft, in a dark cylindrical space called the tunnel, with his electronic gear around him. At the back end of the tunnel, under the tail, a thirty-caliber machine gun, the stinger, was mounted, and he was also the gunner. Campbell was quieter and less distinct—dark, very young-looking (though none of us was over twenty). He was turret gunner, and rode in a glass bowl on the backbone of the plane, with a fifty-caliber machine gun."

What is disquieting to realize is the extreme youth of most of the men who performed these dangerous jobs in World War II. Most of them were little more than kids. During the war years, it was Air Force policy to accept only men between the ages of eighteen and twenty-seven. Any combat airman older than that had probably been in the service before the war, was a commander, or was simply an anomaly. The vast majority of American combat airmen were men in their late teens or early to mid-twenties. It was very common, for example, for every member of a bomber crew to be twenty-one or under. War is always a young man's enterprise, but this was especially true of the air war. The Air Force felt that only the young had the necessary eyesight and dexterity to survive in air combat. Of course, there was a darker side to this as well. The young were usually quite eager and willing to fight, something very true of American combat airmen in World War II. Earl Wilburn, a bombardier in the 331st Bomb Group, summed up this sentiment: "Kids have to do these things [fly combat]. Older people realize how good life is and wouldn't want to do it." The Army found this to be true in its research of combat airmen. It asked bomber crewmen in the European theater if they would choose combat flying if they had it to do all over again. Among those thirty and older, almost 50 percent said they would not. Meanwhile, only 32 percent of the thirty-and-under men said they would not.

Quentin Aanenson was a twenty-two-year-old fighter pilot in the 366th Fighter Group: "We were all so young at the time. Most of us were in our early 20s. A couple of years before, we had been college students, or starting out in our first jobs. Why we had eagerly selected one of the most dangerous jobs in the military may be a little hard to understand, but at that young age, I guess we felt we were immortal. We were forced to grow up fast or never grow up at all. We left much of our youth on those battlefields in the skies over Europe in 1944 and 1945."

James Good Brown, a chaplain in the 381st Bomb Group, was in awe of the youthful airmen with whom he interacted every day. He wrote in his diary that "I should be the one to die, not these young men. Most of them are just 18 to 25 years of age. Only a few are over 25. And believe me: They are the very best of American manhood." James Talley, a navigator in the 306th Bomb Group, shook his head at the youth of his crew: "Most of us were young except the pilot. He was an old, old man. He was twenty-three years old and we thought he practically needed some help to get up and down the steps. I was . . . nineteen." It was not at all uncommon for anyone twenty-two or over to be the oldest on a crew and to be referred to as "Pop." Bob Ferrell, a B-24 pilot in the 458th Bomb Group, remembered one such person on his crew: "We had one guy on our crew we called 'Granddad' and he was 22 years old." John Patterson marveled at the youth of his B-29 crew: "We weren't a bunch of sophisticated, mature guys like you see in the movies. Our bombardier was 22. Our copilot was 21. Our CFC gunner—the guy who sat with his head in the blister and watched the fighters and decided which turrets to connect to which gunsights—the guy up there making these life-or-death decisions was a 20-year-old pinball wizard from St. Louis. Our pilot, now, he was *old*. He was 23!"

Sam Ross recalled that the guys on his crew used to razz their twenty-six-year-old tail gunner about his advanced years: "We called the Tail Gunner 'Pop' because of his old age. I was 19, having a great experience, and didn't understand why my Mother was so concerned."

In spite of their youth, or perhaps because of it, they managed to perform their jobs well and survive the deadly skies of World War II. Julian Rebeles, a ball turret gunner in the 448th Bomb Group, knew that his crew did its job well: "We were all young men in our teens and early twenties with no previous experience in ordeals of battle. Yet we managed to do the best we could to help each other survive. One cannot ask for more." Joseph Beswick, a top turret gunner/engineer in the 483d Bomb Group, found this youthful bravery and dedication truly amazing. Nearly fifty years after World War II, he expressed these sentiments in a memoir: "Now that I look back at it I am amazed that you could take a bunch of kids out of high school, college, off the farm and out of factories, give them about a year's training and send them out to hit targets that looked about the size of a checkerboard at 26,000 feet."

To do this, these American combat airmen had to possess such important attributes as youth, physical fitness, intelligence, and eagerness. But they also had to possess a unique kind of character. What were they like? America's wartime propaganda machine often portrayed them as glamorous, devil-may-care flyboys laughing in the face of death. This is more myth than reality, although a few fighter pilots did fit that stereotype. Most combat airmen, though, were ordinary men from every corner of America who did a tough, dangerous job in the face of mortal fear. Merle Perkins made this point well in a postwar memoir: "Many were enthusiastic about music, poetry, and the arts. They were widely read in philosophy, history, the natural and social sciences. Conversations with them were instructive. They were living under circumstances that forced a probing of the meaning of their existence and endeavors. Between missions they drank a lot, they talked a lot."

havior [the tumbling] tended to panic the pilots. Just cutting the power and taking hands off the controls . . . worked. But pilots were so shocked by the erratic spin that they usually panicked."

Lucky Lester, a fighter pilot in the 332d Fighter Group, did not like the P-39 at all: "The P-39s were dogs if I ever saw one, rickety old things, just lousy airplanes. It had the engine behind the pilot and a shaft with the cannon ran between your legs and shot out through the propeller spinner. It was lousy for air-to-air combat but pretty good for ground support. There were a lot of pilots who were scared to death of it."

Fighter Pilot Hugh Dow's 350th Fighter Group was equipped with P-39s for a time. He did not like the plane much but was nowhere near as ardent a critic as some other men. In a mixed assessment, he noted a few good features of the plane: "It proved to be an outstanding strafing platform—possibly the best anywhere. Visibility was superb and the aircraft was so light and responsive on the controls that it could be flown a few feet off the deck until the target was spotted. On the negative side, the 37mm cannon was a disaster in that it was seldom possible to get more than one or a few rounds off before experiencing a jam. In the case of the P-39 most of the flak hits were in the vicinity of the rear placed engine, making it more vulnerable than most fighter aircraft."

Clearly the plane was adequate for the early stages of the war, but, with its dangerous tumbling characteristic, its low ceiling, low rate of climb, and awkward ordnance, it proved to be one of the least effective fighters in the American arsenal.

Another fighter in service early in the war, but one that performed at a higher level, was the P-38 Lightning. Like many other American planes, it underwent various improvements in the course of the war as updated models rolled off the assembly lines. The Lightning was unique in that it had two engines. It featured a "fork-tail" design with a rear boom connecting the two fuselages, carried a 20mm cannon as well as four .50-caliber machine guns, and could carry rockets and bombs. It had an effective radius of almost 1,500 miles and a ceiling of well over 30,000 feet. At 25,000 feet, it could reach speeds in excess of 400 miles per hour. Wayne Rothgeb, a fighter pilot with the 35th Fighter Group in New Guinea, loved the

P-38: "What lines! What grace and beauty! Just viewing this creation made our hearts beat faster. We were smitten. She had refinement. Switches, levers, and gauges adorned the cockpit. She had graceful power; her two synchronized engines didn't roar—they purred like kittens. When a P-38 lifted off the runway, her wheels didn't klunk [sic] into wheel wells. Rather, like a refined, elegant lady, she slowly lifted her gear and very discreetly tucked them out of sight."

Pilots who liked the P-38 (or other aircraft) commonly described the plane in feminine terms. In the case of the P-38, its advocates thought of it as delicate and refined. Harold Rosser, a fighter pilot in the 33d Fighter Group, echoed this sentiment: "It handled flawlessly. It trimmed well; its props synchronized easily; it climbed with purpose. It was a 'Hollywood' plane . . . beautiful in flight but fragile in combat, like the beauty who had been made uncomfortable by a pea under her mattress. With so many instruments . . . everything would have to go right, or there'd be a peck of trouble."

As Rosser hinted, the Lightning had some serious shortcomings, most centering on durability and sluggishness at high altitudes. Jack Ilfrey flew P-38s in Europe in 1943–44 and commanded a squadron of the 20th Fighter Group. He noted that problems arose during bomber escort missions: "There were some difficulties flying the P-38s at the high altitudes the bombers flew. Some of the pilots got frost-bitten hands and feet, because there was almost no heating system in those models of P-38. And at high altitude, the oil froze up and pistons blew out." Later models of the P-38 did include a heating system, which helped alleviate some of the problem.

Hub Zemke, a famous fighter pilot and commander of the 56th (and later 479th) Fighter Group, indicated in clear detail that the aircraft had problems in Europe and was generally more effective in the Pacific: "The P-38 was not up to conditions prevailing in the north-west Europe winter, particularly its Allison engines with which the extreme cold and damp played havoc. A large plane for a fighter, the P-38 could turn as well as most single-engine interceptors at low altitudes and it had good speed. In the Pacific our people developed a successful technique of employing it against Japanese fighters. It was popular there by virtue of its range, being superior to other American pursuits available during the early war years and, with plenty of over-water flying, two engines were a comfort. The same should have applied in Europe but the operational circumstances and climatic conditions were different. Here the P-38 was a big flop. The design just couldn't take the combination of extreme cold and high humidity that characterized flight over Europe, especially in winter. There was a standing joke that the P-38 was designed with two engines so you could come back on one. A P-38 mechanic's life was not easy, the type demanded a hefty maintenance load."

Zemke's analysis is right on target. The P-38 could succeed in certain conditions such as long-range strafing or escort missions in the warm air of the Pacific. It could hold its own in a dogfight—provided it did not absorb too much punishment and provided it fought at lower altitudes, particularly in Europe. It was a good plane that performed well in the right environment, but clearly its overall performance suffered from a disquieting lack of versatility.

Although the P-39 and the P-38 were primarily Army Air Force fighters, the F6F Hellcat was flown almost entirely by Navy and Marine fighter pilots. Like all American fighters except the P-38, the Hellcat was a single-engine aircraft. It had a radius of nearly 1,500 miles, excellent for an aircraft that would be employed primarily over the vast expanses of the Pacific Ocean. Its ceiling of 38,000 feet proved ideal for combat air patrol missions over the fleet, and it carried six .50-caliber machine guns, along with bombs or rockets. By late 1943 and early 1944, most Navy fighter pilots were flying Hellcats. Most of them loved it because of its flexibility and durability. Karl Smith, a fighter pilot in Navy Air Group 23, felt it was "the best fighter that we had at that time. It was a heck of an airplane. It had so much power. It could just do anything you wanted it to do."

Franklin Shires, a Navy fighter pilot who flew with Fighter Squadron 13 off the USS *Franklin,* loved the Hellcat for the punishment it could absorb: "They could take a lot of punishment. Shoot off half the tail, shoot off the aileron or something, you'd still get them back. They were just tops." The ability to withstand punishment and still make it home was often the top criterion for American combat airmen in evaluating a plane, because it often meant the difference between life and death. Jim Campbell, a fighter pilot who flew with Air Group 5 off of the USS *Yorktown,* loved the Hellcat. He wrote a detailed description of the plane in a postwar memoir: "The F6F was a fighter pilot's dream. It had hydraulic retractable [landing] gear . . . which made it . . . stable in landing and taxiing. In air combat we would use all six guns, but in strafing we would usually cut out two guns and save some ammunition for the return trip back to the ship. Another good feature of the plane was the shield of armor plate both behind and under the pilot's seat. This offered quite a bit of protection from enemy fire, and was something the Japanese planes did not have. Also, the windshield in front of the pilot's face had a very thick glass shield, which . . . did offer some protection. The gasoline tanks were self sealing, in that a bullet could penetrate the walls of the tank and then the hole would soon seal up so that the loss of fuel would be kept to a minimum. We found that we could get a bullet completely through the tank with no ill effect."

The Hellcat performed quite well in what it was designed to do. It afforded close air support to ships while at the same time providing excellent ground support. By 1944 and 1945, when the majority of combat took place in the Pacific, it flew in head-to-head combat with Japanese fighters and also turned out to be quite effective at destroying Japanese ground forces at various islands in the Pacific. By any measure, the Hellcat was a major success.

The P-47 Thunderbolt was one of the most successful American fighter planes of World War II, especially at strafing ground targets. Heavily armored and reasonably maneuverable for a large aircraft, it entered service in significant numbers in 1943 and provided American bombers in Europe with a medium-range escort fighter. The P-47 had a radius of about 700 miles and a ceiling of roughly 35,000 feet. In terms of armament, it was a formidable weapon. It could carry as many as eight .50-caliber machine guns in its wings and was ideal for carrying bombs or rockets. It proved to be a devastating dive bomber and more than satisfactory in air-to-air combat.

Even so, it did have drawbacks. Before his unit transitioned to P-38s, Harold Rosser flew the P-47 in combat in the China-Burma-India theater: "The P-47 had no nose wheel, and instead of leaning forward to take off, it held back, leaning on its tail wheel, its tilted up nose obstructing our forward view until it gained speed. Not until it reached a speed of sixty miles per hour did the tail come up, and until it did, we could not see the runway in front of us. The opposite was true when landing. To compensate for the blind spot, we 'essed' when we taxied, turning from side to side, looking to the front between turns."

Lucky Lester, who flew P-47s in the European theater, pointed out some other problems he encountered: "We'd meet the B-17s at twenty thousand feet, but they would invariably want to keep right on going to thirty or thirty-two thousand because the higher they got, the more protection they would have. Our P-47s struggled to get to twenty-eight; we could go to thirty thousand, but the plane became sluggish and started wallowing around in the sky. And the Jug [nickname for the P-47] used too much fuel. It would only let us go out at the most for three hours, then we'd have to turn around and come back."

In spite of these problems, many fighter pilots loved the P-47 and grew very attached to it, something very common among airmen who liked and trusted their aircraft. Their attachment could sometimes border on the mystical. Will Burgsteiner, a fighter pilot in the 359th Fighter Group, was very reluctant to give up his P-47 when his unit transitioned to another fighter type in the spring of 1944. He wrote in his diary that "everyone is sort of browned-off. We never realized we loved the old barrel and her eight guns so much."

Wayne Rothgeb, like many P-47 pilots, felt that the plane gave him excellent security during strafing runs, and he came to love the machine: "When I was dive-bombing and strafing and saw the smoke from machine guns and antiaircraft guns firing at me, I was happy to have a trusted friend in front of me. I ducked behind my security shield—the P-47's 2,000 HP [horsepower] Pratt & Whitney engine."

Francis Gabreski of the 56th Fighter Group was one of the first American fighter pilots to get to England after America entered the war. The son of Polish immigrants, Gabreski initially flew British Spitfire fighter planes with a Polish fighter outfit. Upon transferring to his American unit, Gabreski began to fly the P-47 in combat and was impressed: "The cockpit had more room than any fighter I had flown, and it gave me quite a sense of power to look out and see the big, four-bladed prop in front and the four .50-caliber machine gun barrels sticking out of the front of each wing. Once airborne I found the handling characteristics of the P-47 to be . . . nice. I immediately forgot about how big the plane was, and I noticed it required smooth coordination of stick and rudder. They turned pretty well for their size, and they would roll with anything in the sky. But the P-47 really shined [sic] when it was headed downhill. The dive performance was truly spectacular. I really liked the cockpit heating system, which kept the pilot reasonably comfortable even at 30,000 feet, where the temperature was minus 60 degrees. The heating system also did a good job of keeping the windshield clear of frost. In a Spitfire, if you made a long dive, the windshield would frost over at about 15,000 feet, leaving the pilot blind until it cleared. That didn't happen in the P-47."

Gabreski also noted that the P-47 could withstand terrific punishment and still bring a pilot home. He claimed, for instance, that one of his comrades had sustained five direct hits in his right wing from a 20mm cannon but had still managed to get home. Such ruggedness led to tremendous feelings of trust and affection for the P-47 among pilots such as Gabreski. He himself would one day become one of the top American aces in Europe, scoring many of his victories in the P-47.

Perhaps the best American fighter in World War II was the P-51 Mustang. In terms of air-to-air combat, maneuverability, range, and sheer joy to fly, the Mustang was unquestionably the best American fighter. It did fall short of the P-47 in dive bombing, and it could not withstand the same kind of punishment the Thunderbolt could absorb routinely. The P-51 entered service late in 1943 and immediately began escorting vulnerable heavy bombers to heavily defended targets in Europe. In fact, the P-51 has often been credited with saving the Eighth Air Force from extinction in the fall of 1943. Before the P-51 came along, the Allies had no fighter that could reliably escort bombers to targets deep into Germany and stay with them all the way back to England. Consequently, the bomber formations were sustaining disturbingly high losses to German fighters. The P-51, with an effective radius of close to 900 miles, could perform the vital escort task so needed in late 1943. With a cruising speed of 360 miles per hour and a top speed of 440 miles per hour, it was fast. In addition, it had exceptional turning and climbing ability. Its range and speed made it a formidable dogfighting adversary and helped American pilots sweep Germany's fighters from the skies in 1944 and 1945. By the end of the war, the Army Air Force used it in every theater for almost every conceivable kind of fighter mission.

Lou Purnell, a fighter pilot in the 332d Fighter Group, absolutely loved the P-51: "If that plane had been a girl, I'd have married it right on the spot. Damn right! It was like dancing with a good partner. You could almost think left turn, and the damn plane was right with you. Good response on the controls, good stability. It was a miracle to get in and fly with all that horsepower at your fingertips. Speed, maneuverability, climb rate, reliability? We had it in the P-51. Anyone who has flown a P-51 will agree with me. And those who haven't, wish they had."

Hub Zemke had an opportunity to fly the P-51 in combat and felt that it was the best all-around American fighter of the war: "While not having the firepower of the P-38 or P-47, it was superior on nearly every other count. The P-51 probably couldn't outclimb a 109 or 190 [German fighters] but it could outdive and outrun them at any altitude. It could usually out-turn these opponents too. The all-round view from the cockpit was excellent, and that was of major importance to a fighter pilot. Best of all, with that large built-in tankage and moderate appetite we did not have to sweat over fuel gauges as had been the case with the P-47 and, to a certain degree, with the P-38."

Robert Goebel, who flew his entire tour of duty with the 31st Fighter Group in a Mustang, found that he loved the airplane. He eventually became an ace in it: "One day, as I sat in the closed cockpit enjoying the warm sun and the quiet, I looked around me and suddenly realized that, more than any other aircraft I had known and flown, I felt comfortable in the P-51 Mustang. It was like a favorite warm jacket or an old pair of shoes; everything was friendly and familiar, the feel, the look, even the smell." He eventually earned the privilege of having his own personal airplane, a real status symbol among fighter pilots: "Having an airplane of your own was an ego trip, to be sure . . . but it was more than that. From flying the same plane so often, I knew exactly how the engine . . . sounded, knew all its idiosyncrasies . . . and knew where I wanted the seat positioned. I took care of it as if it belonged to me, saving the airplane and engine from abuse whenever I could. I didn't want anyone else flying my plane, certainly not any new replacement."

The Mustang was also popular among pilots who flew missions against the Japanese in the Pacific theater. Fighter Pilot Edward Popek commanded a fighter squadron in the 348th Fighter Group. His outfit flew combat air patrol, ground support, and strafing missions in the Philippines and along the Chinese coast. In a combat evaluation report of the P-51's performance, he wrote: "We have found the P-51 airplane very suitable for ground support in that it is extremely maneuverable at very high speed with excellent visibility. It is very good for dive bombing from 4,000 feet to 6,000 feet in about a seventy to (80) degree dive. For the most part, our squadron is well satisfied with the performance of the P-51 in that it is more maneuverable, faster, and has better visibility than our previous . . . P-47 aircraft."

The only serious objection pilots ever had with the Mustang concerned its vulnerability to enemy fire, particularly ground fire during strafing runs. Enoch Stevenson flew bomber escort and strafing missions over Europe in P-51s. He knew his plane was not as durable as the P-47: "The P-51 had a liquid-cooled engine so it was vulnerable from ground fire. If the Germans got one in the radiator you couldn't last, you couldn't fly anymore. If that happened to you, all you could do was turn toward friendly soil, fly the plane until it quit and then bail out." The good news was that the Mustang was so quick and responsive that pilots could sometimes successfully dodge incoming enemy fire. By and large, the P-51 was an outstanding aircraft notable for its versatility and user-friendly qualities. It is safe to say that, without the P-51, the war would have dragged on longer and been much costlier to the United States. Along with the P-47 it proved to be one of the unabashed success stories in American weaponry in World War II.

American medium bombers in World War II were used mostly for low-level tactical bombing missions. They represented the middle ground between high-altitude strategic bombers—which in the doctrinal minds of airpower theorists had the ability to win the war all by themselves by bombing enemy industry—and traditional fighter aircraft. One of the most common American medium bombers was the twin-engine B-25 Mitchell. Named after Billy Mitchell—a charismatic advocate of airpower in the 1920s who had proven through demonstrations the effectiveness of aircraft against sea and ground targets—the B-25 usually carried a six-man crew for its low-altitude, ground-support missions. It had an effective range of 1,350 miles and an average cruising speed of 230 miles per hour; it bristled with guns. The typical B-25 had a dozen .50-caliber machine guns in its nose, two more in the top turret, two more in the tail, and a few more in the waist position. The Mitchell could carry about 3,000 pounds of bombs or eight five-inch rockets. Sturdy, maneuverable, and loaded with firepower, the Mitchell usually did not require fighter escort. It was ideal for low-level strafing missions against precise targets.

David Hayward flew B-25s for the 341st Bomb Group in the Pacific. He was thrilled at its ability to withstand enemy fire: "It is amazing how much punishment the B-25s could take. There were relatively few vulnerable places on the airplane. We had armor plate under our seats. The gasoline tanks were self sealing. What we sacrificed in speed we gained in security." Even so, the aircraft was not perfect. Some early models were fitted with a 75mm cannon in the nose. According to R. W. Blake, a B-25 navigator, the cannons were ineffective and downright dangerous: "Our job, great in theory, was to destroy Japanese railroad locomotives, trains, and bridges with the 75mm cannon. The theory wasn't working out so well in practice. In just 10 days, we had lost three of the four slow-flying craft. Two had been shot down by ground fire, killing all aboard."

Another widespread American medium bomber was the B-26 Marauder. Its mission and physical features were very similar to those of the B-25. Powered by two engines, it carried a seven-man crew. Its range of 1,150 miles was a little shorter than that of the Mitchell, but it carried more ordnance. It could haul up to 4,000 pounds of bombs and a total of twelve .50-caliber machine guns placed at various points of the aircraft. Its cruising speed of 216 miles per hour was a little slower than the Mitchell, but the difference was negligible. Combat units used the Marauder for low-level bombing of precision targets and for tactical support of ground troops. It was not a plane for beginners, though, because it had idiosyncrasies that could cause a pilot to lose control of the plane. This gave it a reputation as a death trap early in the war, but many of the problems were later solved. Thus, like most American combat planes, it ended up being far more effective later in the war than in the early stages of the conflict.

A. H. Albrecht of the 319th Bomb Group piloted various medium bombers in European combat, including the B-25 and the B-26. He was not impressed with the latter. He felt that it was heavy and dangerous on takeoffs and that the engines would constantly threaten to get out of control. He conceded its ruggedness but described it as a serious handful to fly. Another B-26 pilot, Franklin Allen, had a sharply differing opinion. He flew with two medium-bomber groups, the 22d in the Pacific and the 397th in Europe, and logged thousands of hours, most of them in combat, in the B-26. He liked the plane so much that he eventually worked with the manufacturer, the Glenn Martin Company, to encourage the Air Force to continue buying updated models. He was particularly pleased with the updated "G" model produced late in the war: "I find the stepped-up performance of the 'G' model—with its new emergency landing gear and improved gasoline system—far superior to other models. Many of our B-26s have been saved by these improved features. You are able to see a lot better out of the B-26 now, because the large nose no longer obstructs the view. While on a bombing mission . . . my plane suffered a direct hit by a Jerry 88mm shell. It penetrated the right wing without exploding, leaving a huge jagged hole. However, the plane was back in service the day after being hit, which I attribute to the superior design and sturdy construction. Everyone in my squadron feels as I do about the B-26. We consider it the finest combat plane in action today, and hope for nothing better than to continue to fly the Martin Marauder for the duration."

Last but not least in the American aerial arsenal were the heavy bombers, the most expensive and complicated aircraft in existence at that time. They were built to destroy the enemy's vital organs—his industrial resources and infrastructure. Military theorists spent much of the interwar period arguing over whether heavy bombers could effectively win wars on their own. Committed advocates of strategic airpower—the most notable being Sir Arthur "Bomber" Harris of the Royal Air Force—argued that heavy bombers could destroy the enemy's capacity to make war, thus making mass ground armies unnecessary and obsolete. World War II (and almost every other war since then) proved the theories of Harris and his cohorts to be dead wrong, but it is important to understand that American heavy bombers in World War II were born out of prewar thinking about the role of strategic airpower. American heavy bombers were designed to fly at high altitudes and rain destruction upon precision targets such as oil refineries, factories, and railroad marshaling yards. All of this was supposed to happen without the benefit of long-range fighter support because bombers came equipped with multiple guns to defend themselves. In the case of the United States, airpower theories grew partially out of the ambitions of high-ranking generals to one day create an independent air force. In their view, strategic bombing was the best route to their goal because it presented the hope of winning the war through airpower alone. When put into practice over the deadly skies of Europe, however, the prewar strategic airpower theory proved to be a near-disaster.

It was in this context that the four-engine B-24 Liberator was designed and built. More Liberators were built than any other combat aircraft in American history. In fact, it was one of the few planes used by both the Navy and the Army in World War II. Stubby and blunt-nosed, the Liberator was not aesthetically pleasing, but its dependability and durability more than made up for its artistic flaws. It had a range of about 2,100 miles and could carry close to 10,000 pounds of bombs. Its top speed was about 300 miles per hour, with a cruising speed of 210 miles per hour. Like all American bombers, the B-24 bristled with .50-caliber machine guns from nearly every side of the ship, including a top turret, a ball turret, a nose turret, and a tail assembly. Depending on the mission it flew, the Liberator required a crew of eight to ten men. In World War II, more American combat airmen flew into battle aboard Liberators than any other single aircraft. Yet the Liberator often took a backseat, in terms of wartime publicity and postwar discussion, to other American bombers—most notably the glamorous and more physically beautiful B-17 Flying Fortress.

Most Liberator crews liked and trusted their plane and remained fiercely loyal to it. Some of them even developed a resentment toward the more famous B-17 and its crews. They argued that the Liberator may not have been pretty, but that it was faster, had more range, and was every bit as durable as the B-17. This was true, and it was why the Liberator, unlike the B-17, flew extensively in both the Pacific and European theaters.

The Liberator was not without problems, though, and not all B-24 crewmen liked their plane. For instance, it required great strength to manipulate the controls, and its fuel system sometimes had flaws. Guyon Phillips, a copilot in the 461st Bomb Group, certainly found this to be true: "Flying formation for several hours gave your left arm a workout[;] later I found that I could arm wrestle my college roommate (a big football player) left-handed [the hand the copilot used to fly the plane], but stood no chance with him right-handed. You made no sudden moves in a B-24, response time had to be calculated. And then there were the constant gas fumes[;] you would think that all gas lines in airplanes would have been designated to standard, but somehow, the 24 was in a class of its own. I lost several friends from accidents, which were assumed to be from gas leaks. More than once, I had to get on the intercom and tell the guys to put them out—no smoking until the air cleared."

John Charlton, who flew B-24s in the 465th Bomb Group, also disliked the fuel system of the aircraft: "The B-24 had the worst fuel gage [sic] system of any aircraft, before or since. In level flight you were supposed to get a good reading in calm air, but the only few seconds you passed through level was just after bombs away. You weren't level long enough to get a reading. Before bombs away you were reading hundreds of gallons less and on descent hundreds more. You could only tell fuel on board reasonably well coming home alone."

Keith Schuyler had longed to fly beautiful fighter aircraft. Instead he found himself slated for four-engine bomber training and ended up flying the ugly B-24 in the 44th Bomb Group. At first he despised his plane: "They never were a pretty sight at best, those four engines tacked onto a slip of a wing, belly nearly dragging the concrete, and hog-nose stuck way too far forward. And, like pregnant hippopotamuses, they bucked and snorted their way around the hangars, letting out an occasional squeak of rubber, their constant bloat seeming to substantiate the foul odors that drifted from them. Only pride could have dragged me to the flight line for my first trip aloft in a B-24. I wanted no part of them." As the plane brought him home safely mission after mission, Schuyler's tune changed and he came to love the B-24 with a passionate intensity.

Many other B-24 crewmen experienced the same transition. Kenneth Jones, a pilot in the 389th Bomb Group, wrote in his diary about his B-24: "We developed a sentimental attachment to Q-Queenie [their plane] and her sisters. The B-24 could take punishment and forces beyond the designer's dreams and still bring you home. Every future breath you breathe depends on the smooth purring of those Pratt & Whitney engines. I clutch those wonderful engines to my chest like a love-sick Aviation Cadet."

William Shelley, a gunner who flew with the 7th Bomb Group in India early in the war, had nothing but praise for the Liberator: "For us in the Tenth Air Force, the Lib was the best machine with its great range and excellent bomb load capabilities." Shelley's analysis is entirely accurate. The Liberator was the most common American combat aircraft in World War II because it was the most versatile. It could be used successfully over the vast areas of the Pacific as well as over the flak-filled skies of Europe. It fit nearly every type of strategic bombing mission, including low-level strikes against industrial targets, as at Ploesti, Romania, or in Pacific shipping raids. Paul Stevens, a Navy pilot, flew the Navy's version of the B-24, the PBY-1, on many low-level raids against Japanese ships and harbors: "The B-24/PBY-1 Liberator was one of the all-time great combat aircraft. An outstanding performer in all areas, it could take punishment and still get the crew home. It had a high degree of reliability, due in large part to the Pratt & Whitney R-1830 engines. We did operate the airplane well above its maximum emergency war overload in order to achieve the range and carry the bomb load for our missions."

It was valuable, then, because of its range, its speed, its ruggedness, and, most of all, its versatility. The ultimate test of its value came in the sentiments of its crews. Army researchers asked a large group of B-24 crewmen the question, "Do you think you have the best type of airplane for the particular job which you have to do?" A full 76 percent of the crewmen replied yes to the question and only 16 percent no. Such was the satisfaction among American combat airmen with the B-24 Liberator.

The B-24 may have been the most versatile American bomber, but the ultimate expression of America's strategic airpower policy was the B-29 Superfortress. Designed in the months leading up to Pearl Harbor, the B-29 did not enter combat until mid-1944. It was the largest and most complicated of all American aircraft in World War II. Powered by four engines, it had a staggering range of well over 4,000 miles and could carry about 12,000 pounds of bombs, along with the requisite .50-caliber machine guns located throughout the aircraft. Its ceiling was well over 30,000 feet. The B-29 was truly a manifestation of the strategic bombing philosophy of the leaders of the Army Air Force, in that it was designed mainly as a high-altitude heavy bomber. In the minds of those who built it, the B-29 would carry out the doctrine of high-altitude precision bombing and would singlehandedly destroy the enemy's industry, cities, and infrastructure—in theory, his very ability to make war.

Ironically, the B-29, used exclusively in the Pacific theater, experienced its greatest success not in high-altitude raids but on relatively low-level (10,000 feet) strikes. For the first six months or so of the B-29 raids over Japan, crews bombed from high altitudes and remained reasonably safe from Japanese defenses. There was a problem, though. At high altitudes over Japan, American bombers encountered a jet stream of heavy winds. This caused buffeting among the B-29s and took a serious bite out of their bombing accuracy. Upon taking command of most of the B-29 force in early 1945, Gen. Curtis LeMay realized that something had to be done. To the extreme consternation of his crews, he ordered them to fly at night and bomb at altitudes of 10,000 feet or under in order to achieve maximum accuracy. Low-altitude bombing brought better results, but it also made bombing missions significantly more dangerous.

Most men who flew in B-29s liked the plane not only for its reliability but also for its comfort in comparison with other American bombers. The B-29 featured pressurized cabins for its crews. By necessity the bomb bays were not pressurized, but the rest of the plane was, so B-29 crews did not have to worry about braving subzero temperatures and oxygen-poor air on their missions. They could carry out their raids in reasonable comfort—a welcome ability, because their raids often lasted fourteen hours or more. John Patterson, a B-29 flight engineer, described the interior of his aircraft: "Boeing [the manufacturer] knew we'd do a better job if we were comfortable, so they'd pressurized and heated the fore and aft crew compartments and tail gunner's compartment. They didn't pressurize the bomb bays because of the doors. The fore and aft compartments were connected by a pressurized tunnel."

Airmen voiced a couple of complaints about the B-29. First, it was difficult to keep in service because of mechanical breakdowns. Once in the air, it was reliable, but the problem was keeping it flyable. Small armies of mechanics worked on the B-29s to keep them airworthy. Also, it could not take quite as much punishment from enemy flak as could other American heavy bombers. Bob Morgan, pilot of the famous *Memphis Belle* (a B-17), also flew B-29s in the Pacific. He generally liked the airplane but did not think it could have survived in Europe: "The '29 would never have lasted in Europe, and there was a thought to take it over there at one time. We lost more B-29s from mechanical failure than we did from the Japanese. If it had been in Europe, it would have been a dead dog. It was a great airplane, don't get me wrong, but the '29 was built for a particular purpose: long-range, Saipan and Guam to Japan. It could carry a big load, but it was not the airplane that could take the punishment from the accurate German antiaircraft and the German fighters."

Patterson, who loved the B-29, disagreed with Morgan. He argued that it held up very well against whatever punishment the Japanese gave it: "We had engines knocked out, chunks of wing torn off, holes punched in the sides, but the B-29s kept on flying. I thought the B-29 was the most beautiful thing in the world. I lost track of how many times our airplane saved our lives. Sometimes it was a piece of armor plate that stopped a cannon shell. Sometimes it was a fire bottle that snuffed out an engine fire. They weren't 'B-29s' to us. To us, our airplanes were *Southern Belle* and *Miss Behavin'* and *Dinah Might.* You don't give something that's part of you a number, you give it a name."

Morgan's opinion is most likely colored by his extensive experience with the unbelievably resilient B-17. It is almost certainly true that, although not able to take as much punishment as the B-17 or the B-24, the B-29 stood up quite well in the dangerous skies over Japan. Robert Ramer, a B-29 pilot, loved his aircraft because of its reliability and its comfort: "This thing was tremendous. I had to get used to the idea that the rest of the crew was way, way back there somewhere. It was a magnificent plane to fly. We went first class. Warm and comfortable. We even had a food warmer. When we were about an hour from the target, we'd plug in the warmer so when we got done with the bomb run and were coming home, we could eat our dinner. It was very important to us that it got plugged in. The cockpit in the B-29 was like an office. There was more than enough room in there and the visibility was incredible with all that glass. There was a tunnel that went back over the bomb bay to the rest of the plane. Sometimes I'd go in there with a blanket and sleep like a baby. Remember, we were flying missions to Japan that went 15, 16 hours. Like I said, that airplane was very pleasant, especially when you compare it to what else was available."

The crews of America's best-known and most glamorous bomber, the B-17 Flying Fortress, could only dream of such comfort. Their plane may not have been comfortable, but it was among the most rugged aircraft ever produced. The B-17 could withstand terrific punishment and still get its crew home, a fact that bred an almost religious devotion to the B-17 among its crews. A four-engine bomber like the B-29 and the B-24, the B-17 Flying Fortress was designed for deep penetration, strategic bombing raids over the enemy's homeland. High-ranking Air Force officers hoped that the B-17 could fight its way to the target and back with the benefit of more than ten .50-caliber machine guns throughout the aircraft. In reality, it needed fighter escort to escape prohibitive losses over Germany. It had a ceiling of 35,000 feet, a cruising speed of 160 miles per hour, and a range of more than 1,800 miles; it could carry up to 17,000 pounds of bombs on short missions. Late models, called B-17Gs, featured a chin turret of twin .50-caliber machine guns directly below the nose. The chin turret was installed to counter head-on German fighter attacks.

The Flying Fortress proved to be an ideal heavy bomber for America in World War II. It was beautiful and majestic in appearance and handled quite well. Its bombload and its armament made it a formidable weapon. The crews who flew the Fortress thought of it as the perfect aircraft for the kind of missions they carried out. When the Army asked them if they had the best kind of aircraft for the type of job they did, 92 percent of them responded affirmatively.

In spite of the operational and aerodynamic success of the Flying Fortress, most B-17 crewmen loved it mainly because of its ability to absorb a tremendous amount of enemy fire and still get home. Nothing caused combat men to love an aircraft more than its direct contribution to their personal survival. Because the B-17 often returned home safely from the murderous skies over Europe, many of the airmen came to love it. Ray Zuker, a pilot in the 486th Bomb Group, wrote about his crew's attachment to their B-17: "Machines aren't human but we practically believed that *Lady Lightnin'* [their aircraft] had a life of her own. We endowed her with that life since our lives depended upon her mechanical performance. She took us to hell and back." Harry Crosby, a navigator in the 100th Bomb Group, concurred: "Because of the many times a 'Fort' got our crews back when it could have dropped them into the drink, we were grateful to it, and emotional about it. The sound of a B-17 brought tears to the eyes of anyone who ever flew one." David McCarthy, a navigator in the 381st Bomb Group, felt that B-17 crewmen often ascribed human qualities to their planes: "To the men who flew in them, every Flying Fortress had a soul and could feel the pain of a shattered body. To us, they were living, breathing creatures."

Combat airmen were astonished at the sheer punishment the B-17 could endure. John Clarkson, a top turret gunner/engineer in the 34th Bomb Group, wrote to his wife that, when it came to his crew's B-17, "You can shoot the hell out of her, but she'll make it back if the pilot can get her back." Barwick Barfield, a navigator in the 100th Bomb Group, proclaimed: "It was a miracle how some of these damaged B-17s got home—with tails shot off, gaping holes in the fuselage, engines and electrical systems shot out, and with dead and wounded crew members." Another 100th Bomb Group man, copilot Keith Lamb, thought the B-17 was the most rugged airplane he had ever seen: "B-17s seemed to be able to take more punishment and still fly than any other plane built. I saw one come back so riddled with flak that when it landed it broke right in two. But still it came back."

One of the most amazing and compelling stories of the B-17's lifesaving ruggedness occurred one day in the 390th Bomb Group. Pilot John Flottorp and his crew took a terrific beating on a bombing mission, but somehow their B-17 brought them home to their base in England. Flottorp recounted the damage to the plane: "We had landed without brakes with the right tire burned badly after having to crank the gear down. Seventeen 20mm entry holes were counted, along with numerous machine gun bullet holes and too many flak holes to count. The number three engine had the crankcase holed, the oil cooler shot away, a runaway prop, and a fire. The number four engine turbo waste gate had been hit and jammed in a partial power position. Both numbers one and two had burned valves and pistons from overboosting and overheating but had held together. The vertical fin had collected seven 20mm hits that opened up the skin, looking like Swiss cheese. The main wing spar on the right wing had virtually severed in two places along with the right aileron cables. The waist and radio room had been sieved by flak and fighter fire, but no one got a scratch. We were . . . one crew who were inordinately lucky. The incredibly tough B-17 . . . deserves much credit."

The plane was junked, but at least it had gotten Flottorp and his crew home. Thanks to such incidents, the B-17 was arguably the most beloved aircraft of World War II.

What kind of clothing would an American combat airman wear for a typical mission? In most cases, especially among bomber crews in the European theater, warm, layered clothing was the norm.

Temperatures at high altitudes were often well below zero, and most American combat aircraft were not pressurized. This meant two things. First, men had to wear many layers of warm clothing to protect them from the cold. Second, they had to wear oxygen masks, since air at high altitudes is very low in oxygen content. The Army Air Force supplied its fliers with a bewildering array of equipment and clothing that allowed them to survive in such conditions. It is unnecessary to go into elaborate detail about the clothing and equipment. What is necessary is an understanding of the way combat airmen typically dressed for missions.

Fighter Pilot Francis Gabreski outlined the typical fighter pilot's garb: "I wore long underwear and extra socks, along with a thick sweater, under my flight suit. My fleece-lined flight jacket and boots completed the wardrobe. On top of that I would be wearing an inflatable Mae West life preserver and a parachute strapped to my rear."

Bomber crews who did not fly on pressurized B-29s wore tremendous quantities of clothing, including parachutes and flak vests. Often, these pieces of equipment could be the last hope for survival for a combat airman. William Binnebose, a waist gunner in the 95th Bomb Group, described his chute: "This chest chute was a small size chute that snapped on to two hooks on the front of your parachute harness. It was small enough to wear at your position in the plane in case of an emergency. It was only a 22-foot chute and it let you down fast compared to the 28-foot chute that was used by the paratroopers." Because chutes could be very bulky on cramped aircraft, many men did not keep them on all the time. Kenneth Williams, a bombardier in the 351st Bomb Group, did not wear his chute during a mission but kept it accessible at all times: "One wore the harness all the time in the air, but the actual parachute itself was folded up in a neat little package that could be clipped on the chest of the harness if ever needed. I always kept my parachute on the floor close to me in the nose compartment of the aircraft." Airmen commonly put on their chutes during a bomb run, one of the most dangerous moments of any mission. "We have them on usually over the target in the event the plane disintegrates. We are ready to jump," Radio Operator Merle Perkins of the 483d Bomb Group wrote in his diary.

This worked for everyone except the ball turret gunner. The turret was simply too cramped to allow the gunner to wear his chute. To bail out of the plane, he would have to have his turret cranked up, exit the turret, snap on the chute pack, and then jump—needless to say, a hazardous undertaking.

Another piece of equipment airmen wore during bomb runs was the armored flak vest, designed to protect crewmen from low-velocity shrapnel. Roger Armstrong, a radio operator in the 91st Bomb Group, described the flak suit he and others commonly wore: "Our suits were made of strips of magnesium steel sewn overlapping and extended from your neck to your groin in the front. In the back it extended from about the lowest cervical vertebrae to an area slightly below . . . the sacral area . . . protecting much of the spine and interior vital organs. They proved highly effective as they saved many men from serious injury or death. We also carried a steel helmet that fit over our regular leather helmets. Ear flaps were designed to fit over your head set."

Because it was so bulky, the flak suit could at times be an encumbrance that threatened to prevent a man from doing his job. Willis Marshall, a top turret gunner/engineer in the 389th Bomb Group, explained how he improvised to solve this problem: "I could hardly wear it in the turret so I would take it apart. I would set the oval section across the gun cradle behind my head—take the rear half of the flak suit and wire it up to the gun cradle." Edward Schlesinger, a navigator and bombardier in the 379th Bomb Group, would lay flak vests on the floor to protect himself from shrapnel coming up through the floor: "I would put mine down on the floor beneath me to absorb any flack [sic] which might hit the ship. The flack [sic] vests included aprons or skirts which were snapped on. In addition we wore flack [sic] helmets."

So when a typical bomber crewman prepared himself for a mission, how did he dress? William McCormick, a pilot in the 2d Bomb Group, dressed very warmly for his missions over Europe: "I started with undershorts and tee shirt, then long woolen underwear, followed by wool pants and shirt. This was all topped off with a long white scarf. Finally, I donned a winter wool flying suit and a heavy pile-lined jacket. The scarf was not for glamour, but to keep my neck warm. On my feet I wore two pairs of socks and GI brogans. After all the preliminary dressing, another layer of clothing would be put on when we reached the aircraft. There, we would don electrically heated flying suits, boots, and gloves. The brogans were removed and sheepskin boots were worn over the heated boots, but the brogans stayed with us on a cable attached to the parachute harness. In this way, in case of bailout, the brogans were available for walking when on the ground. Topping off all these layers of clothing was a parachute harness and then later, in flight, the flak vest and helmet. The typical bomber crewman, dressed for a combat mission, resembled nothing so much as a rotund pile of clothing. But it had to be when facing temperatures which could be 60 degrees below zero."

Sam Ross, a ball turret gunner in the 384th Bomb Group, outlined in minute detail what he and his buddies wore on missions: "We wore a bulky wardrobe as follows: Longjohn cotton underwear, wool slacks, wool long sleeve shirt. Then a heated suit made of a thin, light weight nylon type material. The suit was like bib overalls with a long sleeve jacket. Small electric wires embedded in the fabric. There was a connection at the ankle to plug in your felt heated shoes. A plug connection at the wrist for your heated gloves. And a connection at the collar for your heated goggles. Small wires passed thru [sic] the glass lens area to prevent fogging. Next layer was a nylon type jumpsuit with numerous pockets and full length front zipper. Topped off with a leather flight jacket. Head: Leather helmet with built-in ear phones. Side tabs to attach your rubber oxygen mask. Heated goggles. Hands: Silk gloves, Electric heated gloves, Fur lined leather gloves, bulky cloth mittens. That's right, four layers. Feet: Wool sox [sic]. Felt electric heated shoe. Leather GI shoe. Insulated cloth overboot. Survival gear. On the outside of the bulky suits we wore a rubberized 'Mae West' vest on our chest. It could be inflated for flotation by pulling a cord that actuated a small pressure cylinder. Next we wore a parachute harness with straps over our shoulders, around the chest, and thru the crotch."

Although they might seem incredibly elaborate, outfits like the ones McCormick and Ross describe were more the rule than the exception for bomber crews, particularly in the European theater.

One of the most fascinating objects in a typical bomber crewman's garb was the electrically heated suit. A very high-tech piece of equipment for the mid-1940s, the suit heated most of a man's body, including his extremities. Jule Berndt, a navigator in the 490th Bomb Group, thought the electrically heated suit was a godsend to him and his comrades: "Personally I feel this article of flying equipment has been the greatest gain in providing for the comfort of the air corps while working under the most adverse temperature conditions. Temperatures at bombing altitudes drop to minus 50 degrees during winter months and exposure can result in severe frost bite in a very short time. This suit not only has its values in comfort for the men, but it increases the efficiency and amount of work capable of being done."

The suits were not perfect, though, especially early in the war, when they commonly shorted out. William Blackmon, a waist gunner in the Eighth Air Force, had one major criticism of the suit: "If any part of it shorted out, then everything shorted out." Robert Bieck of the 453d Bomb Group had so many problems with his suit that he finally gave up wearing it: "I became disenchanted with wearing an electrically heated suit after I burned my right leg from a short circuit in the suit's wiring. I continued to wear the heavy leather sheepskin flight clothing—nothing in that outfit is going to fail." Such a strategy could be risky, though, because in some cases numerous layers of clothing were not adequate for the kind of temperatures combat airmen faced. Donald Askerman, a ball turret gunner in the 461st Bomb Group, noted: "One got pretty cold without them [the suits]. It got terribly cold in the waist when the waist windows were opened which was all the time we were in enemy territory." He continued to wear his suit in spite of one very unpleasant experience: "My heated suit short-circuited. I first noticed something was wrong when I felt the heat burning my arm and when I looked down I saw my sleeve smoking. Gaudio, our bombardier, happened to be in the waist at the time and just stood there staring at me. I jerked off my glove, but that didn't stop it. So, by the time I got around to disconnecting the suit, Gaudio woke up and pulled out the cord from the socket. I was such a sight hopping around that Gaudio and Lukas . . . laughed so hard their sides hurt. Those suits did that quite often."

Airmen in the Pacific were seldom exposed to such dangerously low temperatures. Nonetheless, those who flew in B-24s and other unpressurized aircraft often had to guard against some cold temperatures and therefore dress accordingly. Although he did not wear an electrically heated suit, Navy Pilot John Bradford still dressed quite warmly: "What some of us did was to opt for several layers of thin clothing under our regulation flight suit. If you could keep your ankle, wrist, and neck areas snug and insulated you could stay warm and still be able to move about. Trying to tough it out bare-handed didn't work; your fingers would stiffen and the fine control needed for precise work was lost. Gunner's gloves with an index-finger hole in the palm worked."

Kevin Herbert, a tail gunner in the 498th Bomb Group, was lucky in the sense that his unit flew B-29s. That meant he enjoyed the warmth and comfort of a pressurized cabin. Even so, he had to dress warmly and have enough equipment at hand in the event the aircraft lost pressure. He described what he took with him on a typical mission: "Colt .45, Bowie knife, and canteen attached to our belts; oxygen mask, parachute, survival vest, which was packed with food, a flashlight, a nylon map . . . compass, fish hooks, and the like; the Mae West jacket, individual rubber rafts, and last but not least, our flak jackets and flak helmets. One notable aspect of the night missions was the way we dressed for them. Since they were always at low levels, we simply wore suntans or flight suits with our sleeves rolled up or cut off. I kept my parachute harness on over Japan, but the snap-on parachute I kept at my feet. The flak jacket and helmet were also on the floor. All of this was in direct contrast to the daylight high level strikes which might be at altitudes from 18,000 to 24,000 feet. Here one dressed against the cold."

In World War II, American aircraft and flying equipment generally did a good job. For those who flew the missions, the machinery that got them to and from targets and the clothes that protected them from the elements were vital parts of the fabric of war.

3

People, Places, and Food—Europe

We . . . had to sleep on cots with three square cushions as mattresses. Invariably they split apart before the night was over. Heat was provided by two small coal-fired units. I think we were rationed one coal bucket . . . per day. The building was 50 feet long and about 20 wide. The floors were concrete, with concrete walls, inside and out. Basically . . . nothing more than a shell.
—Willis Marshall, top turret gunner/engineer,
389th Bomb Group, describing his barracks in England

A major part of the combat experience in World War II consisted of the conditions in which you lived, the food you ate, and the people with whom you interacted. For combat airmen in the European theater, living conditions ranged from barebones to extremely comfortable. Almost all combat airmen had roofs over their heads, which was more than could be said for their ground-combat counterparts. Knowing this, airmen considered themselves lucky for whatever shelter they had, even though it was not always ideal.

The most primitive living conditions were in North Africa. In 1942 and 1943, some American combat airmen found themselves in the alien atmosphere of a completely different culture. Lloyd Haefs, a bombardier in the 2d Bomb Group in the summer of 1943, described his unit's living area: "Our pyramidal tents, like bloated mushrooms, covered the area. Mess and kitchen tents nestled near the center with the 'All important' mail shack. Clear of the living area, straddle trenches ran along one side out in the sandy desert. The temperatures by day often reached 115 degrees and the shady tents afforded adequate protection. We slept on cots under mosquito bars, with Arab mats on the sandy floor. Stacked ammo boxes served as dressers for clothing and storage for books, etc. One small bulb hung in the center to illuminate the interior. It was powered by gasoline fueled generators and their incessant 'Put-put' became a part of the normal camp life. A wooden frame, upright in the sand with a slotted grate beneath it, served as a shower. A 50-gallon drum mounted upon it was filled from the water trucks every day. If one waited too late in the day, the water became uncomfortably hot and it took the cool night air to temper it."

As American ground forces captured large portions of southern Italy, the Army set up airbases from which to bomb targets in northern Europe. In terms of living conditions, Italy was a step up from North Africa, although not exactly perfect for American tastes. Leroy Watson, a pilot in the 17th Bomb Group, found himself stationed on Sardinia. He wrote to his mother and described his living arrangements: "We are off in the woods away from anything and the only electricity we have comes from homemade generators and engines so we only have 'juice' in the late afternoon." Robert Goebel, a fighter pilot in the 31st Fighter Group stationed in San Severo, Italy, described his quarters: "Our housing area, eight or nine miles from the town, was formerly an Italian Army post, so there was a cluster of permanent buildings. The spaces between them were filled with enlisted men's tents. The housing structures were masonry with tiled roofs, the long narrow interiors broken up by walls into a series of rooms. They were dark and gloomy inside, devoid of creature comforts other than Army cots. The stark interiors and hard, cold floors, which produced a faint echo when walked upon, combined to give the places a look and feel of monasticism."

Another fighter pilot, J. Fred Baumann of the 52d Fighter Group, understood quite well that, even though his tent accommodations at Foggia were not ideal, they were more than adequate for minimum comfort. This fact became even more apparent to him one day when he escorted an infantry officer around his base: "We showed him around our living area. He snorted when he inspected our showers. He puckered-up his mouth when we demonstrated how we heated our tents, and when we took him to visit our officer's club and mess, his eyes bulged a little bit. After completing the tour, he was heard to say, 'And I'll bet you guys think you have it real rough!' No doubt, he considered us to be a bunch of over-pampered kids."

Airmen in heavy-bomber groups in Italy also generally lived well. Arthur Carpenter, a navigator in the Fifteenth Air Force, wrote to his family and related the conditions in which he and his buddies lived: "Although we are supposedly roughing it living in tents . . . we are gradually getting very comfortably settled. We have electric lights now, a Finnish steam bath, and will soon have our own Officer's Mess with tablecloths, dishes, and everything."

Some American fliers, mainly fighter pilots and light bomber crewmen, lived in France in 1944 and 1945. They regularly moved from base to base as American troops advanced closer to Germany. Thus, their bases tended to be built hurriedly by engineers. Sometimes they resided at former German airbases. Such was the case for Quentin Aanenson, a young fighter pilot in the 366th Fighter Group. His unit spent the fall of 1944 at a former German fighter base in Laon: "Johnny Bathurst, Ray Beebe, and I put together a well equipped, comfortable tent. We scoured the countryside until we could find enough wood to build some flooring. We installed a wood burning stove, and built a wind protected entrance with an actual door. We were quite comfortable." During his tour of duty with the 404th Fighter Group, Fighter Pilot John Marshall's living conditions ranged from tents to castles. His unit went from France to Belgium to Germany, and he wrote to his family at each stage, describing his accommodations. In September 1944, he wrote from France that he was "just now living in a marble winding staircased chateau which is heaven after tents. Fireplace in my room, great huge windows, a basin, and next door my dressing room with tremendous closets, full length mirrors, etc." Two months later, he was stationed in Belgium and wrote that he had been "sleeping in a fine comfortable sleeping bed. This room now looks like a million. Found, or rather had given to me, a fine looking rug and radio." By April 1945, his outfit had moved to Germany, where they lived in tents but still preserved many comforts. He said he and his buddies were "in an open field, tents for everything, plus the shacks and sheds we've built. The pilots built a lounge which is a knockout room to brief in. Fox-holes to be dug, messes to be set up, engineering armament, photographic laboratories, outhouses (among the first things), garbage pits, intelligence setup, map boards . . .

amounts to a small town actually. It is fun and work. We stand short on nothing, eating out of good china and sitting in good chairs, even though they are in a tent. Wood floor in the tent with the sides braced with boards and they are comfortable."

The majority of American combat airmen in the European theater were stationed in England. From that island nation, the Allies hoped to send fleets of heavy bombers to Germany and pound that country into submission through intense strategic bombing. In pursuit of that goal, dozens of American airbases were built in East Anglia and southern England. The region literally crawled with American planes and airmen. Some of those Americans did not like their living arrangements at all. One such man was Franklin Allen, a B-26 pilot and squadron commander in the 397th Bomb Group. He wrote to his wife and unfavorably described his accommodations at his group's base in Rivenhall, England: "I have a bed and an easy chair (very rare) and a table and a dresser and also a tap of extremely cold and terrible tasting water which falls on a slab of concrete with no drain except a hole in the bottom of the floor. The British make cleanliness an extremely difficult thing. Also they don't care much for toilets. The few they do provide generally don't work and the rest are buckets with seats on top."

John Clarkson, a top turret gunner/engineer in the 34th Bomb Group, despised his base and England itself for that matter. In writing in his diary about the nearby town of Ipswich, he remarked caustically that it "isn't worth the founder to blow it to hell. If I ever come back to England after I leave it, it will be in a pine-box." David McCarthy, a navigator in the 381st Bomb Group, did not like the shower situation at his group's base in Ridgewell. In order to take a shower, he had to walk across the base to a poorly insulated, frigid shower room: "With a bar of soap in hand, and in a hopping, quick-step motion, we raced across the cold damp concrete floor to the colder, wet concrete floor under the closest shower head. Either the cold water added to the discomfort already being experienced, or the body turned scarlet from the onslaught of the scalding hot water. Turning the water off and exposing the wet body to the rigors of that cold, damp room was a test of self-discipline and strength of will that only a well-trained fighting man could possess." John Pendleton of the 466th Bomb Group recalled that his group's showers at Attlebridge were located outside: "Four walls and no roof. During cold weather there was always ice on the floor, wall, and pipes. But we were lucky—we *could* shower, shave, and clean up regularly."

Like Pendleton, most American airmen in England felt that the standard of living was lower than what Americans were used to, but they understood that, under wartime conditions, their barracks and showers were about as good as could be expected. Most of them keenly understood that their comrades in the infantry lived outside among the forces of nature. This made most airmen grateful to have roofs over their heads at all, especially ones in the middle of a modern, industrialized nation so similar to America. Keith Lamb, a pilot in the 100th Bomb Group, described his living accommodations at Thorpe Abbotts: "Our . . . Bachelor Officer's Quarters was a small one-story cement building with steel framed windows, partitioned across the center, with a door at each end, making it practically two separate barracks. In front of each door was a ditch which served as air raid shelter. Twelve fellows slept on each side of the building, usually the officers of three crews."

Another officer, Pilot John White of the 448th Bomb Group, described his barracks at Seething: "We slept in Nissen huts. A Nissen hut is made out of corrugated metal and it's half round. They were probably twelve feet high. We didn't have any toilet facilities in there. We had a stove right in the middle of the room and we had cots. The officers of two crews would be in one hut. We had electricity in there."

Quarters for enlisted men were similar, the only difference being the fact that they were slightly more crowded. Jack Novey, a waist gunner in the 96th Bomb Group, lived at Snetterton Heath: "In the non-com areas there were two or three crews—between twelve and eighteen men, all sergeants—in each hut. Our own hut had eighteen beds. These Nissen huts were made of corrugated iron in the form of a half-dome with a wooden wall and door at the front. The floor was concrete. When you opened the door you saw unmade beds and crudely-fashioned shelves illuminated by a single bare light bulb hanging from a wire in the center. The tiny coke stove in

sudden there was a tremendous explosion when a V-2 hit very close to the club, rattled all of the windows, and shook the foundation. As soon as that happened I grabbed my stuff and decided to leave London immediately. I procured a cab to take me to St. Pancras Station and on the way a V-2 bomb went off not more than 100 yards from our taxi cab . . . and dug a huge hole spraying dirt all over the place, but it did no damage to us because of the soft ground in which it hit. I was glad to get out of London after that incident. It was bad enough being fired at when you are over Germany, but I didn't fancy the idea of being fired at while I was in London."

This is not to say that American airbases in England were completely safe. Occasionally the Germans fired buzz bombs at American bases or flew small air raids to harass them. Casualties were minimal, though, causing only slight damage to the bases. Mostly they amounted to nuisance raids. Philip Ardery, a pilot in the 389th Bomb Group, described the extent of the German air threat to his group's base at Hethel: "Once or twice I saw the puny efforts of the Nazis attempting a raid on our airdrome. We would hear frantic calls over the public address system for all personnel to report to the shelters. It was only a cue for us to go outside to see the sight. Twice I watched the enemy planes get shot down." James Good Brown, a chaplain in the 381st Bomb Group, clearly felt that German raids posed no threat to his group's base at Ridgewell. In his wartime diary he wrote: "When the alert is sounded, no one does anything, though there are air-raid shelters all over the base. I have never seen anyone on the base enter a bomb shelter when the alert is sounded. Men just keep on working at their jobs. Occasionally a bomb falls in a field a few miles from the base, dropped at random by a night bomber. If one fell on our base, it would be a mere chance hit."

On rare occasions, though, disaster did occur. One day in the summer of 1944, Keith Lamb and his crew had just returned from a mission to Nantes, France, when German planes attacked their base: "After we landed, a Jerry JU-88 flew over, strafing our field. I . . . saw a JU-88 boring right down on top of us—spitting lead. Tracers were passing about six feet over my head. The Germans had followed us back . . . and were raising cain all over. A group of B-24s were trying to land at their base right next to us, and a bunch of

Focke-Wulf-190s were shooting the devil out of them. I saw three blow up. They were too low to parachute, but guys were jumping out anyway."

Curiously enough, weather often proved to be a bigger threat to the lives of American combat airmen than German bombs. This was true not just in England, where foggy weather is notorious, but also in Italy, where the weather could be atrocious at times. Foggy or inclement weather meant dangerous flying conditions, especially in crowded skies with heavy bombers attempting to get into formation for raids over Europe.

Donald Askerman, a ball turret gunner in the 461st Bomb Group in Italy, wrote that Italian weather was tolerable enough through most of the year except for winter, which could be awful. Italian weather in the winter usually meant cold, rainy, raw days: "The winter weather in Italy . . . was uncertain and usually harsh. Mud was something we had to learn to live with. We tried to keep it out of our tent, but the best we could hope to do was to keep a little area clear beside our bunks. Periodically one of us would go get a broom . . . and sweep it out, but that was a hopeless task with the mess right outside the door and so much traffic in and out of our place."

On days like that, most groups in Italy would be grounded. Since the weather in Italy was usually conducive to flying, bomb groups and fighter groups stationed in that country could afford to stand down on bad-weather days. This was not always the case in England, a country famous for its foggy and rainy weather. Clear days in England tended to be the exception rather than the rule, so fliers had to learn to deal with dangerous weather conditions and fly in them.

Art Gulliver, a weatherman in World War II, described the task of predicting weather for combat air groups: "Predicting weather in England was difficult. The moisture was the problem—there was so much of it. And weather changed rapidly. In the North Atlantic, particularly in winter, the storms came in every eighteen hours on average." Combat airmen rarely found themselves flying in perfect weather. The weather had to be very bad, over England and over Europe, for missions to be scrubbed. But sometimes men would be briefed for a mission only to get the word it was aborted due to bad weather. Even though combat airmen knew in the backs of their minds that the mission would simply have to be flown another day, they could feel a sense of relief when missions were scrubbed. Ben Smith, a radio operator in the 303d Bomb Group, often thought of bad weather as his best friend: "I was always glad to see the mission scrubbed because of bad weather. It meant I had another day to live."

Usually, though, the foggy and rainy English weather was not bad enough to warrant a cancellation. This meant flying in very dangerous conditions. James Good Brown thought of the weather as the flier's worst enemy. He wrote in his diary of the kind of strain poor weather put on combat airmen: "While sitting with the fliers, I sometimes hear the remark: 'The flier's worst enemy is the weather.' What an enemy it can be: strong, defiant, mean, ugly, treacherous, unconquerable. I pity the fliers more when they face this unbeatable weather than at any other time. They come into the room with sweat running down their faces. Black streaks mark their cheeks. Their eyes are red from strain, and they look haggard and worn. If we waited for good weather in England, we would hardly ever fly. It certainly seems hazardous to send men into the air when they cannot see the wing tip of the plane next to them."

Keith Schuyler, a B-24 pilot in the 44th Bomb Group, hated and feared the English weather: "Fighting the weather over England was the most frustrating battle of the air war. It was one thing to risk the wrath of enemy planes and ground fire. But fighting the clammy mists and rolling clouds that covered the British Isles . . . was yet another." Eugene Fletcher, a pilot in the 95th Bomb Group, disliked the weather not only because it made for dangerous flying conditions but also because it could mean uncomfortable living conditions: "Our rooms were heated by a little old stove which was probably twelve inches in diameter and maybe eighteen inches tall. We had a coke ration every three days, but if you had a fire for several hours the ration would last only for one evening. It always seemed colder inside . . . than it was outside. The English weather is very, very damp and all the time we were there I don't remember ever putting on clothes that were completely dry."

With such an inadequate supply of coal or coke, men in England routinely pirated extra fuel from base coal dumps. This was true of both officers and enlisted fliers. By most accounts, almost everyone did it, and culprits were rarely punished. With the frequency of rain, mud could also be a problem at some of the less-developed bases. Dale Smith, a pilot, commanded the 384th Bomb Group. His group's base at Grafton Underwood—the men sardonically called it "Grafton Undermud"—was built on hard clay soil that held rains and generated awful mud: "It was irritating and depressing. Everyone slogged to the mess halls . . . in caked overshoes, parking them inside the doors, but mud somehow invaded every building and dried on the floors. Mud was tracked onto the taxiways and hardstands where the B-17s were parked, and accumulated on the wheels. There were instances of landing gears sticking in the up position when the mud froze."

By and large, American combat airmen in Europe ate well during World War II. Certainly many bases featured poor food, and airmen at those bases usually complained loudly, but most American airmen received reasonably good food compared to the fare for most combatants in World War II. Airmen quickly realized that, as Americans, they enjoyed a higher standard of living than other people. Combat airmen ate in special mess halls reserved exclusively for combat personnel. Combat fliers had the benefit of hot meals, rarely eating prepackaged rations.

Ben O'Dell, a navigator in the 303d Bomb Group, described a typical pre-mission meal for his unit: "Most of the time, we were served powdered eggs with thick sliced streaked side meat (ham). The powdered eggs were prepared in a very large pan. Directly above the eggs, the fluorescent lights gleamed with blue bulbs. This blue light and the yellow of the eggs resulted in lovely green eggs for breakfast! These green eggs were our last meal for a long time. On real long missions a box lunch was prepared which consisted of a sandwich. With temperatures frequently minus 40 degrees C or colder, our food was usually frozen solid."

Used to high standards, some American combat airmen found themselves nauseated by the food served to them, and they displayed little reluctance to air complaints. Franklin Allen wrote to his wife one afternoon that he had just "had an awful lunch—stew consisting of 90 per cent fat and gristle. I told the mess hall that in the future whenever they had ingredients for hamburgers or cheese sandwiches, they were to rush a set over to me so I can stave off starvation." Jack Novey despised the food at his base. It was all he could do to choke it down: "The food was gruesome at our base. All I could get down before a mission was a piece of bread and some coffee." Barney Bussey, a fighter pilot in the 332d Fighter Group, described the food he and his fellow pilots consumed: "The food was piss-poor. Very little meat. Dehydrated food, I'd never heard of it. On the whole we lived a very bleak and miserable life." Tom Miller, a pilot in the 448th Bomb Group, wrote that breakfast before missions usually consisted of greasy, green powdered eggs, fried salami, disgusting chipped beef or "pancakes that certainly would have been satisfactory substitutes for discs . . . in the Olympics! We all eventually concluded that the Army personnel people in all their great wisdom had assigned all the cooks as truck drivers and assigned us the truck drivers as cooks!!" William Cubbins, a pilot in the 450th Bomb Group, thought that the food at his unit's base in Manduria, Italy, was nothing short of a disgrace. He vividly recounted a typical breakfast: "Breakfast was the usual demoralizing affair: powdered eggs drenched in catsup; acid Spam that would sour a goat's stomach; and greasy toast lying limp in its own sweat. The coffee tasted and felt like raw metal."

One way to spice up an otherwise disgusting menu was to procure food from the locals. The most sought-after food was eggs. J. Fred Baumann, a fighter pilot in the 52d Fighter Group in Italy, used to barter with local farmers for fresh eggs: "By being located near several farms . . . we had an abundant supply of fresh eggs. The farmers would frequently come through our living areas to trade eggs for American cigarettes. The exchange rate was three eggs for one pack of cigarettes (they cost us five cents a pack)." Baumann claimed that the farmers accepted all American cigarette brands except one, Raleigh. Apparently a ship loaded with Raleigh cigarettes had sunk off the coast of Italy. Some packages of the cigarettes had been salvaged and circulated. They appeared dry and normal on the outside but were actually soaked on the inside. Word traveled fast about the Raleighs among the Italian farmers, and they refused to accept them in trades.

Jack Lancaster, a fighter pilot in the 350th Fighter Group, recalled eating wild birds in North Africa: "Some of us bought some guinea fowl from the Arabs. We put the tough birds in a pot and boiled them for two days before they could be eaten. Finally they were done enough to chew and were pretty good; at least they were better than C-Rations." Ben O'Dell had a buddy who knew how to cook chicken and dumplings. They found the necessary butter, flour, and salt at the mess hall but still needed the meat. For several days they stalked an elusive rooster. Finally one day, the rooster's charmed life came to an end: "Suddenly the rooster crowed. The barracks doors flew open and out came everyone with pistols, knives, rifles, and even one broom. As the circle closed, the rooster did his . . . disappearing act by flying straight up. Andy Virag immediately ran in, jumped up, and caught the rooster by its longest toe." That night they dined on chicken and dumplings, a welcome respite from the mess hall. In England, local restaurants and pubs provided a major source of alternate food. Roger Armstrong and his buddies used to buy carry-out fish and chips from a nearby restaurant: "At times, the men in my . . . barracks tired of the combat mess-hall food. A number of us would decide we wanted fish and chips. One of us would volunteer to ride his bike to Royston. The owner of the fish and chips house would wrap our orders in old newspapers, due to the shortage of wrapping paper and boxes. Fish and chips shops were the original 'fast food' services in Europe."

Usually the food served to combat airmen was of reasonably high quality and quantity. This is especially true compared to other nations' combatants or even American ground-combat troops, who often had to eat prepackaged, cold rations on the front lines. Vince Cahill, a bombardier in the 491st Bomb Group, knew quite well that he was relatively lucky in the food he ate: "Considering that there was a war on, the food in the mess hall was O.K. One advantage the Air Force had was a hot meal and a bed when you returned from a mission. I didn't envy the infantry living in fox holes and eating out of mess kits or with cold rations." Edwin Anderson, a gunner in the 489th Bomb Group, wrote to his mother and expressed his satisfaction with the food: "The food here is real good. For supper we had ham probably from a fat hog back in Iowa." In writing his postwar memoir, Harry Crosby fondly recalled the hot breakfast he used to eat before embarking on a mission: "At the mess hall, I smell bacon, eggs, pancakes, syrup. The breakfast is good, very good. Real eggs. Canadian bacon, orange juice, oatmeal, pancakes. I eat something of everything the K.P.s put out." Robert Fesmire, a pilot in the 492d Bomb Group, gave the food in his mess hall high marks: "The food in the officer's mess was of the highest quality, and very delicious. While going through the serving line one evening, I saw large, juicy steaks."

As a group commander, Dale Smith made a special effort to improve the food served to his men: "One of our enterprising cooks found that by mixing the powder and water with a high-speed electric heater for twenty-four hours, the eggs and milk lost their offensive odor and began to taste like the fresh articles. We found, too, that delicious omelets and pastries could be made with the treated eggs. Fresh eggs were rare and precious, and were served only to combat crews who were scheduled on a mission. Using our unlimited supply of powdered milk and eggs, we produced tons of delicious ice cream. After a while I was pleased to find people from other groups dropping in to eat at . . . our messes. And when I asked an airman why he had returned early from leave, he told me he got tired of London food and wanted to get home for a good meal."

One perk American combat airmen enjoyed was a hot turkey dinner on holidays such as Thanksgiving and Christmas. In fact, the Army attempted to get hot turkey to all men regardless of rank or circumstance. Infantrymen's meals were often cold by the time they reached the front lines, but airmen had no such problem. Richard Anderson, a navigator in the Fifteenth Air Force, wrote to his family from Italy on Thanksgiving Day and lauded the meal he had just eaten: "It was all white meat and really good with dressing, string beans, peas, and *real* mashed potatoes. We had wine to start on and then minced [sic] pie and a big piece of cheese and sliced pineapple for dessert." William Stafford, a bombardier in the 388th Bomb Group, wrote to his family the day after Christmas and described a similar meal: "We had a terrific dinner last night, it was really nice. Turkey, with all the trimming, even down to candy, fruit, pie, and ice-cream. That's one reason I've always been thankful to be where I am. We at least have a warm bed and good food."

Every bit as plentiful as food on an airbase was alcohol. During World War II, combat airmen had a collective reputation as hard-drinking glamour boys of the sky, and there is a certain degree of truth to this notion. American combat airmen in Europe consumed large amounts of alcohol during their off-duty hours. They had ready access to bars on their bases and pubs or restaurants off base. They also had plenty of disposable cash to spend on drinks. In addition, many combat airmen received a "medicinal" shot or two of whiskey upon returning from a mission. The purpose was to relieve the tension of the mission and loosen their tongues for debriefings. The lion's share of drinking among combat airmen, though, occurred at night at on-post bars or at unit parties.

Lloyd Haefs recalled an instance in North Africa when the men in his outfit, with their commander's approval and assistance, took some aircraft to England to buy liquor from a British distiller: "Our crew whiskey had been depleted for some time and no other sources presented themselves. Locating the main office of a prominent distiller was easy and they proceeded from there post haste [sic]! The CEO listened attentively then made some phone calls. The upshot [was] a truck of various liquors would be loaded and sent to the airfield to be transferred to the bomber. Final amenities were exchanged and the crew soon found themselves leaving the civilized air of London for the dingy atmosphere of the North African desert where they were welcomed with open arms."

Apparently the British distiller, grateful for American help in defending his country, would accept no money for the liquor. At the same time, another group flew to Tunis to procure beer: "A ship load was taken aloft for several hours to accomplish a cooling process so that everyone's thirst could be slaked by the liquid of their choice."

Most units, particularly those stationed in England, had no problem finding alcohol. There was plenty of it to go around, and men drank it in mass quantities as an escape from the horrors of combat. Base parties were very common, as Keith Lamb recalled: "There were dances at both the Officer's Club and Enlisted Men's Club every weekend. We would send out trucks for miles around the countryside to pick up the girls who wanted to come, and it seemed as if they all did. To my knowledge, none of these affairs ever ran out of Scotch or beer; we always had all we wanted. As a result, at the end of the evening there was usually a fight or two—and some would start breaking up furniture—or have a bicycle race around the dance floor."

Units often threw parties to celebrate their 100th or 200th missions. Harry Crosby's 100th Bomb Group organized one such party in September 1944: "Wars being what they are, and soldiers being what they are, we began to accumulate all the alcoholic beverages we could acquire. The party committee commandeered a plane . . . to fly to London to pick up crates and crates of supplies. I was asked to be the navigator." James Good Brown described the alcohol consumption at a typical base party. Nothing in particular was being celebrated or commemorated. The unit simply felt like having a party and had the necessary time and alcohol to do so: "Four kegs of beer were consumed. Each keg holds 240 pints. Four times 240 equals 960 pints; 110 men were present; 960 divided by 110 makes 9 pints per man. Just how any man can get nine pints into his stomach in one evening is a mystery to me. Nevertheless it was done."

Most likely the majority of the drinking took place not at such organized parties but, night after night, at officer's or enlisted men's clubs on the base. After a perilous day in the skies over Europe, many men turned to alcohol as an escape or as a release. They also drank to relieve the boredom of mission postponements or prolonged unit stand-downs. David McCarthy described an instance in which he had too much to drink, something very common in the tight circle of combat airmen at any given base. In McCarthy's case, overconsumption led to mischief: "During the evening after mess, a group of us gathered in the lounge, and in a giddy, hilarious manner we began drinking. Before many rounds of drinks were consumed, we became loud and boisterous, and from that stage degenerated into drunkenness. Realizing I had long since passed the limit of my capacity I found my . . . coat and my cap and left the club. Outside, I hesitated. For some unidentified reason I had to go to the Flight Line. As I walked slowly from the club, passing several parked jeeps, the thought occurred to me that a jeep would get me there faster—so I took a jeep. Not just any jeep—the best jeep, the one with the enclosed cab. Colonel Leber's jeep." Driving way too fast in the pitch-dark night, McCarthy had a difficult time seeing the road, and before long he lost control and crashed the colonel's jeep. Lucky to escape unhurt, he endured a major tongue-lashing in the morning from his commander. McCarthy felt that the colonel never forgave him for the foolish stunt. The combination of alcohol, combat, and high-spirited young men made such instances fairly common among combat airmen in the European theater. The consumption of alcohol was a big part of the culture of flying and the culture of combat.

American combat airmen in Europe had numerous opportunities to interact with indigenous civilians. Combat airmen were stationed far and wide in the European theater, from North Africa to Italy to France to England. By and large, they enjoyed excellent relations with civilians. Americans came not as conquerors but as liberators in World War II, and this guaranteed that there would be very little significant tension between combat airmen and local civilians. Because most combat airmen were white, there was also a shared cultural heritage with Europeans. Moreover, American aviators generally comported themselves with decency and respect toward the locals.

Combat fliers had their own varying opinions of Europeans, although it can safely be said that they generally liked most civilians. In Italy, though, combat airmen sometimes felt contempt for the poverty and filth in which many Italians lived. Americans, used to cleanliness and high standards of hygiene, were at times appalled by the lack of attention some Italian civilians gave to such matters. Merle Perkins, a radioman in the 483d Bomb Group, visited Naples during his tour of duty and described the scene in his diary: "The Naples street scene . . . is miserable. The smell of fish, garbage, and urine is sometimes intense. Men and children seem 'to go' on any available wall. Most people are poorly dressed, undernourished." Donald Askerman generally liked the Italian people, but he was initially revolted at some of the smells emanating from Italian towns:

"It seemed that one could almost smell them before one saw them. This was a smell no doubt formed from the unclean nature of their life-style where rubbish . . . was often thrown out the back door—out of sight, out of mind. One had to accept it as a price for visiting the Italians where and as they lived." Technically, Italy was an enemy country, and there were some areas in which Americans found themselves unwelcome. Askerman recalled that he and his buddies had to wear pistols and travel in groups if they chose to visit the nearby town of Cerignola, a place rife with Fascist activity. On a leave one day, he walked through a small Italian town with a Scottish soldier he had recently met: "As we approached we noticed the populace got quiet. People were gathered on their balconies which projected over the sidewalks. They . . . became noisy with epithets and loud shouts as we passed. It was kind of scary, like we were truly foreigners . . . and very much on our own." It is possible that the civilians gave Askerman and his friend this hostile reception in reaction to Allied bombings of the area. Stray bombs accidentally killed numerous Italian civilians throughout the war, and rumors circulated among American airmen that some Italian civilians would lynch bombardiers (since they were the ones who actually dropped the bombs) if they could catch them alone. Such notions, though, were usually nothing more than rumors.

J. Fred Baumann's 52d Fighter Group moved northward in Italy as the war came to a close. He had a veiled contempt for southern Italians but found he liked the northerners, who were often lighter skinned and culturally similar to northern Europeans: "In southern Italy the people were dark and of swarthy complexions—dirty-looking so to speak. Up here, they were of fairer skin, lighter color hair, and oftentimes they had blue eyes. Moreover, their personal hygiene habits were vastly improved over their southern cousins." Joseph Beswick, a ball turret gunner in the 483d Bomb Group, liked the Italian people very much. Like many other Americans, he and his buddies became especially attached to the local children: "My best memories of Italy were the kids. One young boy by the name of Mario used our tent as his headquarters. He would pick up a lot of laundry from the other tents and would leave it in ours until he was ready to go home. Mario was a real good kid and could speak English very well; it seemed that all the young kids could speak and understand the English language. When we went to the mess hall to eat, we always tried to take some extra food because when we went out to empty our mess kits there was [sic] always some kids waiting for any food that was left over."

Many American light bomber crews and fighter pilots had an opportunity to meet French civilians in 1944 and 1945, and they generally held them in higher esteem than the Italians. Like many of his comrades, Fighter Pilot Francis Mooney of the 324th Fighter Group, was especially drawn to children: "When we were in France, there were always kids hanging around garbage cans looking for whatever they could get because that was the only way they had to survive. That's the tragedy of war that you don't think about. You heard about the guys that were heroes, the guys that got shot . . . but you didn't hear about the poor little kids whose house was blown up or looted or was [sic] starving."

John Marshall lived among the French while his unit was stationed in France, and he came to like them very much. During the summer of 1944, his fighter base was located in the middle of a French farm. He wrote to his parents that he and his buddies "bathe and run around in shorts, regardless. Two gals . . . with two brothers, are always at my plane when I get out and help me off the wing after landing." A few weeks later, he had the wonderful experience of liberating a town, one of the few perks ground-combat troops in World War II normally had over their air brethren: "The people lined the streets and most went wild as we drove through there. I sat in the back seat . . . waving and finally threw kisses while they tossed bunches of flowers to us amidst wild screams and great excitement. Have never had my ego so boosted." Lonzo Hetherington, a Ninth Air Force pilot based in France, also had great affection for the French people. He wrote to his family that "Most of the French people are very friendly with us and treat us swell," and expressed his general approval of French society. Robert Bagley, a ball turret gunner in the 445th Bomb Group in England, had an opportunity to fly supply missions to Allied ground forces in France in September 1944. It gave him the chance to get to know the French people, and he liked what he saw: "It was the most encouraging and heart warming reception I have ever had. I had a whole crowd of smiling kids in to the back hatch of the airplane while I proceeded to tear open the K-rations we had to give them, 'chooin' gum,' chocolate, and sugar lumps . . . and also cigarettes 'pour papa.' They were much more polite than English children. The French people themselves are very friendly and . . . they're cleaner and neater in appearance than the English."

Americans based in England found themselves in the middle of a country with familiar traditions, a similar culture, and the same language. By and large, they enjoyed excellent relations with the British people, although the wartime British complaint about Americans being "overpaid, oversexed, and over here" has been well chronicled.

The general sentiment was that if one had to leave America to go fight a war, the next best place to be was England. With no language barrier, the average combat airman often had the opportunity to get to know civilians very well. Many of them readily took advantage of this opportunity. Some came home with English wives.

Even so, there were a few Americans who did not like the English. John Clarkson, a top turret gunner/engineer in the 34th Bomb Group, freely discussed his loathing of the English in a letter to his wife: "To read the English newspapers, the English is [sic] who won the war. Although some of the English people are nice, you don't run across many of them. The limeys will cut a Yank's throat in everything an American does." American combat airmen rarely fostered such abject contempt for the English, though. More often, the airmen liked the English people but disliked some aspects of their character or English culture. Such was the case with Jack Novey. Sometimes as he and his crewmates waited outside their plane for the go-ahead order to start a mission, they would see English civilians chug by on a nearby train. Novey found himself irritated by their lack of visible support: "These people are going about their business as if we and the war don't even exist. They seem so unconcerned. Aren't they aware that we risk our lives for them every day? Do they care? Why can't they occasionally smile or give us the thumbs-up?" Like many Americans, Fighter Pilot John Ziebell of the 357th Fighter Group found that he disliked and could not understand the British class system: "I was dating a British Red Cross volunteer. She worked as a maid for a wealthy family. When I met the family, I felt very much looked down upon. I was an American officer but was dating their hired help."

Cultural differences aside, most American combat airmen in England had nothing but the highest opinion of the English people. Many Americans admired the quiet courage of the English people in enduring so many years of war. Others liked their industrious, earnest approach to the war, probably since it mirrored America's approach. They were also fascinated with the British tendency for understatement even in the face of great danger. Elmer Bendiner, a navigator in the 379th Bomb Group, met numerous Royal Air Force men and was impressed with their attitude: "The British, I quickly found, play themselves superbly in a nonstop performance. I had been used to watching Americans laugh at their own fears . . . with hilarious mock panic. These British . . . seemed determined to conquer death by patronizing it. It was an elegant approach." Franklin Allen admired the bravery of British civilians in the face of the V-1 attacks in London. He wrote to his wife: "It's absolutely amazing how these people react—or rather don't react to these things. I was having lunch yesterday in the open air patio of a very nice restaurant. At the next table were seated a distinguished looking ole [sic] man and his wife. All of a sudden one [V-1] came very close and the motor cut out and we could hear the thing diving in our direction. Those two acted like nothing happened. Didn't even look up. Just at that time an elderly waiter came out carrying their order. The thing blew up with a helluva crash about a block away. The waiter never even wavered. Hell, I was scared stiff. Later I asked the head waiter why no one seemed alarmed and he said, 'That's just what ol' Hitler wants us to do—take notice of 'em. If they're going to hit you, they're going to, so I don't take notice of the ruddy things.'"

Although Americans were readily recognizable due to their uniforms and their unique accents and mannerisms, they often mixed with local English communities. Kenneth Drinnon, a teenage small-town Tennessean who became a ball turret gunner in the 487th Bomb Group, fondly remembered his trips to neighboring pubs:

"The pubs seemed to be at the center of English social life. The local citizens acted as though they enjoyed our company. Occasionally we were invited to their homes for tea and biscuits. We donated chocolates and American cigarettes to our hosts." James Goodson, a fighter pilot in the 4th Fighter Group, recalled going to nearby towns "where the people accepted us with kindness, courtesy, and friendship." Lloyd Nelson of the 453d Bomb Group had nothing but respect and admiration for the English: "We liked them very much—especially one particular family of kids, whose mother did our laundry. We always felt sorry for the kids, so we paid more than she wanted." Saul Kupferman, who served in the 306th Bomb Group at Thurleigh, formed deep and lasting friendships with the local English people: "They became my 'family' for the eight months I was in England. A true love affair formed. Looking back, I strongly feel that the love and friendship they offered me during those trying times, as well as the home atmosphere, played an important part in my survival."

Hank Koenig, a pilot in the Eighth Air Force, described how the local civilians often became part of the fabric of his base: "Many of our personnel became acquainted with the English families in the local areas, particularly the children. It was not unusual to see children of all ages standing on the outskirts of our bases waving to the passing planes as they taxied to takeoff runways or when landing." Clearly the bond was strong between most American combat airmen and their British hosts. They felt a deep sense of kinship with one another and a shared sense of purpose to defeat the common enemy—the Nazis.

With so many British men away from home during the war, and so many young American men in close proximity to young British women, a great deal of interaction and sexual activity inevitably took place. It is undeniable that during World War II, English women found themselves greatly attracted to Americans, especially combat airmen who had the time, opportunity, and money to find female companionship. Far away from home and from American women, the combat airmen eagerly sought liaisons with British women. For their part, British women were just as eager to meet American fliers. Jack Kirschbraun of the Eighth Air Force wrote to his family about the extensive fraternization between the two groups of young people: "Almost without exception the girls here are more friendly, more receptive than those at home. The girls here like the Americans very much, in fact one of their most entertaining features is their effort to speak the English language as we speak it. Who knows—someday we may teach them how the English language should be spoken?! Some talk like native Brooklynites while others like the Texan brogue."

Harry Crosby described the symbiotic relationship between combat fliers and English women: "American girls were in America. English girls were in England. And so were we. Maybe never in history was there so perfect a fit between the women that men needed and the men that women needed. Reserved? As the expression went, 'We never had it so good.'"

Quite often when a combat unit threw a party on its base, women would be trucked in from miles around. English women rarely expressed reluctance to attend such parties. Dale Smith described the process: "Our fleet of trucks was kept busy and girls were plentiful. Trucks left the station at midnight to return the girls to their towns, but there were never as many passengers returning as arriving. I turned a blind eye to all this hanky-panky." Elmer Bendiner wrote of the results of most of these parties: "Their laughter tinkled from the barracks in the summer night. Some of the girls, with rumpled hair and heavy-lidded, lustrous morning eyes, would kiss the boys goodbye before a mission. It was not good for security, but it was pleasant for morale." Richard Baynes, a pilot in the 466th Bomb Group, remembered that after one party at his group's base in Attlebridge, "It was difficult to walk across the dark field without stepping on bodies laid out along the way. It was reported that it took a week to get all the girls off the base after the party." Robert Fesmire remembered being stunned by a sight that greeted him one morning in the shower: "Suddenly I heard the distinctive giggle of a female. Completely naked, I walked around the partition to take a look. One of the pilots was trying to have sex with an English girl. Both of them were naked and joined together in a way I had never imagined. The pilot grinned, 'Want to share?' he offered politely." Fesmire declined the offer and retreated from the shower immediately. Somewhat amused, he nevertheless could not help wondering about the extent of base security.

Jack Novey had a remarkable range of experiences with English women, everything from brief encounters to a steady relationship. One night he and a buddy got an overnight pass and left the base to go have dinner at a pub. On the way they met two English women, one of whom had a boyfriend in North Africa: "That became common. You'd meet a girl and her boyfriend would be in some other part of the world and here we were, in England and available. English girls found sex very natural. No fuss, no bother. I remember my lady was blond, with blue eyes. Sex was easy with her, natural and wonderful." Another time he was riding through the countryside on his bicycle and spotted three women in Royal Air Force uniforms. He had tea, and a few laughs, with them: "One of them, an adorable girl, said goodbye to her friends, took me by the hand, and led me to an isolated pasture for some wonderful spontaneous love which we both seemed to need badly. Afterward, we parted with a casual goodbye and a promise to meet again. But in those days, promises were just words." Indeed, Novey had difficulty thinking of anything beyond today or tomorrow during his perilous tour of duty in the fall of 1943. This attitude remained even when he began a steady relationship with a young woman who lived near his base: "Margot was twenty-six years old, seven years older than I. She lived about a mile from the base in a little cottage she shared with her two daughters, ages two and four. She told me her husband was an R.A.F. sergeant, a navigator in Lancaster bombers, and had been missing in action for over a year." Convinced her husband was dead, Margot welcomed Novey into her home repeatedly, and before long, a steady relationship developed: "It was great having a lover and a friend so close to the airbase—a refuge where I could have a change of attitude and scenery and escape from the war for brief periods." Novey brought her food from the mess hall to augment her wartime rations. A deep affection grew between them, but it was also painful because of her husband's assumed death and Novey's hazardous job: "She could hear the planes taking off for a mission and watch them coming back. If, after a mission, I didn't visit her that night, she would be afraid that something had happened to me." Because of his youth and his day-to-day existence, Novey was unwilling to commit to anything long term, and his girl-friend did not seem to mind: "Margot and I almost never went out. Her husband was well remembered, and she didn't want to provoke gossip that she was dating an American soldier, even though—or maybe because—it was happening all over Britain. I understood how she felt." One night Novey went to her cottage and heard voices inside. He peeked through a window to see her talking and the children playing with an elderly couple. Novey assumed the visitors were Margot's in-laws and quickly retreated, unseen. After surviving his twenty-five-mission tour, he went home and never saw Margot again. Such relationships permeated England during the war years.

Some combat airmen did end up marrying their girlfriends. One such man was Willis Marshall, who met his future wife at a Red Cross dance one night in December 1944. Near the end of the war, they became engaged: "The wheels turned slow. They [the military] tried to discourage weddings between Yanks and British. It turned out that the wedding wouldn't be able to take place until February 1947. I was returned to the U.S. before permission came down through the channels. Dot had to now start through immigration and get to the U.S. With a lot of headaches, problems, and perseverance, she finally arrived in New York on February 3rd, 1947. We were married the next day." During and after the war, thousands of couples went through this process. Base security and sexual escapades may not have been a deep concern for commanding officers, but the same could not be said for venereal disease. Woe to the commander whose airmen missed raids in order to be treated for sexually transmitted diseases. The Army made a tremendous effort to warn its soldiers of the dangers of venereal diseases—everything from graphic color films to pamphlets to speeches—an effort that was reasonably effective, as Tom Miller attested: "I have had my crotch grabbed, my fanny patted, and all kinds of invitations but I had an enormous fear of venereal disease! The Army movies had gotten to me and I was too deeply in love with my Lyn to risk damaging my most valuable body parts!" Robert Goebel remembered a very effective tactic the Army used to prevent venereal disease in his outfit. The authorities brought attractive women to the base, but these women had been infected with venereal diseases, so the fighter pilots could see firsthand that an attractive exterior sometimes disguised a diseased interior. "Titillating it was not. Revolting is what it was. Each of the women was infected with several different kinds of VD and had been placed in a reclining position with legs apart, displaying the ravages of the diseases in living color. It was pretty bad." In Goebel's view, it was also very effective. Keith Lamb's 100th Bomb Group took precautions to make sure that no diseased women attended base parties: "We chartered a special train to London to pick up 1,000 girls, who were all tested for venereal disease when they arrived at the base. Those who tested positive were of course sent home that same day."

American combat airmen also fraternized with Italian and French women, although not to as great an extent as with English women. In France, John Marshall found himself entranced by the local women: "The local women were sunburned—sexy olive color and I've never seen such legs and short dresses—such done-up and dyed hair. They are cultured to the last degree at the ancient art of love-making and are honored at remarks that would get your teeth rattled at home." Francis Mooney remembered seeing many young French women sleeping with fellow fighter pilots: "We had some live-in girls right in the quarters with some of the pilots. They would promise . . . to marry them and take them home . . . one day, but that very seldom happened."

Such promises were unfortunately all too common. For many Italian women in particular, marriage to an American represented a way to escape the ravages of war, poverty, and privation, and many Americans were all too eager to take advantage of such desperation. This meant making promises they had no intention of keeping. A *Yank* magazine sampling of the opinions of young Italian women questioned about American men reflects this, along with a general amiability toward Americans. The soldier's magazine asked these women what they thought of Americans: "Yole Sperra, 16, minced no words, 'They are the most wonderful boys I have ever seen. I love them all, but one in particular I love the most. I'm going to marry him.' Maria Gemita, 19, replied, 'Americano okey dokey in every respect. They are lovely and perfect gentlemen. My best boyfriend has promised me jeep for after the war.' Diana Bressy, 22, declared she 'liked Americanos very much because they do not act superior. One boy will send me ticket to America after the war. I think I marry him.'"

Like their counterparts in England, a few combat airmen in Italy did plan to make good on their marriage promises to Italian women. One such man was the tail gunner on Merle Perkins's crew. In fact, between missions, this man actually lived with his girlfriend's family: "The one girl he chose during his stay in Italy, Philamena, to whom he remained faithfully and totally attached and planned to take home with him, was not along the lines of the ideal woman you see in American advertisements. She was attractive, had long, thick, black hair, a strong face with heavy eyebrows. The family used up most of his monthly paycheck for food and drink. He sneaked them clothes from the base. They had found a breadwinner in difficult times."

American combat airmen in Europe were truly fortunate in their opportunity to find ready access to female companionship, alcohol, good food, and relatively good living conditions. Such things made their hazardous, difficult jobs just a little more bearable. Facing the terrible odds over the murderous skies of Europe became a little less painful for men who had full bellies, a bed, sheets, and perhaps a girlfriend as well.

4

People, Places, and Food—The Pacific

There were times when I felt regrets that we had been sent to the Pacific rather than the European theater of operations. There one could visit the great cities of London, Paris, and Rome on leave, see the museums and monuments, and enjoy the pleasures of civilization, if only for a fleeting moment.

—Kevin Herbert, tail gunner, 498th Bomb Group

Compared to the shelter that combat airmen enjoyed in Europe, living conditions for combat airmen in the Pacific theater were somewhat spartan. Much of this is simply a reflection of the fact that most of China, Burma, India, and the Pacific Islands—where American combat airmen found themselves based—was not as well developed as Europe. Indeed, some airmen, like those based in New Guinea, found themselves in the middle of some of the most forbidding and inhospitable territory in the world. It is not surprising, then, that the typical American combat airman in the Pacific did not exactly enjoy luxurious living arrangements. George Sheafor, a B-17 gunner stuck on a nameless and inhospitable Pacific Island, wrote to his sister that he hoped the next war would be fought in a place with "no bugs or snakes, no vines or swamps, no monsoon rains, no tropical hurricanes, no mosquitoes, lots of light wines and beer, and at least two days a week off. Also toss in paved roads and concrete foxholes with drains."

Sheafor's experiences notwithstanding, tents and a few necessities became the norm for American combat fliers in the Pacific. Charles Bond was a fighter pilot in the American Volunteer Group, usually called "The Flying Tigers." Even before America entered the war against Japan, he and his buddies flew missions as "Chinese volunteers" against the Japanese. In his diary, he described his living conditions on a base in British-controlled Burma: "The barracks and administrative buildings are made of teak wood frames covered with woven bamboo. Roofs are metal sheets of corrugated iron. Our dining hall serves as the club and bar, and we eat at 6 A.M. [and] 1 and 7 P.M. We have no hospital, only a small infirmary. Latrines are dry outhouses in the rear of our barracks, as are the bath shacks and washstands. Burmese natives take care of the menial jobs and food preparation."

David Hayward, a B-25 pilot in the 341st Bomb Group, found himself based at Chakulia, India, in 1942: "We lived in bashas: mud-walled, white-washed, thatched-roof structures, with mosquito-netted frame beds. On the average, our names were posted for a mission once a week, so the remaining time was often heavy on our hands. We took our daily showers while the sun was up, because after that the malaria-bearing mosquitoes were out. At night we watched old movies and then went to bed and listened to the laughing hyenas outside, hoping the malaria-bearing mosquitoes would not sting through our netting."

Harold Rosser, a fighter pilot in the 33d Fighter Group, lived in similar conditions while his unit was stationed in China. According to Rosser, sanitation proved to be a constant problem: "We washed in the bathhouse, using water drawn through bamboo pipes from an overhead tank which was kept filled by coolies. The water was cool and refreshing when applied externally but was not fit, because of China's fertilizing practices, for internal consumption. We couldn't even use it when brushing our teeth. With the sickening stench of excrement ever-present, it was not hard to believe that the water, though beautiful and clear, was polluted. Even in washing, we used generous quantities of soap in order to assure ourselves that all bacteria were destroyed."

Life on New Guinea for combat airmen was a constant struggle against the elements and the terrain. Even so, they managed to set up makeshift homes. Charles Nickell was lucky in that he had wooden floors in his tent and an air mattress for sleeping. In a letter to his sister, he described New Guinea as a "mass of jungles and swamps." As for his tent, he wrote: "We have home-made double-decker beds and on the other side is a clothes rack, shelves for our clothes and a bench for our stove. It is a small alcohol stove that we bought in Sydney [Australia]. We bargained for a parachute today. We put it up under the roof of the tent." Wayne Rothgeb, a 35th Fighter Group pilot, lived in a basic tent with few amenities for most of his time on New Guinea. He was truly envious of the "luxuries" nearby bomber crews enjoyed: "We Fifth Air Force fighter pilots were jealous of the . . . bomber pilots. It wasn't the planes they flew. No, it was the fact that they had a pot that flushed. At their officer's club, it was a surprise feature attraction, a real show-off piece for bomber squadrons. In New Guinea there were social advantages to having a toilet that flushed. Nurses and Red Cross girls got the news quickly and were always very happy to visit the club. Why did the bomber guys have this luxury? In their bomb bays they had lots of cargo space, and from Australia they hauled to New Guinea civilization's luxuries: a flushing toilet, furniture, fresh food, mosquito screens."

Pilot Dan Sasser's 307th Bomb Group found itself at Noemfoor Island in the fall of 1944. One night he wrote a letter to his mother and described the scenery outside his tent: "I can look out across the sea, it looks wet, nasty, and hungry. Or I can look out across the grove and camp. The coconut trees dripping, the white coral sand stands out clearly. There are a few crickets out, you can hear some talking in nearby tents—low soft toned with no boisterous shouting going on. There are a few lights here and there, but not many."

Combat airmen in the Pacific usually did not have movie-theater buildings on their bases, but they found ways to improvise. Edward Harris described his group's "theater" at Owi in a letter to his mother: "There is sort of a horseshoe curve in the cliff back of our squadron area that makes it a natural theater. The screen is set down at the bottom and the audience sits around on the face of the cliff. Most of the seats are made from empty ammunition boxes and some are thickly padded with cushions stolen from junked planes and torn GI blankets."

As the American war effort moved inexorably closer to Japan, it became increasingly common for fighter groups to set up bases on newly "secured" islands, the better to provide close air support for troops or fly escort missions for bombers striking targets in Japan. For the fighter pilots, this usually meant crude, or even dangerous, living conditions. Walter Springer, a fighter pilot in the 413th Fighter Group, wrote to his parents from Ie Shima, an island off the coast of Okinawa. After American troops captured it in the spring of 1945, the 413th incurred the task of setting up its base and, according to Springer, that usually meant a lot of hard work: "Living conditions are not as good as they have been but that is because we are having to set up camp ourselves. We are living in two-man tents. The food is good except we are eating out of mess kits, which is something we haven't had to do."

In order to provide close air support for the embattled Marines, Pilot Harry Crim's 21st Fighter Group moved to Iwo Jima in the midst of the battle in March 1945—a very dangerous situation for which he and his fighter-pilot comrades were not prepared: "The engineers had rebuilt about 3,000 feet of an existing Jap strip in the center of the island. The Marines owned all of runway number two, but little beyond that. Our camp area was a piece of the island composed of volcanic ash, mines, and dead Japanese, about halfway between two airfields on the west beach. We secured our planes and proceeded to pitch tents, dig fox holes, establish communications, and set up operations. Iwo was perhaps one of the most hostile ground environments a person or plane could find itself in. Dante, in his visions of Hell, could have used Iwo as a model. Nature provided the volcano, and men provided the war. Marine detachments were scattered all over the place. Spasmodic rifle fire and continuous artillery, ours and theirs, thundered across our camp day and night, keeping us alert. We were between our protectors and the enemy."

Although not immune to such dangers, Navy carrier pilots generally enjoyed fine living conditions. In some ways, they were the most important group within the World War II U.S. Navy. They were highly trained men who would carry out the new kind of sea warfare—long-range air battles between opposing fleets, instead of the old battleship duels featuring face-to-face confrontations of great fleets. If commanders learned one major lesson during this war, it was that ships were extremely vulnerable to air attack. Accordingly, a great deal of the damage done to the Japanese navy during the

months later, when Edward Harris wrote to his mother: "The climate can be described in one word, 'wet,' and the camp area can also be described in that word." Torrential rains were in fact very common on Pacific theater bases. Samuel Hynes, a Marine bomber pilot whose unit was stationed on Okinawa in the closing days of the war, described the climate: "We lived in a world of water and mud. The company street ran first in rivulets, then streams, until it became a bog of gluey mud that sucked at your feet as you walked. Tent floors were slick with mud. We were always wet. Bedding never dried, and clothing never dried, so that night and day our bodies were always in contact with something damp and unpleasant to the touch. Rain became the medium we lived in, a part of our air."

As if the rains were not bad enough, energy-sapping heat could also be a common problem. John Patterson, a flight engineer on a B-29 crew, recalled the hot climate of India: "The heat and humidity were exhausting. The simplest task wiped you out. I was almost always with the plane. By mid-morning the aluminum would be so hot you couldn't touch it without getting burned."

Shipboard duty also presented its own set of weather-related problems. Even if naval aviators retreated to the comfort of their cabins, they could not always escape the forces of nature. Gerrit Roelofs, a Navy pilot who flew his missions from the USS *Rudyerd Bay*, remembered when a typhoon hit his fleet in December 1944: "Three destroyers rolled over and sank. Over 180 planes were blown off carrier decks. Our ship was blown to a standstill, and you couldn't stand on the deck. To be in the grip of a storm like that is something that you will never forget. You realize there is something pretty big out there and that your ship is just a little speck on the ocean." Another Navy pilot, Joe John Bond, recalled dealing with fierce cold while aboard the USS *Bennington*. In early 1945, his carrier group cruised into the waters immediately off the coast of Japan and into the teeth of Japanese winter weather: "Well, I've been cold, I've been wet, I've been miserable—but never so much all at the same time. It was 'stormy' inside and outside of Tokio [sic] that day. It was sleeting like mad. The seas were so heavy the waves were spraying over the bow. And our forward speed, plus the velocity of the storm, plus the added wind of the airplane propellers whipped the sleet and salt spray across the flight deck at a velocity ranging between 70 and 100 miles an hour most of the time. Three days later my outer layer of face skin peeled off in tiny chips. In several cases men were blown under whirling propellers. Once I was picked up and blown literally 'through the air' against a gun turret almost 20 feet away."

Clearly, Pacific weather was volatile and dangerous to fliers. It made them wary in the air and uncomfortable on the ground.

Thanks to long supply lines and bases located in rough terrain devoid of modern infrastructure, it was usually quite difficult for the United States to keep its combat airmen supplied with appetizing food. As a result, combat fliers in the Pacific sometimes did not eat very well, at least by American standards. Edwards Park, a fighter pilot in the 35th Fighter Group, had no fond memories of the food he ate on New Guinea early in the war: "I have never eaten such absolute shit in all my life. It was Australian army rations. Front-line stuff. Everything was bully beef and canned salmon. Canned salmon was a huge luxury in Australia and I got so I couldn't stand it because we got it all the time. Breakfast, canned salmon. Lunch and supper, the same. Our poor chef used to try and dress bully beef up. He would say, 'Tonight we are having Boeuf de Bully.'"

Earl Wilburn, a bombardier in the 331st Bomb Group, described the food he ate as "miserably bad. A couple eggs before a mission. I can't eat lamb to this day." Another B-29 crewman, Navigator Kenneth Michel of the 504th Bomb Group, wrote home from Tinian (in the Marianas) and complained about the poor food the mess hall served: "I have lost thirteen pounds in four weeks. The food here is terrible. All I do is fill up on vegetables and bread. I'm constantly hungry. About the only decent meat we get is Spam, then you soon tire of it." David Hayward and his buddies turned to humor in the face of lousy food: "The food was not the best. The bully beef came from Australia, on a reverse lend-lease basis. So did the butter, which was so waxy that it couldn't melt in the hot sun of India. As for the chicken curry, we speculated that the buzzards we saw flying over every day were actually the 'chickens' of our curry."

Hayward, along with most other combat airmen, generally understood that the food was probably the best that could reasonably be expected under the circumstances. Dan Sasser's description, in a letter to his mother, of typical meals on Noemfoor Island sounds palatable enough: "Had canned pears, jam, roast beef and gravy, bread, coffee, for dessert we had Bartlett pears in halves. Had spaghetti with a cooked sauce of tomatoes and peppers to put on it. Then there were diced carrots and jelly, concentrated orange aide [sic] or water. Oh yes, those dehydrated spuds, too. We can eat dinner anytime from 4:00 P.M. until 5:30 P.M. Had roast beef, gravy, good creamed spuds with jelly and bread, coffee or water with mixed canned peaches and apricots for dessert, I love them."

Proving that the Army really did go to universal lengths to supply its troops with proper Thanksgiving dinners, Edward Harris reported in a letter that, even on his remote base in the Philippines, he received turkey with all the trimmings. Beyond that, he genuinely liked his food: "We had a big Thanksgiving dinner with turkey, pumpkin pie and practically everything that goes with Thanksgiving dinners. The food has been exceptionally good lately. We've had fresh eggs every morning for over a week. We've had pork chops twice in the past week and about two weeks ago we had steak. We also get potatoes that aren't dehydrated."

Usually the food served to Pacific-theater combat airmen was not quite up to the level Harris and his buddies enjoyed. One way to improve one's diet was to sample indigenous food, although that could produce mixed results. Paul Stevens recalled eating local fruits: "We had really enjoyed the fresh fruits and vegetables available for purchase from the local Philippinos [sic]. I particularly liked the watermelons. But we paid the price. About 99.9 percent of the camp had diarrhea." Stevens also recalled that, when his unit had access to the sea, some men would obtain explosives, drop them in the water, and have fresh seafood for dinner. David Hayward often ate at a local restaurant: "When the food got too bad, there was always the Wog Restaurant. The water buffalo steaks did not have the benefit of aging, due to lack of refrigeration. So they were tough, but good under the circumstances." Sometimes an airman was lucky enough to have a first-class local meal. Such was the case for Everett Geer, a copilot stationed in China with the 308th Bomb Group. After a fourteen-hour night mission, his plane ran out of fuel, forcing the crew to bail out over Chinese territory within a reasonable distance of their base. After parachuting safely, his crew quickly found each other. Soon friendly Chinese met them and took them to the nearest town for a feast: "A typical Chinese feast consists of some sixteen dishes, all excellently prepared and very tasty, the Chinese being cooks of the first order. We had everything from delicious fried 'drunken' chicken, and partridge, to octopus meat."

One thing Pacific-theater airmen had in common with their European-theater comrades was the constant quest for alcohol. Unfortunately for those in the Pacific, alcohol was not always as readily available at their remote bases as it was for men in Europe. With typical American inventiveness, however, American combat airmen sometimes manufactured their own alcoholic beverages. The flight surgeon in Harold Rosser's outfit turned out to be a master at making home brew, or "jungle juice." He mixed fruit juices with medicinal alcohol to create a potent drink: "So smooth it disguised the alcohol, its smell, its taste—Doc's blend hid everything but the deceiving kick which went unmanifested and unsuspected for two or three glasses and then, like a delayed-action five-hundred-pound bomb, exploded with such impact and fury that it annihilated its partakers for hours. His warning of his mixture's potency fell on deaf ears, for it was something the men had to learn for themselves."

Sometimes airmen, like V. F. Cozad, a top turret gunner in the 7th Bomb Group in India, received beer rations. He wrote home, "Beer is the only thing we get to drink that tastes anything like [what] we have in the states. Our radio operator doesn't drink beer, so that gives me about one and one half bottles per day. Cold beer is unheard of over here. At first I couldn't do it. Now I don't know if I could drink it cold." Robert Nelson stashed two cases of whiskey aboard the USS *Enterprise* during one of his tours of duty. After missions, he and his roommate would pour themselves drinks: "After one flight we invited all the officers up and had a party. They . . . took a picture of about eight of us, all drinking whiskey on the *Enterprise* in my room." Predictably, some problem drinkers did not know when to stop. Kevin Herbert wrote of an instance in which a fellow crewman was dead drunk, and had passed out, the night of a mission: "Fearful that he would be court martialed if he did not make the mission, and with the added factor that no one else in the crew could perform his particular military specialty, we decided to carry him aboard and try to bring him around before reaching Japan. Lifting his dead weight into the truck [to the flight line] was not difficult, but hoisting him up into the plane was a job that required the tugging and pushing of five men. For the next six hours hot coffee, smelling salts, and cold water were administered by a succession of experts in these matters as we flew northwards, and finally he was at his position when the battle was joined."

It is somewhat surprising that Herbert and his buddies did not attempt to sober up their comrade with a common Air Force remedy—pure oxygen. When a crew member was intoxicated or feeling the effects of a hangover, he usually put on his oxygen mask, regulated the mixture to pure oxygen, and simply inhaled. Apparently this could work wonders in such cases.

Although alcohol was not always readily available at Pacific bases, American combat airmen did manage to consume it whenever they could. The rule of thumb was that if it was available, men drank it in fairly large quantities. If it was not available, they simply went without or made their own home brew.

With the exception of Australians, the American combat airman in the Pacific theater had very little in common with most civilians with whom he came in contact. Americans met mostly Chinese, Indians, Filipinos, and Burmese, because there were large American airbases in those countries. But some airmen did get to know Pacific island natives from New Guinea to Guam to Saipan. In spite of substantial language and cultural barriers, the airmen generally behaved well toward Pacific-theater civilians.

They were liberators, not conquerors, and this often showed in their behavior. For one thing, they were typically generous. Allie Lymenstull, a Navy pilot who flew missions in a patrol bombing squadron, recalled helping local fishermen one day off the coast of the Philippines: "We would drop hardtack to them or, as we called it, dog biscuits, and wave to them. This time there were several boats close together. About half a mile away there was a huge school of fish. So we flew over the natives, and pointed . . . to the school of fish which they could not see. We dropped a bomb at the edge of the fish. After it went off there were hundreds of stunned fish floating. They paddled out there and seemed really excited, throwing fish into their boats."

Most Americans were somewhat curious about the inhabitants of South Pacific islands, who came from a completely different world. It was almost like turning back the clock hundreds of years. Wayne Rothgeb described the natives on New Guinea: "The natives, like the fellow we dubbed 'Snowball,' were dark-skinned Melanesians, a Pacific Island people. Their black hair was very curly—even frizzy. Snowball washed our clothes. He couldn't read or write but he never got our clothes mixed up. Some of the islanders helped us, and some helped the Japanese, who had seized the northern part of the island early in 1942. The villages were clusters of huts and ranged in number from fifty to three hundred. Leadership in some villages was based on age and achievement, and in others on prowess in warfare, head-hunting, oratory, and accumulation of wealth."

Even though most Americans' knowledge and understanding of such people and cultures barely extended beyond the pages of *National Geographic,* relations were usually very good. One Marine pilot fondly remembered the people of Guadalcanal: "Those natives were so big-hearted that it made us a little sad. Right away they began bringing us gifts. They came in a long procession. It made a whale of a heap in no time. A chap would come along staggering under the weight of a basket of fruit that was about all he could handle, and I'd pay him with one cigarette. He'd go and sit down on his heels and smoke that cigarette, perfectly happy. When we ran out of cigarettes, we gave them odds and ends and trinkets."

Somewhat better known to Americans were Filipinos, who had been under U.S. control since the early days of the twentieth century. In letters to his family, Charles Nickell described the people he met in the Philippines as "fairly dark. They look something like our light colored Negros back home. Most of them seem very friendly toward us." On another occasion he wrote that "several of the people I have run into can speak fairly good English. Some of them are very intelligent." Upon arriving in the Philippines, native Tennessean Edward Harris was impressed with how westernized some of the people seemed to be: "Calling these people natives would be like going to Tennessee and calling the people there natives. Most of the people have been to school and speak English pretty well. It looks like we're back in civilization again."

Large countries like India and China more closely conformed to the American concept of "civilization." Curiously enough, though, many American combat aviators were not impressed with those countries and looked upon the Indians and Chinese with a detached, albeit benevolent contempt. Mostly they found themselves appalled at the poverty and backwardness of the two Asian nations. Vast racial and cultural differences also led to great barriers between Americans and their hosts. Dwight King, a bombardier in the 468th Bomb Group based in Kharagpur, India, visited Calcutta on leave and never forgot what he saw: "The streets of Calcutta were crowded with pedestrians, rickshaws, ox carts, trolley cars, and taxis, setting up a merry din. When we weren't being accosted by street salesmen we were being pestered by beggars. Some of the little ragged urchins had learned to chant: 'No mama, no papa, no seester, no per diem, baksheesh, Sahib!' They were desperate and would do anything for an anna or two [local currency]. Sometimes they would run beside us on their short legs, polishing our belt buckles. We'd have to shoo them off, even though we did feel sorry for them. Near the central marketplace we encountered many beggars, including the spider men who only walk on their knees to beg. They do this all their lives, and their calves and feet are deformed from lack of use over the years. The sightless, the tongueless, and the fakirs, they were all there. Right along with these, one could see rich merchants in spotless white robes and turban, and neatly kept beards."

If anything, the poverty in China was probably even worse. Some American fliers, like Fighter Pilot Howard Longhead of the 23d Fighter Group, looked at their Chinese allies with utter contempt. In a letter to his parents, Longhead described the Chinese as "dumb ignorant people . . . and they are our allies. They haven't changed in the past thousand years; just doing things the same old way as their fathers did. They don't use shovels at all, but some kind of a hoe. And the clothes they wear when kids are just added to as they grow."

Most combat airmen in China viewed the Chinese not with such hostility but rather with a patronizing mixture of revulsion and sympathy. In the view of most airmen, the Chinese people were the product of a backward and rather incomprehensible Oriental culture. Although based in India, V. F. Cozad often flew cargo missions to supply Chinese troops. His contemporary description of his experiences with the Chinese reveals an attitude of amused superiority: "We pull up to the unloading dock and about fifty Chinese coolies and guards come out to unload the plane. One crew member must stay with the plane to guard the guards, as they will steal the whole plane if they can carry it away. We take turns guarding the plane. The rest of the crew goes in to eat. The Chinese guards and coolies try to talk you into giving and trading them American cigarettes. I have quite a bit of Chinese money and a Chinese inf. [infantry] insignia to wear on my hat. Hot stuff? And how!"

One aspect of the Chinese defied the comprehension of most American combat airmen—the superstitious religious beliefs of the average peasant. John Patterson, whose unit flew out of both India and China, recalled that such beliefs often led to bizarre behavior: "The Chinese believed you could cure bad luck by killing the evil spirit that was following you. They must have figured the best way to kill a spirit was to run over it with a B-29 because they kept dashing across the runways in front of our airplanes. The evil spirits weren't the only losers, though, because occasionally these fellows ended up in the props. It was a bad deal, but we couldn't get them to stop doing it."

Harold Rosser, whose group was based in China for a time, had a range of experiences with Chinese civilians, some of them bordering on the surreal. One day, he and his buddies noticed that the Chinese laborers on their base used incredibly squeaky wheelbarrows. Feeling sorry for the workers, Rosser and his fellow pilots found some grease and showed their allies how to apply it. At first the Chinese were enthusiastic, but that soon changed: "As quickly as the rasping, irritating squeaks stopped, so did the coolies. So did their wide smiles and their excited chatter. Faces that had first registered surprise and glee took on looks of concern, then changed to looks of stark fear and wonderment, as the realization dawned that their evil-spirit deterrent was gone, forever silenced by the squirt cans. Panic-stricken, they dropped the handles as if they had suddenly become hot. Then, fearful of the consequences of lingering, with glowering stares of anger mixed with fear, with their raspy voices laced with hatred for us, they backed slowly away from the deadly scourge and darted frantically away. Bewildered and disappointed, we stood, our oil cans hanging limply in our hands like a pistol that had accidentally emptied its lead into a friend."

Apparently the Chinese workmen believed that the squeaks in their wheelbarrows warded off evil spirits. Although well meaning, Rosser and his friends had unwittingly deprived them of their mental security blanket. On another occasion, however, Rosser and his buddies clearly were not as well meaning. One day, during a ricksha ride, they decided to bet on whose man could pull fast enough to win a race. The result was something straight out of the most backward days of imperialism: "It was a grunting, slipping, no-holds-barred match that would have made the rudest American cab driver look like a Girl Scout. They bumped pedestrians, passed other rickshas, and yelled in what could only have been the spiciest of Chinese curses. With each of us exhorting his man to greater speed, the ricksha boys grunted, hacked, and slashed their way through crowds and at each other. Big Boy's driver . . . forged to the front and finished a full ricksha length ahead. Breathing and sweating heavily, he continued to glower at Big Boy until the seventy-five dollars prize money, equally provided by the three of us, was proffered him. He vented his pent-up feelings in an explosion of Chinese gibberish."

Another time, Rosser met an American transport pilot who had flown Chinese soldiers over the Himalayas, or "The Hump," as Americans called it. Previously, he had flown mules, and the animals had relieved themselves to the point where the stench in the plane was overwhelming. When the Chinese soldiers boarded the plane, the American pilot joked with them through an interpreter that if the stench caused any of them to get sick in his plane, he would have them thrown out. Even though he meant it as a joke, the

Chinese soldiers took him seriously. Rosser recounted the rest of the transport pilot's tale: "'Sure enough,' he laughed, 'one of those poor guys got sick. His buddies grabbed him and very dutifully heaved him through the open door.' His laughter was contagious. I felt shocked and eery [sic]. 'And then those guys,' the transport pilot was not finished, 'stood in the doorway and watched him tumbling end over end toward the mountains. When they couldn't see him anymore, they started laughing and jabbering and applauding. I tell you, it was weird.' He stopped laughing. His voice steadied but remained ridden with surprise. 'Their lack of regard for human life is beyond me,' he said, shaking his head sadly."

This last incident reveals much about American fliers' attitudes toward the Chinese. They felt sorry for them in a way, but they really could not—and almost did not want to—understand them or their culture. The result was an ambivalent, but usually benevolent, brand of revulsion and pity for their Chinese allies.

Pacific-theater combat airmen were not nearly as fortunate as their comrades in Europe when it came to fraternizing with women. Fraternization with women was almost nonexistent on most Pacific Islands and was not very common in India and China. In the latter two countries, American combat airmen usually had little interest in the local women, for two main reasons. First, they feared venereal diseases. The Army's VD films could be a powerful deterrent, especially after an American witnessed the filth of Chinese and Indian cities. Second, most white airmen were not very interested in dark-skinned or yellow-skinned women. Racial and cultural differences were often too vast for white American airmen to have serious interest in Chinese or Indian women. Raised in a segregated society, they were used to the cultural norm of racial separation in sexual matters.

Accordingly, Pacific-theater combat airmen rarely had steady girlfriends. The lone exception to this was Australia, a predominantly white nation. Although very few combat airmen were stationed in Australia, many—particularly those who served with the Fifth Air Force in New Guinea—went there for R&R. Wayne Rothgeb, who, unlike most fighter pilots, was quite shy around women, had no problem finding a date in Australia: "I blurted out something. I was too excited to know what I had said; however her answer was, 'I'd love to.' With her calm help, I was able to purchase a theater ticket. My blue-eyed date . . . had cost me only a theater ticket."

With most young Australian men fighting overseas, and the usual American combination of charm and wealth, combat airmen tended to be quite popular with Australian women. To many combat fliers, Australia was like an oasis in a vast desert. The women were white, friendly, and from a similar culture. Most relationships were quite transitory, because airmen inevitably had to return to their units throughout the Pacific within a week or two. Had this not been the case, however, it is easy to imagine that there would have been many Australian "war brides" similar to the numerous British-American couples in the European theater. But for most American combat airmen in the Pacific, the comforts of good living conditions, good food, and steady female companionship were usually little more than unfulfilled dreams.

5

Flying the Missions

Almost immediately crew members reported enemy aircraft coming in at all positions. I was a teenager. I was scared. I wanted to live. I wondered how the hell I had ended up in this situation.
—Jack Novey, waist gunner, 96th Bomb Group

What was air combat like for those Americans who experienced it in World War II? Often as not, it was both terrifying and exhilarating. Always present was the sense of carrying out a vital job that had to be done for the United States to win the war. Most airmen knew only too well that many fellow Americans, such as ordinary taxpayers, factory workers, political leaders, or ground crewman, had worked hard to put them in a position to do their dangerous jobs. Thus they usually were determined to fly their missions to the best of their training and ability.

The experience of combat varied according to an airman's job. For instance, fighter pilots waged a substantially different kind of war than bomber crews, and their experiences reflected those differences. Ever present for all of them, though, was the constant danger and mortal fear that went with every mission. Air combat was a deadly game played for keeps. You killed him or he killed you, but it usually took American airmen a few missions to get used to this Darwinian state of affairs. Dayton Castor, a fighter pilot in the 353d Fighter Group, described his first mission: "All of a sudden you realize that the man sitting in the cockpit of that little silver job has cannon and machine guns which will blot out your life if he can maneuver into position. Your mouth becomes dry, the hair on the back of your neck stands stiff, and the sound of your breathing is . . . short and raspy. Your eyes are concentrated on that silver streak. There is no feeling of speed even though somehow your eyes have registered that you are doing over 350 [miles per hour] airspeed."

Although it could be very difficult to describe adequately the look and feel of an actual combat mission, many men tried. Howard Kelly, a pilot in the 319th Bomb Group, wrote to a college buddy in late 1942 and attempted to convey the emotions and experiences of combat missions flown in North Africa: "I wish I could describe a raid to you the way it feels, but it is one of those things you have to experience personally. Black puffs of smoke begin breaking in front of the nose, off the wing, right overhead. They break suddenly in clusters and hang in the air like tiny clouds. You are twisting, turning, diving, climbing—anything to keep those clusters from coming too close. They get closer and you hear the whisper of them as they break in close."

Merle Schwartz, a pilot in the 465th Bomb Group, vividly recalled the routine of a combat mission. For him, the icy fear began when he descended a flight of stairs to the briefing room: "You have just walked down 24 steps feeling as though you were a condemned person going to the electric chair, because a percentage of those walking down the steps are going to their deaths. Once the officers on the platform have explained all needed explanations, you're back on the truck to your B-24. The flight is not as treacherous as the final bomb run where the flak is thick. The . . . initial point is where you turn on to the final bomb run. You don't look down, you concentrate on the plane by and in front of you, trying not to see the big flashes of exploding shells which send flying pieces of metal . . . to hit your plane. Back to the field. Back to the Ready room where a critique is held and you get donuts and coffee by a Red Cross girl."

Sometimes combat airmen had the opportunity to describe their experiences as they happened. Such was the case with Charles Murrell, a young radio operator in the Twentieth Air Force, who wrote a letter to his aunt and uncle during one of the March 1945 low-altitude fire-bombing raids of Tokyo. The result is a remarkable window into the world of combat: "2:00 A.M. We are now over the coast. Told by the pilot to put on all equipment—parachute, flak suit, and helmet. 2:30 A.M. I can see big fires up ahead through the breaks in the clouds. Tokyo is aflame. 2:45 A.M. We start our bomb run. We are lighted up like a Christmas tree from the fires below. This is a very critical time for us, for it is at this point we are most vulnerable. Flak is bursting all around us, and the plane is rocking like a cradle, but we go straight in. 2:50 A.M. We are over the target. Below us mile after mile of Tokyo is a solid conflagration. Words alone cannot explain it. I can see block after block of four and five story houses ready to collapse. It is truly like looking in the depths of hell. 2:55 A.M. We break away from the target and are caught in a maze of searchlights. The pilot takes violent evasive action, but they hold us in a cone of light. More and more flak bursting to the front, rear, right, and left of us. On my right there is a sudden burst of flames in the sky. I cross my fingers and hope it is not a plane. I know if it is, there can be no survivors. 3:00 A.M. We are several miles away from the target, but as I look back there is an ocean of fire. 3:10 A.M. Crew members are reporting to the pilot. Tail gunner: 'Everything OK here.' Left gunner: 'Everything OK here.' Every crew member reports the same. We have come through in good shape in spite of everything. I relax and light a cigarette, for we are several miles at sea and headed for home." On another mission soon after this one, things did not work out so well. Murrell's plane went down and he was forever after listed as missing in action.

Every mission began with a briefing. The goal was to inform the fliers about their mission and the kind of enemy opposition they could expect, as well as any other pertinent information. For most daylight missions, combat airmen needed to be awakened in the middle of the night for their briefing. Such was often the case with bomber crews who flew daytime missions. Jack Novey of the 96th Bomb Group never forgot the feeling of being awakened in the dead of night: "When I close my eyes, I can still see it and hear it. The time is 0300 hours on a cold, rainy morning in England in the fall of 1943. I lie in my bunk, listening to the rain. Other men are snoring. Before long the sergeant called the Charge of Quarters comes tromping down the walk, opening the doors of other huts, and shouting out names. Then he opens our door and calls the names of those scheduled to fly today. We're all grumbling as we get up. We go to the bathroom, wash up, come back to our bunks, and get dressed. It's dark, cold, and raining. We're wondering who's going to live and who's going to die this day."

The next stop was usually the mess hall, where crews ate a pre-combat breakfast, usually eggs and sausages washed down with coffee. At later times of the day, most commonly in fighter groups, commanders simply sent a messenger from dwelling to dwelling summoning fliers to the briefing room in anticipation of a mission.

The briefing was a ritual in and of itself. Lloyd Haefs, a bombardier in the 2d Bomb Group, recalled being awakened in the middle of the night and told to report to briefing. He shrugged off the cold of a North African desert night, dressed, and made his way to group headquarters: "All awaited the announcement of the target with great curiosity which the Colonel promptly dispelled by pulling the drape aside to reveal a map of northern Italy. The City of Bologna was highlighted as the primary target and he went on to describe a six-storied factory used for the manufacture of ball bearings."

James Campbell, a pilot in the 380th Bomb Group in the Pacific, wrote a detailed description of his unit's briefings: "The squadron commander would start the briefing by telling us where we were going (e.g., Lombox Straights [sic], Ambon, Rabaul, etc.). He would also announce the flight leaders and the others in the formation. The next briefer would be the intelligence officer. He would have aerial photos of the target and also tell us how many Jap fighters could be expected, how many ack-ack batteries were there and their locations, and where escape submarines and . . . rescue planes were located and how to contact them. One of the things the intelligence officer was required to tell us: 'If you are captured, tell only your name, rank, and serial number.' I used to think to myself, 'bull shit, if some slant-eyed bastard is going to drive bamboo slithers under my fingernails because I won't talk, all he's got to do is ask the questions and I'm a singing son-of-a-bitch.' The next briefer would be a meteorologist. He would present the current weather enroute to the target and forecast weather conditions including the amount of cloud cover expected over the target. The next briefer would be the squadron commander for the final briefing. He would point out our IP [initial point] . . . where the bomb run would start, bombing altitudes and heading, engine starting time, taxi-out order, frequencies to use and answer any questions from any crew member. We would then synchronize our watches."

Ever attuned to the dangers of any given target, crews usually reacted positively or negatively upon being informed of their mission. An anguished groan arose from men slated to go to a target such as Berlin, Bremen, Vienna, or Tokyo. By contrast, relieved sighs or chuckles filled a room if a unit was headed for targets in France or northern Italy. Occasionally, tremendous excitement arose over a special mission, regardless of the dangers. Wilbur Morrison, a bombardier in the 462d Bomb Group, recalled one such instance. He and his buddies crammed into a briefing room in China and heard some very welcome words: "'Gentlemen, I know you have waited a long time for this. But the months of training and the sacrifices you have undergone will bear fruit tonight. At last we can say, tonight we bomb Japan!' A roar welled up and thundered against the rafters. I felt a mixture of emotions: joy, fear, and consternation." This mission, flown in the early fall of 1944, was the first bombing raid against Japan since the famous Doolittle raid of April 1942. Philip Ardery, a pilot and squadron commander in the 389th Bomb Group, flew on the first mission to Ploesti, Romania, a raid notorious not just for its heavy casualties but also for its importance in attempting to knock out a vital source of Germany's oil. In view of the mission's importance and the dangers it presented, Ardery told his men that the night before he had "said a prayer for myself and in it I included a word for all of you, my good men and great friends. I would like to be able to tell you how deeply my feelings will be tied up today in the welfare of each of you. I can't. Good luck. Let us say we'll see each other here tonight."

Few missions, however, were so dramatic. To combat airmen, most missions were merely part of the routine of existing, fighting, and hoping to survive. Roy Wehman, a copilot in the 464th Bomb Group, flew missions out of Italy. He remembered getting up around three in the morning, eating breakfast, and hustling over to the briefing room: "You go down, check in, and have a little [religious] service. Then they would lock the doors and pull back the

potentially thousands of planes. Tom Miller, a pilot in the 448th Bomb Group, recalled the next part of the laborious process: "The forming ship was flown by an experienced crew including sometimes the group commander. It was painted garish colors that were distinctive to each group and had a large number of 'Very' flare pistol ports. If the weather was poor as it almost always was, the flares were vital. Forming always was done above the main cloud deck but not infrequently below other cloud decks. Visual sightings obviously were vital. Each aircraft of the group formed on the forming ship in his assigned, as-briefed slot/position. Each group would then set a course and pattern to arrive at a given point over the English coast so as to join, in their proper place in line, the air division leader. He then led his bomber stream in such a timed pattern so that he could enter his division into the proper place in the Eighth AF bomber stream if all three air divisions [that made up the Eighth] were going to hit the same target. If not, each air division leader would strike out for his briefed target."

Naturally, this protracted process took a great deal of expert planning and execution. Since formations and timing proved so important, lives were riding on how well leaders carried out the formation process. Often as not, carefully laid plans unraveled on mission days. Harry Crosby, whose proficiency as a navigator led to his rise to the rank of group navigator of the 100th Bomb Group, nonetheless recalled a maximum-effort mission when a joint error by the command pilot and him nearly led to disaster: "So here we are. Every aircraft and crew that the U.S. Eighth Air Force can get into the air . . . are flying right at each other. Maelstrom. The three divisions converge. Their command pilots yell at each other and at their formations. Dozens of flares . . . all the possible combinations as the lead planes try to identify themselves and keep their formation together. Fourth of July. I cover my ears to keep out the sound of the crashes I expect. Planes veer in every direction to avoid smashing into each other. Suddenly we are in the clear. We have made it through the melee. God seems to have been with us. No losses. A miracle. Then, Colonel Jeff [the command pilot] wants to know what happened. I tell him, and he gets mad, and then I get mad, and we start shouting at each other."

A simple miscommunication between Crosby and his colonel had led to the near-disaster. With such a delicate balance between efficiency and failure, it is amazing that the Eighth Air Force did not experience a crippling number of midair collisions during the formation phase of its missions.

Forming up for fighter pilots was usually a much simpler process. Blessed with more maneuverable craft and not saddled with the necessity of tight formations, fighter pilots could take a more low key approach to formations. Karl Dittmer was one of those rare pilots who flew both bombers and fighters: "Flying a bomber in tight formation was hard work. Formations in fighters was [sic] much easier. We didn't expend nearly as much effort concentrating on keeping position. Plus, most of my missions in fighters were less than five hours long. In bombers, I had one mission ten hours long and several that were nine—a lot of that time and energy spent in forming up before we even began across the Channel."

The problem for fighters was not forming up prior to combat but getting into formation after having hit a target or engaging in a dogfight. Lone aircraft, even fighters, could be extremely vulnerable in hostile skies. Hub Zemke, the legendary ace commander of the 56th Fighter Group, explained how he and his pilots got together after a dogfight had scattered them all over the skies: "A major difficulty following a bounce or break in air fighting was re-forming a flight or section. This was normally achieved by radioed directions to form over a prominent landmark—if the ground was visible—or by a bearing reference to the bombers we were supporting. Even so, until pulling into a position where the letters on the next P-47 could be clearly seen, it was often a matter of luck if one was joining the correct slot."

Even after the briefing, takeoff, and formation process, some fliers still did not proceed with the mission. Instead they aborted, meaning they turned around and headed back to the base and received no mission credit, the usual justification for aborting being mechanical difficulty. Aborting a mission was usually controversial. Most units attached a stigma to anyone who aborted with any frequency. Mechanical difficulties or not, commanders nevertheless wondered if cowardice had been the pilot's true motivation to abort. In some fighter groups, it was common knowledge that some pilots simply could not bring themselves to fly into enemy skies. Such pilots would find any kind of excuse to turn back. Ordinarily these men did not last long in a unit. The same held true in bomb groups, where abortions tended to be more complicated and even more stigmatized because of numerous factors. First, the average bombing mission was significantly more dangerous than the average fighter mission. Second, a bomber pilot had the final say as to whether or not to abort, and most had no desire to appear cowardly to their crews. Third, heavy bombers by their very nature required extensive maintenance. This meant that many things could and did go wrong with the average heavy bomber, such as engine flameouts, oxygen system failures, and hydraulic failures. All of these problems justified aborting a mission.

Even so, the frequency of mechanical troubles did not make abortions any more acceptable. Most commanders, under intense pressure from superiors to keep abortion rates low, viewed any aborted mission as having one of two causes—either the pilot lost his nerve or the ground crew failed to do its job. Needless to say, the specter of crewmen losing their will to fight was unacceptable to bomb-group commanders, especially in the face of appalling losses on daylight raids over Europe in 1943 and 1944. So, if a pilot chose to abort, he was in effect saying that his ground crew had not done its job properly. Keith Schuyler, a B-24 pilot in the 44th Bomb Group, recalled seeing the disappointment on the faces of the ground crew when he chose to abort a mission. Upon landing at his base, he saw the ground crewmen on the tarmac: "There was nothing to ease the obvious pain showing in the crew chief's face as he signaled us to our dispersal area. Obviously we were bringing back a black mark on his record. I explained our problems to the chief. He listened politely to my full report, but I thought I detected a certain incredulity in his attitude, more of a resignation to the authority that flew his airplanes than a real belief that one of them could fail to perform to perfection."

At times, there was little doubt that a plane needed to turn back. John White, a pilot in the 448th Bomb Group, remembered one such instance when his bomber's oxygen system failed: "We took off, joined the formation, and were part way across the Channel when our oxygen system developed a leak and we lost all the pressure at five stations in the ship. You can't fly at 23,000 feet without oxygen, so we had another abortion chalked up to our credit." Knowing the terrible stigma associated with abortions, most pilots agonized before ordering their plane to turn for home. R. H. Tays, a pilot in the 392d Bomb Group, only aborted once, but it led to a falling-out with his squadron commander: "Number-three engine started to trail smoke—a constant gray stream, never increasing or decreasing. We could see no fire, but where there is smoke, there is fire. Fire is a real concern in the air with all that hundred-octane fuel around. He [the squadron commander] reported seeing no fire and told me to continue on the mission as briefed. This didn't sit quite right with me. Fire is fire, respected by every flier. I reported my analysis to the squadron commander; he did not show concern and threatened me with 'Cowardice before the enemy.' I offered a deal. If I was right, we would forget the incident; if not, he could do as his conscience dictated. Documented evidence proved I was right. We never had the same relationship again. The crew thought I was terrific."

Sometimes crew members disagreed among themselves as to whether or not a mission should be aborted. The pilot, of course, had the final say, but most of them took a great deal of input from the rest of the crew, especially the top turret gunner/engineer, the man responsible for the in-flight mechanical health of the aircraft. Bill Chamberlain, a tail gunner in the 96th Bomb Group, recalled an instance when his pilot and engineer had serious differences about whether to abort. Their plane could not seem to stay in formation: "The pilot refused to turn back and . . . then finally I remember the engineer telling him, 'If you do not turn back, I will bail out.' With that the pilot turned the plane around and went back with a full bombload. This is an action that is not looked upon with favor by the officers of the base. They raised particular hell with my pilot. The ground crew checked the plane out and they said it was perfectly alright, no reason for us to come back. The upshot of it was the second time we took off. We had started over toward

France and the same thing happened again. Again with a full bombload we came in and landed at base. Word got all over the base. When we went out to get a beer, the men didn't want to talk to us. They were calling us 'abortion kings.'"

There is a postscript to Chamberlain's tale. Not long after his crew aborted these missions, another crew took their plane up for a mission. It exploded in midair, killing everyone aboard. In spite of the stigma Chamberlain and his crew endured, their engineer's refusal to fly may well have saved their lives.

In carrying out their missions, bomber crews endured two major threats—enemy fighters and enemy antiaircraft fire (usually called flak). Both could be quite deadly and could strike fear into the hearts of even the most veteran crews. On almost every bombing mission of the war, American combat airmen found themselves threatened by one or the other. Bristling with heavy machine guns at nearly every station, American bombers were designed to ward off fighters. In reality, bombers, especially when alone, could be quite vulnerable to enemy fighter attacks. Combat airmen, particularly gunners, often had to fight for their lives during missions. The speed and violence of enemy fighter assaults left a deep impression on most combat airmen, including Philip Ardery: "I particularly noticed how suddenly an enemy fighter attack materializes. Usually with practically no warning, you look to see a bunch of 20mm cannons blazing at you. Attack after attack can come within a matter of seconds. If your ship is flyable, you are lucky. But if you have really been taken by surprise, there isn't much chance that it is flyable."

By most accounts, the outcome of World War II air battles often depended upon the element of surprise. Those who got the jump on the enemy usually won, especially in fighter combat. This meant staying alert. On bomber crews, the gunners strained their eyes at their posts in enemy skies, constantly hoping to catch a glimpse of a fighter plane before it was too late.

A large group of Japanese fighters jumped Pilot Tom Young's B-29 one day in 1945 while his 468th Bomb Group bombed the docks of Singapore: "One fighter came up from below and laid an explosive shell in my nose wheel well, damaging both tires, tearing away the linkage on my throttles, and blowing a hole through the side of the fuselage. Another fighter had come from above with an explosive shell that put a nine-inch hole in the top of the left wing above a gas tank."

With no friendly fighter escort, Young tried something unorthodox. He turned into the remaining attacking fighters and ordered his gunners to open fire when in range. It worked. His nose turret gunner shot down two Japanese fighters and the crew made it home safely. Another pilot, Maxon Wotring, flew with the 43d Bomb Group in the South Pacific. One day, a group of Japanese fighters attacked his plane: "He opened fire with four guns around a thousand yards and stayed in his pursuit curve. Number-three engine was knocked out. I hit the feather button and shut down the engine. I felt something warm on my stomach and groin. I looked down and saw red from my waist to my thighs. I had no pain, and then I saw a wounded hydraulic line alongside my seat spurting red fluid on me. I looked out again in time to see red yolks as the other Zero [Japanese fighter plane] . . . began his pass. I turned around and saw the round wing tipped Zero high above us dipping his wings, weaving back and forth, taunting us. Suddenly he rolled over on his back and came straight down at us." Although one of his crewmen was killed, Wotring managed to ward off the fighters and get back to his base.

The 494th Bomb Group flew B-24 bombing missions to Formosa, the coast of China, and Japan itself during the last year of the war. Its crewmen came under frequent fighter attack. In July 1945, they hit an airfield on Kyushu, Japan. Bombardier Neil Goodrich recalled the ensuing fighter attack. His group had no sooner dropped their bombs than the Japanese fighters pounced: "As the bomb bay doors were closing, the enemy fighters struck. The lead Zero, with guns blazing, broke out of the sun and Cannon [their top turret gunner] was ready. He fired a long burst from his twin fifties, point blank at the first one, which immediately spiraled earthward. Others reported seven Zeroes attacking. Our crew counted two attacking and one shot down. The attack was over in seconds. No one saw the overall picture. It was over so fast."

Pilot James Culliton also flew on that mission: "I felt our B-24 shudder as our nose gunner . . . fired his twin .50s with a short burst followed by a long burst. The Zero's right wing was severed and the fuselage was rolling. The wreckage of the Zero passed our right wing, estimated at 50 feet. Our tail gunner saw the remains of the Zero falling into the ocean. There was no parachute observed. We assumed that he was on his way to greet his ancestors."

Navy B-24 pilots often flew dangerous solo missions bombing and strafing Japanese shipping and installations. Their stripped-down B-24s had enough firepower nominally to defend themselves against Japanese fighters, but they still sometimes became vulnerable. Off the coast of Vietnam one day, enemy fighters attacked the plane of one such naval aviator: "I turned the airplane around very sharply and dove to 4,000 feet with military [emergency] power on the engines. At 100 feet above the wave tops, Bill Wales in the waist hatch reported that the Oscar [Japanese fighter] was performing acrobatics. I was . . . varying my altitude up and down, skidding and whatever to deny them setting up for an accurate firing run. Then a Tony [Japanese fighter], painted red, came boring in our tail, firing all guns from a very low altitude. His gunfire churned up a terrific spray to such a degree that I thought we had got him. Not so, and as I continued jinking around every which way, the red Tony came pulling alongside so close we could have thrown a rock and hit him. Then they all turned away and headed back to Saigon."

As this account proves, sometimes the best course of action for a bomber was to get away and live to fight another day.

In the European theater, enemy fighters presented an even greater danger. During the violent air battles over Europe, German fighter pilots sometimes wreaked havoc on American bombers. Most American bomber crewmen regarded German fighters with a wary respect and a healthy dose of fear. Ken Bragg, a pilot with the 97th Bomb Group in North Africa, recalled an intense fighter attack on his group during a daylight mission to Bizerte (Tunisia): "In what seemed to be seconds, they were upon us, diving through our formation out of the blinding sun, their guns spurting death. Our big bomber, *All American*, trembled with rage as her .50-caliber guns vibrated in answer. On they came with one plane about thirty seconds behind the other, ready for a one-two punch with their terrific firepower. Brilliant tracer bullets flew in both directions, as though a score of boys were fighting it out with Roman candles. The first attacker half rolled into our flight to make a quick getaway. As he did, I saw Captain Coulter's bomber burst into smoke and flames and start earthward in an uncontrollable spiral. The second enemy fighter was now our primary concern. As he followed his leader into a roll, our gunners found the mark. Fifty-caliber bullets ripped into the pilot's cockpit. The Nazi pilot was disposed of, but his ship streaked on toward us. I rammed the controls forward in a violent attempt to avoid collision. I flinched as the fighter passed inches over my head."

Beginning in 1944, sallying from airbases on Italian soil, the Allies carried on an air offensive against southern Germany, the Balkans, and, most important, Romanian oilfields. The Fifteenth Air Force combat crewmen who flew these missions were sometimes trapped in the shadows of their better-known comrades in the Eighth Air Force in England, but they experienced equivalent dangers during their missions over Nazi-controlled Europe. Pilot William Cubbins was one of these men. He flew with the 450th Bomb Group, a unit known as the "Cottontails." Cubbins had a great deal of respect for the skill of German fighter pilots, especially after an intense attack they made on his formation: "I'd never seen or envisioned anything like it. It was beautiful airmanship, a veritable flying circus. So daring were their maneuvers, so great our surprise, that I doubt that a single gunner got an effective shot at them. I tracked one fighter. He came racing through . . . a shiny yellow-nose [Messerschmidt] 109 dancing on air as the pilot skillfully avoided colliding with the bombers. The sunlight reflected from his face, a face that seemed to look directly at us as his oxygen mask dangled to one side. I saw him for only the briefest moment, but I was certain that he'd smiled as he sped by. Wave after wave of yellow-nose 109s . . . and Focke-Wulf 190s [another type of German fighter] came screaming by. In less than a minute's time, between forty and fifty enemy fighters had hit us. Low and to my right were six parachutes of men leaving a smoking B-24."

The 483d Bomb Group also flew missions from Italy. Merle Perkins, a radio operator with that outfit, wrote about a fighter attack on his formation over southwestern Germany. As the bombers began their run to the target, German fighters appeared: "Systematically, in close arrow-head formation, with cannon and rockets firing, swarms of six fighters at a time would curve into the lowest box. After six of these attacks, that squadron's planes and crews, seventy men, were gone: one plane exploded, another was totally shot to pieces, a third . . . went into a spin. Lumbering off the target, we were braced for follow-up attacks, and they came with intense ferocity. An FW-190 curved toward our midsection from eight o'clock high. I gave the FW steady and repeated bursts of five rounds, and I scored. His engines smoked, then flamed. My wild shouts and screams, my howls of rage and triumph were demented. 'You bastard, I got you! You've had it now! I hope you fry in hell, you Nazi bastard!' I must have said this many times."

Joseph Beswick, a top turret gunner/engineer in the 483d, also experienced the demented exhilaration that came with shooting down an enemy plane. His prey was the rarest of all—a German jet fighter: "An Me-262 jet attacked a B-17 on our left wing. When he hit him, I saw the propeller fly off the number-four engine. The jet had to back off on his power to keep from ramming the B-17 he was attacking. That gave me the chance I was looking for and I poured .50-caliber bullets into him. He just sat there like a sitting duck. I had to quit shooting for fear of burning up the gun barrel. Finally, he rolled over into a dive and I watched him go down trailing smoke. I am sure . . . the pilot was dead in the plane."

The Eighth Air Force also dealt with powerful fighter attacks. In fact, the effectiveness and ferocity of German fighter attacks nearly threatened to annihilate the Eighth Air Force in 1942–43, the early stages of the American air war over Europe. This was before the United States possessed a long-range fighter to escort the bombers to long-range targets and ward off enemy fighters. The brass had put their faith in unescorted, deep-penetration daylight raids, and the terrible and unacceptable casualty lists quickly proved them to be completely wrong. Jack Novey served his tour of duty during this time and ended up as one of the lucky few who completed his missions unscathed. One morning in September 1943, German fighters jumped his group as it prepared to bomb a factory outside of Paris: "I was leaning against my gun, looking out, when, all of a sudden, right in front of me appeared an Me-109. I swear that if my gun had been three feet longer, I could have touched the fighter with it. I could see the pilot looking at me through the canopy. I let loose a burst from my .50-caliber machine gun, and shells exploded around the cockpit. The pilot blew his canopy and ejected. His suit was on fire. His parachute opened up, burned away in an orange-yellow blaze, and he came out mouthing a scream. I'll never forget the image of him freezing in front of me in slow motion. It was as if time stopped. It took me more than thirty years to forget that horrible moment. I can only hope the pilot was dead before he started to fall in flames—but I don't think he was."

John Gabay, a tail gunner in the 94th Bomb Group, also flew some of his missions during this difficult time. In early December 1943, his crew flew a mission to bomb Kiel in northern Germany. Immediately after the American bombers crossed the coast, enemy fighters attacked: "Four of them attacked our ship from the tail, one at a time. The flame from their cannons, tracers from their machine guns, and rockets from under their wings made the situation a bit hairy. All I could do, besides being scared, was to spray each one as they came in and call for evasive action. I hit the second one, and he rolled over and burned. I saw my tracers slam into the cockpit of the third. I may have hit the pilot, as the ship started to go out of control. I poured more into it, knocking off the canopy under the nose. It looked like a leg hung out of the ship for an instant, then fell out."

Edward Hearty, a bombardier in the 95th Bomb Group, recorded in his mission diary a remarkable play-by-play description of a desperate German fighter attack over Muenster in October 1943: "The Jerries attacked in force after we left the flak area. B-17s are going down in flames all over the place. The formation in front of us are getting shot to pieces. Eight of them have gone down so far. Our ball gunner has shot down 2. The tail 1, the waist 1 each. The radio 1, the top turret 1. I used 1,700 rounds of ammo and couldn't hit the side of a barn."

The Eighth naturally could not absorb such punishment for very long. Mercifully, by the end of 1943, fighters such as the P-51 Mustang could escort bombers to and from the targets. This helped curb bomber losses, but it did not mean the threat from German fighters had ended. Larry Wallerstein, a pilot in the 381st Bomb Group, was nearly blown out of the sky by German fighters over Berlin in 1944: "They all flipped over and . . . came at us from 12 o'clock level, in two waves in a head-on attack. At that point I began my daily combat prayer, 'Dear God, please get us safely home. Our lives are in your hands.' The first line of German fighters began firing into our formation. They got the pilot in number-three position in our element. As his B-17 flipped over, it collided with the element lead plane. Both B-17s blew up and *Sweet Patootie* [his plane] flew through the smoke and debris. As we emerged, I saw another line of German fighters approaching head-on with their wings flashing like blinking headlights. One came straight at us. I sensed when he came into range and began to squeeze his triggers. At that instant, I pulled *Sweet Patootie*'s nose up, turned the wheel to the left, kicked right rudder in an attempt to evade his line of fire."

His crewmen, particularly his waist gunners, tumbled all over the plane, but the German fighter missed. Lloyd Martin, a B-24 pilot in the Eighth Air Force, wrote to his parents about a harrowing mission to Gotha, Germany, in February 1944. As soon as they hit Germany, the fighter attacks began: "This attack was the first of many starting a two hour and twenty minute airial [sic] battle. During this melee I saw men die, live, work, and pray. I saw fighting men turn heros [sic]. We had endless attacks from single-engined fighters and rocket-carrying twin-engined fighters. The target comes into view. 'Will these attacks never stop? Please God help us!! Why don't they stop? There goes another B-24 down burning' came as a constant flow over the interphone. The German fighters were using what seemed to be suicidal defense tactics. From the moment we crossed the Nazi coast, relays of fighters started this endless pounding."

It is important to understand that most fighter attacks probably were not this intense or protracted. But such attacks happened often enough, especially for beleaguered combat airmen expected to fly at least twenty-five missions. As 1944 unfolded and American fighters escorted bombers to their targets in Europe, the threat of

German fighters diminished in favor of the threat of flak. In fact, in both the Pacific and Europe, flak probably brought down more bombers than fighters. It was a hated and dreaded foe. C. L. Anderson, a ball turret gunner in the 390th Bomb Group, feared flak above all other perils: "My greatest fear in combat was flak. With fighters, you had a chance to fight back. With flak, you were like a duck flying over a blind. When you started on the bomb run, you didn't alter course or altitude, so they could zero in on you." Bob Ryerson, a pilot in the 96th Bomb Group, completed a tour of duty of thirty-five missions over Europe in 1944–45. In his opinion, flak posed a significantly greater threat than fighters: "There were two kinds of flak, high velocity . . . and low velocity. If you were close enough to hear the shell go off, that's high-velocity flak. If you couldn't hear it and all you saw was the puff . . . then it was low velocity. If it was high-velocity flak, your bulletproof glass, your armor plate, you could stick it in your ear. It was not going to stop that from going right through it just like a hot knife through butter. Low-velocity flak it would stop."

Philip Ardery braved flak many times on his numerous missions against targets in German-occupied Europe: "Usually the worst flak we saw was while we were on or closely approaching the bombing run, when we could not afford to make any turns for any reason, except to put the bombardier over the target. After the bombs were away, if the formation was one of medium or larger size—that is, twenty-four ships or more—the wisdom of turns . . . was questionable. If fighters were about, such turns might loosen the formation. Loosening the formation meant greater vulnerability to fighter attacks. There was really nothing you could do when the flak started breaking around your ship but sit and look at it—and pray."

The inability to do much to avoid flak led to a helpless feeling among bomber crewmen. Many felt like mere pawns caught in the clutches of blind luck or fate. Arthur Carpenter, a navigator in the Fifteenth Air Force, mentioned flak in a letter to his family in the spring of 1944: "Surprisingly enough, it isn't the enemy fighter planes that worry us (we have seen very few and our own escort takes care of them)—it's the flak that has everybody buffaloed. You just can't do a darned thing about it. You feel just like a duck during hunting season." Another Fifteenth Air Force man, Pilot Lon Lilley, also wrote to his parents about flak: "That flak really gets on a guy's nerves at times. When you approach a target, you look out ahead and see the entire sky filled with those little black puffs of smoke. When you are about to enter it, you start praying and trying to convince yourself that your ship won't be hit, and at the same time they are coming so close that the explosion of the shell is heard even above the roar of the engines. Every time an explosion is heard, it sounds as if one of them connected with you."

John White kept a diary during his combat tour. After returning from a tough mission to Bremen, Germany, he took refuge in the diary, writing candidly of his intense fear of flak: "I don't mind saying I was plenty scared [of the flak over Bremen] and the thought kept going thru [sic] my mind that this might be the day we get it. It's not very pleasant to wonder and think that at any moment . . . a shell may hit you and blow your ass out of the sky or a piece may come tearing through the ship and rip off your arm or leg. We just have to sit there and take it and I for one don't receive a bit of satisfaction out of the fact that 5 miles below us our bombs are knocking hell out of the guys who are doing this to us. It seems as tho [sic] we have no way at all of fighting back."

Perhaps the inability to fight back substantially against flak accounted for why combat airmen so feared it. For young men accustomed to taking the war to the enemy's vital organs of warfare every day, flak could be frustrating because it offered no immediate way to strike back beyond dropping bombs on a distant target.

Naturally, the intensity, accuracy, and deadliness of flak varied from theater to theater or even mission to mission. In the Pacific, Japanese flak was largely inconsistent. At times, it could be shockingly effective. Other times, it was nearly nonexistent. It all depended on the luck of the draw. David Hayward, a B-25 pilot in the 341st Bomb Group, flew missions against the Japanese in the early days of the war. He recalled a bombing mission to destroy a bridge in Burma during the Allied retreat in 1942: "Black puffs of smoke were starting to appear ahead. But on our bomb run we could not alter our altitude, direction, or air speed. The ack-ack had our altitude and course well figured out. All we could do was fly into the black puffs, grit our teeth, and hope for the best. When an antiaircraft shell goes off under your airplane, you feel a sharp buffeting and then you hear what sounds like buckshot being fired against a galvanized iron building."

Sometimes, bombers took flak from Japanese warships. This happened to Tom Young and his crew one morning over Singapore. On the bomb run, they started taking intense fire: "There, below us, sat a Japanese warship throwing up the most accurate flak pattern I have ever encountered. This was pinpointed directly in front of us. We would see the burst, flew [sic] through the puff of smoke, and listened to the shrapnel clatter. We had one shell go through our radar compartment and burst above us." John Olson, a radio operator in the 494th Bomb Group, had a close call with flak on a mission in early 1945: "Flak was thrown up like hailstones and it was the first time I really got scared. During the bomb run we were hit. Our number-four engine was shot out plus the hydraulic system and the electrical system. The flak was a solid wall and there were fighters too. The hydraulic fluid was blowing all over and our bomb bay doors would not close. They had to be cranked shut by hand. Paisley [one of the gunners] put on a parachute and stood on the slippery catwalk doing this with nothing but space below him and with little to hang on to."

The intensity level of flak over Japan itself varied substantially. Some missions, particularly those flown near the end of the war, encountered little resistance. Others weathered devastating fire. Ray Ebert, a navigator in the 498th Bomb Group, recorded in his mission diary a frightening encounter with Japanese flak: "Just after leaving the target, a burst of flak caught us just aft of the camera doors and nearly turned us over. We depressurized so fast I'm sure there must be a few popped ear drums in the crowd. When the pressure seal broke, our cabin temperature dropped from +20 [Celsius] to −37 [Celsius] and I'm shivering so bad I can hardly write. I didn't think to bring winter clothes."

Bombardier Wilbur Morrison wrote about the intense flak (aided by ever-present searchlights) his unit encountered while on the first post-Doolittle bombing raid to Japan: "Mingling with the searchlight beams were curving arcs of tracer bullets and wicked red flashes of heavy ack-ack firing at an invisible B-29. The darkness was rent wide open and batteries of searchlights combed the sky for us . . . swinging straight toward us with unerring accuracy. They enveloped us in blinding light. We felt naked and alone. Red flashes appeared all around us and long strings of tracers arched up from the small-caliber guns on the ground. The searchlights never wavered but followed us with maddening intensity. Thicker and thicker grew the puffs of antiaircraft fire as we neared the bomb-release line. 'Bombs away!' I quickly salvoed and pulled the door handle up as . . . we dived away from the target. After what seemed like an eternity, the refreshing blackness closed in on us again and we were safe."

Richard Fisher flew thirty missions to Japan as a gunner with the 444th Bomb Group. His hatred for flak and the danger of a typical mission in the night skies over Japan are evident in a letter he wrote to his parents: "There's those bursts of flame from flak below, off the wing and up above. You hope one doesn't burst in the nose, the bomb bays, or the tail. You hope *that* all the way to the target. Then there's tracers coming up from the smaller weapons on the ground. Then you hope a fighter doesn't find you, sneak up under the tail, and rake you from front to rear. You hope too that one of the four or five hundred other '29s doesn't decide to cross your path at the same altitude at the same time. Nice these night missions. I could have mentioned searchlights, but they don't hurt—ha."

There is little doubt that German flak was even more deadly. Germany produced a tremendous number of antiaircraft guns, most notably the 88mm, to counter the Allied air threat. This meant that combat airmen routinely braved devastating, accurate flak over German skies. Robert Bagley, a ball turret gunner in the 445th Bomb Group, described in a letter to his parents the kind of flak he encountered and his reaction to it: "It comes in various sizes, explodes in different colors, and the puffs are rather pretty, at a safe distance. On the way in and over the target you always sweat the damn stuff out. When you are in a turret . . . all you can hear is hm-ump, hm-ump, as each shell explodes. No matter how cold you have been up to the time of the bomb run, you'll invariably get a hell of a lot warmer and even sweat a little wondering when they are going to start shooting, but from the second you see the first burst until 'Bombs away' . . . you know where you stand. During the flak periods on the bomb run, there's not much talk. I think there is a prayer on everybody's lips. But the minute 'Bombs away' comes over the interphone, everybody hollers simultaneously, 'Let's Get the Hell Out of Here.'"

Bagley's description is fairly typical of flak opposition on missions in Europe, although obviously the degree and accuracy of flak varied according to how many guns happened to defend the target of the day. Usually the flak reached peak intensity during the bomb run. The Germans knew which factories, airfields, railroad marshaling yards, or petroleum refineries would attract Allied interest and defended these valuable targets accordingly. Joe Kenney, a radio operator in the 99th Bomb Group, flew his missions out of Italy with the Fifteenth Air Force. In late July 1944, his group attacked the Hermann Goering tank works in Austria. The flak was withering: "In one instance one whole wing was blown off a B-17 with no survivors. Several other planes exploded with the same 'no survivor' results. Any place you looked . . . you could see a trail of smoke and a ball of flame. There were many, many parachutes from planes going down." As a general rule, the lower the altitude that a bomber flew, the more vulnerable it would be to flak. For that reason, the low-level Ploesti, Romania, oil-refinery raids proved especially costly. American commanders hoped to sneak their planes in under German radar and achieve the element of surprise. It didn't work, and the results were nearly catastrophic. Philip Ardery's description of his experiences on a 1943 mission to Ploesti reads like a passage out of Dante's *Inferno:* "The first ships dropped their bombs squarely on the boiler house and immediately a series of explosions took place. Already the fires were leaping higher than the level of our approach. We found ourselves at that moment running a gauntlet of tracers and cannon fire of all types that made me despair of ever covering those last few hundred yards to the point where we could let the bombs go. From the target grew the column of flames, smoke, and explosions, and we were headed straight into it. As we were going into the furnace, I said a quick prayer. During those moments I didn't think that I could possibly come out alive."

Radio Operator Ray Hubbard of the 98th Bomb Group also flew on that 1943 Ploesti mission. He never forgot what he saw: "I looked through the open bomb-bay doors and could see flames from exploding gas tanks shooting right up into the bomb bay. It was like flying through Hell. We could see fuel tanks exploding with fire shooting up like ruddy tongues in the middle of the smoke. It was so hot the hair on my arms was singed. I could smell it burn. German ack-ack batteries were firing in unison. We were so low that they were actually trained down on us."

Eighth Air Force crews were also no strangers to flak. As Allied fighters increasingly drove German fighters from the skies, flak opposition seemed to get stiffer. John Clarkson, a top turret gunner/engineer in the 34th Bomb Group, wrote to his wife about the flak over Hamburg: "The sky was black with flak. You can usually tell what the Germans guard the most by the amount of flak they send up. The bursts were so close. You could hear them explode, raising the ship up in the air and then down again." Men often described such flak as being "so thick you could get out and walk on it." Radio Operator Roger Armstrong did not like to sit passively while flak rocked his aircraft. Unfortunately for him, radio operators usually did not have any specific duties to perform during a bomb run, the time when flak was at its most intense, so he volunteered to throw "chaff" out of the plane. German radar would often identify each strip of foil as a plane. By disseminating these radar-confusing strips of foil, Armstrong felt like he was fighting back. He also took other precautions to protect himself: "I had a piece of armor plating approximately 4 x 4 feet. I kept it underneath my chair, at the radio-room table. When it came time to throw chaff I would push it over to the chaff chute, across the radio room, and sit on it. Then I made myself a flak hut by piling boxes of chaff on one side. I also acquired an additional flak suit and placed it against the right wall. Then I pulled my steel helmet over my eyes and started throwing chaff. The busier you were, the less you thought about being shot at."

E. T. Moriarity, a waist gunner in the 306th Bomb Group, felt particularly vulnerable to flak as he stood at his open waist door in his B-17: "The closer we moved to the target, the more flak bursts there were. At times it seemed the ship was dancing with the up and down

and sideways motion. My stomach muscles tightened and I started
to sweat. Will it always be this way?" Jim Lynch, a radio operator in
the 379th Bomb Group, kept a diary of his combat experiences. On
a mission to Cologne, Germany, flak caused a fire in the bomb bay
(an exceedingly dangerous situation) before the bombs had even
been dropped: "The flak began. It was sudden and dense, with
bursts so close the smoke of the spent shells drifted into the bomb
bay and the smell of Cordite permeated the oxygen masks. At that
moment we caught flak under the bomb bay. We popped into the
air like jumping jacks. White smoke was pouring into the radio
room! I grabbed the fire extinguisher and moved into the door
leading into the bomb bay. Blinded by the smoke, I made my way
along the narrow catwalk, until I was about halfway into the bomb
bay. I . . . blasted the foam toward the front of the bomb bay, spraying it wildly." As he did this, the bombardier salvoed the bombs.
Lynch had the spine tingling experience of actually being in the
open bomb bay as the bombs dropped from their racks around
him.

Dale Smith, a career military man who eventually rose to command the 384th Bomb Group, flew dull antisubmarine missions off
the American coast in the early days of the war. The missions he
later flew over Germany were a far cry from those fruitless days
searching for German subs. In March 1944, he led a mission to
bomb a ball-bearing plant outside of Berlin: "I had never seen such
accurate enemy fire on the first salvo. It was phenomenal. Unfair!
Before I could even think of taking evasive action with the formation, a shell went through my left wing and exploded a few feet
above, rocking our ship and sprinkling it with metal fragments. I
stared in chilled alarm at the gaping hole. Carefully I tested the controls. The wings dipped normally. A miracle! It didn't make sense
but I thanked God and breathed a sigh of relief."

Lonnie Osborne, a B-26 waist gunner in the 394th Bomb Group,
also dodged a tremendous amount of flak during his tour of duty.
As a medium-bomber crewman, he knew that his plane flew faster
than the heavies, but it also flew lower, and that meant braving flak
in large quantities: "I swear we could have put the wheels down and
rolled on the stuff. Worst of all, an 88mm shell went right through

our aft bomb bay! It made a hole in the bottom and top of the fuselage big enough to put your head through; fortunately it missed the controls. And fortunately too, it didn't explode on impact. If it had, I'm afraid our pieces would have been flying around in space. The smoke and noise of the bursting 88mms was fearful when you thought about it."

As in the Pacific, combat airmen in Europe sometimes received flak from enemy warships. This often happened to those who flew low-level medium-bomber raids. At times the flak could be deadly. William Redmond, a navigator/bombardier on a B-26 in the 387th Bomb Group, saw German flak boats shoot down several aircraft on D day. While they were en route to bomb targets in support of the invasion, the flak started: "Four flak boats opened fire with deadly tracers. The 394th lost 3 ships in rapid succession, one disintegrating in a ball of flame. Apparently its bombs exploded. I became very mad at those Germans so I yelled, 'Get the dirty bastards, Kestner [his tail gunner].' All tail gunners returned fire upon these boats. Our bombs knocked out the machine gun and mortar nests in the target area."

Robert Fesmire, a pilot in the 492d Bomb Group, had an unusual tour of duty. He flew top-secret OSS missions over occupied territory. Flying a black-painted B-24, his missions consisted of sneaking into enemy skies at night and dropping supplies or agents to local Resistance groups. Although he studiously avoided enemy flak concentrations, one night he mistakenly blundered into one: "It was dark, since the lights in Nazi-occupied countries were always blacked out. We strained our eyes to see the underground [Resistance] fighters at the target area. Suddenly brilliant flashes of tracer fire lit up the sky in front of us. Pete George . . . screamed, 'Turn left fast!' I immediately made a steep bank to the left. With a heavy load, flaps down, and reduced airspeed, we were a sitting duck for the German guns below. We found ourselves surrounded by enemy fire. The dense flak and .50-caliber tracers lit up the sky all around us, and we were so low we could hear the explosions of gunfire."

With the help of expert navigating, they vacated the area and avoided other German guns. If bomber crews could successfully negotiate enemy flak and fighters and fly away from enemy-controlled territory, the rest of their missions consisted mainly of flying back to their bases to rest, regroup, and prepare for the next time they laid their lives on the line.

Nearly all American fighter missions in World War II consisted of one of the following three jobs: air-to-air combat, or "dogfights"; strafing missions designed to destroy ground targets; or escort missions to protect American bombers from enemy fighters.

Most fighter pilots preferred air-to-air missions in which they flew into enemy skies attempting to induce enemy fighters to come up and fight. The result was a so-called dogfight. Aggressive in nature and supremely confident in their piloting skills, most American fighter pilots eagerly sought to test themselves against enemy pilots in life-and-death struggles. Fighter pilots took pride in their ability to fight in this one-on-one, *mano a mano* type of combat. Some saw themselves as modern-day knights. The typical fighter pilot felt that he had been trained primarily to engage in dogfights with enemy fighters. Most of these young men had been raised on tales of World War I aces, and they were all too eager to pursue their own personal glory in the skies. Some pilots—particularly those who served late in the war, when enemy fighter strength had been dramatically reduced—never got the chance to engage in dogfights. For those who did, though, dogfights brought immense excitement.

Although dogfights tended to be fights to the finish, sometimes engagements were inconclusive. John Brown, a fighter pilot in the 78th Fighter Group, encountered two German fighters over Cologne, but he could not be sure he had shot down either one: "The second 'hun' I chased for about six or seven miles down at zero feet, tearing in and out of factories over bridges, down one back of a river and up the other (the Rhine River, to be exact). I fired about ten to twelve short bursts at this fellow, and finally hit him. He started streaming black smoke and I tho't [sic] I'd be able to close right up and 'clobber' him, but at that moment several ground batteries opened up on me, and so I was forced to pull up. At that time the ole 'hun' dived into this thick cloud of smoke, and I lost him."

Clarence Jamison, a member of the African-American 332d Fighter Group, engaged a German fighter formation over Anzio but could not confirm a kill: "I . . . was right on the top of one of the German flight leaders. We were about one hundred feet apart . . . and I looked right in his cockpit. I gave him a blast with all six machine guns in my wings. Then my guns jammed. I know I hit him, he was smoking, but I don't know if he went down or not, so I got credit for a damage." One day in the late fall of 1944, a German jet attacked Quentin Aanenson, requiring him to fight for his life: "We could see the flashes as he opened fire with his cannon. My wingman and I rolled upside down and pulled into a high-speed dive to the left. Our other two planes did a hard right turn. The German plane made a sharp turn and followed us down—closing fast. Cannon shells were going past my plane, but in the next instant, the jet overran us, and for a very few seconds was in front of us, but pulling away fast. I fired a three or four second burst, and saw pieces of his right engine fall off. Even with his right engine smoking and probably out of commission, he was able to outclimb me, and head for home. This whole action took place in about twenty seconds."

William Pickron, a P-51 pilot, flew his missions from the small island of Ie Shima just off the coast of Okinawa. One day he and his buddies had no sooner finished shooting up a Japanese airfield on Kyushu than Japanese fighters jumped them. Low on ammunition, they had no choice but to run: "We dived for the deck with throttles bent full forward. This is where the 'Pucker Factor,' on a scale of one to ten, hovered around nine for what seemed like an eternity as we were fired on from the rear. We must have inherited the luck of the Irish or they were very poor shots, because we finally outran them and made a safe return home."

Far more exhilarating, at least to the narrator, are the tales of victories told by American fighter pilots. It is important to remember that victory stories represent the survivor's view of combat. Those Americans who ended up on the short end of dogfights and lost their lives obviously have no way to tell their stories. Those who survived such defeats usually ended up as prisoners, providing accounts more appropriate to the next chapter than this one. In the confusion and speed of aerial combat, how could a pilot verify shooting down an enemy aircraft? Robert Goebel, a 31st Fighter Group pilot who became an ace (five or more kills), explained the process: "To claim a confirmed victory, one of the following must have occurred: a. The enemy fighter must have crashed into the ground; b. The enemy pilot must have bailed out; c. The enemy aircraft must have been enveloped in fire; d. The enemy plane must have lost structural parts, such as a wing or tail surface. These conditions had to be either corroborated by another pilot or clearly visible on the gunsight . . . film. A lot depended on who was making the claim; more leeway was generally given to veterans who had already scored several victories."

Francis Gabreski became a famous and high-scoring American ace during the war, with close to thirty victories to his credit. How did a pilot enjoy such phenomenal success? Being in the right place at the right time helped. He served his tour of duty at a time when the Allies took on the brunt of the German fighter force. That made Gabreski's success possible, but his unique understanding of how to survive and succeed as a *combat* pilot accounted for most of his victories and hence his success: "When the fight started, you obviously got excited, but you couldn't let yourself stop looking around. Even if you got an enemy plane in your sights, you couldn't fix your attention on it. You had to remain completely aware of what was going on around you, and fire only when it was expedient. Otherwise, there might be someone else on one side or the other coming in on your tail. I took a long time to hold fire until I was completely in range. Once I learned how to get in close before starting to shoot, I began to have some success as a fighter pilot." He recounted an instance when these qualities helped him shoot down an enemy plane. By remaining alert and constantly scanning the skies around him, he spotted a large formation of German fighters. Taking their time, he and his wingman sneaked up on the end of the formation: "I picked out a straggler and opened up on him at 600 yards. He still was carrying his belly [fuel] tank, and it burst into flames when my shots hit it. I continued firing short bursts . . . and could see that he was a goner. I swung away to the right and picked up four more enemy fighters. I was dead astern when I opened fire on another one carrying its belly tank, and again it burst into flames. Smoke and glycol poured from the 109 as it dove . . . straight down into overcast trailing smoke and fire. Another sure kill."

Gabreski's group commander, Hub Zemke, also became an ace. In fact, his 56th Fighter Group became the highest-scoring group in the European theater. The press took to calling them "Zemke's Wolfpack." Shortly after D day, Zemke led a fighter sweep into German-occupied France. These missions were designed to induce enemy fighters into the sky. Zemke scored a rather unusual victory that day: "I saw a single FW-190 trying to sneak up on one of our lower elements. Turning right and down to attack him, he saw me coming, changed his mind, and fled to the west. Because of my superior altitude I rapidly overtook him in a dive. The Focke-Wulf pilot then broke right to engage me, and as I came in behind him he tightened his turn, suddenly losing control and spinning down straight into the ground. I never fired a shot."

Even though he never had to shoot, he still received credit for a kill. Zemke's story demonstrates the fact that there were many ways to record an aerial victory. Combat meant confusion and chaos. All that mattered was downing enemy planes, regardless of how a pilot did it. The winning pilot usually held some major strategic advantage, such as seeing the other pilot first, maneuvering into an altitude advantage before engaging, or simply possessing a superior aircraft. Even the best pilot in the world could not consistently overcome the major strategic disadvantages of flying an inferior aircraft or yielding the first shot to the enemy.

Poor aircraft in particular represented a major challenge, and danger, for American fighter pilots in the early days of the war. Some of them did not survive the handicap of inferior airplanes. Others managed to survive and even find ways occasionally to destroy enemy planes. Hugh Dow of the 350th Fighter Group flew hopelessly outclassed P-39s against German fighters in North Africa in 1942. He managed to score a victory one day by trailing a German fighter during the enemy pilot's strafing run, a vulnerable time for any aircraft: "I don't believe the 109 pilot knew I was there. He had drifted up to two or three hundred feet by now and must have finally seen me, because he suddenly hit the deck again. I dropped down immediately and, as I bounced around in his slipstream, finally squeezed off a burst. There were strikes all over the aircraft and I overran him as his power came off. A few seconds later . . . he hit the ground in a ball of smoke and dust."

Marine fighter pilots flew inferior Grumman F4F fighter planes against far more maneuverable and swifter Japanese Zeroes during the desperate days of the Guadalcanal campaign in 1942. In spite of their disadvantages, the Marines managed to fight the Japanese to a standstill. Fighter Pilot Doc Everton flew with Marine Squadron 212 on Guadalcanal. One day he shot down a Japanese Zero: "They were all over the sky. One of them turned back into me from above, and it seemed to me that I could feel the bullets from all six of my guns smashing into him. He exploded; I flew through smoke and flames and bits of shattered plane. The Jap pilot fell, dead of course. I saw him splash into the sea." Jack Conger recorded numerous victories during the campaign. One time he engaged in a protracted one-on-one dogfight with a Japanese Zero. After twisting, turning, and maneuvering all over the sky, he got close enough to shoot: "Finally I got up to twenty or thirty yards—just like opening a door and walking into a room it was so close. Then I fired the shortest burst I ever used, not more than twenty or thirty shots, but they were all smashing right home into him, and he blew up all over the sky. I was hoisted up in my seat by the force of the explosion. I saw the pilot blown up thirty feet in the air. The chute he had didn't open, and then he dropped. I came clear down and watched him hit the water. The shroud lines of the chute were holding him, and he was lying there as though asleep."

The consequences of losing in World War II aerial combat were clearly severe. Red Jackson of the 332d Fighter Group won a victory one afternoon near the Alps and also had the opportunity to observe his quarry. The enemy pilot got the jump on him but missed on a shooting pass. It gave Jackson the chance to counterattack: "I fell in behind him. Realizing I was on his tail, he began weaving from side to side. Every time he turned, I gave him a short burst of fire. On the fourth burst, his plane began to smoke. I saw the canopy come off the Me-109 in two pieces. A little later, I saw the pilot jump and his parachute open. I circled the helpless pilot for a while."

Another 332d man, Bobby Williams, downed two aircraft in one day: "I dived into a group of enemy aircraft. After getting on the tail of one of the enemy planes, I gave him a few short bursts. My fire hit the mark and the enemy plane fell off and tumbled to the ground. On pulling away from my victim, I found another enemy plane on my tail. To evade his guns, I made a steep turn. Just as I had turned, another enemy plane shot across the nose of my plane. Immediately, I began firing on him. The plane went into a steep dive and later crashed." Yet another member of the dramatically successful 332d, Johnny Briggs, scored one of the group's many victories. During a mission to Germany in the late summer of 1944, an enemy fighter attacked his formation: "He leveled off and made a turn to see if anyone was back there, a slow turn to the left. I said, 'No, you don't,' and I shot—Brrrt. He started a slow turn to the right. Brrrt—I let him have it again. Bullets bounced off him. I pulled up beside him and above him, and he went into a spiral, going down, and I saw his chute open. He was probably saying, 'Well, you got me today, but I'll be back tomorrow.'"

Most American fighter pilots had a soft spot for front-line troops. They especially relished catching enemy aircraft in the act of strafing U.S. troops. Charles Mott of the 33d Fighter Group recalled flying combat air patrols over Salerno, Italy, to protect American troops desperately hanging on to their precarious beachhead. Mott and his flight leader spotted German planes strafing American troops. They quickly gunned their engines in the hopes of eliminating the German planes before they did much damage: "We were doing about 400 mph. Bishop and I rolled in behind one and started firing. We saw smoke coming from the German plane, and we both gave him good solid blasts. The German peeled off to the right and went into the ground. Bishop and I pulled up sharply with heavy G-forces."

Japanese fighter pilots usually proved to be every bit as dangerous as their German allies. The same principles that made for success in Europe also worked in the Pacific. American fighter pilots craned their necks in search of Japanese fighters and constantly looked for any speed or altitude advantage. Charles Bond, who flew with the American Volunteer Group (the "Flying Tigers"), shot down a Japanese plane during an attack on his airfield in January 1942. In the middle of a swirling mass of American and Japanese planes, he made several fruitless passes. Finally, he succeeded in cornering one plane: "I bore in and fired. He started downwards toward a cloud. I stayed above in anticipation that he would come back out of the cloud. He did, climbing back up and leveling off squarely in front of me. He must have been within two or three hundred yards as I closed in and opened fire with all six guns. My tracers tore into his cockpit and engine. I had to raise my left wing to get over him as I zoomed past. His cockpit was flaming. I squealed in delight, laughing aloud."

Wayne Rothgeb, a fighter pilot in the 35th Fighter Group, did not become an ace, but he did shoot down a Japanese navy fighter over New Guinea: "I looked up and didn't believe what I was seeing! Right in front of me, a Zero—spread-eagle. He had shot up and into my path. Someone had been on his tail. His evasive, straight-up-in-the-air maneuver was dying in front of my guns. For me, a sitting duck. It was automatic. My guns came to life, spitting lead and orange-red, whirling tracers, not the prescribed short bursts. I was determined. I held the button down and let the guns run. The shells tore into him as he topped out his climb, paused, shuddered, and then did a cartwheel. Black smoke billowed as he turned, head over tail, and went straight down under me."

The Navy also accounted for its share of downed Japanese aircraft. Fighter Pilot Charles Moutenot flew his missions from the USS *Essex*. One day he and his buddies overflew Truk, a major Japanese base. Before they knew it, Japanese fighters attacked them. The American formation scattered. Two enemy planes made a run at Moutenot and he hid in a cloud. When he emerged, he spotted a lone Japanese plane, most likely a straggler: "He came around and made a run on me. I kicked the rudder and put the plane into a skid, and it slowed down abruptly. He went charging by me and I slid on his tail. I had a good shot at him and there was an explosion. I ran through the smoke and debris." Moutenot saw no sign that the enemy pilot had escaped from his plane. Fighter Pilot Roland Baker flew missions from the USS *Hancock*. One day he and several other pilots were circling a downed flier floating in the sea. As rescue planes attempted to get to the flier, eight Japanese navy fighters attacked Baker's flight: "One of the Japs peeled off and started a strafing run on the raft, but he never pulled out of his dive, as Davis got on his tail with an accurate burst. A Zeke [Japanese fighter] flashed in front of me, presenting a perfect deflection shot. I then looked over my shoulder and saw a Zeke diving down on me. Wrapping up my turn, I climbed to meet him head on, both of us firing. As the Jap passed by, I turned hard over to observe him go straight in. I now found a Jap on my tail, sustained a few hits, and then he was gone. Klinger had shot him off my tail just in time. Seven Japs went down before it was all over."

Baker's account communicates the importance of teamwork among fighter pilots. Even though they thought of themselves as individuals and fought a one-on-one type of war, their best chance of survival came about through teamwork. The reliance on teamwork for survival was something fighter pilots had in common with bomber crews and ground-combat soldiers. American fighter pilots flew in two-man teams and constantly attempted to keep enemy planes off their buddy's tail.

Navy pilot Bill Burch flew missions in the South Pacific in early 1943. During a combat patrol near New Georgia, he and his wingman became separated. As he attempted to find his buddy, he spotted a Japanese fighter and caught the enemy pilot completely by surprise: "I don't think he ever saw me as I made my run on him from the stern. I was aiming a little far ahead with my first burst, but the second burst went right in the root of his left wing and an explosion occurred immediately." Navy Fighter Pilot Jim Campbell of Air Group 5 flew many combat air patrols high above his carrier, the USS *Yorktown*. On combat air patrols, Navy fighter pilots patrolled an area above the fleet, constantly on the lookout for enemy planes that might pose a threat to the ships below. The vast majority of the time, no such planes appeared; this meant combat air patrol could be quite boring and, at the same time, nerve-racking. One day, Japanese fighters jumped Campbell's group as it protected American warships. The U.S. warships had engaged a Japanese fleet when the air attack on Campbell's force began: "It was while watching this surface engagement that we were jumped by four Jap Zeroes. I picked out one and got him in my gunsight. When he approached in range of my guns, I opened up on him. He was headed almost directly at me. Finally I saw my tracers going directly into his engine and cockpit and he burst into flames. I believe he tried to crash into me, and as he was almost on me I turned violently to the left and Carmen dove to the right and he passed between us. I can't describe the elated feeling I had when that Zero burst into flames."

If the prospect of dogfighting provoked elation and excitement among pilots, then strafing usually evoked the opposite. Strafing meant dive bombing or shooting up ground targets. It was deadly, dangerous business—not just because of the threat of flak but also because missions were flown at such low altitudes. If you got hit badly, you had little room to maneuver and very little time to get out of the aircraft safely. Sweeping enemy fighters from the skies was important, but so was lending close air support to ground troops. Even though most of the Army Air Force's leadership felt that high-level strategic bombing held the key to victory, close air support—strafing—proved to be the most effective use of airpower in World War II. As devastating as heavy-bomber raids were to Germany, they did not destroy its capacity to resist. In fact, Germany's production of almost all vital materials of war reached their highest levels in 1944–45, after years of strategic bombing. By contrast, tactical bombing (the use of airpower for direct support to ground troops) proved to be extremely effective, perhaps the best example being the Falaise Gap in France in which Allied fighter-bombers turned the German army's avenue of retreat into a boiling cauldron of death. Allied fighters shot up trains, trucks, tanks, bunkers, communications centers, soldiers, and many other targets. The fighters provided crucial support for the ground troops. This pattern held true for the entire war. Effective use of aircraft in support of ground troops helped win many battles for the United States and turned many battlefields into death zones for enemy soldiers.

Fighter pilots more commonly engaged in the less glorious and more dangerous job of strafing rather than dogfighting, especially late in the war in Europe when German fighter capacity had been crippled by years of attrition. Frank Harrington, a fighter pilot in the 78th Fighter Group, mostly flew strafing missions. He resented the fact that the aces received most of the attention: "For reasons I cannot understand, the 'glamour' is accorded to fighter pilots who were involved in aerial combat. Yet to my way of thinking and experience, it was far more dangerous to be sent on strafing missions in support of ground troops." Most fighter pilots, even the aces, would probably agree with Harrington. Strafing, not dogfighting, presented the greatest danger to the pilot. At low levels, enemy flak could be intense, and most fighter aircraft, with the notable exception of the P-47, could not absorb the kind of punishment that heavy bombers flying at high altitudes could withstand. Fighter Pilot Jack Ilfrey flew many strafing missions during his time in the 20th Fighter Group. Although he understood the vital importance of such missions, the dangers could be disquieting: "That type of combat was the worst. You can't do anything about people shooting at you from the ground, like you can when someone is shooting at you in the air. German trains had flak cars, often pulled immediately behind the engines. The flak cars were somewhat disguised like boxcars, but we knew they were there. One day I spied one and went down to blow up the boiler, but the flak cars were ready for me—they shot me down." Ilfrey survived the crash and evaded capture. He disguised himself as a French farmer, bicycled to American lines, and eventually returned to his unit.

Clifford Harrison flew P-47s with the 86th Fighter Group. On his first mission, he and his buddies dive-bombed a German locomotive. As he followed his wingman, he could not believe the steepness of his dive: "Quite a bit of flak was being thrown up at us, but the thing on my mind was when to pull out of the dive. It seemed I was flying right into the ground when I finally decided that regardless of where my leader was, it was time to release my bombs and pull out. I found that one hand pulling back on the stick was not enough. I took both hands and pulled back with all the strength I had. I blacked myself out and when I recovered consciousness I was going straight up. I saw the other P-47s in my flight and quickly and happily rejoined them." Harrison's account highlights a crucial fact about strafing missions. A large part of the danger came from the steep dive necessary to attack a target. These dives exposed pilots to extreme forces of gravity (usually called G-forces) that put immense strain on their bodies, often causing them to black out. The chance of losing control and crashing was quite high. Pulling out of such dives required strength, timing, and skill. Thus, every time a pilot went down on the deck to destroy a ground target, he stood a good chance of crashing or being hit by enemy fire.

In spite of the dangers, many became masters at strafing. Hannibal Cox of the 332d Fighter Group once led a strafing mission that completely destroyed a German airdrome: "It was impossible for the enemy to get planes off the ground. One plane was taxiing . . . and my number-three man clobbered him before he got into position. I hit a revetment that had aircraft in it and pilots attempting to get in the aircraft. The .50-caliber shells just lit up when they hit the enemy." Danny Davis of the 364th Fighter Group also wreaked havoc on a German airfield: "As I came into sight of the airplanes, I started firing my guns in short bursts, at the row of Me-110s. Chunks came off them, but no fire or explosion. I noticed small red objects going by me . . . about the size of golf balls. It was 20mm cannon ground antiaircraft fire." Davis then flew between a pair of aircraft hangars and made his way out to sea, where he escaped the deadly fire. Ken Smith, a P-39 pilot in the 350th Fighter Group, flew a strafing mission to Italy one day in 1943. He and his buddies flew around for a time, looking for anything worthwhile to shoot. He blew up some power lines before they found a railroad line and some boxcars: "We . . . were having a ball shooting up boxcars parked on the line. I was really plastering one when Ben Jones cut across from the side right into my line of fire. I quit firing as soon as I saw him coming, but he still flew through a line of tracers. I anxiously called to him, 'Are you OK?' He replied, 'Thanks, Ken, you just scared the hell out of me.' He continued on and Pee Wee hit a small Fiat on the road beside the rail line. When he hit it with a 37mm shell, it just disappeared."

Smith's account makes two points very clear. First, it shows how dangerous strafing missions could be: Smith nearly shot his own friend right out of the sky. Second, it provides a glimpse of just how devastating strafing could be to the enemy. Almost effortlessly, Smith and his friends blew apart several Italian trains, power lines, and automobiles.

Quentin Aanenson survived many close calls while strafing. Flak hit his aircraft many times but did not shoot him down. He dodged every danger from flak to high-tension wires to blackouts during dive-bombing runs. He realized intellectually the effectiveness of his guns and bombs in destroying the enemy, but one particular incident afforded him the opportunity to experience firsthand how indispensable strafing could be in saving the lives of American infantrymen. In November 1944, he and his wingman were strafing German positions on the edge of the Hurtgen Forest when they received a distress call from an infantry captain whose unit was about to be overrun by a German tank. He had no choice but to drop his ordnance right on the captain's position: "I told him to disperse his men as much as possible. I came in on my dive from a lower altitude than normal, so I could see the tank all the way, and I made my dive as slow as possible to try to improve my accuracy. I was scared to death I might overshoot and hit our guys. When I released my bombs, I poured the power to my plane to try to get clear of the explosion, but I ended up flying through a big part of the blast and took a lot of damage. I can't describe the great feeling I had when I looked back and saw the German tank on fire and totally out of commission. The infantry captain was on the radio shouting with excitement, and I could see some of his men waving at me."

There is an eerie postscript to this story. Two years after the war, Aanenson met a new neighbor, a fellow veteran who had been an infantry captain. As they talked, Aanenson discovered that his neighbor was the very same infantry commander whom he had helped save the day he destroyed the German tank: "By an unbelievable combination of circumstances, the infantry captain and the Thunderbolt pilot, who had shared a dramatic and emotional moment in their war, had now come together, face to face. As we discussed that day, we both came close to crying."

Aanenson's experience of saving the infantry unit may have brought home to him the importance of close air support, but it did not make him any less fearful of the dangers. By contrast, John Marshall, a fighter pilot in the 404th Fighter Group, actually seemed to enjoy strafing missions. His aggressiveness and eagerness to obliterate the enemy by strafing shone through in the letters he wrote to his parents. In the summer of 1944, he wrote a letter describing his job satisfaction: "This dive-bombing I'm a fiend about is deliberate, hell-raising destruction, which . . . I took considerable part in with joy. Like vultures we go out just looking for trouble. An even temper and good judgement is all you need, with reasonable luck. Now and then some poor fool gets caught walking down a road or bailing out of a car—my Quaker background goes all to hell if the situation is right. When these guns bark, it has a faint resemblance to smashing a tomato with a ball bat—rough talk but they are paying us pretty good money to do that job which I'd gladly do for nothing."

On another occasion, he wrote to express his exhilaration at saving a pinned-down infantry unit. His fire effectively destroyed German resistance in the infantry unit's sector: "When I landed, the armament Sgt. looked at my guns, pushed his hat to one side, and said, 'Jesus, Captain Marshall' with a broad grin. The guns were just about melted. The ground unit practically cried on my shoulder over the radio with 'thanks for the support—Jesus, thanks a lot, those guys just threw down their guns and left.' Seems we put an Infantry Division into a completely disorganized retreat, plus some 'just right' bombing on some gun positions. Never enjoyed anything more."

Strafing missions were every bit as important in the Pacific theater. Sometimes tough, well-entrenched Japanese troops could be defeated only with the help of close air support. Boyce Holleman, a Navy pilot, remembered attacking enemy positions on Saipan in direct support of Marine combat troops: "We just laid those eight-inch rockets . . . one right behind the other and you could just see the Japs coming out of the trenches, blasting them out." Japanese trains, trucks, ships, and airfields were also fair game. Charles Bond cornered a Japanese supply column in Burma in 1942: "We practically obliterated them. After our first pass, the road was smeared with blood, dead oxen, and riddled caissons. God, what a mess! Man, what those .50-calibers will do! It was a sickening thing to think about at the moment but those thoughts are fleeting." Harold Rosser, a pilot in the 33d Fighter Group, spent much of his combat time strafing Japanese troops. One day his unit bombed a bridge in Mawlu, Burma: "The Japs' groundfire was a dreaded thing. Having learned not to attempt to hit streaking fighters by aiming at them, they concentrated . . . on a point in front of the plane, a technique that assured them of strikes. Groundfire was what I worried most about when strafing. I followed Ruddy [his flight leader] into his bomb run. Beginning my own pullout, I released my bombs just as the bombsight on the windshield raised above the target. Groundfire was heavy. Skidding, twisting, and turning, we used all the evasive maneuvers we had been taught with some extras thrown in. Turning in time to see one bomb explode in the embankment at the end of the bridge, blowing out the foundation, I watched a large chunk of the span fall into the water. It left a yawning opening."

Navy fighter pilots often found themselves providing close air support for amphibious invasions. Franklin Shires, a fighter pilot based on the USS *Franklin,* flew many such missions: "We always chose a target, usually around an airfield, hangars or something like that, shot our rockets, dropped our bomb, and strafed. When we would escort dive bombers and torpedo planes . . . we would always take the antiaircraft position and strafe them. You're shooting down at them and they're shooting straight back at you. The only protection you had was speed and jinks, going in all over the sky, turning and diving and zooming and trying to keep them from getting a lead on you."

Jim Campbell flew strafing missions against Japanese-held islands, destroying anything and everything: "There was some AA [antiaircraft] fire and you could see the bullets coming up at you like they were sort of floating up. They appeared as orange and white dots and looked very harmless, but of course they weren't, they were quite dangerous, and for the ones we could see, there were many others we couldn't see, for we could see only the tracers. I could see my tracers lining out from my six guns and as they tore into the target area on the ground. We didn't open fire until we were down to about 3,000 feet and then fired in short bursts. We would pull out at about 1,000 feet or sometimes lower and then make a fast getaway."

Some fighter pilots, like Marine Pop Flaherty, especially enjoyed shooting up Japanese ships. He found a Japanese cruiser one day off the coast of Guadalcanal: "When I strafed, I went right down over the ship, not more than two hundred feet above it. The decks were just covered with men trying to get off the cruiser, and with those six .50-calibers I carved a passage right through the middle of the crowd. I saw the men falling, some of them knocked right over the side of the ship. That was about the most fun I ever had. In fact, I was so interested in it that I damned near hit the water."

Medium-bomber crews also did their share of strafing. Much of their job involved low-level strikes on tactical targets in direct support of ground troops, the kind of tasks for which the twin-engine B-26s, A-20s, and B-25s had been designed. Robert Quinn flew A-20s against ground targets for the 417th Bomb Group in the Pacific. In a letter to a friend, he described his experiences on a typical mission: "You approach the target. Your bomb-bay doors open with a swoosh! You flick on your gun switches, and now you are all set. Then suddenly there it is, your target! Those houses in the clearing, with all those tiny figures running about like rats caught in a trap. You feel an immense satisfaction and grit your teeth. You squeeze the trigger and out go six streams of copper-clad steel 'fifties.' You spot a big shack and kick rudder to get over it. Now! You press the little black button and a 500-pound bomb drops; you don't know if it hit or not but photos will tell later on. What are those red balls hanging there in the air? Ack! Ack! With that, they begin screaming past your wings. You instinctively crouch closer to that bulletproof glass, then you kick one rudder, then the other rudder. You slip, you skid. Be careful, those trees are close. You keep low and fast."

Even though he flew a B-24, George Stevens found himself on many strafing missions in the central Pacific. In fact, he and his crew did almost all of their damage at low altitudes. Enemy fighters were a constant worry, but so were enemy ships, as he found out one day in late 1944. He had just strafed an enemy harbor when his plane overflew a Japanese heavy cruiser: "She fired her main batteries as well as the antiaircraft big guns at us. My first thought was one of extreme flattery, quickly replaced with stark terror! I executed a violent diving turn. This maneuver was of such magnitude that the explosions of the shells were not seen (and just as well, from my point of view)." Stevens and his crew managed to escape to fight another day.

Not all strafing missions were harrowing. Some, particularly in remote areas of the Pacific, could be almost boring. Early in his service, Marine Torpedo Bomber Pilot Samuel Hynes flew such missions, including one to destroy a bypassed Japanese airfield on the island of Yap: "Nothing moved below us. Nothing suggested any life at all there. I saw no installations, no people, not a hut or a kitchen garden. The island seemed uninhabited and forlorn. We circled . . . and made our bombing runs. As I dropped my bombs, I could hear the hard rattle of Campbell's gun, and high, tinny popping of Edwards's .30-caliber [these two men were his crewmen]. 'What the hell were they shooting at,' I wondered. Just shooting, because they were in combat now."

Escort missions were the third and final type of combat mission that fighter pilots flew. On an escort mission, a fighter pilot accompanied bombers on their missions and protected the bombers. This meant flying in formation with them and destroying any enemy fighters that threatened their safety, a less hazardous task than strafing or deliberately engaging enemy fighters. Alone in enemy skies, bombers could be quite vulnerable. But with friendly fighters at their side, bombers became far more effective. When long-range P-51s and P-47s came into service in the Army Air Force in late 1943, they unquestionably changed the entire course of the air war in Europe and broke the back of the German air force. From that point on, German fighters usually had to battle their way through American fighters to get to the bombers they so desperately wanted to destroy.

Armed with this security blanket, bombers could drop their bombs more accurately and take fewer casualties doing it. Bomber crews referred to their fighter pilot brethren as "Little Friends" and held them in the highest esteem. Fighter pilots returned that respect. Most of them could not help but have tremendous admiration for the courage of the bomber crews, who faced so many dangers to get their bombs on target. Fighter pilots particularly admired the bravery it took among bomber crews to fly straight and level through flak during a bomb run while the fighters flew high above, out of danger. J. Fred Baumann, who achieved his lifelong ambition of becoming a fighter pilot, originally had a condescending attitude toward bomber pilots. He thought of them as inferior pilots lacking the ability to fly fighters. Then he began to fly escort missions, and his attitude changed dramatically: "It did not take much of watching those poor devils flying so steadily and slowly into the heart of the heavy antiaircraft defenses for me to develop an entirely different attitude regarding bomber pilots. I'll always take my hat off to them. They were the boys with the real guts!"

Warren Johnson, a fighter pilot in the 4th Fighter Group, also had tremendous respect and affection for bomber crews. On escort missions, he knew that his job was to protect the bombers at all costs, even if it meant sacrificing himself. On an escort mission over Mannheim, Germany, one day in April 1944, enemy fighters attempted to attack the bombers. Johnson's group shot down five of them and drove them off, but they could not do anything about flak: "When the bombers lined up on their IP . . . all hell broke loose. It was murderous and devastating. Although we had to climb up and away from the B-24 bombers, we nonetheless had to clench our teeth and still try to pray for those poor souls who were now on their assigned target run. Many of the bombers received direct hits, rolled over, and began plunging towards earth as they left a trail of flames."

After the bomb run, the German fighters returned. Johnson's group shot down more, but some got through to the bombers. After a running air battle, the Germans broke off their attacks. At this stage, Johnson began to hunt for crippled bombers, knowing well that the enemy preyed on wounded planes separated from the main formation. On the return leg of any escort mission, the fighter pilots, fuel permitting, scanned the skies in search of cripples they could safely escort home. On this day, Johnson found plenty: "I came upon twelve badly damaged . . . B-24 bombers, most of them trying to make it on two engines and leaving numerous trails of smoke. They were sure glad to see me; they knew they were sitting ducks for an attack. I . . . put out a call for P-51 fighters, giving them our heading, speed, and altitude. Within several minutes eleven Mustangs arrived on the scene, none too soon. We saw . . . Kraut fighters swooping down to kill off the near-helpless . . . B-24s. Somehow, those Hitler-loving SOBs didn't see us in time. We quickly split them up, shot down six of them, and gave chase to the rest in such a manner that none of them even got near the crippled bombers.

Sometimes close calls were not quite this personal. Occasionally, planes went completely out of control, plunging toward certain doom, only to recover in time for the crew to survive. Hiram Drache of the 457th Bomb Group remembered a mission in which flak hit his bomber's oil lines, causing the controls to freeze and the plane to dive headlong toward the earth: "I found myself standing in a horizontal position, looking straight down at the earth. I couldn't move. In my mind, I saw my folks' house and my hometown. My thoughts were, 'Gee, it's too bad my folks are going to get this telegram saying I'm missing in action.' I knew I was going to die and that telegram is what I felt most badly about. Then, at about 4,000 feet, the pilot was able to pull us out of the dive. After we got on the ground in England, they told us it was aerodynamically impossible. I got the feeling I was destined to lead a long, productive life, because we had faced sure death and survived."

Tail Gunner Kevin Herbert and the rest of his crew nearly went down one night off the coast of Japan when their plane ran directly into a violent thunderstorm. The force of the storm completely flipped over the seventy-ton B-29 and sent it spinning toward the sea: "The initial thrust of the G-forces seemed to all but crash me against the ceiling, then as we flipped up and over, I was pinned to the floor. My first reaction was disbelief, for I could not even move my hands, which seemed fastened to the ceiling, and then I realized we were in deep trouble. Up in the cockpit Lt. Tunnel [the pilot] was fighting for . . . our lives. He managed to lock his legs around the wheel and then as the ship looped and started down, he and the copilot found the strength needed to pull us out to level flight. But it was a very near thing."

During low-level incendiary raids over Japan, B-29 crews often endured major buffeting in their planes from thermal heat blasts. Sometimes the thermal heat caused a momentary loss of control, but nothing like what the thunderstorm did to Herbert's plane. Fighter pilots also had many near-crashes, especially during strafing runs. Johnnie Corbitt, a pilot in the 48th Fighter Group, came very close to going down one day in Belgium. As he strafed a German column, he smashed into a tree: "The plane came out of the tree almost upside down, just above treetop level. I reacted instinctively with full throttle, full left rudder, stick left and back. To my amazement, the plane righted itself and was straight and level barely above ground. While this was going on I thought, 'My parents will be so sad,' and I felt very badly about the ugly attitude I had used to badger them into giving permission for my entry into the Air Corps. I also thought that the Germans would be watching and laughing at my predicament after what I had just done to them. I also thought I was floating in the air above all of this and watching the plane crash and roll up into a ball of aluminum with flames coming out. It was a very weird experience and just as vivid today as it was then."

One peril that belonged exclusively to bomber crews was the danger of an undropped, or "hung," bomb. If a bomb failed to drop, it had to be forced out of the bomb bay or disarmed as soon as possible; otherwise, it could explode, killing everyone. Incredibly courageous combat airmen routinely climbed into open bomb bays, sometimes with no oxygen, and kicked hung bombs out of the bay. Because of the confined spaces in the bomb bays, they often wore no parachutes. Dick Lincoln, a bombardier in the 486th Bomb Group, found that only half his bombs had released one day during a mission over Germany. He had no choice but to go to the bomb bay and release them by hand: "I hooked on a walk-around oxygen bottle and without a parachute went to the open bomb bay. I found that with a wrench I was able to release each bomb by crawling precariously on the catwalk with one of the gunners holding me by my shoes. Suddenly he grabbed me and pointed. The wind had caused the cord of my heated suit to wrap around the fin of the bomb I was about to release. If the gunner had not stopped me, I could certainly have gone out with the bomb. That is what generates camaraderie."

Other crewmen—especially radio operators, waist gunners, and ball turret gunners—often handled the dangerous and tricky business of going into the bomb bay to release hung bombs. Radio Operator Jim Lynch had to do so one time during a mission to Cologne: "At the far end of the bomb bay . . . one 1,000-pound bomb was tilting, nose down, and the arming prop was spinning. [After a certain number of arming prop revolutions, a bomb exploded at the slightest pressure.] I grabbed a walk-around oxygen bottle . . . and threw off my flak vest. As I stepped into the bay, the and later on I found out that they were shooting at me and the rest of us. I hit the ground with a severe jolt. My head hit and I was knocked cold. I haven't any idea how long I was out, but when I woke up I was bleeding and surrounded by American soldiers. I remember my first words were, 'Thank God you're Yanks.' They treated us as if we were kings."

Many other perils went along with flying combat missions. For example, anoxia—lack of oxygen to the brain—could be a real problem. Sometimes anoxia proved fatal. Many combat missions, particularly in Europe, were flown at high altitudes (above 10,000 feet) in unpressurized aircraft. In those conditions, men needed to wear oxygen masks, because the air was too thin to provide them with enough oxygen to survive. At high altitudes, anoxia was a persistent threat. As Jule Berndt explained, anoxia could be staved off only by constant vigilance: "Starting from 15,000 feet until the assembly altitude is reached, oxygen checks on the crew are taken every 2,000 to 3,000 feet of ascent. The checks are usually called by any one of the four officers. The purpose is to see that the crew is obtaining oxygen and no one has lost consciousness from anoxia. Anoxia can result in the death of a crew member within a few minutes when the flight level is above 25,000 feet. The symptoms of anoxia are not too evident; and by the time a person recognizes them, it may be too late for self-help. Whenever a crew member does not check in, the man nearest his station is sent to him for any possible aid. A person suffering from anoxia is given pure oxygen so that his body does not have to work for it."

Top Turret Gunner/Engineer V. F. Cozad of the 7th Bomb Group wrote that anoxia "effects [sic] you like getting drunk. First you get dizzy, feel tired, and then pass out. No pain whatsoever. I passed out at 18,000 feet. It was a very queer experience." Radio Operator Earl Benham's 100th Bomb Group crew—like many other crews—routinely checked the oxygen status of every crew member. The bombardier called to each man every few minutes and expected a response. One day the ball turret gunner failed to answer, and Benham went to investigate: "I saw Goodman's face and skin was [sic] a blue color, indicating he was completely out of oxygen.

We thought he had 'gone to the great beyond.' We plugged his oxygen hose . . . into an oxygen bottle, turned it to full rich mixture. To our happy amazement, Goodman revived and was in good shape."

Joseph Beswick, a top turret gunner/engineer in the 483d Bomb Group, gave his buddy the best gift of all on Christmas day 1944— he saved his life: "When the ball gunner was getting into the turret at high altitude, he was supposed to unplug his oxygen tube from the waist and plug it into the ball turret before he attempted to get into the turret. Erik would not do that. The first time I found Erik passed out, he had not been out long. The second time I noticed him sitting in the turret and not moving. I tipped his head back and the oxygen mask was loose on one side. His face was covered with frost from his breath. It scared the hell out of me. I thought he was dead. I put his mask back on and turned on the emergency oxygen and Erik regained consciousness. I gave him hell that time and Erik never did do that again."

Ben O'Dell was a navigator in the 303d Bomb Group. On his first mission, his crew demonstrated their inexperience. Their oxygen problems would have been a comedy of errors if they had not been so potentially serious: "The engineer, attending to his duties, did not connect his walk-around oxygen bottle and passed out, falling full length across his turret. The pilot called for help and the copilot turned and stretched toward him to fasten his oxygen mask. In doing so, the copilot pulled loose his oxygen supply hose (he did not realize this) and fell down through the catwalk from lack of oxygen. I unhooked from oxygen, crawled to the catwalk, and with my hands under Bergeron's [the copilot's] chin, pulled him into the nose compartment. I put the oxygen regulator in the emergency position and alternated the oxygen mask between us. He had turned blue and I was concerned. Finally he revived and returned to his position. While I was reviving Bergeron, the radio operator came forward through the bomb bay to revive the engineer. After reviving the engineer, his supply line became loosened and the radio operator was revived by one of the gunners."

Harry Crosby recalled a mission when the entire crew of his lead plane had oxygen deficiency. A malfunction in the plane's oxygen system caused them to get just enough to stay alive, but not enough to stay alert or function properly: "I began to have an excruciating headache. Everything was black. The crew navigator and bombardier were just sitting on the floor, slumped over. The radar operator stopped giving me fixes. Colonel Harding [the pilot] was gradually losing consciousness. His intercom made little sense; mostly he just mumbled." German fighters attacked them and still they flew on aimlessly. After the attack, Crosby heard the radio operator call the pilot: "'The waist gunners are acting strange. They seem to think they are drinking beer. They keep holding up their relief cans and toasting each other.' 'Anoxia.' It was Colonel Harding, barely audible. 'That's what's wrong. Walk-around bottles, all stations.'" They made it back to their base, physically exhausted and completely dispirited.

But simply wearing one's oxygen mask was not enough to prevent anoxia. Airmen also had to make sure the oxygen line was clear at all times. Otherwise the oxygen supply would gradually dwindle, strangled by frozen saliva from a man's exhalations. This happened to Sal Leotta, a navigator in the 491st Bomb Group: "I was jumping from one side to the other of my compartment and identifying incoming fighters for the Gunners. Unknown to me, this activity was pulling my oxygen mask away from my face, permitting enough cold air to enter and freeze the moisture in the mask, restricting the flow of oxygen. Over a period of time I . . . became disoriented and slowly lost consciousness. Fortunately, Jack Fitzgerald, our Bombardier, was alert and quickly took action. He . . . got his spare oxygen mask, connected it, and turned on the emergency oxygen. As I recovered consciousness, I had a fit of coughing. He saved my life."

For obvious reasons, it could be especially dangerous if a pilot fell victim to anoxia. This happened to Philip Abbott of the 489th Bomb Group during a mission on the eve of D day: "I had commented to Lt. Hansell [the other pilot] that my oxygen mask felt a little loose. Excessive ice had formed under my chin. The oxygen-flow indicator near my right knee blinked with each breath I took, though, and I forgot about my concerns. Next, I was aware of a cold, steady stream of oxygen hitting my face. Our flight engineer . . . was leaning over me, working on the oxygen regulator. I had lapsed into unconsciousness from anoxia (called hypoxia now).

Hansell was shouting at me . . . because I had not released my grip on the controls."

John Williamson, a pilot in the 461st Bomb Group, experienced the giddy euphoria that sometimes comes with anoxia, and it nearly cost the lives of his entire crew: "I . . . remember trying to touch our wing tip to that of the lead plane in our box, a feat that seemed inordinately amusing to me. When the euphoria suddenly stopped, something made me glance down. I saw the nose of my oxygen mask dangling free, hit the other pilot, and passed out. A savage burst of pain in my head accompanied by a simultaneous bright red flash were my next sensations as the engineer gave me oxygen from a portable bottle."

Fighter pilots also fell prey to anoxia. Joe Boyd flew P-38s out of North Africa and Italy. He noticed that the plane did not have a very reliable oxygen system. One day it almost cost him his life: "I suddenly found myself blacking out. We had a flexible tube under the oxygen mask and this tube had come loose. I immediately had to yank off my oxygen mask and put this tube in my mouth. I went through a fight . . . like that. A lot of people got killed before they figured out what was happening." Louis Purnell of the 332d Fighter Group flew P-51s. Its oxygen tube could also get blocked, and it happened to him one day without his knowing it: "All of a sudden, I felt like this was the best day I had ever lived in my whole life. Everything turned beautiful, I could hear music coming out of nowhere. I wanted to roll back the canopy and climb out on the nose of the plane and direct all 64 pieces of the orchestra. Then, about five minutes later, it felt as if someone had lowered a great mosquito netting right in front of my eyes. I began to get really sick to my stomach. It was an effort to do the things that should have been second nature. I got to the point where I said, 'I don't give a damn.' I had a feeling as if I was going to sleep." Luckily Purnell realized he had anoxia, took steps to correct the problem, and eventually landed safely at his base.

Temperatures at high altitudes were extremely cold. The vast majority of American combat airmen flew combat missions in unpressurized aircraft, and extreme, biting cold was a constant source of misery and worry. If you did not dress warmly enough, you could get frostbite or even freeze to death. Temperatures often reached thirty to forty degrees below zero. According to Edward Hearty's mission diary, sometimes it got even colder: "At an altitude of 27,000 feet the windows continually froze up due to the severe cold. 51 degrees below zero was today's temp."

Bomber crews in the European theater bore the brunt of the cold temperatures. Not only did they operate in a cold climate, but they all flew in unpressurized aircraft, and usually at very high altitudes. John Crowe, a copilot in the 491st Bomb Group, wrote that "the unbearable cold at altitude was ever present, along with the long hours breathing pure oxygen. After an hour or so, the condensation inside the mask, mixed with nasal discharge, dripped out and formed small icicles which hung down and fell or broke off, landing in one's crotch—not altogether very glamorous." As a waist gunner, Jack Novey was probably the most exposed member of his crew. One time, his gun even froze during combat. Novey, a Chicagoan, could never forget the feeling of standing at the open waist of his B-17 in the middle of the iciest winds and most terrible cold he had ever experienced: "The air temperature is anywhere from thirty-five to fifty degrees below zero—not counting the chill of the wind, which whistles through our waist windows at 150 miles per hour and more. Freezing to death is a constant hazard at these altitudes. It's cold. It's the kind of cold that creeps into every pore of your body and freezes the sweat on your back. If you pull off your glove and touch the metal of the plane, it will take the flesh off your fingers. If you have to pee, the urine freezes before it hits the fuselage floor. In an attempt to protect our faces, we wore big black masks with holes cut out for eyes, nose, and mouth, but they're terribly uncomfortable. You could die quickly from the cold. Sometimes the air temperature was sixty or seventy degrees below zero Fahrenheit. Our primitive electric suits and all the heavy clothing we could put on just barely kept us from freezing to death. The cold hurt; it penetrated with an intensity that was the same as pain. The cold was like a serpent, crawling over my body, enveloping and numbing my mind, roaring into my ears, 'Let me in. Let me in and I'll kill you.'"

Ball turret gunners like Robert Geraghty of the 381st Bomb Group also bore the brunt of the fierce cold. The turret provided little or no shelter from the elements: "The numbing coldness whistled in through cracks in the turret. It froze the moisture on my eyebrows and eyelashes and stiffened the anti-frostbite grease smeared on my face. My breath, exhaled through the oxygen mask, condensed, froze, and formed a thick, icy breastplate on my chest. My feet were heavy with numbness."

Combat airmen in the Pacific often flew at lower altitudes than in Europe and in warmer climates, but cold temperatures could still be a problem. John Bradford, a Navy B-24 Liberator pilot, remembered the uneven nature of the cold in his plane: "The Lib's fuselage admitted numerous small blasts of chill, icy air and its thin aluminum skin possessed little insulation ability. Temperature changes from the deck to altitude were often extreme; this was particularly noticeable in the tropics. There, the greenhouse effect of the cockpit enclosure had the pilot and copilot sitting in sunny warmth wearing short-sleeved shirts while their feet, in the perpetual shadow (and cold) . . . would be encased in fur-lined flight boots!"

Even fighter pilots, whose planes often came equipped with heaters, had to guard against the cold. There was no certainty that, even if a heater worked well, it could keep the whole cockpit warm. J. Fred Baumann wore heavy, fleece-lined flying boots on high-altitude escort missions, despite the fact that the boots took away his feel for the rudder pedals: "The cockpit itself was heated adequately. But the heat entered into the cockpit near my left foot. That foot was always cozy, but the other one could get awfully uncomfortable without the boot on it. Therefore, I always put them on when heading . . . up to altitudes . . . as high as 38,000 feet." Francis Gabreski also took precautions against the piercing cold prevalent at high altitudes: "It was plenty cold in the cockpit of my P-47 at nearly six miles above northern Germany. I had the heater on full blast and, of course, I was bundled up in heavy flying gear and my thick boots. Still, I had to keep wiggling my toes and fingers to keep the blood running through them."

The cold temperatures, and the clothing airmen had to wear to protect themselves, made relieving themselves quite difficult. Answering the call of nature could be a real challenge for a combat airman in his freezing, buffeting aircraft miles above the earth. As

C. L. Anderson made clear, anyone who tried to do so quickly became disabused of the notion that war in the air was glamorous: "Hollywood made the life look glamorous. I've laughed at their portrayals. Here's what it was like in a ball turret. There was a relief tube under the seat. It was a plastic line funnel, chamois-lined, that ran outside the turret. Using the tube at that altitude, the hose would freeze up and back up to the funnel. If it spilled on the sighting glass, it would turn instantly to ice and obscure vision."

Jack Novey had nothing but contempt for the relief facilities on his B-17: "Between the waist compartment and the tail, there was a tin can with a lid on it. You were supposed to sit down and defecate into that can. But on a mission, even if we managed to find the time to go—remember that meant peeling off a number of layers of clothing—at high altitude, when you put your butt down on the toilet, the frozen metal would take part of your skin with it. So we just threw the damn thing out of the airplane. Then, in the bomb bay, there was a . . . funnel with a tube running out. You were supposed to make your way across this narrow catwalk with bombs hanging on both sides, unzip yourself in this extreme cold, aim into the funnel, and urinate. But if someone had already used it and if some of his urine had frozen and stopped up the tube, your pee splashed right back up in your face. So we abandoned the tube. If we had to go and if we had time, we unzipped and peed on the floor or out the waist window. I've seen urine freeze before it hit the waist window, then rattle around like tiny ice cubes. If you were desperate, there was only one place to take a crap: in your pants. It was an uncomfortable solution, to say the least. It was a common thing. As a result, there was no smell like the smell that greeted the ground crew when a combat crew came back from a particularly long and harrowing mission. No one writes about this in the books that try to make war glamorous."

Such were the everyday realities of flying combat missions. R. H. Tays flew with a copilot who had a small bladder. Despairing of his relief tube, he took to urinating in an extra shoe, and the urine would freeze at high altitudes. However, when they descended on the way home, the temperature dropped, melting the urine, thus causing it to splash on him: "On all subsequent missions, he saw to it that empty gallon cans were located fore, aft, and on the flight deck. This item became a part of the check list." Jim Bakewell, a nose turret gunner in the 459th Bomb Group, once had a powerful and irresistible urge to urinate while his plane was on a bomb run: "There was no way to wait until we had pulled off the target; I had to do it immediately. With great effort, I stood up with my five-foot-eleven frame hunched up against the Plexiglas roof and doubled over in a 'half-moon' shape. With greater effort, I extracted my 'apparatus' through my heavy flying suit and flak jacket, and I proceeded to make a 'direct hit' on the Plexiglas covering the front of my turret. All hell was breaking loose outside our plane, but I didn't care about the flak or anything else. I had to do what I had to do."

B-29 crews had the advantage of flying in a pressurized airplane, which meant not having to deal with cold temperatures or oxygen masks. They could dress normally and move about their heated cabin without the need for any breathing assistance. They could also relieve themselves conventionally. Every B-29 came equipped with its own toilet. Kevin Herbert remembered it as "a single round container, with a seat and a cover on top, no chemicals of any kind, and it was placed in the far end of the radar section." Most of the crew members used it at least once during their long missions to Japan.

Fighter pilots found themselves provided with a funnel and relief tube, hardly adequate for the task, in their small aircraft. As Robert Goebel explained, using the device took the contortion skills of a magician: "The device consisted of a plastic cone fitted with a small rubber tube, which, in theory at least, conducted the urine to a vent on the underside of the fuselage. Using the tube involved undoing the lap belt and the leg straps of the parachute, unzipping and peeling back layers of flight clothing, finding the plumbing fixture (no small feat in a sitting position), and tucking into the cone—all with the left hand while flying with the right. To maintain formation, however, the throttle had to be tended almost continuously with the left hand. I didn't even try."

Joe Boyd dreaded having to urinate during missions in his P-38 fighter plane: "I'm here to tell you that sixty below zero will make a little boy out of a grown man and you start digging through all those clothes and then you had a little tube . . . that would come out from under the seat. If you could get it, you had to pinch it here 'cos [sic] that's all you could find. Then you'd try to put it into that little tube and of course it'll freeze and throw [the urine] back at you. Those were . . . smelly airplanes."

Sometimes the difficulty of evacuations for crewmen during missions made for humorous incidents. Kenneth Jones was a pilot in the 389th Bomb Group. His copilot forgot his relief can one day on what was supposed to be a "milk run"—the term bomber crews used to describe easy missions. Unable to hold it any longer, the copilot urinated in his flak helmet, figuring he would not need it that day: "A short while later, we turned on the IP and started the bomb run. An eight-gun battery of 88mm tracking flak opened up, very accurate and right on our formation. We all grabbed flak vests and helmets. Strong [the copilot] plopped his helmet on his head. The frozen contents occuppied [sic] head space and he had to balance the flak helmet on his head with one hand. The body heat under the helmet caused melting conditions and a small trickle . . . was coursing down his left temple. He snatched the helmet off in a hurry. I informed the other crew members about the comedy . . . and they razzed him the rest of the way home."

Ron Bereman, a B-17 pilot in the 486th Bomb Group, had his ground-crew chief place special relief cartons under the pilots' seats in his plane. One day he decided to do some special "bombing": "On an extremely cold day, outside temp was –55 degrees, I filled a carton to the brim, put the lid back on, then checked for planes behind us. With none visible, I decided to throw a frozen brick on some German's head. With the pilot's window back, I proceeded to eject the missile. The lid . . . came off in the slipstream, and my face and oxygen mask were immediately covered with salty ice as well as the window. I started chipping the ice off my face and mask. I took a quick look at the copilot . . . only to see him going into hysterics over my most embarrassing moment. To make matters worse, my pilot's window did not clear off until we reached a warmer altitude. Needless to say, that incident was not reported at the debriefing."

The debriefing was the last stage of any combat mission. Upon their safe return, combat crews met with intelligence officers who questioned them about every detail of the mission. No matter how harrowing their mission may have been, crewmen, if uninjured, went straight from their planes to debriefing, because intelligence officers wanted to speak to them while the mission was fresh in their minds.

At debriefing, crews could find out the "big picture" of how their mission had gone, and they could relay information that might be useful for future missions. For example, navigator Ben O'Dell spotted a group of flak guns firing at his plane from a wooded area one day. He noted the location in his logbook and relayed the information to the intelligence officer during debriefing: "Being convinced that I was correct, the debriefing officer forwarded the information to Fighter Command. The next time we flew over the same location, we were not fired upon. Instead, there was a large burned-out area around the former Gun Emplacement Site. Fighter Command did its job!"

Fighter-pilot debriefings usually centered on strafing results, downed enemy planes, and the fate of escorted bombers. Robert Powell, a fighter pilot in the 352d Fighter Group, said that debriefing officers gave returning pilots a shot of Scotch to loosen their tongues. Then the debriefing began: "Our interrogations were . . . informal. We'd tell the intelligence officers about anything unusual—sightings of unusual aircraft, etc. If you had strafed an airfield, you could make a sketch showing positions of enemy planes and those that were destroyed, along with your route of strafing." Navy Pilot Jim Campbell often flew several missions a day from his carrier. This also meant going through several debriefings: "Each returning pilot had to take his turn with the Intelligence officers for a de-briefing session. He wanted to know what you did and what you saw. If you made any strafing runs, then how many and in what direction and what did you hit. They wanted to get the information while it was still fresh in our memory."

James Good Brown, a chaplain in the 381st Bomb Group in England, sat in on many debriefings and observed the returning crews: "They can hardly walk; they are stiff from the cold. Their feet are quite numb, perhaps not frozen, but lifeless. They laugh; then they laugh again; and then they laugh some more. They are happy that they are back. They gather around in a circle. They pat each other on the back. They throw their arms around each other. They act as though they have not seen each other for six months, yet it has only been six hours. What? Only six? Those six have been ages."

Jule Berndt described in detail a typical mission debriefing at his base: "As the complete crews gather, they are taken to a table by a member of the intelligence section for interrogation. All the information that can be given to this officer is of vital importance in planning following missions, and so thoroughness and accuracy is [sic] required. Two important questions are on the appearance of fighters and flak. Concerning fighters, the type and tactics used is [sic] the information desired. If a fighter is to be credited to a bomber, there has to be verification of its exploding, spinning down out of control, or if visibility permits, its crashing by some other members of the crew. Information on flak deals with intensity, accuracy, and, most important, the location. Intelligence is also interested in finding out from the crews the results of the bombing. The ball turret gunner and the bombardier are in the most favorable positions for observing where the bombs hit and so usually can offer the information wanted. Additional information is wanted concerning the extent of danger to the plane, presence of wounded or fatalities aboard, and then . . . any suggestions by anyone on the crew. Here any person on the crew can get rid of any bitch or complaint he has concerning the mission."

Roger Armstrong described a debriefing in which he participated one afternoon upon his safe return from a mission to Merseburg, Germany. It is very typical of what most crews experienced after they had landed and deplaned: "Our crew sat together at a separate table from other crews. The Intelligence Officer came over and sat down. He asked a number of questions on what we saw in the air and in the target area. We soon learned that he had a set of questions all crews were asked. The Eighth Air Force had learned that the crews would open up more if they had a couple of stiff shots of Scotch or whiskey. So he poured out a double-shot and everyone, except the copilot, drank them a little bit faster than normal. This was to loosen our tongues. He received a lot of rapid-fire information after that drink. In fact he tried to slow down our conversation a bit. At interrogation, the crews were always in a hurry to get back to the barracks, clean up, eat, and go to town."

When a combat airman walked away from debriefing, he could go back to his bed, change clothes, eat, and rest. With the mission finished, he could relax until the next time, when he would have to lay his life on the line all over again. Such was the nature of flying the missions that made up a tour of duty in World War II.

6

Going Down

You can't fight a war without someone getting hurt and I am no better than my buddies that fly next to me. Try not to grieve over me as that isn't the way I want it. I have had a good life and a lot of fun, so I don't have any regrets. Always remember me in your prayers . . . I'll be waiting for you in the Heavenly City.
—Joe Boswell, fighter pilot, in a letter to his family written on the eve of his death over Ploesti, Romania

Untold thousands of American combat airmen experienced the sick feeling that came with the realization that their plane could not get them home. Most of the time, enemy fighters or flak did the fatal damage to their aircraft, but far too often the damage came from a midair collision with another American plane, mechanical problems, or even fire from one's own antiaircraft, fighters, or bombers. Often combat airmen were grateful to survive their dying planes long enough to become prisoners of war. A lucky few managed to evade capture and make it home. In Europe, those who escaped with the assistance of local underground fighters usually were discharged from further combat flying duties and sent home. No one wanted to take the chance that they would be shot down again and forced to incriminate the underground.

The Army Air Force alone sustained more than 112,000 casualties in World War II. In addition, Navy and Marine aviation suffered several thousand fatalities. The vast majority of Air Force casualties were killed, missing, or captured, but about 25,000 were wounded and made it home to their bases to be hospitalized and treated. Combat airmen had no equivalent to the ground-combat medic, so if an airman was wounded, he either treated himself—very common among fighter pilots—or, in the case of bomber crews, one of the injured airman's untrained buddies tended to the wounds. This lack of on-site medical assistance existed out of necessity, because bombers barely had enough room to fit their essential crew much less a medic. Wounded fliers often had to hang on for hours during the return trip to base, sometimes inside grievously damaged aircraft. Upon approaching the base, planes with wounded aboard shot special flares to alert the tower and then received first priority in landing, where an ambulance and trained medical personnel would then be waiting. Ambulances moved wounded men to medical facilities that were usually located close to airbases. If you were wounded, the key was to make it home. If you could do that, your chances of survival were good.

Combat airmen may have been highly trained for their flying jobs, but most had little training or skill when it came to first aid. Roger Armstrong, a radio operator in the 91st Bomb Group, took care of a wounded comrade on a mission to Cologne, Germany. A burst of flak hit the man in his right thigh: "The hole was about the size of a silver dollar. I used my 'Boy Scout knife' and proceeded to cut the leg of his heated suit open. There was an ugly wound, but I saw no pumping blood so assumed it was not the femoral artery. I had to take off my heated gloves to work on Ralph's wound. When my glove was off, the cold air caused my fingers to stiffen to the point I could not bend them. Beicker came back and the two of us, working in relays, put sulfa in the wound and bandaged the anterior part of his thigh. We two lay doctors weren't sure if he was going into shock. Since we weren't sure, I said we should give him a shot. So, it was decided I would give Ralph a shot of morphine. I warmed it under my heated suit then started to push it through the skin of his thigh. At first it wouldn't go. So . . . I shoved hard, and it went into the muscle. Then I squeezed the morphine into his body. In a few minutes he was asleep." They made it back to base on two engines, and the waist gunner survived.

As a bombardier on his 390th Bomb Group crew, it often fell to H. C. White to tend to wounded men, since he had few duties after he had dropped his bombs. One time, immediately after he had released his bombload, he received an urgent call to administer first aid to the waist gunner, who had been hit by a hunk of flak: "I crawled to the waist section and found my left waist gunner with his leg almost severed from a flak wound. Remembering my Boy Scout training, I fashioned a tourniquet from a handkerchief and a .50-caliber shell and soon the bleeding stopped. I then gave him Morphine in his leg. Later back at the airfield I was called to the medical barracks. The Doctor said . . . 'that morphine goes directly to the brain and it was a miracle that the man had not died of trauma. From now on give the shots in the upper arm.' 'Doctor, no one ever told me where to put the stuff,' I said. As I was leaving the room, he was shaking his head and I heard him say, 'Well, he's a bombardier.'"

White's account, and the doctor's final words, illustrate the fact that most combat airmen simply did not know what they were doing when it came to first aid. They did the best they could, but sometimes they could do more harm than good for their buddies. To make matters worse, they often administered first aid in extremely cold temperatures aboard gravely wounded aircraft at oxygen-poor altitudes, conditions that would challenge even the most highly skilled physician. It is truly remarkable that so many wounded combat airmen lived.

Elmer Vogel, a ball turret gunner in the 307th Bomb Group, had to care for his plane's nose gunner on a mission to Miti in the Pacific. Japanese fighters attacked their plane and a piece of shrapnel hit the nose gunner in his back and chest: "When we got John out of the turret, I thought he was dead. He was hit in the right chest, and his right arm was dangling. Pfirman and I proceeded to give John some blood. This wasn't easy as neither of us knew how to do this but realized it had to be done, or he would die. Pfirman and I read the instructions on mixing the plasma with the water. We knew we couldn't have any air in the lines when we inserted the needle in his vein, but we had a difficult time getting it done. We would look at each other as we tried unsuccessfully to insert the needle in his vein. John said, 'Elmer, let's pray . . . we need help.' After we had prayed aloud and cried out for God's help . . . a miracle did happen. We gave him six pints of blood and kept him alive."

Prentiss Burkett, a pilot in the 499th Bomb Group, had to fly his B-29 alone after his group bombed the Nakajima aircraft plant in

Japan. Soon after they hit the target, Japanese fighters wounded his copilot. Burkett and his crew knew the copilot needed blood but had no idea how to give it to him: "He had lost quite a bit of blood from multiple fragment penetrations of his right arm and shoulder and upper chest. He was obviously suffering from shock. Charlie Ball, the radar operator as well as the first-aid man, was called in to give the plasma injection. He came through the tunnel with his first-aid kit, and as he came out of the tunnel he was very pale, almost white in color, and we knew he could not do it. All the officers discussed the problem and no one thought he could press the sternum needle into the soft bone above the solar plexus, as the plasma was given in those days. The idea was finally abandoned. We covered the wounds as best we could and the morphine seemed to control his pain." In spite of the fact that his crewmates were too unskilled and too squeamish to administer proper medical care for shock and loss of blood, the copilot lived, although it took him the better part of a year to recover from his wounds.

Fire may well have been the combat airman's greatest enemy and his greatest fear. According to Tail Gunner Kevin Herbert of the 498th Bomb Group, fire stood above all other dangers when it came to striking abject fear into the hearts of fliers: "More than death, most air crewmen truly feared permanently disfiguring or disabling injuries. Here the chief danger was from fire caused by explosion of a fuel tank. Enemy fighters, flak, the sea, bad weather, and all operational problems were rated as nothing compared to the hazards of fire." J. Fred Baumann, a fighter pilot in the 52d Fighter Group, saw firsthand what fire could do to human beings. While recuperating from wounds he sustained in a flying accident, he roomed with a fellow fighter pilot who had been horribly burned: "His face was a scarred tight-skinned mask. He had to use taped-over goggles in order to sleep—he had no eyelids, they had been burned away. The burns themselves had healed before he was brought here, and other than his scarred face, he was in pretty good shape, but . . . was horribly disfigured. It was said that after he had been returned to the States, new eyelids would be constructed, skin grafts would be performed on his face, and that he would not look too bad . . . but I've always wondered about that poor fellow. The same thing could have happened to me just as easily. He was a real trooper [sic]; I never heard him complain, not once. He never said much, which was certainly understandable."

Wayne Rothgeb, a fighter pilot in the 35th Fighter Group, experienced engine failure one day during a takeoff. His plane caught fire and he was burned, although not as badly as the man Baumann met: "The flames followed me as I skidded down the runway, then off into a ditch. The heat was all around me. It took my breath away. I had to get out. The emergency release handle . . . was overhead. I touched the handle; the canopy literally exploded up into the vacuum created by the rising, furnace-hot air. The heat was intense. I lay down and tried to roll, but couldn't. The heat had sapped my strength. I heard the medics arrive. They seized my parachute shoulder straps and frantically dragged me across the rough ground into the ambulance. Suddenly, above the roar of the raging fire, I heard the erratic chattering of the plane's machine guns. The fire had gotten to them, and they dug a hole three feet deep in the exact spot where I had been lying. I was perspiring. My burns were starting to sting. When we entered the emergency tent, a call went out for a Dr. Schmidt. A needle was put in my arm, and they asked me to start counting. I never got to forty-five." Sometime later, Rothgeb awoke at the field hospital and discovered he had been completely wrapped in bandages. The medics had left two eyeholes and another hole for his mouth. Rothgeb had nothing but admiration and gratitude for the nurse who lent him moral support the night he awoke from surgery: "She gave me a gentle pat and a little personal squeeze that was worth a million dollars to a frightened guy entombed in bandages and lying on a cot at the 166th Station Hospital somewhere in the New Guinea jungles—a fellow who was putting on a brave act."

Boyce Holleman, a Navy torpedo bomber pilot, suffered burns when his plane was shot down during a strafing run along the coast of Saipan. With his two crewmen dead, he crashed the plane into the sea, a mere two hundred yards offshore. Unable to prevent his life raft from floating toward the Japanese-controlled shore, he jumped into the salt water and suffered excruciating pain as the salt ate away at his burns. At one point, Japanese soldiers jumped into a boat and attempted to row out to him, only to be strafed by an American fighter. Finally Holleman heard a motorboat approaching him: "I heard a voice say, 'Just stay there, Mac, we'll get there.' I knew that was a sailor. I . . . swam toward them. They picked me up and then I asked for morphine. That night I spent on an army troop carrier. A doctor . . . took a bucket on each side and pulled all the burned skin off . . . to keep from infection and keep from scarring. Then they wrapped me up like a mummy. A doctor came and . . . he said, 'I'm going to take care of your face.' Every morning he came and pulled dead skin off my face and . . . that's the reason I didn't have any extensive scarring. I had thirty-six skin-grafting operations, twenty-three of them under total anesthesia and I had another great plastic surgeon who did that in California."

Charles Bond, a fighter pilot in the Flying Tigers, was shot down in a dogfight with Japanese fighters. Bullets struck his fuel tank, it exploded, and the ensuing cockpit fire threatened to engulf him. He contemplated giving up and crashing, but somehow he found the strength to fight his way out of the burning plane. He managed to bail out and landed in friendly Chinese territory: "I felt a burning sensation on my neck and shoulders and suddenly realized that my scarf and flying suit were on fire. I hurried to a small stream . . . and laid down on my back and wallowed in the water. My head ached. I looked down at my hands. They were badly burned, and the skin had been torn loose in several places. Blisters were forming. My face and neck and upper shoulders were scorched; my eyebrows were gone. Pain was setting in. The agony of my burns had me on the verge of passing out. I wanted to die to get out of the pain. I would lie down, get up, walk around, lie down, get up, hold my hand in the air to reduce the circulation and throbbing pain, cry out aloud, and pray." A doctor gave him a shot of morphine and treated the burns, including prying off his partially melted Air Corps ring. Even with the morphine, Bond felt incredible pain. He eventually recovered, though, and returned to flying duty.

Charles Meyer, a B-26 pilot in the 319th Bomb Group, suffered flak wounds on a low-level bombing mission to Sicily. To make matters worse, his plane could not make it all the way home to his base in North Africa, and he had to crash-land it in the Mediterranean:

"We got a direct burst of flak. The plane gave a violent lurch. My right eyeglass (sun glasses) was shattered, and blood was pouring into my right eye from flak wounds on my forehead. The right side of my face and neck burned like the Devil. I noticed that my right forearm was badly swollen, that blood was running from my sleeve, and that it was becoming so stiff I could hardly move it. Tommy gave . . . me sulfanilamide tablets and poured sulfa powder [to prevent infection] on the wounds. Glancing down, I found that I was sitting in a pool of blood." After the crash, Meyer and his crewmen swam to shore, where they found a British hospital. A few days later, the British operated on him and cut flak shrapnel from his right arm and left thigh. After a short recovery period, he returned to flying duty.

James Barison, a pilot in the 485th Bomb Group, made a grisly discovery during a mission to bomb a bridge on the German-Italian border. He was in the middle of taking evasive action to escape heavy flak when he noticed that the right rudder pedal did not seem to be responding: "I looked down to see why . . . and saw that my right flying boot was doing little hopping motions at the end of a bloody stump." To make matters worse, the plane had taken serious damage and could barely make it home, with the copilot and another crewman (a pilot-training washout) flying the plane. Two hours later, they finally made it to the base, but Barison's ordeal was only beginning: "The medics could not bring the stretcher into the flight deck because the opening under the bomb-bay door was only about twelve inches from the ground. I could not climb out through the hatch above me. Tom Moore, who had been attending to my wound, agreed to hold my partially dismembered foot while I slid down from the flight deck to the space under the bomb-bay door. I squeezed through that opening and when outside the plane, I was placed on the stretcher. Because of the sedation, I can remember very little about the ambulance ride to the hospital. Three days later, I came out of unconsciousness. There was only a stump below the knee where my right foot had been, but I was still alive."

Roger Sandstedt, a central fire-control gunner in the 468th Bomb Group, was shot by a Japanese fighter plane. Bullets tore through his compartment: "I lost the left side of the tip of my nose, my left eyeball was cut, and I had cuts and metal particles around both eyes and in my forehead. I had a near-fatal wound in my left shoulder. The main blood vessel was not severed or I would have bled to death, so the doctor told me later." His buddies treated him with sulfa powder and morphine and watched him closely the rest of the trip home. After two months in the hospital, he returned to combat duty. Reuben Martin, a top turret gunner/engineer in the Eighth Air Force, wrote during his hospital stay to a friend about the wounds he suffered: "The nerve in my jaw was obliterated by that peace [sic] of shrapnel. However, I shall be wired for about two more months. It is not healing as rapidly as expected because the hole is larger than usual. Will merely have to sit it out. The doctors are performing miracles. They have my utmost admiration and respect." Most combat airmen agreed with Martin's assessment of medical personnel. They had nothing but the highest respect for doctors, nurses, and orderlies. They had the comfort of knowing that, should the unwanted day ever come when they required medical attention, they would receive the best and would stand an excellent chance of survival.

Those who were wounded and survived were the lucky ones. Many more did not survive. In ground combat in World War II, it could be safely assumed that for every soldier killed in action, three or four others would be wounded. Air combat was completely the opposite. For every man wounded, three were killed. The Army Air Force lost 54,700 men killed in action as opposed to 17,900 wounded. Very simply, this meant that the average combat flier stood a significantly better chance of being killed than wounded.

Death in air combat was usually ugly, brutal, and violent. Often combat airmen suffered great pain and horror at the moment of their demise. In real warfare, unlike much cinematic warfare, death in combat is not glorious and romantic. It is ghastly and dispiriting. Fighter Pilot Alexander Jefferson of the 332d Fighter Group described the kinds of deaths he saw in the skies of southern Europe. "Planes fell in flames, planes fell not in flames, an occasional one pulled out and crash-landed . . . sometimes they blew up. Men fell in flames, men fell in parachutes, some candle-sticked [chute not opening]. Pieces of men dropped . . . pieces of planes. Have you any idea what it's like to vomit in an oxygen mask?" Edward Hearty, a bombardier in the 95th Bomb Group, kept a mission diary. One day, after yet another perilous mission, he recorded a mournful entry: "The tail gunner and the waist gunner were both killed by 20mm shells. That is the penalty you pay for being in the Air Corps. Show me the glory in such a ride and I'll show you a damned fool." Those who died were not mere props on the stage of war. They were living, breathing, dreaming, hoping, flesh-and-blood human beings whose deaths brought unspeakable grief to their buddies and their families. In a letter to his parents, Blaine Briggs, a navigator in the 451st Bomb Group, wrote about the effect of seeing the deaths of friends: "We have seen battle in its action and in its results—both immediate and permanent. It is no pretty picture to see the fleecy black and white puffs that look like innocent puffs of mother's powder, knowing they carry with them the sting of death and destruction. Airplanes cease to look beautiful . . . when you see their wings, looking as though they are on fire, and knowing that those wings are spitting death to you and your buddy. It is no happy sight to see a plane explode and know the Bill, Bob, and Jim with whom you had your pre-flight breakfast will not return with you for your evening meal. We know what it is to count the returning planes and know that one . . . missing . . . means that ten of your brothers are also missing."

Those who were killed had postwar plans like everybody else. Nolan Ducote, a navigator in the 459th Bomb Group, looked forward to seeing his wife and son after the war. He wrote letters to them and expressed just how terribly he missed them: "I miss you, my darlings. I never knew time could become so slow. I patiently await the day when I can hug you two in my arms—tears mixed with kisses, as I cling to you two. I find myself imagining I am coming home finding both of you asleep. I hope I can drink in the sight, peacefully and quietly. Let's hope we can be altogether for my birthday." Sadly, he never made it home.

Men who were killed in action had likes and dislikes and their own motivation for doing their dangerous jobs, the same as anybody else. Joe Stalder, a young top turret gunner/engineer in the Eighth Air Force, had a happy-go-lucky attitude toward life. He wrote to his sister about his mindset in combat: "You may think me crazy, Sis, for saying I'm thankful for the opportunity to flirt with death. However, this is a great experience, and if I come through this OK I'll never regret my part in this war." He did not come through the war OK. Stalder was killed on March 24, 1945, on a mission over Germany.

When an airman was killed, his family received a telegram from the Army informing them of the death of their loved one. The telegram, delivered by Western Union, usually contained only a couple of sentences. The parents of fighter pilot Charles Nickell of the 348th Fighter Group received a typical killed-in-action telegram in April 1945: "The Secretary of War desires me to express his deep regret that your Son, 1 Lt. Charles L. Nickell, was killed in action 11 April '45, confirming letter follows. Ulio, The Adjutant General." After the arrival of a consoling postcard from General George Marshall, the Nickells received a letter from General Hap Arnold, commander of the Army Air Force. Arnold's office made a sincere attempt to write personalized, sensitive condolence letters: "With deepest regret I have learned of the death of your son, First Lieutenant Charles Lafayette Nickell, which occurred in action on April 11, 1945, in the Southwest Pacific Area. His high standard of proficiency as a pilot reflected the conscientious and thorough preparation he had made in the Advanced Single Engine School at Marianna, Florida. He was a loyal, aggressive officer who long will be remembered by associates for his ability and sound judgement. Although mere words cannot allay your sorrow, I hope pride in the memory that your son made the supreme sacrifice for our cause will afford you some measure of consolation. My heartfelt sympathy is extended to you and other members of the family."

One family, the Marshalls, lost two fighter-pilot sons to aerial combat. The older son, Dick, was killed in the Pacific and the younger son, John, was shot down and killed in the waning days of the war in Europe. When General Arnold learned of John's death, he wrote to the Marshalls: "My attention has been called to the fine reputation Major Marshall established in the Army Air Forces, and to the singleness of purpose that characterized him throughout his military career. An able leader of men, possessed of unusual initiative and a pleasing personality, he was a credit to this organization, and the excellent manner in which he performed assignments attests his ability as an officer and pilot."

Sometimes families received condolence letters from their son's commanding officer or comrades. Dick's commanding officer wrote to the Marshalls and gave them the details of his death, something highly prized and appreciated by grieving families. After John's death, they received numerous letters from his many buddies in the 404th Fighter Group, including one from a fellow fighter pilot: "Ashby [John's middle name and nickname] was a son that any mother and father can well be proud of because, as a friend, a soldier, and as a well liked admired gentleman, he had few rivals. I always will count him as one of my life's best friends as well as . . . my 'best man' [in his wedding]. Ashby and I lived together . . . and I feel as much toward him as I would toward my own brother. I know how deeply trenched your sorrow must be to have lost two fine boys like Dick and Ashby. I can only say that there must be a greater work some place other than our existence here on this earth. I truly believe this for I have seen several good boys leave this earth for no apparent reason."

Naturally, the aftermath of such tragic deaths brought acute grief among families and buddies in a man's unit, but what did death in combat look like when it happened? Sometimes it could be impersonal. Airmen would watch another plane go down and know in their hearts that no one could have survived. Chester Marshall, a pilot in the 499th Bomb Group and no relation to Dick and John Marshall, remembered seeing a Japanese kamikaze plane make a beeline for a neighboring B-29: "All the planes . . . brought their guns to bear on him and filled the sky around him with tracers, but he kept bearing in. As he struck the B-29, on which one of my flight school classmates . . . was pilot, the wings of both the B-29 and the Jap fighter plane crumpled and flew off. Both planes started spiraling, breaking up and exploding as they plummeted toward the ground 25,000 feet below. We watched closely for parachutes opening, but there were none."

Keith Schuyler, a B-24 pilot in the 44th Bomb Group, watched in horror as flak blasted another bomber from the sky: "Suddenly the picture, hellishly fascinating, assumed its true identity. There were ten kids burning up inside that aerial blast furnace. Flames were blocking the exits for any still alive. I could hear myself screaming into my oxygen mask, 'My God, my God, my God!' The doomed B-24 gave up. It didn't blow; it just melted apart. Like a bird caught by a blast of shot, the heavy parts fell first, and feathers of debris followed in a long string of smoking wreckage."

Far too often, death in aerial combat meant not only watching faceless planes crash but also watching your buddies die before your eyes. Milton Many, a waist gunner in the 464th Bomb Group, saw his fellow waist gunner and friend hit by a hunk of flak on a mission over Germany. He desperately attempted to save his life by applying a tourniquet below his buddy's leg wound and giving him morphine, but the man still passed in and out of consciousness: "He complained of only one thing, that his hands were cold, but I remedied that by unbuttoning my clothing and placing his hands against my warm body to keep him comfortable. His eyes were the things he spoke with and to my dying day I shall remember his look of gratitude and helplessness. About 15 minutes before we landed he . . . passed into a very deathlike coma. As soon as we landed, an ambulance rushed him to the hospital. That evening, we were informed that he had died from loss of blood without even regaining consciousness. Believe me when I say that we were all heart-broken. I cried like I never before in my life cried. I've never been quite the same."

John Abney, a Marine pilot, rode along with a friend and fellow pilot one day as an observer/gunner on a South Pacific mission. His friend never made it home. Japanese antiaircraft fire hit the cockpit, killing him instantly: "I stepped up into the pilot's compartment with one foot and looked at Eric. His head was rolled back, his mouth open with a small, thickish trickle of blood down his chin. His eyes were closed; there was some trickle of blood from each nostril. I rolled his head over. Blood oozed out of his left ear and there were several holes in that side of his head. I was glad it had been quick for him and not drawn out. Goddamn every Jap. I wanted to see a buck-tooth face leering before me right then. I swore mightily and hoped we had left some Japs in pieces but not to die quickly."

John Wood of the 381st Bomb Group also found his pilot dead in his seat after German fighters attacked his plane head-on: "It was unbelievable. The pilot was just sitting there with his hands in his lap. And it wasn't like his head was cut off. I didn't see it laying on the floor—it just wasn't there. I wiped the blood off the instruments so that the copilot could see." The flight surgeon later wrote, "There was hardly a square inch of the entire cockpit that was not covered with blood and brain tissue." Enemy 20mm rounds had completely disintegrated the pilot's head. Other members of the 381st also witnessed their share of death. Their unit flew missions to Europe for almost two and a half years and sustained heavy casualties. After a difficult mission one day, the chaplain, James Good Brown, had to pull his dead friend from the cockpit of a plane. He wrote about it in his diary: "A crew becomes a little family. It is common to see the entire crew, officers and enlisted men, talking to each other in off-hours. This friendship only adds to the pain when a crew does not come back. Ten men missing at the evening table, twenty men, seventy men, one hundred men. We were pals. It hurts. My very close buddy, a co-pilot, is removed from the plane. His head has been severed completely, as though cut off with a knife. I stood underneath the door, taking hold of his legs as they came out of the plane. When he slid out, the blood came pouring out of his heavy flight suit which had held it in. The blood ran down and flowed over me. My hands were red with blood. His face had no life in it. It was the face of death."

Another 381st man, Navigator David McCarthy, went to check on his crew's tail gunner during their first mission when he failed to respond to an oxygen check. McCarthy never forgot what he found: "Steve was dead! The force of the projectile had knocked him onto his back with his head toward the nose of the ship. Kneeling in blood an inch deep on the deck, I placed my hands under his shoulders, and pulled—but his left shoulder was destroyed and it started to slide from the applied pressure. So I grasped him on both sides of his head. But his throat and the back of his neck were also destroyed. Covered with his blood, I returned to my station and reported his death to the crew. I was stunned and shaken by the sight of Steve's torn and shattered body."

Radio Operator Merle Perkins, who ended up being the only surviving member of his 483d Bomb Group crew, helped pull a dying man from a wounded aircraft at his base one afternoon. What he saw never left him: "His phrases, slow, fragmented, were low, hissing, delivered in gasps. They marked my memory with deep imprints. I keep hearing them. They shudder within me, still at times hold my thoughts and feelings in suspension: 'Shit . . . no more . . . shit . . . die . . . not live . . . like this . . . night . . . fall . . . want nightfall . . . far beyond . . . stars.' His face of chalk, filled with revulsion, the eyes averted upward and away from the caved in, bloodied lower torso, was a grimace of pain and disgust for his new identity, monstrous in his mind's eye. Our own eyes were riveted on his bloody middle, entrails exposed, private parts destroyed. Nausea filled me. We stood dumb, paralyzed."

Although fighter pilots saw fewer up-close-and-personal deaths, they often witnessed the violent deaths of their buddies as they happened. Such was the case with Quentin Aanenson. On one terrible mission, he witnessed the deaths of two of his friends. The first man was hit on a strafing run and did not have enough time to escape his mortally wounded aircraft: "I watched him frantically trying to disconnect everything and bail out—I was just a few feet away from him—but he was too low. He waved to me an instant before his plane crashed into the trees and exploded. To this day, I can still see the expression on his face as he looked directly at me. In that instant, he knew he was dead." As Aanenson's unit returned from that mission, another man announced that he had to bail out due to heavy flak damage to his plane: "His chute wasn't opening as it should have. He just kept falling—and we kept screaming for him to pull the rip cord. He fell 8,000 feet, and we could see his body actually bounce several feet into the air when he hit the ground. We were almost crazy. It was a terrible day."

When men were killed in action, those left behind could at least take the small consolation that they knew what had happened and knew the man would never come back. The mourners could grieve and move on with their lives. The same could not be said for the families and friends of those airmen listed as missing in action. Very often, when a plane went down in combat, no one really knew if the men inside that plane had gotten out. Three possibilities existed. The crew of the downed plane could be dead, captured, or evading capture. Until commanders knew for sure what had happened, they listed the crewmen of the downed plane as missing in action. Within a few days, if the fate of the downed airman still had not been determined, his family received a telegram much like the one sent to the mother of 100th Bomb Group Top Turret Gunner Chuck Sewell in June 1944: "The Secretary of War desires me to express his deep regrets, that your son Tec Sgt Charles B. Sewell has been reported missing in action since 24 May over Germany. If further details or other information are received you will be notifyed [sic] at once. Ulio the Adg General." Two days later, Mrs. Sewell received the confirmation letter from Ulio: "I know that added distress is caused by failure to receive more information or details. Therefore, I wish to assure you that at any time additional information is received it will be transmitted to you without delay, and, if in the meantime no additional information is received, I will again communicate with you at the expiration of three months. The term 'missing in action' is used only to indicate that the whereabouts or status of an individual is not immediately known. It is not intended to convey the impression that the case is closed. I wish to emphasize that every effort is exerted continuously to clear up the status of our personnel. Under war conditions this is a difficult task. Experience has shown that many persons reported missing in action are subsequently reported as prisoners of war, but as this information is furnished by countries with which we are at war, the War Department is helpless to expedite such reports." A few weeks later, she received the welcome news, under the circumstances, that her son was a prisoner of war in Germany.

Some families never heard any more information on their loved ones. They had apparently disappeared. This happened to John Crowe's brother, who had been a P-38 fighter pilot. In fact, Crowe joined the Army Air Force and ended up as a copilot in the 491st Bomb Group largely to avenge his brother's presumed death. Since it could never be conclusively determined that Crowe's brother had been killed in action, their father always held out false hope: "I think he knew, but was unwilling to accept the facts. He never gave up hope that someday his oldest son would come home from the war. Dad passed away in 1985 still believing and hoping. The absence of remains under such circumstances created the illusion of false hope; but in the end there was only a foot locker with personal effects and a Purple Heart, given posthumously."

Sometimes combat airmen wrote letters to the families of buddies listed as missing in action in order to provide them with information they could not obtain from official sources. William Faulkner, a fighter pilot in the 332d Fighter Group, wrote to the wife of a good friend who had gone down with mechanical problems in Italy: "He called in that he was bailing out and a fix (by radio) was taken on his position. Some of the men in the squadron following his formation saw his plane strike the water about five miles from shore in the midst of about 100 small Italian fishing boats. None saw a parachute. I got two fellows to go with me over the water to look for him. For three hours, the limit of that plane's endurance, we searched a 50-mile radius about the point down on the water, but saw no rubber boat, no parachute, no oil slick. Since then, we've heard nothing."

The man was never heard from or seen again. He simply disappeared. The same thing happened to a friend of Marine torpedo pilot Samuel Hynes, who never returned from a close-air-support mission. No one could find any trace of him or figure out exactly what had happened: "Our friend Bergie—the church-in-the-wildwood tenor, the gentle husband—had simply vanished from our lives. There was no body, no grave, and no funeral. T and Joe and I put his possessions together—there was almost nothing worth saving—and gave them to the Adjutant to send home."

As Hynes indicated, the usual protocol with respect to missing men was to remove their possessions from their living space. In the Eighth Air Force, where casualties were alarmingly high, ground personnel removed the possessions of missing crews within a day or two. Waist Gunner Jack Novey of the 96th Bomb Group vividly remembered the eerie emptiness of his hut when other crews did not come home: "The quartermaster came by after a day or two and picked up all their clothing and personal effects. During the interim before he came, looking at the photos and other things of

your . . . buddies was very demoralizing. We were not too sentimental to avoid helping ourselves to better equipment. We knew our
buddies would have wanted it that way; they had done so themselves
in many cases."

Sometimes missing crews did come back, though, only to find
that all their possessions had been pilfered or removed. Harry
Crosby, a navigator in the 100th Bomb Group, survived a harrowing
mission that saw his plane crash-land at an emergency landing strip
near the southern coast of England. Because the emergency strip
had no phone, they were not able to communicate their whereabouts to their base at Thorpe Abbotts. In the interim, their unit
listed them as missing in action. When Crosby and his crew returned to the base, they found that someone had already come for
their possessions: "When we walked into the Quonset hut . . . our
beds were stripped. My radio and record player were gone, my picture of Jean [his wife] was gone, my footlocker was gone. On the
bare cot were two clean sheets and two pillowcases, two blankets,
one pillow all neatly folded. Ready for the next crew." In these instances, airmen usually acted expeditiously to send telegrams to
loved ones, telling them to disregard any official missing-in-action
notification.

Sometimes men listed as missing in action were very much alive
but unable to get word to their units or their families because they
had been captured by the enemy. More than 40,000 combat airmen
became prisoners of war, most captured in the European theater.
Combat fliers stood an excellent chance of becoming POWs just by
the very nature of their jobs. If they were shot down, they often parachuted or crashed in enemy-controlled territory, with little or no
way of evading the enemy. The Air Force even issued escape kits for
just such an eventuality. Kenneth Williams, a bombardier in the
351st Bomb Group, recalled that his escape kit contained "a photograph of us in civilian clothes, maps, compass, chocolate, German
and French money, and other items. My flight coveralls had a large,
buttoned pocket on the right leg below the knee where I kept the
escape kit." Williams had occasion to use his escape kit when his
plane went down in occupied Europe, but it did not prevent him
from being captured.

Almost every airman who became a POW first had to find a way to escape from a dying aircraft. Most men preferred to parachute to the ground rather than take a chance on crash-landing. Roy Kennett, a radio operator in the 392d Bomb Group, described what it felt like to jump out of an airplane: "If you're traveling down the road in an automobile and you throw a piece of paper out the window, you notice how it flutters and turns and does all kinds of whirligigs, and then all of a sudden it just calms down and very gently falls to the ground. Well, the initial reaction to a jump is very much the same. When I rolled off that catwalk and into the slipstream, it just turned me every which way but loose for a few minutes. Then it sort of comes down to your normal falling speed—around 120 miles per hour. But you have no sensation of falling, because you have no reference point. When you're five miles up in the air you're not passing anything. It isn't noisy; you don't hear anything but the wind whistling next to your ears."

Barwick Barfield, a navigator in the 100th Bomb Group, had to bail out of his stricken B-17 somewhere near Berlin: "I was in the air about 15 minutes. During the first few minutes, I could not sense any movement. I gradually sensed some lateral movement during the last 4,000 to 5,000 feet. I had an increasing sensation of falling. I was still surprised to hit the ground so fast. Within a few minutes, a German Luger was pointed at my head and I heard, 'Raus' (get up, and fast)."

Milton Abernathy, a navigator in the 303d Bomb Group, was captured in France in early 1944. His plane made a bomb run on a German airfield and encountered terrific flak. He barely managed to escape from the burning bomber: "I felt an unusual sense of relief from all personal responsibilities. It could no longer be my fault if we flew over heavy flak or got lost. My total concentration was on escaping after landing . . . in a plowed field. Quevado [their top turret gunner] landed near and wanted to stay with me. In a few minutes I heard gun shots whistle close to my head and 'I see you.' Luftwaffe cadets took us at gunpoint to the rest of our crew. My refusal to answer questions got me a solid slap to the head by one German officer. It made me very angry but after looking at guns pointed at me, I made a lifetime decision to hold my temper from then on."

Richard Klocko, a fighter pilot and commander of the 350th Fighter Group, was shot down in North Africa, where evading capture could be quite problematic. If a downed airman managed to survive long enough in the desert, he could make contact with nearby Arabs. Some of the Arabs were friendly to Americans, while others did not like Americans because they associated them with their French colonial overseers. Klocko had the misfortune of meeting up with one of the latter groups—as he found out when he offered his escape cards, written in French and English, promising a reward for his safe return: "These cards were ground underfoot by the Arabs. It soon became apparent that the Arabs despised the French and hence the Americans, who were considered French allies. On the other hand they seemed to like—or at least tolerate—the Germans, who had treated them much more civilly than their French landlords. A German jeep soon appeared, driven by an officer accompanied by an armed guard. The Arabs had obviously notified the Germans of the downed American pilot."

John Moulton, a waist gunner in the 381st Bomb Group, went down on the first Schweinfurt mission in August 1943. His wounded bomber limped as far as occupied Belgium before he and his crew had to ditch. Bracing himself against the waist door as the plane bucked violently, he managed to fling himself into space: "For awhile there was no feeling except the rush of wind pulling against me, but in a few seconds, this slackened and I noticed I was falling feet first, arms still folded. I reached the rip cord and started to pull . . . the 'chute' opened so gently, I was surprised; it was like sitting in a rocking chair. The ground was flying up fast now, and . . . I hit the ground on my right foot, falling backward like a ton of bricks, with an awful pain in my right ankle. Some people from the next field rushed upon me and grabbed me. Removing my chute, they proceeded to kiss me on the cheek and ask me questions about the war and who I was." The friendly Belgians helped him evade capture and put him in touch with the Belgian underground. For a time, he hid in the house of a young couple, then he rode to Paris by train. He planned to make his way to the Spanish border, where he could then be interned or repatriated. However, he had no sooner arrived in Paris than the Gestapo captured him: "I took one side step towards the door, when something slammed my head back into the wall. I saw a small snub-nosed gun pointed at me. The man behind it acted as though he would enjoy using it. They were a happy group of Gestapo, seventeen in all, who rode us to the Paris prison, La Frenz. We were in a sightseeing bus, and they were shouting and singing." Clearly someone had betrayed him.

American combat airmen could expect fairly decent treatment from their German captors. As a signatory to the Geneva Convention, Germany had, at least in theory, committed to humane treatment of prisoners, although German troops showed no enthusiasm for extending such treatment to Soviet prisoners, who were routinely starved and tortured. By contrast, German soldiers normally treated captured British or American servicemen far better. If a combat airman fell into the hands of the German military, he was usually disarmed, relieved of all valuables, and taken to the nearest interrogation center. At the interrogation center, an English-speaking German officer questioned the airman about anything of military value. The experiences of Richard Child, a 487th Bomb Group tail gunner, were typical: "I landed in a soft plowed field. My feet hit, knees bent, and my head hit the ground hard. I was dazed for a few minutes and lay there without moving. When I looked up, I saw soldiers in blue uniforms and civilians from a nearby village. Guns were pointed at me and I raised my hands. A soldier quickly took my .45 [pistol]. I was then marched to a village and held for a few minutes. There was quite a crowd around me; I must have been quite an attraction to those Germans with helmet, oxygen mask, and heated suit; a typical 'Man from Mars.' At camp we were interrogated by an officer from the Luftwaffe. He asked several questions of military importance, which I refused to answer. He threatened to shoot me but I doubted if he would. He asked me where I came from and I replied, 'America.' I was rewarded with two sharp slaps across the face."

Although the Germans did not exactly present airmen with gourmet meals during their initial captivity, they normally provided the basics. Even so, being a prisoner of the Germans could be very difficult for American combat airmen, especially when they moved on to permanent camps, where they often experienced hunger, privation, and misery. Although it was somewhat rare, airmen at times endured mental torture. Wayne Livesay, a navigator in the Eighth Air Force, was shot down in Holland and captured within a few minutes of hitting the ground. His German captors incarcerated him in a small local jail for the night. In the morning, they woke him and told him to board a truck. They rode for about twenty minutes and then stopped and forced Livesay to stand against a large stone wall. Handing him a "last cigarette," they lined up and pointed their rifles at him, apparently planning to shoot: "My emotions at that time were a mixture of anger, prayer, and regret as I thought of many things I should have done in the past as well as numerous things I should not have done. Only one who has experienced a similar sensation can truly empathize with my feelings at that moment. There was no doubt in my mind as to what was about to happen, and my final decision appeared to be whether I should look or close my eyes. I decided to assume an erect position as if someone had called me to attention. I stood there for what seemed like minutes but, in reality, was not more than 10–15 seconds. Suddenly the officer raised his hand and motioned for me to go back to the truck. About twenty minutes later, I was placed back in my cell and given breakfast, which consisted of a slice of black bread and a cup of barley coffee."

Livesay's experiences notwithstanding, such feigned executions were rare. Even more rare were actual German military executions of captured combat airmen. The Germans sent to Dachau some downed American fliers—ones with no identification who had attempted to evade capture with the assistance of local underground fighters—but most airmen under military control underwent an orderly, if unpleasant, path to permanent prison camps.

In fact, for any American airman bailing out over Germany, the greatest danger was not the German military but German civilians, who were often enraged at the deaths of friends or loved ones or the destruction of homes and property by American bombs. Sometimes these civilians formed vigilante mobs and lynched any American flier they could find. In this atmosphere of vengeance, downed American airmen who had no hope of escape naturally wished to fall into the hands of the German military, which generally observed the practice of not harming helpless American prisoners.

George Iles, an African-American fighter pilot in the 332d
Fighter Group, crash-landed near Munich, Germany. The German
Home Guard picked him up within an hour or so, which suited him
just fine because he had heard plenty of stories about civilian
reprisals: "I was fortunate to be grabbed by the military. One of our
pilots . . . was beaten severely by civilians before the German military got him. The civilians had been bombed and shot, their homes
had been burned, and they were more angry than the military, who
thought of war as a job." The Germans took Iles to an interrogation
center in Frankfurt and treated him well. During his interrogation,
a German officer claimed to have lived in Chicago before the war
and asked Iles "why you fellows choose to fly and fight, and perhaps
die for a country that treats our German prisoners better than it
treats you." Iles found the question thought-provoking and considered it quite ironic that the German POW camp afforded him his
first glimpse of a life without segregation. Another African-American who became a POW got along very well with white Southerners
in prison camp: "They treated me as one of them. Each man performed a duty, we combined our rations, cooked our meals together, and shared equally." Wilbur Long, also a fighter pilot in the
332d, survived a very close call after crash-landing his plane in Germany. He recalled nothing about the crash but remembered "running with a large gathering of civilians chasing me. I was overtaken
and beaten by the angry mob. However, a group of soldiers arrived
in time to save me."

Many other downed American airmen had similar close calls.
John Boisseau, a top turret gunner/engineer in the 92d Bomb
Group, bailed out of his plane and landed at an airfield near
Nuremberg, Germany. Soon a knife-wielding civilian came after
him, but he warded the man off with his service revolver: "I had carried the pistol with mixed feelings. We'd need them, so we'd been
told, as protection against civilians, who could be nasty if they got
hold of us. On the other hand, if we were armed when captured by
the German military, we could be executed, according to the
Geneva Convention. I really believe having it saved my life, pre-
venting a stabbing, but now it was time to get rid of it [as German
troops were approaching him]. The angry civilian, seeing me un-

armed . . . started to come after me again. But the soldiers intervened and stopped him from doing me any harm."

As a bombardier, George Collar of the 445th Bomb Group had special reason to fear German civilians, because they often searched specifically for the man whose job was to release the bombs on them. After bailing out, he landed in a plowed field. A man on a bicycle and two farmers with pitchforks apprehended him and took him to a village about half a mile away: "The whole village turned out to line the streets to get a close-up look at the '*Amerikanische Terrorflieger.*' It was like walking down a gauntlet, with people glaring at me malevolently. One teenager stepped out and gave me a swift kick with his big rubber boot. They marched me into the courtyard of the Burgermeister's [mayor's] house, and all the people flocked in and surrounded me. They made me take down my pants and hold my hands out while they searched me. An ugly-looking farmer with big fists swung from left field and planted his fist right between my eyes. He started swinging again, and I kept dodging out of the way as I attempted to get my pants back up. I had a funny feeling that if I went down, that the whole crowd would jump me. He finally broke away and picked up a long-handled, square-nosed spade. He swung at me, and as I ducked, I felt it whistle over my head. I knew at that moment I was fighting for my life. I . . . closed in, and as we were grappling for the spade, an old man with a walrus mustache and a green felt hat stepped in and started to help me. After that, the crowd seemed to cool down somewhat."

Bob Ferrell, a pilot in the 458th Bomb Group, was shot down in western Germany. He bailed out and landed a few feet away from someone's house. A group of Germans jumped him, loaded him into a wagon with two other members of his crew, and took them into town: "We were held up in the square and the crowd began to assemble and it got worse and worse. There was a woman out in the crowd who was leading the anti-American, 'Kill them, hang the scoundrels' chant. We understood later that her child had been killed in the raid the day before. Things were getting pretty nasty and we knew we were getting ready to be hung. Out of the crowd appeared an old . . . fellow. He was a . . . reservist. At riflepoint he took us away from the crowd and saved us." The man turned Ferrell and his buddies over to the German army, and they ended up in a prison camp for the rest of the war.

Only a miraculous appearance by German soldiers saved Walter Mayberry, a waist gunner in the Eighth Air Force, from being lynched: "When I hit the ground, people of all ages were upon me. They hit, kicked, and beat me with shovels, rakes, sticks, and rifle butts—even small children were attacking me. I could see members of the crew also being attacked. They fashioned a hangman's noose and placed it around my neck. Fortunately, I landed in a field, so there were no trees near. They dragged me to the nearest town. I remember the intense pain and then I lost consciousness." German soldiers came along and cut him loose before the noose strangled him.

Leon Berkovsky, a navigator in the 463d Bomb Group, faced a different and more deliberate peril from the civilians who caught him. On his fiftieth and final mission, he was shot down and fell into the hands of pro-Nazi Croatian nationalists, who planned to try to execute him for "war crimes." Of Czech extraction, he understood Slavic languages and thus could make out much of what was being said around him, although he concealed this from the crowd. From overhearing their conversations, he knew their deadly plan: "It was 'now or never' for me. I . . . became very vocal, emphasizing that I was not a volunteer (this was not true) but was in college studying to become a schoolteacher when I was drafted. I told them I was born on a small farm and about the crops we grew. I described how hard we had to work to make a living . . . and that my great grandparents on both sides emigrated from Czechoslovakia to Texas. For the next thirty minutes or so, I heard arguments from the 'jury room,' and they weren't discussing the cost of a new roof. Finally, total silence. I was told that there was good news and bad news. 'Give me the bad news first,' I said. They told me that they had voted to turn me over to the Germans, who had a garrison in a nearby town. That was the best news I could have hoped for, because the Germans observed the Geneva Rules of Warfare on captured prisoners. I asked them what the good news was. The reply: 'They've decided not to shoot you.' The following day, I became a prisoner of the Germans."

Sometimes European-theater airmen were captured by German allies, such as Romanians or Italians. These nominal Axis partners usually treated Americans well. William Cubbins, a pilot in the 450th Bomb Group, could not save his damaged aircraft after it was hit by flak over Romania, so he and his crew bailed out. Cubbins landed in a field and began to nurse a slight shrapnel wound he had incurred before bailing out. He heard airplane engines, looked up, and saw most of his group heading home: "'They'll be home in a few hours,' I thought. The thought became a burden, a crushing depression. I sat quietly, trying not to think of home. Hopelessness overwhelmed me, leaving a cold vacancy in my mind and body." A few minutes later, he noticed a man with a shotgun advancing toward him: "I'd moved no more than a few yards when my excited captor caught up with me. I rolled over and looked up into the smiling face of a man who seemed to regard me with the honest joy of someone who had found a treasured friend. He obviously had no fear of me nor intended any harm. He laid his shotgun on the ground and helped me sit up. His smile and demeanor were so infectious, I forgot he was the enemy." Although he insisted on turning Cubbins over to the authorities, the man treated Cubbins like a friend. He even fed him what he considered to be a grand meal of cornmush and soup.

Fighter Pilot George Fitzgibbon was captured by Italian troops while flying close air support for Allied ground troops during the invasion of Sicily in July 1943. He landed in the sea, a few hundred yards offshore: "Soldiers were waving for me to come in and soon fired shots on both sides of me with more waving. I think I made a wise decision when I laid my '45' on the floor of the Med. [Mediterranean] and walked in. The Italian sergeant said, 'For you the war is over.' They walked me inland to the small city of Castel Vetrano, where I made a brief appearance before the Colonel at the Officer's Club. Two Italian guards were assigned the task of watching over me, which they did quite well. A couple of hours later, they brought me some dinner. A piece of Salisbury steak, some spinach and bread, and a third of a bottle of red wine. My immediate thoughts were that if I had known the food was going to be this good, I'd have come sooner." Unfortunately for Fitzgibbon, he, like many other

Americans in Italian custody, was turned over to the Germans after Italy surrendered.

Some combat airmen had the dual misfortune of both capture and wounding. After all, most of those who ended up as prisoners had escaped from dying aircraft. Some had been injured by flak or enemy fighters. Others hurt themselves bailing out or crash-landing. Lloyd Haefs, a bombardier in the 2d Bomb Group, was shot down over German-occupied Greece. A burst of flak caught his plane and mortally wounded it within seconds. He knew he had to bail out—quickly. The last thing he remembered was standing and preparing to jump: "I awakened in a hospital with severe face pain. My lower mandible was broken vertically, the skin split apart to the corners of my mouth. Most front teeth, upper and lower, were missing or broken. To my probing fingers, the rest were a dentist's nightmare. The right cheek bone was also broken. My only garment was a ragged blood-soaked pajama top." Haefs apparently lost consciousness while bailing out, and his face smashed into the ground when he landed, causing the damage to his jaw. He lay in a coma for more than two weeks before waking up. A German dentist then roughly, and painfully, wired his jaw, but the damage was permanent. Bill Stafford, a bombardier in the 388th Bomb Group, sustained a badly broken leg when his stricken plane crashed just a few yards off the German coast. Within three minutes of the crash, German soldiers showed up: "They were all armed with rifles and had full battle equipment. There were at least fifty. With various shouts and motions from a distance of perhaps fifty yards, the troops made the crew climb out of the ship and wade to them with their hands high." Since he could not move, Stafford waited for the German soldiers to come and get him. After yanking him from the water-soaked plane, they took him to an aid station and questioned him and the rest of the crew. An hour or so later, a doctor performed surgery on his shattered leg: "They bound my leg up in a metal brace using paper bandages. Pain . . . blinded my eyes as jagged bones were ground against torn flesh." Sometime later, when the Germans allowed him to write home, he explained to his mother that "My navigator and I were both wounded and are in the hospital now. Mine was in the right leg and I expect the worst. Just thank

God it wasn't something worse." Luckily for Stafford, his leg healed and the Germans released him from the hospital and sent him to a permanent camp.

Andrew Schindler, a fighter pilot in the 350th Fighter Group, was captured in northern Italy after flak downed his P-51. When he hit the ground, he fractured his hip: "I lay there until two Jerry troopers arrived. They commandeered an Italian with a wagon and took me to their unit. I was shifted three times [to different hospitals]. The first couple of hospitals were for Axis troops. They were loaded with patients and German nurses. The individual next to me must have had a lung wound and the doctor was lifting his rib cage up to drain the lung cavity. Well, I turned my head away from him and a sweet young Jerry nurse turned my head back so I could see what they had to do to the wounded Jerry. She held my head in that position. She wanted to make sure that I saw what we had done to the young kid. 'Real nice people,' I thought." Schindler hastened to add that the Germans did give him basic medical treatment. Wounded combat airmen normally received this kind of rudimentary care from their German captors. Hard-pressed to treat their own casualties, German medical personnel provided the minimum care for wounded American fliers within the dictates of the Geneva Convention and not much more.

In the Pacific, the Japanese made no efforts to be helpful and had no pretensions about humane treatment of prisoners. In their view, anyone who surrendered had forfeited his dignity as a human being and had no right to be treated as anything other than chattel. Their cruelty in starving, torturing, and neglecting Allied prisoners of war knew no bounds. Because Japanese brutality toward prisoners was common knowledge among American combat airmen in the Pacific theater, most of them dreaded and feared the prospect of capture. Some, like Pilot James Campbell in the 380th Bomb Group, preferred death to captivity: "One of our fighter pilots had been shot down while on a strafing mission to Wewak, New Guinea. He was found by our infantry after he had been captured and hung between two trees by his wrists and his stomach cut open. While flying my fifty-six combat missions, I never worried about instant death but was really afraid of being captured alive. My plan was if I ever got in that situation where I saw I was going to be captured, I would use all of my forty-five [caliber pistol] bullets . . . on the Japs and use the last one on myself."

Luckily for Campbell, he never had to put his plan into practice. Others were not so fortunate. Milton Woodside, a fighter pilot in the 24th Pursuit Group, surrendered in the spring of 1942 along with the rest of the American and Filipino force on the Philippine island of Luzon. He and his comrades were shocked at the brutal treatment they received from their Japanese captors during the notorious Bataan Death March. In the first few days of his captivity, Woodside witnessed numerous atrocities: "Jap soldiers continually passed among us looting, beating, and abusing the prisoners for no reason whatsoever. I was clubbed severely when a Jap guard found me with a small can of beans which I had managed to hide during the looting." Woodside said that Japanese guards delighted in urinating and defecating into water the thirst-crazed Allied soldiers were forced to drink. After executing some of the sick and wounded, Japanese guards forced Woodside and the others into a small area off the road and told them to close up to each other until their chests and backs touched: "Sanitary measures were impossible. Men caught out of formation evacuating themselves were either severely clubbed with rifle butts or bayoneted. Quite commonly, men were forced to sit or lie down in fecal matter and urine where some sick prisoners were unable to control themselves. We had no water for about 12 hours. Thirst was unbearable. Screaming and crying of thirst and sickness was so great as to make sleep impossible, even though every one was exhausted. Most of us had not eaten for four days."

The next day the march continued: "Even though there was a river fifty yards away, we were not allowed to get water. We were kept sitting in the hot tropical sun until hundreds began to faint. Screaming and moaning of thirst became so great that Jap guards came among us bashing people's heads and prodding with bayonets to quiet them. These 'sunning out' treatments were continued throughout the whole march. By this time I was partly delirious from fever and exhaustion. Any prisoner becoming exhausted and falling out was either shot or bayoneted. An Air Corps 2d Lt. marching next to me became exhausted and could go no further. Unable to carry him, I helped him over behind some bushes to lay down. The follow-up Jap guard saw us and motioned for me to go on. I left the man my canteen of water and moved on. About 100 yds. on, I looked back to see the guard repeatedly bayoneting the sick man in the chest. About 30 minutes later, I saw an American soldier lean up against a building beside the road. The Jap guard shot him repeatedly then bayoneted him in the neck. Dead bodies lay all over the area and in the building. Many not quite dead were laying in feces, covered with flies, moaning in delirium. It must be understood that all of the atrocities I witnessed on this march are not related, since they are so many and diverse as to require hours and pages of relating. Suffice to say that I have seen every atrocity including murder, brutality, maltreatment of every description, and indignity possible for the human mind to conceive."

Woodside and the other Death March survivors could look forward to more than three years in Japanese prison camps and similar treatment nearly every day of those three years.

Lou Zamperini, a bombardier in the 11th Bomb Group, went through a terrible ordeal even before the Japanese captured him. His plane crashed in the South Pacific early in the summer of 1943. For forty-seven days, he and two buddies drifted in a raft, baking in the sun, with little water and almost no food. To make matters worse, on a number of occasions sharks came very close to swamping their precarious raft and mauling them. About a month into the ordeal, one of the others died and the two survivors buried him at sea. After finally spotting land, they made the horrible discovery that they had drifted into Japanese-held territory. A Japanese patrol boat snagged them and took them ashore: "On the beach, we couldn't even stand. We could barely crawl. I weighed between 60 and 70 pounds, I think. They kept us there two days, then took us to Kwajalein, to a prison camp. I was put in a two-by-six-foot cell for 43 days. Next they took me to . . . Yokohama. The chief interrogator at the prison camp turned out to be a guy I'd gone to SC [University of Southern California] with for four years. He was friendly to me at first, and we talked about people we knew. But my relationship with him didn't help. The guards beat us up all the time. Once, they forced me to run a race against a Japanese runner when I weighed about 80 pounds. They took pictures of him beating me."

Francis Sawyer, a gunner in the 7th Bomb Group, bailed out of his plane seconds before it exploded over Rangoon, Burma, in October 1943: "Shortly after I landed, I was picked up by Burmese villagers who turned me over to the Burmese police, who were working with the Japanese. The police took me by boat to the village where they were holding the four officers of my crew. The Japanese took us to a nearby jail where we stayed for 4–5 days. Every day we were questioned. We were put into solitary confinement for two months. Interrogations and beatings were followed by more of the same. In December of 1943 we were finally put into a compound with other prisoners."

Martin Govednik, a B-29 radio operator in the Twentieth Air Force, was shot down and bailed out over the Malayan peninsula during a raid on Singapore. With the help of a Malayan civilian, he met up with another member of his crew. Because they had no idea where they were, or how best to evade the Japanese, they had little choice but to trust the Malayan: "Just before dawn I heard a noise like rustling brush. Then a Jap was on me with a rifle across my throat. They tied my wrists, and Dana's, behind our backs. How could a Jap patrol find us in a jungle on a dark rainy night? The Malayan turned us in to the Japs!" Govednik endured weeks of interrogation and a starvation diet during his seven months in Japanese captivity.

American combat airmen who went down over Japan in 1944 and 1945 also had a perilous ordeal in front of them. Lynchings were common among Japanese civilians and even Japanese military personnel. Most showed little or no compassion for the American airmen who were bombing their homeland. If downed Americans managed to avoid being lynched, they had to endure the typical Japanese maltreatment of enemy prisoners—beatings, starvation, torture, interrogation. Sometimes prisoners even found themselves under the bombs of their own planes. Naturally airmen who flew missions to Japan dreaded and feared the very notion of capture.

For some, like Navigator Hap Halloran of the 499th Bomb Group, fears became reality. During a January 1945 mission to Tokyo, Japanese fighters attacked his B-29 and put two engines out of commission. Soon a third engine quit. If possible, crews usually tried to fly out to sea in stricken aircraft, in hopes of being picked up by American submarines or rescue planes. But Halloran's plane could not make it that far. They could either bail out or go down with the plane. Halloran chose the former: "In the free fall, I did slow rolls over and over, and I would estimate I was between 5,000 and 7,000 feet when I pulled the ripcord over suburban Tokyo. I was not fired on by fighters after I opened my chute, but I was circled five times by two Zeroes." When he landed, civilians quickly surrounded him and began to beat him—until a military truck arrived on the scene and took him away: "I was put on exhibit at various street corners where large crowds had congregated. One civilian took a pair of scissors and tried to cut off my little finger to get the ring I was wearing as a souvenir. I was treated extremely bad, degradation, beatings, mostly with rifle butts, no medical attention. I went from 212 pounds to 125 pounds in 67 days of solitary confinement; barefooted walks for interogation [sic] through snow in February and March." About five members of Halloran's crew survived their captivity. According to him, most of the others had been lynched by civilians.

Forrest McCormick, a Navy fighter pilot who flew missions from the USS *Hornet,* was also one of the lucky few who survived going down over Japan. He crash-landed his fighter near a small farming village and proceeded to tend to his wounds. Before long, a group of Japanese men approached the plane: "One of them approached cautiously and gestured for me to surrender my weapon but I was unarmed. I had my left arm in a sling and gestured back that I was unarmed. When they were convinced, I was quickly surrounded and marched down . . . to a truck. I received a few blows to my head." Soon a crowd gathered and screamed for retribution. Just as the crowd seemed ready to kill him, McCormick saw a woman jump forward and protect him. Because of her intercession, he survived the initial threat of lynching. Seven months later, the war, and his captivity, came to an end.

• • •

A fortunate minority of combat airmen who went down in enemy territory managed to evade capture and return to their units. If you were shot down, your first thoughts upon hitting the ground probably centered on escape and evasion. Naturally, some men enjoyed better chances of success than others. For example, fliers shot down in occupied Europe before the Normandy invasion faced long odds of making it across the water to England. But those who went down later in the war, when Allied troops occupied much of western Europe, stood reasonable odds of evading capture. In the Pacific, those who went down in Japan itself or deep within Japanese-occupied China had almost no chance to get away. By contrast, men who bailed out over the ocean or close to American lines in any one of the numerous Pacific battlegrounds could and often did return to their units.

E. T. Moriarity, a waist gunner in the 306th Bomb Group, was shot down in the spring of 1943 on his ninth mission, a supposed "milk run" to France. Had he gone down over Germany, he would have had no hope of evading capture at that time, but landing as he did among a group of French people, he had the opportunity to escape. The French hid him in the woods until darkness, when a guide from the Resistance showed up. So began a three-week odyssey that saw him meet many different people—most of whom, for security reasons, he did not know by name—who helped him evade capture. During his nomadic existence with the French underground, he developed strong feelings of gratitude and love toward those who helped him. One example was a middle-aged woman who took him in for a few days and fed him well. Before long, the guides came back to move him on to the next hiding place, and the parting became emotional: "Millions of words flowed to each other through our looks, though not a word was spoken. I gave her a big hug and a kiss and walked through the door. I felt as if I had just kissed my mother and left my own house. If I had to speak, I would have broken down and cried like a baby." At one stop on his escape route, Moriarity hid right next door to the German military police. He began to think about all the people who had helped him: "I counted eighteen people, not including any relaing area. They put us up in an old hotel for about three weeks while most of our crew joined us there." Finally, after about forty days, the Russians returned them to their base in Italy.

Fighter Pilot George Blackburn of the 57th Fighter Group was shot down in northern Italy late in the war and escaped with the help of a colorful group of anti-Fascist partisans, including a young woman named Louisa who had a passionate hatred for the Germans. Blackburn stayed with Louisa's family, and she told him that the Germans "came through here, raped me, stole everything we had, took our one cow with them. Now we have no milk. I was once an educated person. I went two years to the University of Pisa. I have studied English since [I was] a little girl." Curious, he asked her about the band of partisans she led: "We are well organized. We kill Germans wherever we can. I have killed one myself. I killed him with scissors. He raped me. While he [was] raping I plunged the scissors into his back." Blackburn was relieved that she was a friend and not an enemy. During his stay with the partisans, he even witnessed the trial of a man who had betrayed them: "The young man broke into loud sobbing . . . and then raised his head with tears in his eyes, put out his hands, and began to obviously plead for his release, but to no avail. All he did was provoke even more shouts and angry words. Then suddenly the young man who had brought the accused . . . grabbed him by the arm and took him through the door from where he had entered and a hush came over the group."

Blackburn assumed the man was executed. The next morning, Louisa informed him that an American plane would retrieve him that day. Before the plane arrived, she expressed her gratitude that Americans were liberating her country: "She said, 'Georgio, I like you, I like Americanos and we thank you . . . for what you have done for our country.' I felt a certain amount of pride of course but I also was . . . a little startled by her philosophic conversation and how mature and intelligent she seemed. I felt deeply indebted to her and frankly an affection for her, but when I thought about her scissors story I decided that was as far as I would like to go with this young lady."

The Dutch underground helped Quilla Reed, a top turret gunner/engineer in the 91st Bomb Group, to evade the clutches of the

Germans. After he bailed out and landed, the first people he met were women interested in his silk-and-nylon parachute. Then two people on bicycles came and guided him into a nearby forest, where he and another crew member hid. They waited in the woods until Dutch Resistance fighters showed up, fed them, and gave them civilian clothes. Reed knew that he was lucky to have made contact with the underground, because they were a distinct minority: "About 5% of the Dutch people worked with the underground. 85% of the Dutch people really didn't care. About 10% of the Dutch people were sympathizers." He ended up hiding for a couple of weeks in a crawl space in the home of a doctor. The Germans apparently suspected the doctor's family of harboring the Americans, because one night they burst in looking for Reed and his buddy: "They came in screaming and yelling, talking about 'Amerikaners.' They beat the mother—they dragged her through the house by the hair of her head and they beat the sister, and they killed the father." As all this happened, Reed could do nothing but remain as quiet as possible in his special hiding place. The Germans took away the entire family and stayed in the house much of the next day. After getting drunk, most of them left—all except one man. The youngest son of the Dutch family had been hiding with Reed. Suddenly he fell through the floor of their hiding place right onto the German soldier in the kitchen: "Kobus jumped on that guard and took his knife and cut his throat, right there in the kitchen. That was the only thing to do. When that happened, we all fell out of there. We all went in different directions." They met up again with the underground and eventually moved from hiding place to hiding place until finally, after weeks of waiting and unbearable hunger, they heard nearby sounds of combat and made their way to the front lines, where they found a Canadian unit. A Canadian colonel gave them a hearty welcome: "That colonel looked at me and he said, 'I'll bet you fellas are Americans, aren't you?' And I said, 'YOU'D BETTER BELIEVE IT!' And we hugged and shook hands with him, and cried and yelled."

Robert Yowan, a ball turret gunner in the 487th Bomb Group, escaped German capture when his plane went down in Belgium near American forces during the Battle of the Bulge. After a rough para-

and accidentally hit him instead: "I floated down and was subsequently picked up by apologetic Englishmen. They bandaged me up, fortified me with rum-laced tea, and rigged a stretcher in a jeep. Moments later, the jeep hurtled over an embankment and I was . . . catapulted out, adding a fractured ankle to my injuries." The British treated Thyng's injuries and then dropped him off at his unit.

Some American airmen accidentally shot at their British allies. Ken Smith, a fighter pilot in the 350th Fighter Group, spotted a submarine off the coast of Algiers one day. He radioed an Allied antisubmarine control center and asked if any friendly subs were in the area. They told him that no Allied subs were in the area and that he should use his own discretion about opening fire. After buzzing the sub, he could not make out any identification and decided to attack it: "I hit the conning tower with at least five cannon shots before it [the cannon] jammed as usual. I then went home and filed a report. About two or three weeks later, we received a request through channels, asking if anyone knew of a plane that had attacked a submarine east of Algiers harbor. It seems the British wanted to file a formal complaint against the pilot who had damaged their submarine in an unprovoked attack." Luckily for Smith, no one aboard the sub was hurt.

Fighter Pilot Quentin Aanenson often had great difficulty determining which ground targets to attack during strafing missions: "A serious problem for us was trying to tell the Germans from the Allies from the air. Tanks, armored vehicles, and troops look very much alike when you are traveling over them at high speed. On a couple of occasions, we ended up attacking our own people. One day I was making a broadside attack on what I thought was a German halftrack. Just as I was bearing in for the kill, I recognized British markings on the side. My bullets were already hitting it, but the full convergence of my eight guns had not yet reached the vehicle. Apparently none of the bullets had penetrated, because it kept rolling along. It was a disturbing experience for me. If I had fired just a couple more seconds, I would have killed those guys."

Smith and Aanenson were lucky. No one was hurt, so their experiences could be chalked up as close calls brought about by mistaken identity. Not nearly as fortunate was a man in Robert Goebel's

31st Fighter Group. He had the worst kind of friendly fire incident imaginable—the accidental killing of a friend: "Harry didn't come back from a mission one day. Although such things happened and we were geared for them emotionally, this loss was truly tragic. He was shot down by his own flight leader. As they converged, Harry slid over into his leader's line of fire. He took the full brunt at close range and just blew apart. There was something unsettling about the whole affair. The pilot who had shot Harry down acted as if nothing had happened. I don't know what I expected him to do—he couldn't very well go around in a sackcloth and ashes. It wouldn't have done Harry any good." Perhaps the flight leader's sense of guilt did not permit him to acknowledge that anything had happened.

It seems there was no end to the ways combat airmen could be hurt or killed in World War II. As troubling as friendly fire could be, accidents presented an even bigger peril. The volatile combination of teenagers flying high-performance aircraft loaded with explosives and high-octane fuel under wartime conditions led to numerous accidents. These casualties were the most preventable, because they almost always came from carelessness, fatigue, or recklessness. Few things frightened Eugene Fletcher more than midair collisions: "These thoughts were never out of our minds and they preyed on us constantly—the pilots especially because they were responsible for the safety of the crew, not to mention their own necks. From a safety standpoint, our flight procedures left a lot to be desired. To say it was a harrowing experience would be an understatement of gross proportion."

Philip Ardery, a pilot in the 389th Bomb Group, witnessed a fatal midair collision over England: "One Liberator pulled up to one side and too close under another. The wings of the two airplanes touched and crumpled; for an instant, neither plane seemed to change its direction of flight. Then the wings began to come off both ships. Another instant and the whole part of the sky was aflame as the gasoline and bombs exploded. One big fire gently descended. Falling from it could be seen engines, props, wheels, bits of wings, and some bundles that might have been men. I was sick.

Here were twenty men, trained arduously for years, who had at last reached the combat zone and who never helped their country."

Sometimes accidents happened on the ground. John Gabay, a tail gunner in the 94th Bomb Group, recalled an incident when a waist machine gun accidentally went off and hit a man as the group prepared for a mission: "When we got to him, he was bleeding badly. We gave him first aid, and by then the ambulance came and took him away. I cleaned up the mess afterwards and found pieces of meat and brains. They operated on him and took out the shell casing that had pierced his skull." Amazingly, and fortunately, the man lived. Accidents frequently happened during takeoffs when planes loaded with ordnance and fuel struggled to get off the ground. Harold Rosser, a fighter pilot in the 33d Fighter Group, kept a meticulous record of the number of comrades killed in accidents. Over the course of his tour of duty, he compiled a distressingly high tally, including the day two of his buddies collided while attempting to take off at the same time. They died fiery deaths: "That . . . smell, the sweet, sickening smell of burning flesh, had permeated the air. Above the roar of the fires, I could hear the boys vomiting, their stomachs heaving as if to rid themselves, once and for all, of the source of nausea. I couldn't get away from the thought that it was my buddies who were burning, that it was they whom we smelled, that they were being cooked. Slowly, we began to . . . huddle in little groups. Most were crying, but some were in shock, their tears held back, not by will power, but by a paralysis that numbed them."

Seeing their comrades die so foolishly and avoidably took a psychological toll on those left behind, particularly those who cleaned up afterward. As a chaplain, James Good Brown felt it was his duty to assist in cleaning up after fatal accidents, and there were far too many in his unit. The terrible sights he saw marked him for life. One day in early January 1944, a plane crashed on takeoff, killing everyone on board. At the crash site, Brown helped extract the remains of the dead, most of whom he had known personally: "A head lay among the wires, steel, and heap of unnamed bits. How awful to probe in this mess trying to extricate the bodies! All of the charred stuff around the bodies had to be carefully picked off with the fingers to discover letters, envelopes, or dog tags. I cannot describe the ghastliness of this experience! One must see the charred bodies . . . to know the horror. One thing we cannot erase from our memory is the smell of the scene. It pierces down into one's consciousness and stays there. The shriveled-up body 'talked' to you through the sense of smell. I had been speaking to them only an hour before. They were my friends. Something says within me: 'This is not the person you talked to an hour ago. He is not here. He is in Heaven.' But that, I submit, is an easy way out. That is just a way of softening my hurt. And I certainly will not say, 'This is the will of God.' That is one explanation no one will ever hear me say."

A few months later, another plane crashed shortly after takeoff. Predictably, the results were grisly: "To see a body sprawled out on the ground, lifeless, ripped to pieces, black with burns, is an ugly sight that will never leave the memory. One by one, we picked them up. Most of them were beyond recognition, with faces blown away. I was so sorry for them! And I was sorry for their families back home! Another body was together, but the head was a jellied mass, not recognizable. Identification was difficult. We picked up chunks of flesh mixed up in fliers' clothing. We put together six bodies as best we could. The remaining four, we could not find at all. Parts of legs and arms and fingers and intestines were strewn over the entire area and into the woods beyond. Far into this woodland, we found a head. The whole head was soft and spongy. There was no jaw left to identify the teeth. We had the head, but no body to which to attach it. It had to be placed on a pile. The entire afternoon was spent picking up and identifying bodies. They were taken to the base hospital. The hospital staff had to undress them, removing the shreds of clothes. The underclothes were inside the compound fractures of the legs, tangled up with large bone. They were my men. I had loved them. They were somebody's son, husband, or brother. They were robbed of life. They wanted to live. They cherished life as much as I now cherish life. And—they deserved to live."

Not surprisingly, such terrible events took a serious toll on the psyches of young airmen. Amid the violent world of air combat, it was only natural for some men to break under the strain and experience combat fatigue. Among American ground-combat troops in

World War II, combat fatigue was quite common. Airmen did not experience combat fatigue with as much frequency, but it did happen to some. They came to feel they could no longer fly combat missions just as some infantrymen felt they could no longer function in battle. In Europe, about 3,000 combat airmen had to be removed temporarily from flying status. Many of them eventually returned to combat duty. About 1,500 men, representing just over 1 percent of the total combat force, were removed permanently from flight status because of combat fatigue. The other theaters combined had similar totals.

In spite of the low overall numbers, most airmen witnessed some form of combat fatigue during their tours of duty. Kenneth Jones, a pilot in the 389th Bomb Group, employed a typical airman's description of men with combat fatigue, calling them "flak happy," a condition caused by "the accumulation of hazardous takeoffs with maximum loads in adverse weather, sweating under an oxygen mask at subzero tempetures [sic] at high altitude and the tension of getting there and coming home. It grinds away at your mind." Combat-fatigue casualties in the ground forces were taken off the line, sedated, fed hot meals, and given new clothes. Most were then sent back to their units as soon as possible. The Air Force had no such elaborate procedure. Combat-fatigue cases were dealt with differently from unit to unit. Harry Crosby's 100th Bomb Group, which took terrible casualties in the air war in Europe, removed men with combat fatigue immediately: "When a flyer was undone by missions, when he saw too many planes blow up in front of him, when his tail gunner was cut in two on a mission, when too many of his friends were killed, he sometimes quit. We did not call them 'cowards,' we called them 'combat failures.' Since 'combat fatigue' . . . was so contagious, the flyer was whisked off the base immediately and sent to the nearest General Hospital. Here in a special ward he was given psychiatric and religious counseling. After that he usually went back to the States, was reclassified, and usually demoted. In some cases, he was court-martialed. Some returned to duty. While he was gone, to preserve our own courage, we never mentioned him, not once."

Roger Armstrong, a radioman in the 91st Bomb Group, remembered seeing official orders to his unit outlining clear and somewhat harsh policies with respect to combat-fatigue victims: "Enlisted combat crew members: Lack of Moral Fiber or Operational Fatigue—Reduce to lowest grade and put on least attractive duty possible. Officer crew members: 1) If individual has less than 18 sorties to his credit or has been subjected to very severe battle damage less than three times—Reclassify without mercy. 2) If individual has over 18 sorties to his credit or has been subjected to very severe battle damage more than three times be as lenient as possible consistent with the morale of the organization."

Upon reading these policies, Armstrong felt it was "very apparent that if a person felt he could no longer handle the stress of combat flying . . . the Army Air Corps was very harsh in their treatment of that crew member." It is of course an open question as to whether commanders truly enforced such strict regulations. Fighter outfits, for instance, usually grounded or quietly transferred those pilots who could not cope with combat. Even so, the Army Air Force did seem to adopt a fairly hard-line stance on the acceptability of combat fatigue, especially compared to the lenient attitude of the ground forces. Perhaps Air Force combat commanders felt that, as highly trained, motivated volunteers fighting an episodic war with basic comforts and a prescribed tour of duty, their men should not succumb to the physical misery and hopelessness that often caused combat fatigue among infantrymen.

Armstrong's order prescribed different treatment for officers and enlisted men who suffered from combat fatigue. Kevin Herbert found that, in his unit, enlisted men who could no longer continue were dealt with much more harshly than officers with the same problem: "Inevitably there were some who could not stick it, but they were not many in our squadron. If a flying officer cracked up psychologically, his treatment was quite different from that of an EM [enlisted man]. One officer . . . quit cold after his first mission, which admittedly was a rough one. He simply refused to fly again, and as a result within hours was heading back for Honolulu and some rear-echelon desk job. But a sergeant who could take no more after a few missions was reduced to private and put in charge of . . . trash collections in the area. This poor soul walked about in continual silence, neither speaking nor being spoken to."

As Herbert indicated, anyone who could no longer bear combat risked being ostracized by combat crews. This kind of humiliation and separation from the group naturally was a major deterrent for anyone tempted to succumb to combat fatigue. Some were too far gone to care and others simply wanted to survive too badly to worry about their peers. Combat airmen did not ostracize men with combat fatigue out of scorn or disdain for supposed cowardice or lack of moral fiber. In fact, most had great sympathy for men with combat fatigue but feared it could spread to them if they had too much contact with the afflicted. Most airmen wrestled with the same terror, doubt, and fatigue of spirit that felled psychological casualties, so they knew the same fate could also happen to them. Robert Goebel knew a fighter pilot who quit in the middle of a mission. He simply informed his flight leader that he could no longer bear to fly, then he headed for home: "He told me he was so shook and lacking in confidence that he even considered bailing out. He remained in the squadron as a ground officer and no one thought the less of him for his trouble. We all knew that he had given it his best shot but had lost the battle with whatever demon was tormenting him. George was an honest man whose time had run out."

Earl Wilburn, a bombardier in the 331st Bomb Group, recalled the day his tail gunner went to pieces after a mission to Japan. The man could no longer control himself: "He was talking nonsense, like in a coma but walking and talking. It was sad. We felt bad for him and for anyone who got like that." The man was removed from combat duty immediately. Elmer Bendiner, a navigator in the 379th Bomb Group, had no hard feelings toward combat-fatigued men who refused to fly: "They had an overriding personal necessity to preserve their bodies intact. It is hard to argue against such an order of priorities." One man who fell into this category was a waist gunner on Bendiner's crew: "He made up his mind to survive. In refusing to fight, he stood his ground with indomitable spirit. One summer morning when we were not alerted, Snuffy went to see the squadron CO. Our tail gunner, Mike, went with him and so could tell us precisely what happened. Snuffy saluted with that casual wave to the forehead that was our bow to protocol. 'I ain't aflying anymore,' he said in his own blend of Kansas and Oklahoma accents.

'I'm ascared. That fuckin' flying's for keeps. I'm agoing to the kitchen.' At that point, Mike says, Snuffy began to tear his sergeant's stripes from his sleeve by way of emphasizing the finality of his decision and his acceptance of the consequences. Theoretically, of course, he might have been given far worse than a demotion—anything from a dishonorable discharge to time in a stockade. Snuffy won. He went to the kitchen. Mike commented to me years later, 'It took a lot of guts on his part to admit that he was scared shitless.'"

Many combat airmen would have agreed with the tail gunner's comment. To some, enduring ostracism from one's combat brothers and the humiliation of being unable to stand up to the rigors of battle took more guts than risking one's life. Even so, most airmen did not want to fly with such men because they could not depend on them to do their jobs, thus endangering the whole crew. Hub Zemke, an ace fighter pilot who commanded two different fighter groups in Europe, refused to fly with a man who fled from combat one day, leaving Zemke alone to face an enemy fighter attack: "My immediate reaction was to have Murray transferred. Once a man breaks under duress, no one is going to trust him again. Some of the kinder hearts in headquarters reminded me that others who once panicked had later proved their worth. So I relented, although Murray never flew as my wingman again."

William Cubbins came face-to-face with combat fatigue one night in the officers' club at his base. In this case, the victim did not go to pieces. Truly fatigued, the pilot simply could not imagine summoning the energy and courage to face enemy flak again: "The man was near tears. He'd flown over forty missions and was questioning his own fitness for combat. His friends knew that he'd had a particularly rough combat tour and sympathized. However, I think we were all shocked when he blurted out, 'I can't take it anymore. If tomorrow's target is near Switzerland, we're going to get ourselves interned.' After a moment's pause, all those in attendance agreed with him. Various members of the group suggested that he reconsider. They well knew how his actions would be viewed. I became convinced that the man was not a coward, but he obviously feared being branded one. He was simply fatigued, combat fatigued. And as is usually the case with fatigue under conditions of great stress,

P-40 fighters take off from an American escort carrier in support of the invasion of North Africa. In the course of the war, close air support from fighters became an invaluable asset to ground forces.

B-17 Flying Fortresses from the 91st Bomb Group, home of the famous *Memphis Belle,* drop their bombs over a target in Europe. To achieve maximum accuracy, bombers had to fly as straight as possible in the midst of sometimes intense flak. Fliers loved the B-17 because it could withstand terrific punishment.

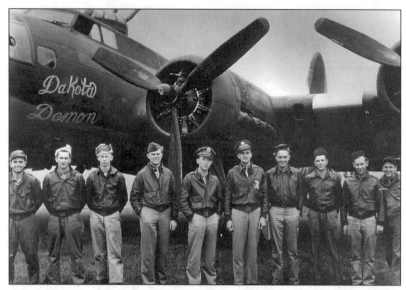

This crew from the 92d Bomb Group, standing in front of their plane *Dakota Demon*, is about to meet the King and Queen of England in the spring of 1943. The crew of *Dakota Demon* was sent to the 91st Bomb Group's base at Bassingbourn so that the English royalty could view this particular model of B-17.

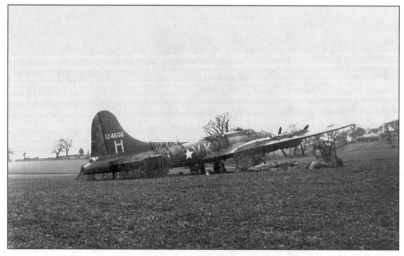

A crash landed B-17 at its base in England. Frequently, combat airmen barely made it home from their perilous missions. Often as not, they had to turn around and fly another mission the next day.

Oily clouds of smoke drift high above Mannheim, Germany, during a raid by the 303d Bomb Group in mid-January 1945.

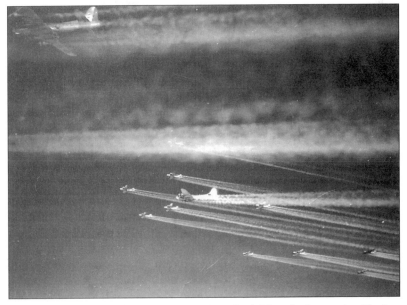

Less than one week later, the 303d bombed Mannheim again. Notice the vapor trails or "contrails" emanating from the four engines of each plane. Contrails were caused by engine exhaust making contact with cold air at high altitudes. Crews hated contrails because they were "like beacons in the sky" for the enemy.

An oil refinery burns in Misburg, Germany, during a daylight raid. American strategic bombing doctrine placed a high premium on oil related targets.

Snub-nosed B-24 Liberators dodge flak over a target. The United States produced more B-24s than any other combat aircraft in its history. In all, some 18,313 were built, many of them originating from Henry Ford's famous Willow Run plant in Michigan. Although not as sleek and beautiful as the more glamorous B-17, the B-24 Liberator proved to be nearly as durable and more versatile.

A B-17 from the 95th Bomb Group completes the ultimate task of every bomber crew on every sortie—namely dropping the bombs as close to the target as possible. This particular aircraft is a later model B-17G which featured a chin turret to provide firepower against head-on fighter attacks, as well as enclosed waist windows so that gunners could be shielded from the swirling, icy winds common at high altitudes.

A view of a typical target in Europe. Notice the multiple puffs of flak. Airmen would often describe flak like this as "so thick you could get out and walk on it." Enemy flak and fighters, along with primitive technology, human error, and the escalating barbarity of the war combined to make precision bombing, even in daylight, extremely difficult.

This is what it looked like when a bomber got shot down. This B-24, piloted by Lt. John Hansen, has just been hit by flak over Fallerslaben, Germany, and is about to go down. When a plane got shot down, an airman faced three possible fates: death, captivity or, in the case of a lucky few, escape and evasion through the efforts of local resistance groups.

A P-51 fighter pilot chats with his two man ground crew as they reload the fifty caliber wing mounted machine guns on his plane. Fighter pilots had the highest regard for their ground crews and often worked very closely with them. Fighter groups were one of the few places in the military in which officers assumed the risks of combat while enlisted men were mostly safe.

Pilots of the 357th Fighter Group pose for a group shot at their base in Leiston, England. Fighter pilots usually ranged in age from 19 to 25. While bomber crews placed a high premium on group cooperation and chemistry, fighter pilots valued independence, creativity and aggressiveness.

Lieutenant Richard Peterson of the 357th Fighter Group pilots his P-51 Mustang. Fighter pilots flew three basic kinds of missions: air to air sweeps designed to destroy enemy fighters; strafing missions in support of ground or naval forces; and escort duty, sometimes termed combat air patrol.

Fighter pilots had their share of close calls too. The pilot of this 354th Fighter Group Mustang barely made it home.

Almost every combat sortie began with a briefing. These naval aviators aboard an escort carrier in the Pacific are being briefed in the ready room for their day's mission.

American planes strafe a Japanese destroyer escort vessel in Hokkaido Bay in the closing days of the war. Aircraft proved to be remarkably effective at sinking ships during World War II.

U.S. Navy torpedo and dive bombers release their bombs over a target in Mokodate, Japan, in July 1945. By this time, American airpower had reduced most Japanese cities to burnt-out wastelands.

A Navy fighter pilot aboard the *USS Lexington* poses with a bomb his F6F Hellcat will carry into combat. Notice the anti-Japanese scrawlings on the bomb. Most combat airmen in the Pacific had no love for the Japanese, although they did not always share the intense racial and cultural hatred of the Japanese exhibited by American ground combat troops.

Crash landing aboard an aircraft carrier was among the most dangerous things a combat airman could do. This pilot sustained heavy flak damage to his plane during a strafing mission in support of American ground troops at Leyte in October, 1944. He managed to escape unscathed after setting down his damaged Hellcat on the deck of his carrier.

A common expression among airmen after tough missions was that they had made it home "on a wing and a prayer." The predicament of this American plane and its crew illustrates that this expression was not always hyperbole.

A Marine fighter pilot prepares to take off from his base in the Philippines and fly close air support of American ground troops. Although strategic airpower advocates did not look kindly on the employment of airpower for ground support, combat airmen often derived the most satisfaction from these missions.

Navy dive bombers prepare to attack Japanese ships during the pivotal battle of Midway.

This was the fate of most American combat aircraft after the war air-craft graveyards in the southwestern deserts and left to rot. Over the years they were often cut up or sold for scrap. In this photograph B-24s, having faithfully performed their service, live out the rest of their lives under the burning sun in Kingman, Arizona. Only a tiny handful of World War II combat aircraft survived to see the end of the twentieth century.

7

Thinking of the Enemy

In an air war, you are not very conscious of your enemies as human beings. We attacked targets—a gun emplacement, a supply dump, a radar station—not men, and succeeded or failed in terms of the things we destroyed. If I thought of the men down there at all, I thought of them as ordinary, like us, men who ran supply dumps and radar stations, and who manned their guns and shot at us when we attacked them.

—Samuel Hynes, Marine torpedo bomber pilot in the Pacific

Although aerial combat, by its very nature, was largely impersonal, every American combat airman knew that on the ground thousands of feet below, or off in the distance in the foreign planes he tried to destroy, the enemy existed in real human flesh and blood. From day to day, this realization ebbed and flowed within each man's consciousness. Fighter pilots wondered from time to time about their adversary's personal character and background, even as they sought to destroy as many enemy planes or as many enemy ground targets as possible. Bomber crewmen knew that their bombs meant death and destruction not just for military targets in the enemy's warmaking arsenal but also for enemy civilians. Combat airmen did not have the same level of antipathy for their enemies as did their ground-combat counterparts. To be sure, numerous fliers despised the Japanese and some did have a significant degree of hatred for their German adversaries. But, by and large, the impersonal nature of air combat modified feelings of intense hatred and vengeance. Some airmen thought, perhaps naively, of their form of warfare as chivalrous or even romantic. They liked to think of themselves as modern-day knights of the sky, but in reality they were simply soldiers in the sky fighting for their lives against skillful, determined enemies whose courage and prowess they generally respected and sometimes admired.

More than historians have previously believed, airmen grappled with the moral consequences of strategic bombing. They knew that, even in the most surgical strikes against war-related targets, errant bombs could take the lives of civilians. As American strategic-bombing philosophy evolved during the war to include area bombing against enemy cities, combat airmen found themselves increasingly troubled by what they were doing—but not quite to the point of refusing to fly their missions. In spite of their personal misgivings, they carried out their orders to the best of their abilities. Even so, many of them wondered, along with later generations, about the morality of their actions.

The Japanese

It is no secret that the Pacific war was fought with a great deal of racial and cultural hatred. During the war years, most Americans had nothing but outright hatred for the Japanese. This fact has been well chronicled in such books as John Dower's *War Without Mercy* and Ronald Spector's *Eagle Against the Sun*. Both books argue that numerous factors led to this antipathy on the part of many Americans. These included cultural and racial differences, Japanese atrocities such as the Bataan Death March and the Rape of Nanking, and, of course, Pearl Harbor. Clearly, the Pacific War was a kill-or-be-killed kind of war fought between two diametrically opposed cultures, both of whom despised the racial makeup of the other side. Upon entering World War II, most Americans thirsted for revenge against Japan. They reasoned that Japan had (treacherously, in their view) started the war and now must pay the consequences, while Germany could be dealt with later. Grand strategy, however, dictated otherwise. Correctly considering Germany to be the more dangerous enemy, American and British leaders carried out a "Germany first" strategy for winning the war. This meant that the majority of American resources would go to the war in Europe. Once Germany was defeated, then Japan could be dispatched. Although this made good strategic sense, it flew in the face of American public opinion, which burned to make Japan's defeat the highest priority.

In this context, then, it is only natural that many American combat airmen in the Pacific would harbor feelings of hatred against the Japanese. Franklin Allen, a B-26 pilot in the 22d Bomb Group, resented the Japanese for starting the war and thus forcing him to be apart from his wife, to whom he wrote: "I'll hate the Japs to my dying day for causing this separation between us. I want you to have the realization that your husband is really doing something worth while. The Jap is a foe that must be annihilated before we can be safe and it's going to take some time to do it." Harold Rosser, a fighter pilot in the 33d Fighter Group, had nothing but enmity for his Japanese foes when he entered combat, and this endured throughout his entire tour of duty. This hatred boiled over one day into vengeful feelings when the Japanese set up a booby trap for American fighters. They parked a truck in the open, knowing it would attract American fighters, and then opened up on the fighters with concealed antiaircraft weapons, killing an inexperienced American pilot who failed to sniff out the trap. Rosser took great pleasure in leading a flight to destroy the Japanese positions around the truck: "Even with a seething hatred for the Japs, I had maintained a calmness, deliberateness about the missions I flew, seeing the most rational way to accomplish the objective. That was in the past, but the rules had changed. The Japs had booby-trapped Stisson [the dead pilot]. With a vengeance that surprised me, I led the men in repeated strafing passes until at the end I could report with certainty: the booby trap at Gokteik has been destroyed."

Earl Wilburn, a B-29 bombardier in the 331st Bomb Group, loathed the Japanese, even at the end of the war, when he flew the bulk of his missions. On the final day of the war, his crew was sent on a raid to Japan. The briefing officers told his unit that the war could be over at any moment but, if they had not heard official confirmation of the war's end by the halfway point of the mission, to go ahead and drop their bombs. He and his buddies had their own plans, though: "We were still a bit pissed at the Japanese. We decided to drop our bombs come what may, so we went ahead and dropped them. On the way back, we heard on an L.A. radio station that the war was over. Successive generations [of Japanese] have no concept of what their country did in World War II. The Japanese are the racists of the world."

For some fliers, hatred continued unabated many years after the war. Karl Smith, a Navy fighter pilot, never forgave the Japanese for the undeniable brutality with which they fought the war: "I hate their guts. I don't buy anything Japanese. I've seen too many tricks that they've pulled, like shooting a guy in a parachute." Another Navy fighter pilot, Eugene Pargh, felt exactly the same way. Upon visiting Nagasaki, long after the war, he felt completely unsympathetic to the suffering the Japanese atomic-bomb victims had endured: "A Japanese lady gave a speech describing the bomb blast and the horrible damage it did. I wanted to tell her about the Navy pilot who crash-landed at sea near one of the islands held by the Japanese. When our troops invaded a week later, he was found with his head chopped off. I'm sure there were thousands of stories like that. As we wandered through the park, one old-timer about my age asked me what I thought about all this. I said it served the bastards right. He said he felt the same way, but stronger. Very few people in the present generation of young people would ever know or understand how we feel."

If it is true that succeeding generations did not understand the enduring residue of wartime antipathy among some combat airmen, it is also true that many fliers with no love for the Japanese still had mixed feelings about the hatred they felt in their hearts. To them, the Japanese may have been despicable, but they were still human. Charles Moutenot, a Navy fighter pilot who shot down two enemy fighters during the war, including one over Truk, had mixed feelings about it many years later: "I don't like to think of it now, but I hated the Japanese. I shot that guy down and one other plane, and I hate to think that I killed anybody. I didn't see any 'chutes so I don't know if they bailed out or not. That bothers me now, but it didn't then." Charles Bond, a fighter pilot in the American Volunteer Group, or "Flying Tigers," fought against the Japanese in the early days of the war, when Pearl Harbor was fresh in the minds of many Americans. After strafing an enemy supply column, he returned to base and described his mixed feelings in his diary: "What a business. Like beasts. No thought for life whatsoever. Instead, a

feeling of hatred for the Japanese that becomes deeper day by day."
In spite of that growing hatred, he found he could not rejoice in
some of the grisly emblems of Japanese death he saw around him:
"An RAF airman held up a leather helmet with a Japanese pilot's
head still in it with parts of his throat hanging down in a bloody
mess. With his other hand, the airman pointed two fingers . . . in the
usual V-for-victory sign. I returned the V-sign. I could not, however,
return his broad grin."

Marine Fighter Pilot Jack Conger, of Fighter Squadron 212 on
Guadalcanal, shot down a Japanese fighter one day and helped fish
the live pilot out of the sea. The pilot, like most Japanese in World
War II, resisted capture and did so with obvious hostility. The
ground-combat Marines in the boat with Conger wanted to shoot
the Japanese pilot, but Conger prevented them from doing so, even
though he felt little more than hatred for the man: "It made me feel
a little queer. I suppose it's alright for a fellow to be willing to fight
until he dies, but war shouldn't be just plain murder. In a way it
ought to be just a game that you play extra hard."

John Filbrick, a 35th Fighter Group pilot, strafed Japanese troops
on New Guinea one day and then wrote about it in a letter to his
parents. Although he clearly had contempt for the Japanese, he also
had mixed feelings about killing them: "Went on a strafing run the
other day and blasted a bunch of Nips to wherever Nips go when
they die for their Emperor. I caught quite a bunch trying to get away
down a beach-head, 'so sorry' to disappoint them. When I pulled up
off the beach, they were all good Japs—dead ones. These 'fifties'
[his plane's guns] leave a nasty mess and, like it or not, I'm wondering if your little boy is a murderer now."

Like many other American combat airmen, Filbrick did not like
the Japanese but recognized intellectually that they were human beings who hurt and bled just like Americans. Where ground-combat
troops in the Pacific often dehumanized the Japanese, preferring to
think of them as fanatically dangerous animals, combat airmen,
fighting a more detached, less savage war, thought of the enemy as
human but nevertheless flawed due to his race, culture, or outlook.

Some combat fliers actually bore no particular hatred toward the
Japanese. Chester Bennett, a Navy psychologist who spoke with and

evaluated hundreds of naval aviators during their time in combat, wrote to a friend: "You seldom find them expressing vindictive personal hatred for the enemy. It's a contest of mechanical skill and grand strategy. And if anyone can jump the net and shake hands with the opponent after it's all over, I think it may well be some of the fliers." Dick Marshall, a Fifth Air Force fighter-bomber pilot who flew countless missions in the South Pacific before his death in 1943, did not exactly like the Japanese but neither did he have any strong feelings of hatred toward them: "I find the Jap wholly human and subject to fear and, of course, his stomach needs food and his humor and stamina is [sic] considerably altered without it." Franklin Shires, a Navy fighter pilot, never thought of the Japanese as objects of hatred. Rather, he thought of them as enemies to be defeated—nothing more, nothing less: "You don't think of them in terms of individuals. You thought of them . . . as a group, as something you wanted to get rid of before they exterminate you. I don't have any animosity, I never had any, toward the Japanese. It's like a mechanical thing to me. You try to knock . . . them down or shoot them down . . . before they do the same thing to you to get this thing over with to where the world can be normal again."

How difficult did combat airmen feel it was to accomplish that goal of defeating Japanese airmen? Although most had a healthy respect for the fighting spirit, courage, and determination of Japanese airmen, they felt themselves to be superior combat fliers. Based on his combat experiences, George Sheafor, a B-17 gunner, figured American victory was inevitable, but not without a great deal of bloody combat. He wrote to his sister, "The war in Europe must have been a walk-away compared to the hell we have with these babies. You have to kill a hundred to take a square mile, and you don't capture them by the thousands, either." His respect for the Japanese was limited to their tenacity and not their prowess in battle, something true of many combat airmen throughout the war.

Bruce Holloway, a future Air Force general, flew fighters with the Flying Tigers in the early days of the Pacific war and ended up shooting down thirteen enemy planes. He came away admiring Japanese courage but disdaining the lack of initiative among enemy pilots: "The Jap is courageous. The Jap is probably the best-disciplined soldier in the world. In fact, he is so bound by the rules of discipline that as an individual he is lost. He knows nothing except to obey. As long as his plan is in order, as long as he can follow instructions given to him by his superiors, he is a good soldier. But knock out his plan, put him on his own for survival, and you've got him. He has no initiative and no resourcefulness when circumstances make him his own boss. He fights by the book. The Jap goes to pieces when he is scared. Two of us cornered a Zero in the mountains. He turned left and my buddy headed him off. Then, obviously in a panic, he turned directly into my guns. I shot him down. The way he fights will puzzle you at first. When you dive on him, he will pull up into you, and you will think that in spite of all you can do, he is going to ram you. Frankly, I don't know how good the Jap is as a gunner. I never let one get close enough to me to find out."

The Japanese undoubtedly had lost many of their best pilots by the middle of 1944. Many of those who flew against American combat airmen simply did not have the training or experience to be very effective, particularly against highly trained, well-equipped American fliers. E. H. Bayers, a Navy fighter pilot in Air Group 3 who fought against the Japanese in 1945, found that the enemy fliers he encountered lacked aggression, a sure sign of inexperience: "There was nothing wrong with Jap tactics or with their gunnery. The great weakness of the Japs lay in the fact that they were not aggressive enough. Numerous times they initiated an attack, only to break it off whenever a defending section came within 90 degrees of bearing on them." Clearly, American combat airmen respected the dangers with which Japanese bravery could present them, but, when it came to airmanship, tactics, and initiative, they usually felt themselves to be markedly superior to the Japanese pilots.

The Germans

Most combat airmen had mixed feelings about their German enemies. On the one hand, they detested the Nazis and knew they had to be destroyed. On the other hand, they often did not feel much personal hatred for the German people as a whole. Even in the Pacific against the despised Japanese, American combat airmen did not risk their lives out of hatred for the enemy. They fought for each other. So, in Europe, where the enemy came from a similar cultural background and racial origin, airmen sometimes found it difficult to muster much outright hatred for the Germans. Even so, a significant minority did have fairly strong anti-German feelings. For some the feelings grew out of contempt for German militarism and lust for conquest. Others loathed the Nazis so much that they blamed the entire German nation for bringing them to power. Rarely, though, did American airmen express feelings of contempt for the Germans as a race or culture, and even those who hated the Germans found themselves admiring much about German culture.

John Clarkson, a top turret gunner/engineer in the 34th Bomb Group, did not like the Germans because he had heard stories of civilian lynchings of downed airmen. In a letter to his wife, he referred to the enemy as "those bastard Jerries. Excuse the lingo, but the Germans are one hell of a bunch of fighting men. Civilians and soldiers alike. You ought to hear of some of the monstrosities done to some of our . . . airmen." In order to "get back" at these unseen civilian lynch mobs, combat airmen sometimes dumped rocks, airsickness bags, or even the contents of their relief cans out of their bombers. Richard Baynes, a pilot in the 466th Bomb Group, recalled that dumping rocks became standard operating procedure for his crew: "John, Harvey, Lyn, and Harold would load 5 or 6 of these big chunks of concrete near the camera hatch and when they saw the first flak, they would kick them out of the plane. Les Walters continued to gather . . . rocks, on his own, and load them right in front of the bomb-bay doors. After 'Bombs away,' Les always unleashed his rocks, and Lyn Wheeler would always call on the intercom to make sure the rocks went out."

Tossing rocks not only was a mentally comfortable way of getting back at potential lynch mobs or flak gunners, it also was a way for American airmen to express hatred for their German enemy. Merle Perkins, a radio operator in the 483d Bomb Group, saw one of his buddies tossing rocks from his waist gun position one day and immediately convinced him to stop: "I drew him aside once we landed and told him never to do that again. He agreed readily but didn't show any shame. In my own mind, I am still debating the difference between dropping our bombs, some of which might, against our wishes, go astray and kill civilians, and tossing rocks. Jim was personalizing the war, making the objective mean, evil, personally vindictive, a far cry from our 'precision' bombing. Throwing rocks was a horrible, independent initiative."

Realizing that rock throwing was nothing more than an extension of personal hatred, Perkins could not help but disapprove. To him, there was no room for such bitter feelings in carrying out the job of modern war. Others disagreed. Harry Crosby, a navigator in the 100th Bomb Group, knew men who routinely dropped rocks during missions: "One aircrew gunner kept a gunnysack to collect about fifty pounds of rocks. Every time he went on a mission and wasn't firing a gun, he dropped the rocks out, one at a time, over what he called 'Krautland.'" Another man liked to collect full relief cans and drop them over Germany. Routinely plagued by airsickness, Crosby himself jettisoned his vomit bag over enemy territory many times: "When I salvoed one of my number-10 sacks, filled with the produce of my airsickness, I . . . always hoped, without thinking much about it, that it would hit someone on the ground."

A few airmen, such as tail gunner Richard Child of the 487th Bomb Group, had feelings of deep hatred for the Germans. Child's hatred began on the day he was captured, when he witnessed the lynchings of two members of his crew: "I will always remember that the German people were directly responsible for the death of two of my very close friends, the injury of two others, and the endurance of hardship and suffering of my fellow crew members and myself; not to mention the hundreds of thousands of indescribable and grotesque atrocities committed throughout the course of the European war. The majority of the American people will soon forget this, but those few Americans who have witnessed and experienced them will never forget."

Child's hatred grew primarily out of atrocities the Germans had perpetrated on him and his buddies. John Marshall, a fighter pilot in the 404th Fighter Group, suffered no such calamities at the hands of the Germans, but he nevertheless shared Child's abject hatred for them. In letters to his family written in the fall of 1944, he repeatedly expressed his loathing of the enemy. On the subject of strafing, he wrote: "I care not where my bombs and bullets fall nor what they hit. I'd like to see them [the Germans] stay in the fight long enough for the Allies to completely wipe out the German Army. Their minds are poisoned and they've got to be killed in large enough numbers to thin it out." Like many American airmen, Marshall particularly hated the SS [Schutzstaffel, the German security forces]: "They are a stinking goddamn lot who have no right to breathe the air that the rest of this confused world breathes, and each day we are thinning their ranks." Knowing that his bombs and bullets led to death and destruction below him, Marshall's enduring hatred acted as a kind of shield to protect him from potential pangs of conscience: "There is nothing difficult mentally about killing a Hun. If the Jap is hated any more than these people, then God help them." As Marshall gained more missions under his belt, any sympathy he had left for the German people evaporated. If he hated the SS, he also came to despise the average German on the street: "I, each day, feel less and less sorry for the German element which is not Nazi. Nazi or not, they are Germans and they are trouble causers to civilization." By December 1944, after five months of combat, he expressed the opinion that "Any thinking man gives the Hun credit for a lot of things . . . but just for the time being they are good for not a damn thing but to kill."

Men like Marshall, though, were the exception. Those who had hard feelings toward the Germans usually did not express such hatred for all the German people. Instead, their hatred was pragmatically confined to those who tried to kill them day after day. Hub Zemke's parents were German immigrants, and he grew up speaking German. But when he became the commander of the 56th Fighter Group, any ties of kinship with his native country were forgotten. He and his fellow fighter pilots often threw parties to celebrate their aerial victories—not necessarily out of delight that they had killed fellow human beings but because of their pragmatic instinct for survival, which could be achieved only by killing the enemy: "Perhaps another, softer generation yet unborn might be appalled that we could celebrate actions which had extinguished many lives of young men just like ourselves. But as we saw it then, the pilots of the Focke-Wulfs and Messerschmitts were not like us; they were the hated enemy who gave no quarter and had to be defeated."

Most American combat airmen in Europe would have agreed with all of Zemke's statement except the inclusion of the word "hated." In fact, the majority of airmen had no particular feelings of hatred for the Germans. They were simply the enemy who had to be defeated in order to get the war won so everyone could go home. G. W. Pederson of the 306th Bomb Group expressed a common sentiment among American combat airmen in Europe: "I had no feeling of hatred for Germans. Aerial combat was more like fighting a machine than a person. It was a very impersonal war. I had difficulty connecting it with people actually firing at me." Earl Benham, a radio operator in the 100th Bomb Group, wrote in his memoirs of his respect for German airmen: "The German flyers [sic] were fighting for their country, right or wrong, as we were. I felt no hatred for the German pilots." Airmen were even comfortable enough with these sentiments to talk about them during the war. Beirne Lay, a pilot in the Eighth Air Force whose experiences would one day lead to the movie *Twelve O'Clock High,* wrote about the infamous Regensburg mission late in 1943 in the *Saturday Evening Post.* In the article, he referred to German fighter pilots as "German boys in single-seaters who were probably going to react to us in the same way our boys would react, emotionally, if German bombers were heading for the Pratt & Whitney engine factory at Hartford or the Liberator plant at Willow Run."

Wesley Wells, a ball turret gunner in the 379th Bomb Group, also saw the Germans as fellow human beings doing nothing more than fighting for their country: "I found the German people and soldiers to be just people and that, even at the time, I could relate to their situation. I remember after a briefing, the Chaplain gave his little spiel to urge us on, 'Go over and destroy the den of iniquity.' I remember thinking that probably right now on the other side of the Channel, there is a German Chaplain giving a similar spiel, but he has a more compelling story, as we were about to bomb their homeland and families. This is not to say that I didn't feel that it was necessary to go and rid the world of Hitler and his gang, but I met no men in combat with hate but only with respect as soldiers."

Bob Ryerson, a pilot in the 96th Bomb Group, even went so far as to say that he did not feel the war was necessary. He actually liked and admired the Germans. Even though he flew thirty-five missions against them in combat, he always felt that America should not have entered the war in Europe: "I joined the Army to fight Japan for having the audacity to attack the United States. I had no reason at all to dislike the Germans or want to fight the Germans. They did nothing to the United States, absolutely nothing. The Japanese were the ones I wanted to get." Ryerson of course conveniently ignored the fact that Germany declared war on the United States. His pro-German sentiments even blinded him to the crimes of the Nazis.

Very few American combat airmen, even those who had positive feelings about the Germans, would have agreed with Ryerson that the war in Europe was unnecessary, especially after the war, when the terrible crimes of Nazi Germany became widely known. The vast majority of American fliers would have articulated their sentiments toward the Germans the same way Fighter Pilot Al Alexander of the 350th Fighter Group did in a postwar memoir: "You have to figure that while you were shooting those people, they didn't want to be there any more than our guys wanted to be there. But they had guns, we had guns, and it was a question of 'Let's get this thing over with as expeditiously as possible.'"

The lack of much deep hatred toward their German foes meant that American combat fliers rarely concealed their almost-universal high opinions of them as adversaries. It is fair to say that airmen usually had great respect for the fighting qualities and courage of their German opponents. They had a much higher opinion of their German enemy than men in the Pacific theater had of their Japanese antagonists. James Good Brown, a chaplain in the 381st Bomb Group, recorded in his diary a conversation, toward the end of the war, with his group's lead navigator. They both marveled at the fact that the Germans continued to fight in the face of hopeless odds. Finally, the navigator said, "'Only a people who . . . believed firmly in their cause would continue when they know that they are licked. But we must admire any people who are courageous, who are determined, and who believe with conviction.' This is true. One must admire the determination of the German people." David McCarthy, also a navigator in the 381st, admired the bravery of German fighter pilots, who showed no reluctance to fly into the middle of B-17 formations: "I still marvel at the apparent fearlessness of the German fighter pilot. Between five hundred and six hundred .50-caliber machine guns present an almost impenetrable curtain of death. Still, once committed, those young airmen showed no hesitation. They risked all in their effort to kill one of our Forts [B-17s]."

Bill Winchell, a waist gunner on the famous *Memphis Belle* in the 91st Bomb Group, also could not help but admire German pilots: "I had all the respect in the world for them. The pilots that we ran across . . . were top-flight pilots and tough, and determined." E. T. Moriarity, a waist gunner in the 306th Bomb Group, had fearful admiration for one particular group of German fighter pilots known as "The Abbeville Kids." These men, who flew yellow-nosed fighters, were said to be *Reichsmarschall* Hermann Goering's handpicked pilots. Based at Abbeville, France, they flew countless missions against American bombers early in the air war. They reminded Moriarity of skillful boxers: "Their favorite ploy was to fly around us up high so they could look us over like a boxer feeling out his opponent. Jab and jab, move in and out, and then throw the right. When they decided to move in, they spread out and came boring in from the front and usually went right through the formation. If a B-17 was hit and could not keep his place, he was an instant prey. On one mission, a German pilot in an FW-190 joined us. He flew into the middle of our formation, dropped his landing gear and flaps, and flew with us for a couple of minutes. No one could fire at him lest they hit a ship in the formation. All of a sudden, he retracted his gear, pulled up his flaps, snap-rolled 180 degrees, and dove from view, attesting to the skills and courage these men possessed."

Robert Bieck of the 453d Bomb Group respected the German pilots because they had no tour of duty like the Americans. If an American airman could survive his prescribed number of missions or combat hours, he could go home. By contrast, German pilots flew until they could no longer fly: "German pilots were well disciplined, aggressive, and very brave. For the German pilot, there was no such thing as a tour of duty. You simply flew until you were wounded or killed. It's no wonder their top aces had over 300 planes to their record." James Goodson, a pilot in the 4th Fighter Group, even went so far as to say that German pilots were better than their Allied opponents: "German pilots had, on average, much more experience than ours and were therefore superior. Their best were . . . superior to our best."

Most American airmen would have shared Goodson's healthy respect for German pilots, but they would have strongly disagreed with him that the Germans were better overall. Goodson, Moriarity, Winchell, McCarthy, and the others had one thing in common— they mostly flew against the Germans early in the war, when Germany had committed its best pilots to the air war over Europe. By the middle of 1944, however, Germany, like Japan, had lost many of its best pilots in the war of attrition against the Allies. Correspondingly, the quality of German opposition to Allied airmen declined.

Joe Boyd, a Twelfth Air Force P-38 pilot, witnessed this transition in the German fighter force: "As the war went on, a lot of their good pilots had been killed. They got less aggressive. They were never anxious to come into battle unless they had every advantage in the world." One 332d Fighter Group pilot was mildly surprised at the low quality of opposition he faced in the skies over Italy in 1944: "The German pilots at Anzio must have been young guys who didn't have experience; they didn't know how to veer or take evasive action. They were sitting ducks." Their lack of aggressiveness betrayed their inexperience, making them that much more vulnerable to increasingly proficient American pilots, who pursued them for easy kills. Hub Zemke recalled the erosion of German airpower in 1944: "Since the early spring, we had noticed a general deterioration in the quality of the fighter pilots we met, and this became more pronounced as the weeks went by. A great many showed poor airmanship, pathetic gunnery, and lack of tactics, all indicative of insufficient training, which proved to be the case. The P-51 groups, with their range and endurance, had some spectacular turkey shoots at this time, intercepting huge enemy formations where the majority of pilots seemed to blindly follow the formation leader and make only clumsy attempts to avoid the attack. This was in marked contrast to the high calibre [sic] of the average German fighter pilot when we had arrived on the scene the previous summer."

In that sense, the Anglo-American strategic-bombing campaign of 1943–45 was a success. The bombing of occupied Europe and Germany itself clearly succeeded in breaking the fighting quality of the Luftwaffe and its capacity to defend its country effectively. This meant that the quality of German opposition declined dramatically as the war years continued. Even so, American airmen rarely failed to look upon their German opponents with anything but fearful respect.

One form of respect and decency toward the enemy was to refrain from shooting at helpless aviators who had bailed out of their aircraft. Shooting at a man in a parachute was a lot like shooting at a medic or a hospital. In Europe, neither side professed to approve of the practice, but it still happened from time to time. In the Pacific, shooting at parachuting aviators happened all the time, par for the course in the ruthless death struggle between the United States and Japan. Beyond the vengeful aspect of it, some argued that shooting at enemy bailout victims made good strategic sense. What was more valuable to the enemy, the pilot or the plane? In many cases, one could be as valuable as the other. In fact, it probably helped the Allied war effort more to eliminate an experienced, skillful enemy pilot. The plane he flew could be replaced fairly easily, but the pilot's experience and know-how could never be replaced.

Even so, most American combat airmen in World War II frowned on shooting at helpless enemy airmen. Some, like Edwards Park, a fighter pilot in the 35th Fighter Group on New Guinea, found it extremely distasteful. He maintained that his unit often had standing orders to shoot down any parachuting Japanese aviators. One day he shot down an enemy plane and had a good look at the enemy pilot as he parachuted: "He was hanging on his shrouds watching me. He had short . . . black hair and sideburns. A flying suit like ours, but he'd lost his helmet and goggles. He looked like a nice little fellow. I was supposed to shoot him, but I couldn't get my sights on him. I was glad because I didn't want to do it anyway. If there was disputed land under you, the rule was to shoot him." Cloudy Faulkner, a Marine fighter pilot at Guadalcanal, knew that some American airmen shot at parachutes of Japanese pilots, but he could not bring himself to do it as he watched a downed enemy fighter pilot descend toward the sea one day: "I circled the Jap as he was floating down, but I didn't shoot him. That sort of thing may be war, but it makes you sick."

If pilots in the Pacific could sometimes be reluctant to shoot at helpless enemy airmen, the same was very true in Europe. It was an unwritten rule of the air war in Europe that, once a man bailed out, he had become helpless—the equivalent of a prisoner—and should not be harmed. When American airmen witnessed German fighter pilots shooting at helpless parachutists, they became quite angry. Charles Olson, a lead bombardier in the 379th Bomb Group, saw this happen one day over Stettin, Germany: "I saw a JU-88 shoot up 4 Americans as they hung in their chutes after they bailed out. The barbarians. I hope the P-51s got [them]."

Incidents like the one Olson witnessed were the exception, though. Robert Goebel's attitude reflected the conventional thinking among most of those engaged in the European air war. One day, he shot down an enemy fighter and watched as the pilot bailed out and descended: "I made a pass at him, being careful to break off so my slipstream would not collapse his [parachute] canopy. As I passed to the side of him, I raised my gloved hand in a half wave—half salute. He may have thought I was going to shoot him out of his harness when I lined up on him. I knew for sure that nobody in our group did it, and I never heard of an instance of it in our wing. I don't think we would have tolerated anyone who pulled a trick like that."

Most airmen regarded the war they fought as a throwback to an earlier, more honorable chapter in warfare's history. Fighter pilots commonly thought of aerial combat as a gentlemen's game, vastly more civilized than ground combat. They often made the point that in combat they sought to destroy the enemy plane, not the enemy pilot. Even though this is a somewhat romanticized version of what really went on in the violent death skies of World War II, there is little question that airmen on both sides, especially in Europe, did share a common bond and did sometimes go about their jobs with real humanity. Peg Magness, a B-17 pilot in the 97th Bomb Group, saw a classic example of this mutual humanity during a mission to Germany. A nearby B-17 was hit by flak, causing a fire that forced its crew to bail out. One crewman pulled his rip cord too soon and snagged his parachute on the dying bomber. For a few awful moments, Magness watched the man hang helplessly as the fire began to consume him. Clearly he was doomed: "All of us were anguished since we were helpless to come to his aid and could only watch his agony. Then the war kind of hesitated because here came a German Me-109. He flew into the middle of the B-17s and everybody quit shooting. We were all amazed that he had the guts to fly into the middle of our formation with all those guns pointing at him. He then eased up to the boy that was whipping in the parachute and shot him. Not another shot was fired. The German pilot peeled off and left our formation. All of us let him go and then the war started again. The boy was doomed to a horrible death, but we just couldn't shoot him. It was a humane thing [for the German pilot] to do."

Mutual humanity notwithstanding, a combat airman's job was to kill the enemy and destroy his capacity to make war. Some airmen came back to base knowing for certain that they had killed enemy fliers. For some, this elicited little thought or remorse. To them, the killing was all part of the job. For others, it could be troubling, especially for those who got a good look at their victims.

Robert Goebel shot down a German plane over Romania and actually saw the pilot fall thousands of feet to his death. Goebel always wondered if his .50-caliber bullets had shot the German as he attempted to bail out of his burning plane: "I let up on the trigger as quickly as I could, but some of my rounds were still on their way as he separated from his machine. I . . . watched him tumble end over end. I waited for his chute to blossom, but it never opened. He hit in a ploughed field not far from where a Rumanian [sic] farmer was working with his horse. I had never seen the actual death of one of my adversaries before; it was unnerving."

Quentin Aanenson, a fighter pilot in the 366th Fighter Group, saw many Germans die from his lethal strafing runs. It ate away at him during his time in combat and in the years thereafter. On a mission early in his tour of duty, he saw his shells ripping apart German soldiers and realized he was responsible for their deaths: "I will always remember the feeling I had when my bullets smashed into them. Some just crumpled to the ground, but the tremendous impact of .50-caliber bullets at 120 rounds a second threw most of the bodies several yards. I got sick when I landed, and that night as I sat in my tent, I had to keep reminding myself that I had to do it, that I had probably saved some American boys' lives by killing Germans that day."

Another time, he caught a German truck convoy in the open and shredded it with everything in his arsenal: "They never had a chance. My bullets tore into them and blew things apart. I made three passes, firing until I burned out my gun barrels. My wingman and I circled the mess and counted forty bodies. I don't know how many more were in the ditches that we couldn't see. The emotional impact on me was terrible. My right hand and trigger finger wouldn't function. I couldn't grip the control stick. I had to land by laying my arm on top of the stick and shifting my left hand back and forth between the throttle and the stick. I have recurring nightmares about that mission." The more strafing missions he flew, the more he realized that he regularly had the power of life and death over enemy soldiers, something that deeply disturbed him: "A guy might run to the left to escape my guns—should I let him go or not. Just a touch of my left rudder would aim my guns at him and pound him into the ground. Or I could choose not to fire. If I didn't, that German might kill an American soldier tomorrow. But I never felt good about it."

Some airmen shared Aanenson's sense of guilt over killing the enemy, especially face-to-face, but they also felt very elated for having done their jobs and survived. Howard Moebius, a fighter pilot in the 357th Fighter Group, experienced those kind of mixed feelings the day he shot down his first enemy fighter: "At the time it was happening, you had so much adrenaline flowing . . . that you don't have any reaction when you place bullets in an enemy's canopy. Your life is on the line. In later reflection . . . it occurred to me that he might have been married, might have had kids. I thought about him as an individual like me." Lou Purnell of the 332d Fighter Group went through the very same gamut of emotions after making a grisly discovery upon his return from destroying a German troop column: "When I got back to the airfield, as after every strafing mission, I checked the plane for bullet holes. Hanging over the edge of the scoop on the intake under the P-51 was a strange object. On closer inspection, it looked like a black-brownish glob, wet in some

intentional or not, weighed on their collective conscience. Keith Schuyler, a pilot in the 44th Bomb Group, agonized over it many times: "It was an impersonal thing to fly above even the smoke of flaming homes and factories; above the explosions which would bruise a man's face purple from concussion alone; above the frantic cries and screams of women and children caught in this horrible thing known as modern war. I felt my part in this great sin. My part carried a weight on my conscience that was inconsistent with my feelings toward all people."

Jim Lynch, a radio operator in the 379th Bomb Group, wrote in his diary about his feelings and those of his crew: "I know that our entire crew despises every mission we fly. We are aware that we may be killing innocent civilians. We know it does happen. This makes it more difficult with each passing day to fly the next mission. Long after this war is over, we know we will have to live with our consciences. We may try to stuff awareness into our subconscious, but it will always be lurking there waiting for something to trigger it, such as the plaintive crying of a little child."

A tail gunner who had just returned from the infamous Dresden mission in early 1945 confided to his diary that he felt he had just participated in something terrible: "I hope God will forgive us for this unnecessary bombing of innocent civilians. Dresden was known worldwide as a very beautiful city." John White, a pilot in the 448th Bomb Group, told an interviewer that bombing women and children still bothered him long after the war had ended: "I have a kind of hard time accepting that that was the right thing to do. When we went to Hamburg, we bombed the city [rather than a military target]. We started firestorms in Hamburg. The fires must have been terrible. I have to live with that."

George McGovern, a pilot in the 455th Bomb Group who later became a U.S. senator and Democratic presidential candidate, wondered for many years what had happened to a hung bomb his crewmen kicked out over Austria. He saw the bomb land near a farmhouse and worried for many years that it had killed a family. In 1985, he told the story during an interview on Austrian television and soon afterward received a phone call: "An elderly Austrian farmer telephoned the TV station and said that the farmhouse I had described bombing was his. He saw the bomb coming and sought safety. No one was hurt, the man said. So after 40 years I was exonerated from the incident that had bothered me since World War II."

McGovern, though, was one of the lucky few who could be sure that he had not killed innocent civilians, at least on the mission he mentioned. Other men, like Eighth Air Force Pilot Ken Tichener, knew for a fact that civilians had died under their bombs. In March 1945, Tichener wrote to his parents and described the ugly side of the air war: "I'm plenty sick of this destruction and death. Not so long ago, we hit a target in the center of the prettiest little town you ever saw. Some of the bombs fell past and some were short. So with our own hands we wiped the people and buildings off the earth. The people happened to be German and committed the crime of living near a legitimate military target. I never want to see a sight like that again. I would much rather go thru [sic] all the flak and fighters the Germans have and bomb a bridge or warehouse, than to go over undisturbed and accidentally destroy the lives and dreams of the little guys."

Stray bombs and accidental deaths were one thing, but what about those missions actually designed to destroy entire cities and, in effect, civilians? With many of their cities in ruins, the British had little compunction about using these kinds of "terror bombing" methods. They reasoned that the Germans had pioneered the practice and would now reap their just desserts. American air commanders initially sought a more pinpoint type of air warfare. They hoped to spare civilians while they destroyed military targets, but this naturally proved to be quite difficult. As the war continued, American commanders began to order more terror bombings, and these missions were always unpopular with combat airmen. William Cubbins, a pilot in the 450th Bomb Group, recalled his reaction the first time he was briefed for such a mission: "I didn't like it. Heretofore I'd never thought of our raids as being against people. We bombed targets. I'd never liked the obvious side effect, but neither had I tried to fool myself. I'd accepted the certainty that civilians would be killed by our raids against military targets. But to bomb them intentionally—the idea was reprehensible. That was the sort of thing the Nazis did in Holland, at Coventry [England]; the list is long. But this wasn't a game we were playing. We could well die on this or the next mission. With that rationale reinforcing my will, I directed my thinking to mission details."

Occasionally during briefings for such missions, airmen voiced their objections. Dan James, a top turret gunner/engineer in the 100th Bomb Group, remembered this happening during a briefing for a terror bombing of Muenster, Germany: "I will never forget this briefing officer saying, 'After today you're going to be called women and children killers. We're going to bomb the workers' homes, Sunday afternoon at three o'clock. We're going to try to catch them taking a nap.' A little sergeant stood up and said, 'Sir, what about the little babies and children?' I'll never forget the briefing officer's words. He said, 'Goddamn the little babies and children. They're Germans too. Kill them!' Everybody was saying, 'No, no, we didn't come over here to fight that kind of war.' Our radio operator . . . to the very end said he wouldn't do it, but he finally did agree to it."

The last sentence of James's story is illustrative. The radioman strongly disagreed with the terror bombing but still ended up flying. Distasteful as the mission may have been, he could not bring himself to refuse to fly. Either his sense of duty to his buddies, or his fear of the consequences of refusing to go, motivated him to fly a mission of which he strongly disapproved.

Most airmen wrestled with the morality of destroying civilians but few, if any, refused to fly missions because of it. The attitude that one Twentieth Air Force combat airman articulated in a letter to his parents mirrored the sentiments of many of those who flew missions to Japan: "To be sure, we destroy cities, men, women, and children indiscriminately, but that isn't because we so desire it. If we could win the war without killing a single one of them, I'd be for it. But every Jap is in the war effort. Eight-year-old kids at school must make war weapons. It's a war between two different races, between two different religions, between two entirely different concepts of life. And I am all for any means that will hasten the day of victory or save one American life."

The same duality existed in the attitudes of those who flew against the Germans. Jack Novey, a waist gunner in the 96th Bomb Group, participated in one of the early Hamburg fire-bombing raids. Upon returning to base, he found himself deeply troubled by what had happened: "I silently thought of excuses. 'I'm not the one who dropped the bombs,' I said to myself. But I couldn't ignore the fact that I had helped fight our way to the target and back, so that excuse didn't work. I couldn't help picturing children down below. I told myself that they were fanatical young Nazis like the ones in the newsreels, tens of thousands of them, eyes shining, arms raised in salute to Hitler. But still, I thought, they were children. At that time I didn't know about the planned destruction of whole races of people . . . which was going on in concentration camps in Germany and Poland. I knew the Jews were being mistreated, that they had to wear yellow stars, that they were being locked up and beaten up, but I did not know of the genocide. If I had known, I probably would have volunteered . . . for whatever destructive mission I could go on against Germany."

For most American airmen, the bombing of civilians was a terrible fact of war, something that unfortunately went hand in hand with winning the war. Elmer Bendiner, a navigator in the 379th Bomb Group, pondered these issues in a memoir written years after the war: "Many of the men who . . . manipulated the primal elements of fire, earth, air, and water were mild and tender fellows. I knew them well; I was one of them. We were not unconcerned with the hell we left behind us. If, decades after the war, one looks back at Hamburg and Schweinfurt, a terrible equation threatens to rise from the ruins. Were we and our enemies really one and the same? My own answer is an emphatic No. The equation is false and a phantom. Hamburg and Schweinfurt may be equated with London and Liverpool, but none of these with Dachau. It is smug to say that their cause was damned and ours was blessed. Yet what other words will do to chop the truth to digestible size? We were not an ideological army. Actually, those who spouted political convictions of any sort were suspect. But neither were we altogether mechanical in our loyalties. Most of us would have preferred a surgical technique by which we could excise the vital organs of Nazi Germany without unnecessary bloodshed. We clung to the theory that this was possible and that we were trying to accomplish it. I cannot take seriously those who adopt the pose of the disenchanted without having experienced the prerequisite enchantment. World War II had less starry-eyed enchantment than most wars. We were not gulled by slogans. Hitler was real and his victory had to be prevented. For many of us that was the only point of the war."

For most American combat airmen, the moral quandary of killing enemy civilians came not out of disapproval or condemnation of the cause for which they fought but rather from hatred of the barbarism, destruction, and tragedy of modern total war. The evil of total warfare forced these men face-to-face with that which they had been raised to believe and trained to believe was morally wrong—the wanton destruction of civilians. Although they sometimes agonized over their own role in this historical tragedy, they nonetheless felt that—the negative judgment of a more cynical and sensitive postwar world notwithstanding—their ends ultimately justified their means.

8

Leadership in the Air

The commanders in the Air Corps, unlike the commanders in other services, led their men into combat. They did not remain safely ensconced behind their desks and order us to go. From Squadron Commander to Group Commander, to Wing Commander and to Division Commander, our senior officers flew combat missions. They didn't choose the easy missions by rank. They were all leaders.
—David McCarthy, navigator, 381st Bomb Group

Perhaps World War II combat airmen thought of their type of warfare as cleaner and more civilized because of one simple fact—in stark contrast to most other forms of modern warfare, senior commanders led their men into combat, thus harkening back to the days of medieval and ancient warfare, when kings and generals routinely fought beside their troops. Even as recently as the Civil War, generals shared the dangers of battle. In fact, they were 50 percent more likely to be killed in battle than privates. By World War I, all that had changed. The massive carnage of industrial warfare demanded that high-ranking officers remove themselves from the most dangerous areas of combat because modern war now inflicted such high casualties that senior commanders were considered too valuable to risk at the front. Thus was born the image of the chateau general pushing pins around maps, ordering thousands to their deaths while he sat in regal comfort. World War II American ground-combat commanders were not quite so aloof, but by necessity they rarely ventured into true danger. In the Navy, senior officers either remained safely at port or resided aboard the largest of the capital ships (usually aircraft carriers or battleships), which minimized their dangers—much the same way that a division or regimental headquarters located miles behind the lines minimized dangers for colonels and generals on the ground. If the admiral's capital ship was attacked or sunk, he could, and sometimes did, transfer his flag to a safer ship.

By contrast, the aerial branches of the Army, Navy, and Marines quite often sent their senior commanders into battle. For example, in the Army Air Force, it was not uncommon for division commanders—men with hundreds of planes, thousands of men, and dozens of bomb groups under their command—to lead missions to Germany. They risked the same hazards as everyone else, and perhaps even more, because the Germans learned to concentrate their attacks on lead ships. This practice of leading from the front also proliferated farther down the chain of command in the Army Air Force. It was almost unheard-of for group commanders, usually full colonels, not to fly at least one out of every three or four missions. The bravest and most effective often chose to fly on the most dangerous missions. Squadron commanders, usually majors or captains, flew all the time. This contrasted sharply with ground-combat units, whose field-grade officers rarely ventured to the front lines during intense combat.

Then too, at the most basic level, junior officers shared danger with enlisted men. On each bomber, for instance, four officers and six enlisted men on average made up the crew. The pilot, a lieutenant or captain, had overall command, with the copilot being second in command. With remarkable unanimity, bomber pilots accepted the mantle of leadership and the sense of responsibility to their crews. By the very nature of aerial combat, they had no other choice. They had to fly the plane to and from the target. Even if tempted to flee from their responsibilities, they had nowhere to go. Most would rather have died than have their crew think them cowards. Instead, they "led from the front" mission after mission, narrowing the gap between officer and enlisted ranks.

Further contributing to the relative closeness (at least compared to the rest of the military) between officers and enlisted men in the aerial branches of the service was their lack of a separatist tradition between the ruling officer class and its enlisted subordinates. As a newer service, aviation lacked deeply rooted traditions of separation and subservience. In addition, men were chosen for combat aviation on the basis of merit rather than soldierly discipline. Most of those who flew combat missions for the United States in World War II did so because they had proven they could skillfully perform the tasks necessary to succeed in aerial combat, not because they had been the most disciplined, by-the-book soldiers, sailors, or Marines.

Combat airmen, then, existed within their own unique meritocracy in which crewmen demonstrated loyalty and obedience to their combat officers, but rarely to anyone else outside of that sphere. Kevin Herbert, a B-29 tail gunner in the 498th Bomb Group, described how he and his fellow enlisted crewmen viewed authority: "The first loyalty of an aircrew was to the airplane commander, and when not in the air, that relationship continued. As a result, though the ground officers technically had authority over the aircrews in the Group areas, they tended to give the enlisted aircrewmen wide latitude of action in order to avoid confrontations. Rated pilots in the upper ranks were of course responsible for the combat operations of the Group, and here too the tactical [ground] officers had to defer at every turn."

Rare indeed was the enlisted combat aircrewman who possessed anything below the rank of sergeant (or the naval equivalent) himself. The aviation branches of the service rewarded their combat fliers with rank and a certain degree of autonomy in doing their specialized jobs. Thus, it is not surprising, in this relaxed atmosphere, that enlisted combat airmen would have high opinions of their officers. For example, a survey by Army researchers found that, when asked the question, "How well do you think your officers know their stuff?" only 15 percent of enlisted combat airmen answered negatively, compared with 44 percent of enlisted men in service units and 35 percent in ground-combat outfits. In the same survey, researchers also found that enlisted combat airmen felt that their officers knew the abilities of their men and utilized them accordingly. Only 16 percent said that their officers "know little or nothing about my abilities."

So most airmen had loyalty and admiration for their pilots as officers and as fliers. Jack Novey, a waist gunner in the 96th Bomb Group, revered his pilot: "He was superb at the controls of the plane. He could lead, or he could hang on to the element in front of him. He could fly a formation as tight as the Blue Angels'. In combat, if I asked him to drop down ten or fifteen feet to give me a better field of vision or line of fire, he would do it almost as soon as I spoke. I sincerely believe he was one of the main reasons our crew survived and finished its tour of duty. His skill, alertness, and cool head pulled us through many a tight situation."

Claude Basler, a radio operator in the 484th Bomb Group, had similar feelings about his pilot and aircraft commander. In Basler's view, his pilot was a fine leader because he "was most seriously aware and concerned about all the details and functions of the plane and each crew member. He was a task maker of the first water, firm, but not in an offensive manner, always able to win everyone's whole-hearted cooperation without any shape or form of resentment . . . and respected by all his crew." Another enlisted man, Radio Operator Merle Perkins of the 483d Bomb Group, reflected on his crew's pilot. Perkins thought that combat had shaped the pilot into a fine leader: "I don't know precisely what leadership is supposed to be, but I would call Link a good leader. From a shifting, argumentative type, he became a source of stability. He just did the job at hand and saw that we did ours. When I think of Link, I know patience, endurance, strength, competence, practicality."

Bomber pilots served as the leaders not only for the enlisted men but also for the three other officers on an average bomber crew. In some ways, this presented an even greater test of leadership. Even in the relaxed Air Corps, enlisted men were trained to obey the commands of officers in combat. But the copilot, navigator, and bombardier often possessed the same rank as the pilot. Copilots sometimes pined for their own planes. As qualified pilots, they wondered why they had not been made aircraft commanders. Bombardiers and navigators were often washed-out pilot trainees, and a few resented being under the command of someone who had demonstrated greater flying aptitude but not necessarily greater leadership ability. Robert Fesmire, a pilot who flew covert missions for the 492d Bomb Group, dealt with a resentful and rebellious navigator for much of his tour of duty. The man could never come to terms with the fact that Fesmire, as the pilot, was the leader of the crew. One time, during a mission to resupply a Dutch Resistance group, this insubordination exploded to the surface when flak peppered their plane. Fesmire and the navigator argued over how best to get to their drop zone: "Suddenly the frantic voice of Calhoun came over the intercom. 'Take a heading of 270 and let's get the hell out of here! The nose of the plane is hit!' 'We're almost to the target. I'll stay this course, then take 270 back,' I replied. Calhoun screamed back, 'I'm taking control of this plane, Fesmire! I order you to take 270 now!' 'Oh, shut up, Calhoun,' I growled back. 'We're almost to the target. When we get there, we'll make our drop. Then I'll take 270 home.' Two minutes later, we saw the signal lights. We made the drop and I turned the plane around to a perfect course for our return flight. After we returned home, Calhoun reluctantly admitted that my decisions had been correct during the mission. I was pleased that he had apologized for his actions, and I thanked him. He was an excellent navigator, and I thought he learned who was captain of the plane."

Far more often, though, the other officers on bomber crews recognized the pilot's authority and did everything they could to carry out his orders. Abe Wilen, a navigator in the 453d Bomb Group, had the highest opinion of his pilot. Time after time, he saw the man demonstrate leadership to his crew. In an account written decades after the war, Wilen shared his opinion of what made his pilot a good leader: "He listened to his crew's problems and tried to help with them. He was a perfectionist. Everything had to be just right on our plane—our lives depended on it. After missions or between missions, Dick was relaxed and he relaxed his crew. When we were on a bombing mission, he was all business. Everyone had to be alert and doing his job." Wilen's respect for his pilot also grew after he witnessed the man perform an act of selfless bravery when they were shot down and captured: "Our crew was united in a dungeon cell beneath an airfield. Our tail gunner was badly shot up and bleeding profusely. Dick knelt to help him. A German told Dick to move away, and . . . Dick did not move. The German went over and kicked Dick violently in the side of his head and sent him sprawling. Years later, Dick woke up one morning blind in that eye."

Roco Work, a navigator in the 95th Bomb Group, spoke for his entire crew when he praised the leadership of the crew's pilot, Eugene Fletcher: "He was admired and trusted by each of us. We knew he was loyal and would fight to protect our interests. The longer I live and the more people I observe, the more certain I become that Fletch was an exceptional leader; he is an extraordinary man!" Most bomber crewmen felt the same way about their pilots. It is very clear that the Army Air Force in World War II succeeded in producing a remarkable number of excellent leaders among its junior-officer pilots. These men, who often were well short of their twenty-first birthdays, took on the awesome responsibility of flying dangerous, overloaded aircraft to well-defended targets while at the same time they functioned as leaders for their fellow crewmen. They knew that the ultimate welfare of their crewmen, often their best friends, was in their hands. Under these adverse circumstances, they found copious reservoirs of maturity and performed up to the very highest standards of military leadership.

For their part, most fighter pilots were officers, but they nonetheless had element and flight leaders who performed tasks roughly equivalent to those of bomber pilots. These junior-officer leaders led small flights of anywhere from two to a dozen aircraft. Although they usually achieved their leadership roles by combat experience, they still sometimes made mistakes. J. Fred Baumann, a fighter pilot in the 52d Fighter Group, became quite angry at his flight leader one day when the man blundered in his navigation and took his flight right over Venice (Italy) Harbor, a notorious flak concentration. They took evasive action and, almost miraculously, no one was killed. When they returned to base, Baumann and the other pilots gave the flight leader an earful of recrimination: "He was only a first lieutenant, but I do believe that if he had been a general, it wouldn't have made any difference, because the other two pilots and I were steaming. We called him every name in the American vernacular, plus a few choice ones borrowed from our British allies. In plain language we told him, 'You had your damn head stuck straight up your ass!' All he did was to stand there and take it. I do believe that if he had responded defensively, one of us might have decked him. He had been the flight leader, and it was his personal responsibility to avoid such stupid mistakes."

Most flight leaders, though, performed much better than Baumann's leader. As experienced fighter pilots, they usually knew what they were doing. Charles Nickell, a fighter pilot in the 348th Fighter Group, became a flight leader in early 1945 and relished the responsibility. He wrote to his family about it: "I am a flight leader now. Have 10 men in my flight. They are all nice guys and are really good pilots. It makes me feel good to have a responsible job for a change." By all accounts, Nickell proved to be an excellent flight leader. A few months after Nickell was killed in action, one of his men even wrote to Nickell's family about their late son's leadership abilities: "He was a wonderful pilot and personally one of the finest fellows I ever knew. He was the kind of fellow a guy would follow anywhere and have complete confidence in him to bring you back safely. He was my flight leader."

Robert Goebel became a flight leader and ace during his tour of duty in the 31st Fighter Group. As he explained, a flight leader had more to worry about than simply leading other fighters on combat missions: "We decided who was to go and what position each was to fly. When we were satisfied with the lineup, we took it over to the squadron CO for his approval and then posted it on the board in the quarters that evening. I found scheduling a trying task. We tried to give everyone a fair chance, balancing the need for putting up the best pilots in the key slots against letting some of the newer pilots get lead experience."

The squadron commander had even more responsibility in American aviation. Roughly equivalent to a ground-combat battalion commander, the squadron commanding officer oversaw dozens of pilots in a fighter group and hundreds of crewmen in a bomb group. Plus, he flew missions alongside his men. In bomb groups, squadron commanders mostly achieved their rank on the basis of experience and combat know-how. This meant that most bomber crewmen trusted and respected their squadron commanders, although there were exceptions. Edward Harris, a radio operator in the 43d Bomb Group, found that when his crew's pilot was promoted to squadron commander, his leadership left much to be desired: "He thought that since we were in a civilized area, it was time we tightened up on discipline and abandoned our sloppy ways. I think this was a mistake. We had always worked very efficiently with everyone doing his job. Brownfield decreed that the enlisted men should fall out at six o'clock every morning for roll call and the assignment for the day's duties. We resented this. In order to get to the place where roll was called, we had to pass through the area where the officers had their tents. We always made as much noise as possible, since the officers did not have to get up."

Most squadron commanders, though, had little enthusiasm for such military rituals. Stiff discipline was reserved for missions, not for ground duty. Squadron commanders cared about producing a smoothly functioning team in the air, one that could take off, get into formation, fly to the target, drop its bombs, and get home with minimal casualties. With that achieved, most commanders cared little about what crewmen did during their down time.

The typical bomber-squadron commander held the respect of his men through his words and his actions. Like any effective air leader, good squadron commanders rarely shied away from rough missions. Chaplain James Good Brown of the 381st Bomb Group knew many such men during his two and a half years with that outfit, but, in his diary, he recorded a detailed description of one whom he knew particularly well: "He always has the interest of the men at heart. He works for them, and they know this. I have heard him go to bat for them before the group commander [a typical bomb group had three or four squadrons]. Here is a squadron leader who can stand up against any commanding officer and not wilt. This is because he is big in character. He is honest. If he can do a thing, he will do it; but if he cannot, he says in bold language that he cannot do it, and there is no mincing of words. He is one leader of whom we say, 'We cannot do without him.' I have seen him lead his men in the air time after time. How fortunate that the 381st has men like this!"

Squadron commanders in fighter groups played to more mixed reviews. Some were career military men who achieved their positions not through experience or acumen as fighter pilots but rather through connections. These types usually did not fare well within the ruthless meritocracy of a fighter group in combat. Fighter pilots evaluated their leaders on the basis of their aggressiveness, flying abilities, and understanding of fighter tactics. Unfortunately, some did not perform well. During his tour of duty, Robert Goebel had several squadron commanders, some better than others. One had difficulty picking up enemy aircraft on the horizon. Fighter pilots routinely strained their eyes for a glimpse of the tiny dots on the horizon that often turned out to be enemy fighters. Another CO had plenty of flight time in fighters but no combat experience, and it almost led to tragedy during one mission: "He had the notion that he was above serving a combat apprenticeship but could step right into the thick of it. The result was a disaster. Before anyone knew what the novice was doing . . . he called for his flight to jettison [extra fuel] tanks. He went barreling after a [British] Mosquito, thinking it was an Me-210, which it vaguely resembled. The 'Mossy' fired the colors of the day, a recognition signal consisting of three closely spaced colored flares. 'Watch out, he's firing rockets!' the tyro warned as he made a firing pass. When he got close in . . . he must have seen the RAF roundels, because he quietly re-formed the flight and went home. I heard later that a British squadron leader came by the bivouac area that evening and asked to meet the chap who had fired on him. When he was introduced to the embarrassed senior officer, he said with the reserve so typically British, 'I say, your line of flight was all right but your deflection was a bit off.'"

Goebel hastened to add that both new squadron leaders ended up improving dramatically with experience. Without doubt, the Army Air Force, in order to avoid such problems, should have made sure that only experienced fighter pilots became squadron COs.

Harold Rosser, a fighter pilot in the 33d Fighter Group, served under a squadron leader who did not improve with experience. Like one of Goebel's erstwhile leaders, this man had a great body of experience in fighters but none in combat, and that led to problems. Rosser clashed with him repeatedly. One day during a briefing, the CO announced that, on that afternoon's mission, they would strafe an enemy target out of the sun rather than into it. Strafing into the sun had proven highly effective for the group in the past, but it did not conform to regulations. Rosser felt that the CO's order "was a senseless concoction, and it smacked of textbook philosophy. It was dangerous. Restlessness betrayed me. I said, 'Major,

I suggest we follow the plans that were so successful before. You can't knock success, Sir.' 'Let's do it my way for a change,' he replied, smiling tolerantly, but his voice icy; his eyes . . . cold." Rosser then suggested they make only one pass on the target, since it was considered suicidal to attempt any more than that. As it turned out, the major ordered numerous passes on the target, losing a pilot and incurring Rosser's increased wrath in the process. As time went on, the major did not even attempt to listen to Rosser and other experienced pilots: "He clung stubbornly to his stateside tactics, not speaking of them, but demonstrating them with his every flight. We dreaded to fly with him. We . . . didn't like the feeling of make-believe flying. We were combat pilots, not actors, and we felt safer doing it our way." Relations worsened to the point where Rosser wrote a scathing indictment of the CO and posted it on the bulletin board for all to see: "ATTENTION: The outfit has gone to the dogs, but don't despair. All we have to do is forget about the enemy and fly nice stateside formations to impress the superiors of our superior. If we do well enough, we will earn for him the promotion he has been bucking for. That is our first duty. If we are still alive after that, we can settle down and fight the Japs."

When the major saw the note, he exploded. After trying to get Rosser transferred to a transport unit and being refused, he arranged for Rosser to be sent home. Before Rosser left, he saw his squadron commander one more time. The man said he was sorry for their differences but that he could not afford to become emotionally involved in whether his pilots lived or died. To him they were just numbers to be erased when they were killed. In the next breath, he asked Rosser to get in touch with his family when he returned to America. Rosser clearly remembered his reply: "'Why don't you send 'em your number, Sir. They'll know by that that you haven't been erased. I won't be writing letters when I get home. Neither will I be making any phone calls.' I gave an exaggerated salute, wheeled, and left the tent."

Luckily, most fighter-squadron commanders performed much better than Rosser's. In fact, many did excellent jobs, especially those who earned their rank through experience and combat success. Such was the case for Fighter Pilot John Bernstein's squadron commander. Bernstein's 343d Fighter Group flew missions against the Japanese from a base on the Aleutian Islands in Alaska. Bernstein extolled the virtues of his commander in a letter home: "He has a lot of experience that is just now paying off, but nevertheless his advancement is rapid. He is full of life, the best flier in this group or probably any group, and can sweep the floors like one who has known how to work."

The Marine fighter pilots who flew with Squadron 212 on Guadalcanal had the highest respect for their squadron commander. Pop Flaherty thought the CO demonstrated good leadership by taking him up to show him effective combat tactics: "He showed me just what position to get in when you fight a superior plane: behind, below, and always turning so that when he's shooting at you, you're shooting at him. And always be aggressive; never hang back." Another fighter pilot held the CO in such high esteem that he could not bear the thought of disappointing him, as he did one day when he broke off an engagement: "He was so mad that he was boiling. He walked to his tent . . . and threw one sentence over his shoulder, 'If you boys don't want to fight, I'm going to start weeding you out and sending you home.' If other men had talked like that, it would have made you sour. But from the colonel it was talk that made us feel pretty rotten. His opinion meant more to me than any medal the president could pin on me." The opinion of the colonel meant so much to the pilot because he respected the colonel's leadership. If not, he would not have cared what the colonel thought. Such was the essence of good leadership. Whether by instructing or shaming his men, the colonel knew how to motivate them.

Navy Fighter Pilot Charles Moutenot's squadron leader also constantly strove to motivate his men by taking them up for one-on-one instruction in their flying techniques. Moutenot found that he had enormous respect for the man: "I don't think there was a better skipper in the whole fleet at the time. He was an Annapolis graduate, but he had such a way about him that everybody just loved the guy. He checked everyone out that way. I thought it was great. It gave you a little added confidence in your flying, and you also felt closer to the Old Man. That's the way it always was in the Navy. Proficiency. They were always striving to be better. If you reached a certain level, that wasn't good enough. You had to go up to the next step. Your flying was always getting better and better."

David Kipp, a fighter pilot in Air Group 6 aboard the carrier USS *Hancock*, never forgot his squadron commander's courage and calm demeanor in getting the unit home one day while it was lost and low on gas in the middle of a storm: "Our skipper came over the radio, clear, calm, and with all the reassurance of a father to his sons and said, 'This is what we will do, I have the carrier on my radar screen, they are into the wind and ready to take us aboard. I want all of you to get behind me in single file. I will let down through the storm and as I approach the ship, I want the last plane in the string to land. I will see the last plane clears the water by 100 ft. and we will make eight passes at the carrier.' He was so calm and sure of himself that we almost believed him. We started down in the driving rain and lightning, all each of us could see was the trail of lights of the plane above us. Down, down we went and finally he said for the lowest plane to leave us and land, which he did. I landed aboard safely and parked my plane. That one man saved all eight of us that terrible day. None of us will ever forget him."

Higher up the chain of command were the group commanders, who also flew missions in spite of their lofty position. A group commander in the Army Air Force was roughly equivalent to a regimental commander in the ground forces. Most group commanders did a fine job, but some had to learn on the job and others simply did not have what it took to lead men in combat. The Army usually slated career officers for group commands, and this guaranteed that some would be inexperienced or poor pilots with little or no acumen in combat tactics. DeWayne Bennett, a pilot in the 384th Bomb Group, had a low opinion of his senior commanders, including Col. Dale Smith, his group commander, and Gen. Robert Travis, his wing commander. Travis and Smith led their wing (several groups) on a mission to Germany in the spring of 1944. Bennett understood all too well the deep responsibilities of command, because they weighed heavily on him as plane commander. Even so, he maintained that the inability of Travis and Smith to keep the bomber stream in an effective formation throughout the mission had led to terrible casualties and had stemmed from poor leadership qualities: "You would think that General Robert Travis would have realized that the 41st B Combat [Wing] was in trouble on left turns. He had observers in his plane telling him that: 41 B was out of position, and they must be taking heavy losses. The Combat Wings behind us did not maintain the echelon position but pulled into the bomber stream. Colonel Dale O. Smith could have pulled us into the bomber stream. At one time he straggled so far he was behind the 40th Combat Wing, which was six miles behind the 41st 'A' Combat Wing. These two intrepid leaders led a charge like 'The Charge of the Light Brigade.'"

In fairness to the reputations of Smith and Travis, they did make mistakes but eventually became effective combat leaders. Harry Crosby, a navigator in the troubled 100th Bomb Group, saw both good and bad group commanders during his long combat tenure. According to Crosby, one careerist CO lasted just one week. The man apparently had far more bravado than sense: "Although he had never flown a mission before, on the first mission after he arrived, he put himself in the lead ship, right seat. Air Force macho. I began to wonder whether West Point taught its cadets the difference between bravery and bravado. Between courage and brashness. When the group got to the target . . . they were so far off that the bombardier had to hold his bombs. The 100th floated over the target with their bomb-bay doors open. No bombs dropped. With incommendable brashness and derring-do, the inexperienced colonel decided to go around again and make another pass at the target, same altitude, same speed, same direction, same wind deflection. Down below, ack-ack corrected their settings—and blew the 100th out of the air. The lead plane went down, taking with it a splendid crew [and the colonel]."

Luckily for the 100th, the next commander proved to be much better. He whipped into shape what had been a loose unit with a penchant for abortions, accidents, and terrible casualties. The new CO ordered inspections and base cleanups and even closed down the bar. Then he relentlessly drilled his men in formation tactics until they got it right. Many years later, Crosby still felt gratitude toward the commander for turning the group around: "The 100th stopped losing more planes than other groups. Our bombing got

better. Our gunners reported more kills. We felt better about ourselves. I doubt that any one of us ever thanked John Bennett
enough for what he did. For our successes. For the lives he saved."

Philip Ardery, a bomber pilot in the 389th Bomb Group and a
squadron commander, held in the highest esteem his two immediate superiors, the group and wing commanders, because they maintained positive, upbeat attitudes throughout their entire time in
combat: "They were the only two officers whom I knew well over a
period of time who never showed the slightest evidence of low
morale. I consider such forbearance to be one of the greatest assets
a commander can have. His command will love him if he can carry
the gripes of all those under him with never a complaint of his own.
Under the pressure of the continued strain of war . . . an officer's
mettle can be sorely tested."

One quality of good leadership found in abundance in World
War II American aviation was the courage to lead from the front.
Airmen could criticize their commanders over a litany of petty
gripes, but they could rarely ever say that senior officers did not expose themselves to the same dangers as their subordinates. This
gave them credibility among their airmen and promoted good
morale and teamwork. Many fliers saw their senior commanders
leading tough missions and reasoned, "If he can do it, I can do it
too." For instance, Jack Novey vividly recalled the prevailing sense
of dread and cold fear among the combat crews when they found
out they were bound for Schweinfurt in October 1943. He and his
buddies knew just how badly the Eighth Air Force had been crippled on the first raid to hit the vital ball-bearing target two months
before, and they knew the upcoming raid would be rough. At briefing, an officer read them a foolish and insensitive message from Air
Force Chief of Staff Hap Arnold: "'You who are about to die today
will not have died in vain.' I thought that was a hell of a stupid message, and I'm sure I wasn't the only one who thought so." Novey and
his comrades could not have helped but wonder how much purpose Arnold would have felt his own death to have had if he had
been risking his own life over Schweinfurt that day instead of sitting
safe and sound back in Washington. By contrast, Novey noticed that
his wing commander, Col. Archie Old, had scheduled himself to

lead what could well be the most dangerous mission the group had ever attempted: "As I waited in the drizzle, I didn't talk to anybody. I didn't even look at anybody. I was just trying to cope with my own private terror. Then a jeep drove up, and Colonel Old got out. He came over, looked us all in the eye, and talked to us for a moment, wishing us Godspeed and good luck. I thought to myself, 'He's got guts. He's the commanding officer of the Bomb Wing, and he didn't have to fly, but he chose to lead this one.'"

Fighter pilots also admired commanders who led by example and understood the intricacies of combat. John Marshall was a fighter pilot in the 404th Fighter Group, which was part of the Ninth Air Force, a command roughly equivalent to an army regiment in the ground forces. Marshall gave Ninth Air Force Gen. Pete Quesada high marks in command abilities because he flew missions himself and because he seemed to understand the world of fighter pilots. Marshall wrote that Quesada had "delighted us in the way we have been handled. If the luck seems to hit our Group a bit off color, they change the assignments . . . which is only fair." One time, he even met the general: "Gen. Quesoda [sic] was in this afternoon and we kids with gold leaves [rank of major and up] got with him for a good chat. He is a remarkable person. He knows the game and our problems. He laid himself wide open to everything we had on our minds and that is what he came for. He likes you to argue with him if you feel like it. He has a darn fine outfit and we are all 100% behind him. Looks as though he could handle his fists too."

One fighter-group commander who proved to be phenomenally successful was Hub Zemke, who commanded both the 56th and the 479th Fighter Groups. His 56th became the highest-scoring fighter outfit in the European theater and featured such aces as Francis Gabreski and Robert Johnson. Like many fighter pilots, Johnson could be a bit on the wild side, but Zemke knew exactly how to handle him. Years after the war, Johnson attested to Zemke's leadership skills: "I had broken the rules on several occasions and received sharp reprimands from him. He probably thought I was trouble. He had a mission to perform and was quite serious about it. Very stern but also fair. He was not an easy man to get to know. He didn't socialise [sic] much at the Officer's Club and had little contact with the Lieutenants outside working hours. But somehow I got the impression there was a guy just like us imprisoned inside that disciplinarian. Despite my misdemeanors, I learned that our Colonel could and would turn a blind eye to doubtful activities if he thought they were of benefit to our combat mission."

Robin Olds became a leading ace in the 479th after Zemke took command. In his opinion, the efficiency and aggressiveness of the unit changed for the better almost immediately after Zemke's arrival: "You could feel things changing; a presence, a leader. Soon after he arrived, I shot down my first two FW-190s. I really thought I was going to get a royal ass chewing for barging off on my own; but I sense Colonel Zemke knew why I did it, was tolerant of my frustration, inwardly amused at my attempt to hide my elation, and pleased that the two victories were confirmed, all the while looking at me with wise steely eyes that made me inwardly squirm and vow to myself not to push this man. Hub was respected at high command too, and as a consequence, we were accorded better positions on the daily missions. Our admiration for the man kept soaring, as did our morale. He challenged us to do better, to study (literally), and gave us the rope we needed to put it into practice. We tried our best to live up to what he expected of us and earn his respect, which was the reward we sought."

Aerial combat leaders often employed another advantage in exercising leadership. They got to know their men. In ground-combat units, enlisted men did well to know their company commander on a personal basis. In combat air groups, officers constantly interacted with enlisted men. This, coupled with the fact that aviation had no long-standing traditions of separation and subservience of enlisted men, meant that officers and enlisted men sometimes enjoyed very informal, even close relationships. This was especially true among bomber crews, where boundary lines between officer and enlisted could sometimes be next to invisible. Ben Smith, a radio operator in the 303d Bomb Group in England, remembered that in his unit "There was almost no distinction between officers and noncoms. The lowest grade on a crew was staff sergeant. The officers and men went on pass together and chummed with each other. There was not much saluting or military formality." The same low-key atmosphere existed in Pilot James "Pete" Campbell's 380th Bomb Group in the Pacific: "We never had personal or quarters inspection except by medical personnel. We wore what we considered comfortable and were not rank conscious at all. My crew members called me 'Pete' or 'Skipper,' and we didn't . . . require bowing, scraping, and saluting everything that moved like some of the services." Clair Alexander, a pilot in the 461st Bomb Group in Italy, knew that he was the leader of his crew but also hastened to add that this brand of leadership was more informal and democratic than the rest of the military: "Leading a bomber crew was an entirely different task from that of other military officers. The four officers and six enlisted men became a unit whose relationship was quite informal. This was typified by the fact that we called each other by our first names. I was known as 'Alex' by all of the crew." Alexander felt that this relaxed and friendly relationship between officers and enlisted men could exist because every crew member was a volunteer and had been chosen for his job on the basis of merit rather than soldierly discipline. Alexander's ball turret gunner, Donald Askerman, also attested to the informality among the crew. One of the officers spent more time in the enlisted men's quarters than in his own tent. He told Askerman that officers' country was boring. There was more activity with the enlisted men. One day, a fellow enlisted crew member even played a joke on the officer, a man named Chuck. Chuck had spent months cultivating a mustache and wanted it to have the proper Air Corps flourish. The enlisted crew member, Bill, agreed to give him a "trim": "As he worked, he gave Chuck the impression that he was really giving him a top-notch job. What Bill managed to do was shave off all the mustache on one side. After working so hard for over a month, Chuck only had half a mustache. He was anxious to look at his new trim and called for a mirror as Bill edged toward the door. Chuck let out a yelp and started hollering. 'I'll have you court-martialed, I'll have your stripes . . . ,' and on and on until he ran down. Meanwhile, the rest of us were laughing so hard we were weak. Finally Chuck saw the humor of it, too, and joined in."

John Crowe, a copilot in the 491st Bomb Group, also hung around with the enlisted men in his crew. He became especially close friends with the radio operator. They shared mutual interests and enjoyed hunting and drinking together: "The matter of rank, sergeant and lieutenant, never even occurred to either of us as an obstacle to a close friendship."

Jack Novey addressed his pilot as "Sir" only because he was senior in age and the boss of his crew. He addressed the other crew officers by their first names and observed no military formalities. Like most enlisted combat airmen, he endured very little of the petty harassment (usually called "chickenshit") that officers sometimes dealt out to enlisted soldiers in the Army. Among combat fliers, such things simply did not happen.

Sometimes, though, ground officers attempted to burst the egalitarian bubble in which combat fliers operated. Novey recalled being awakened and briefed for a mission one morning only to see it scrubbed. He and the rest of the crew went back to bed. A few hours later, they received a rude awakening: "The door opened and somebody yelled, 'Atten-shun!' We looked up out of the bed and saw a full colonel at the door with a major and two MPs. In our groggy state, none of us moved. Then the colonel said to the MPs, 'I want these men lined up and placed under arrest.' He was screaming at the top of his lungs. We found out that he was from the Inspector General's office. We had never had any kind of an inspection while we were in combat. It was something that just didn't happen. Our purpose was to fly, fight, and die. Who was this silly ass anyway? Didn't he know we were risking our lives every day?"

Colonel Old soon arrived on the scene and put the inspector in his place, explaining that Novey and his buddies were combat crewmen and could not be treated in such a manner. In no uncertain terms, Old told the inspector to leave and forget about his inspection and his arrests, music to the ears of Novey and his pals: "This amusing incident . . . was, for us, high comic relief. Of course the service is full of self-important jerks. But after facing Me-109s, we were in no mood for boot-camp B.S. on the part of some creep colonel." Jim Lynch, a radio operator in the 379th Bomb Group, was stuck with supervising a make-work cleanup detail during a group stand-down, very unusual for combat fliers. Naturally, Lynch was not pleased, and he expressed his displeasure by finding a shaded area and lounging around with his detail instead of doing the work. The sergeant of the guard caught him and informed his supervising officer, who flew into a rage: "Me, being a flyer [sic], was just what he needed to take out his jealousy and frustrations. The nit-picking 'shave-tail' said I should be grounded (a punishment?). I was told to report that evening to my commanding officer for proper disposition of my case. In the meantime, Russ [his pilot] heard about the incident and damned near died laughing about the whole asinine affair. He let me sweat a little and then went to the CO. They both had a good laugh. The CO . . . told him that I never should have been on the detail to start with and to forget it."

Bomber crewmen truly lived in a different world from the rest of the military. Their unique skills and combat status afforded them insulation from the usual officer-enlisted relations and the disciplinary world of the rest of the service.

Fighter groups tended to be somewhat similar, although they featured a unique situation in which officers braved almost all of the dangers. In fighter groups, most pilots were officers, while their ground crewmen were enlisted men. Since pilots were the only ones who faced aerial combat, this meant that a fighter unit's officers constituted its combat force, almost a complete reversal of the typical setup in every other branch of the military. In fighter units, relations between officers and enlisted men were usually good, but the fact that they did not share a combat bond meant that the two sides could only become so close. Unlike bomber crews, officers and enlisted men in fighter outfits tended to live separate lives. Robert Goebel knew an enlisted mechanic from his hometown, and he cultivated a friendship of sorts, but the two could not become very close in the context of their situation: "Certain lines between officers and enlisted men were never crossed. We ate and slept separately. Only in the line of duty was there personal contact. Petersen was from Racine. He received occasional copies of the hometown newspaper, which he offered to lend me. I stopped over at his tent sometimes (never the other way around), and we developed a friendly—albeit correct—relationship. I liked Pete and I enjoyed talking to him about common acquaintances and interests back in Wisconsin, but I realized that my presence was an imposition on his tent mates, who must have been uncomfortable while I was there. I never stayed long."

In some Marine aviation outfits, the schism between officer and enlisted could be quite pronounced. Samuel Hynes, a torpedo bomber pilot in Squadron 232, had almost no relationship with the enlisted men on his base, even his own gunners. In fact, he had almost no memory of either of his enlisted gunners, even though they flew with him on nearly all of his missions: "They rose with me on every flight, but they were back there in the guts of the plane, two people I was responsible for but didn't really need, or not very often. Flying in the same plane with them was not at all the bond that flying beside other pilots was. The pilots were my friends, but the crew was just a responsibility, like relatives or debts. On the ground we separated at once, to our segregated quarters, two areas that were as remote and isolated from each other as two countries that have cut off diplomatic relations. I never saw where my crew lived, and they never came to my tent. We never ate a single meal together. We never discussed any human problem."

Hynes's distant and vaguely contemptuous relations with his enlisted crewmen of course contrasted greatly from the intimate friendships shared between officers and enlisted men on Army Air Force bomber crews. Kevin Herbert's crew even voted on important decisions in the air, something quite common among bomber crews: "In the air the commander often permitted discussion of problems and we talked to each other as equals." The pilot, of course, had the final say in any decision, but, like Herbert's, many chose to temper that power by affording each crew member equal say in important decisions.

Even so, rank had its privileges, especially away from the combat zone. Officers and enlisted men on bomber crews may have treated each other as equals on missions, but the military world outside of aerial combat operated under different rules. Herbert remembered an instance when he and some of his crew members visited their colonel's tent to pick up some documents: "There in the center of the room stood an Army nurse hanging up some freshly laundered bras and panties on a rack. She seemed not to be embarrassed in the slightest at our entry and she continued about her domestic chores while we gathered up what we were sent for. Another colonel turned a former Japanese blockhouse into a shelter for his amours, and what had once been a center of war now saw campaigns of another kind."

As a field-grade officer, Harry Crosby enjoyed a much richer social life in London than his enlisted friends: "I had gone from a second lieutenant to major in eleven months, a phenomenon rare if not impossible in the infantry, navy, or the British [armed forces]. In London, officers had advantages over enlisted men. The USO and Red Cross, as democratic and equalitarian as they admirably tried to be, had to hand out invitations to English parties, some of which were open only to officers. Now that I was 'field grade' I got . . . interesting invitations. In London there were clubs for British, American, and other Allied field grade officers."

Even back at the base, combat officers performed some of the supervisory duties associated with their rank. For example, the military had a policy that all enlisted letters had to be censored for any potentially useful military information before they could be sent on to wherever they were going. The task of censoring letters fell to officers, whose letters were not, in turn, censored. Donald Askerman, like many enlisted fliers, somewhat resented this intrusion of privacy. He also did not like the implication that enlisted men could not keep their mouths shut while officers, who usually knew far more sensitive information, had no restrictions on their letters: "This . . . did not go over very well with any of us at all. So, we started forging our officers' names on the outside of our envelopes signifying that they had read the contents and they were OK."

Most of the time, though, enlisted men could not get away with such schemes for long. The vast majority had to submit their letters to their officers for censoring, a job most officers despised as boring, invasive, and tedious. R. H. Tays, a pilot in the 392d Bomb Group, dreaded censoring his men's letters: "What a miserable duty befell my lot to censor my crew letters. I always felt it was none of my business what they wrote to their . . . loved ones. My scissors was active and cruel. They soon learned what was acceptable and what was not." Other officers, such as Robert Goebel, were far less strict. He outlined the main guidelines he followed: "Taboo were the exact location of the unit, details of the aircraft's performance capabilities, and mission details. Lest any amateur censors sign and seal the envelope without carefully scrutinizing the letter, we were assured that all censored outgoing mail was rechecked on a spot basis. If any forbidden information was found, the squadron censor and the writer would be court-martialed. Although this sounded a little farfetched, the threat was sufficient incentive for thoroughness."

In the course of his censoring duties, Harry Crosby came across a curious mixture of dull and spicy letters, probably typical of most units: "Some enlisted men wrote interesting letters, keeping their wives, sweethearts, chums, parents informed at least of their morale and yearnings. Some writers were hopelessly inarticulate, resorting to every cliché and banality. Every drama of wartime played itself out before us. Worried husbands awaited news from pregnant wives. Back home, fathers became ill and died, and I read their sons' halting attempts to console their mothers. At first, our soldiers wrote to their chums about their conquests of females in London and Norwich. A few months later, we began to read love letters, often in almost the same wording, written by the same man to two women, usually one on the Home Front and another in England. Later, when married men began to succumb to their urges, we read letters written by one man to his wife and, with the same fervor and maybe the same words, to a girlfriend in London."

Samuel Hynes, raised in a middle-class home in which the topic of sex was taboo, never felt comfortable gazing at the love letters enlisted men wrote: "Sometimes their amorous feelings for their wives and sweethearts were expressed with a forthrightness that seemed pornographic to middle-class young men like us. We'd be sitting in our tent, each with a pile of letters to be censored, and someone would begin to laugh, 'Hey, listen to this guy,' and he'd read out some mechanic's fancy, addressed to his wife, of what he'd do to and with her when he got home. It was funny, and it was astonishing, that there were marriages in the world in which a man said *cunt* to his wife, and in which sexual relations were apparently conducted with such violent and inventive enthusiasm."

Censoring letters was just one example of the myriad aspects of leadership young officer/aviators accepted during World War II.

Combat leadership presented numerous challenges to officers, and most proved worthy of meeting these challenges. John White, a pilot in the 448th Bomb Group, shared the sentiments of many other first pilots in that he worried more about letting down his crewmen than about dying, a trait present in most good aerial leaders: "I didn't want to make any mistake flying that airplane that would get the guys in my crew killed. I worried more about them. They were young fellows. The gunners were all like nineteen or twenty years old. I worried that something would happen that I . . . maybe wasn't good enough to handle that would get all the guys killed. I don't think I worried as much about dying as much as I worried about getting them killed."

Robert Ramer, a B-29 pilot in the Twentieth Air Force, had similar concerns, but, like most, he learned how to become an effective leader in spite of his youth. He remembered meeting the mother of his tail gunner before his crew went overseas: "Here was this woman telling me to take care of her son and I'm twenty years old. On top of that, he was older than me. What a blow it must have been for her to see me. She must have gone home and gotten sick." Luckily for Ramer, wisdom, character, and experience counted far more than age in combat. He got his crew home from the war safely and learned many valuable lessons of leadership that helped him both in combat and later in life: "Another officer . . . gave me some advice that's stayed with me my whole life. You give the order to the copilot and let him execute it. Let him do the yelling and cursing. I've remembered that . . . and it has come up any number of times in business. I learned a lot in the Air Force about being in command and being an executive. The pilot was an executive in a way."

Ray Hann made friends with his crewmen, but he never hesitated to lower the boom on them when he felt it was necessary. On the way back from Cologne one day, he ordered them to clean up the interior of the plane. He later wrote in his diary about what happened: "When we landed I went through the plane and they hadn't cleaned anything. I ordered them back to the plane after we had eaten and made them wash the entire ship with gasoline and old rags. I had a meeting in the hut later and made it clear that when we're on the ground I am one of the boys, but in the plane I would tolerate no fun and games. Our lives could hinge on a missed order by any one of the crew."

Joe Boyd, a fighter pilot in the Twelfth Air Force, found himself in the unique and unwelcome situation of having the responsibility of leadership but without the privileges and prestige of rank. For much of his combat tenure, he was a so-called flight officer, a shadowy rank above most enlisted men but below all commissioned officers. In spite of his vast combat experience, it took him a long time to be commissioned. In the meantime, he led flights full of higher-ranking pilots: "Probably the last thirty missions I flew I was leading the squadron and sometimes the group and sometimes the wing. They'd call me over and say, 'Now, Boyd, this is Major So-and-So. He's on a very important assignment today. He's going to be flying your wing. You be sure nothing happens to him.' As if I didn't have enough things to do. Two weeks later, when the decorations would come through here, the guy would get a Distinguished Flying Cross. When I see a general on television with eight rows of ribbons, I know how he got them. Every combat man knows the same thing."

Being responsible for other men was the centerpiece of leadership, and it could be difficult and frustrating. William Cubbins, a pilot in the 450th Bomb Group, held himself accountable for the death of one of his men. Limping home from a tough mission one day, Cubbins's plane was in such poor shape that he had no other choice but to order the crew to bail out over Vis, a tiny island off the coast of Yugoslavia under the control of friendly partisans and a skeleton British detachment. Vis offered shelter, food, and even a small airstrip from which downed Allied fliers could be evacuated and returned to their units. As the crew bailed out, one of the men, who had been deathly afraid of jumping out of the plane, opened his chute too soon, drifted out to sea, and drowned: "I should have been more attentive to him, made certain during our months of training that he had no unreasonable fear of jumping, that he knew the proper procedures. Anger gave way to sorrow, then to a numbness that went beyond sorrow. I felt frustrated, defeated. An easy jump had turned into a tragedy. I rationalized every aspect of the bailout. My only acceptable conclusion was that I had somehow failed him."

Cubbins's self-criticism notwithstanding, at a certain point a good leader had to know when to let go and allow his men to do their jobs. He had to know when to articulate and when to delegate. This fact hit home to Eugene Fletcher during a difficult mission in which the crew had to pull together quickly to survive serious flak damage and make it home. Fletcher was amazed at how well his crew performed without any orders or prompting from him: "I was isolated—they could survive and continue without me. This is a terrible blow to one's ego, but it gave me a feeling of pride that these men knew their jobs and could perform them under any circumstances, with or without me." What Fletcher either did not realize or did not care to mention is that his crew most likely could not have performed so well if it were not for his first-rate leadership in training and preparing them for battle—not to mention his role in flying home a crippled bomber.

The best leaders in the air knew that successful combat leadership nearly always meant leading by example. Francis Gabreski, a 56th Fighter Group ace who achieved legendary status as a squadron leader, explained his simple but effective philosophy: "Basically . . . you can't lead from the rear. You've got to get up front and have your team follow you. Those people behind you must have respect for your abilities, and you can't impose that on them. They have to see for themselves how good you really are, and when they find that out, they'll follow you no end." Bomber Pilot Philip Ardery also made a practice of leading from the front during his days as a squadron leader. Along with flying most of the tougher missions, he made sure to appear loose and calm in the tense moments before a mission began. Ardery knew all too well that men often noticed the moods of their leaders. If they saw that those in command were uptight, they would worry: "I always tried to get the serious job of checking ship and equipment done thoroughly but quickly. After that, I would try to fill any spare moment with light banter in order to get a laugh if I could. At that moment, a laugh means everything. Signs of nervousness on the part of the ranking officer immediately infect all others, and so I tried to play clown."

For leaders higher up the chain of command, responsibilities were even greater, presenting even more challenges. Group commanders perhaps had the most difficult jobs as overseers of the largest operational combat units in American aviation. Not only did they have to supervise the day-to-day workings of ground crewmen, they also had to function as the leaders of the combat crews, which meant proving their worth and courage during missions. They had to juggle the precarious balance between providing sorties and positive results to their superiors while at the same time maintaining the morale and effectiveness of their combat crews. For example, if they decided to have their group fly missions every day, they could probably inflict great damage on the enemy—but at what cost in casualties, fatigue, or morale among their own men? Group commanders had to find the right balance, even as they had to summon the courage to lead their men into battle.

Dale Smith, a West Point graduate and pilot who commanded the 384th Bomb Group, had a difficult time winning the confidence of his airmen. For many months after he assumed command, he lived with the fact that the majority neither liked nor trusted him. This unhealthy situation stemmed from two unpopular policies he had instituted. First, he held group critiques in which he questioned pilots about poor formations. If they had no valid excuse, and if the engineering section revealed no problem with their plane, he mandated that the pilot and crew would not receive credit for that mission: "At one of these gatherings, with about five hundred combat crewmen present, the pilot explaining his actions reported that he had 'intended' to fly closer but he thought he detected too much prop wash from airplanes ahead of him. To this I responded with one of my more asinine remarks, 'The road to hell is paved with good intentions.' Someone in the back of the room piped up in a loud voice: 'So is the road to heaven.' It brought down the house. Everyone enjoyed making me the butt of the joke, and I stood there like a wounded bull with nothing to say. If I had had any sense, I would have laughed with them, but in those days I took my duties so seriously that nothing much was funny, particularly when it was on me."

Second, Smith's policy of requiring ground officers to fly a combat mission was quite unpopular, particularly with those ground officers who now had to risk their lives. Not long after Smith instituted the policy, a popular ground officer was killed: "Those in the group who considered my policy unnecessary and heartless were highly critical. My stock dropped; some few regarded me as no less than a murderer. But I weathered the storm." Eventually Smith became a highly effective leader, but it took a great deal of time on the job and a number of mistakes, proving that good leaders sometimes are made rather than born.

One of the most successful group commanders of the war, Hub Zemke, summed up the daunting stress and multiple tests of character that went with a group command. In doing so, he articulated most of the basic elements of effective leadership in the air: "Command of a group, the Air Force's principal operational unit, was a prized appointment that most seasoned officers sought. To be honest, I was proud to have achieved this status and intended to do my utmost to make my group the best, as I'm sure did every other man given a similar assignment. There were a great many difficulties to overcome, and in my determination to succeed, my command became the paramount concern in my life at that time. When not actually dealing with day-to-day problems, I spent much time thinking how I should conduct myself. There may be born leaders but for me good leadership was a skill to be acquired. It was necessary to distinguish one's [good] qualities and weaknesses, to trade on the former and hide the latter, to endeavor to be firm yet flexible, to be receptive but decisive, to earn the respect and trust of my men. A demanding role, and you can only try to carry the majority with you. Human nature being what it is, however good your performance, there will always be detractors."

Detractors or not, Zemke and thousands of others proved to be courageous, effective air leaders for America in World War II. Most of them distinguished themselves by blending with their men, sharing the same dangers and the same camaraderie. American air leaders in World War II were truly unique modern warriors because they led by example, right out in front where the danger was greatest. As a result, American combat airmen had the privilege of first-rate, on-the-spot leadership—something that led to excellent group cohesion and highly effective air warriors.

9
Morale, Deep Thoughts, and Tours of Duty

War, with its inherent risk of sudden death, affects different people in different ways. Some men became hyper and did everything at a faster pace. Some drank . . . to cover their fears and anxieties. Others withdrew into themselves and became loners. In spite of their fears, most of them did their jobs quite well.
> —Quentin Aanenson, fighter pilot, 366th Fighter Group

In July 1944, the Army conducted a survey among experienced combat airmen. The goal of the researchers was to gauge morale among combat crews by asking them a prescribed set of questions. One particular question went to the very heart of the issues of morale, willingness for combat, and attitudes about facing danger. The surveyors asked the combat airmen—all of whom had a significant amount of missions or combat hours to their credit— if they would choose to sign up for combat flying if they had it to do all over again. The vast majority, ranging from 66 percent of heavy-bomber crewmen to 93 percent of fighter pilots, answered affirmatively. This meant that combat airmen, even though they risked their lives routinely and often dealt with some of the worst horrors of combat, still felt by an overwhelming margin that they had made the right choice in volunteering for aerial combat.

The survey is an excellent indicator of one basic fact about combat airmen—as badly as they all wanted to survive and go home, most felt proud of their status as combat aviators, did not actively seek ways to avoid combat, and were determined to do their jobs come what may. Coping with the incredible stress and soul-sapping exhaustion of war and still emerging with such attitudes did not come easy, though. Surviving a tour of duty and dealing mentally with the effects of combat was, for most men, an internal struggle that required tremendous reserves of mental energy. A man's state of mind and his attitudes could change from day to day, depending on his last mission and his estimation of the chances of survival.

Most grasped at anything that might help them cope and, by most accounts, maintaining a good sense of humor could be very important. Keith Lamb, a pilot in the 100th Bomb Group, found humor to be indispensable in retaining his sanity in an insane situation: "Discovering, remembering—and sometimes creating—humor in an otherwise deadly serious situation was a great help in coping with the daily realities of war." Joe Curley of the 486th Bomb Group remembered some "hilarious times. In wartime, your sense of humor is accentuated. You laugh at things that as a civilian in peacetime, you would not."

Indeed, wartime humor could be somewhat macabre at times, as those facing death laughed at their circumstances if not death's consequences. Robert Goebel and his comrades in the 31st Fighter Group noticed that pilots who had dated one particular woman back home had been dying on missions—all except one. Soon they referred to the woman as the "Jinx Woman" and ribbed her former suitor mercilessly: "We all thought it was a great joke, all except Carl. His discomfort was our cue, and we showed him no mercy. We reminded him with mock seriousness that his contact with the Jinx Woman had been a fatal mistake; he would surely be the next to die. Carl would become visibly shaken and agitated. 'What do you keep saying that for?' he would blurt out. 'I don't want to hear it. That's all bullshit and you know it. And anyway, I never slept with her.' This announcement produced such a chorus of incredulous hooting and jeering that poor Carl would go off muttering, his face a few shades whiter. I suppose it was a cruel trick. Humor in an operational outfit could get macabre at times."

Bathroom humor, often a favorite of young men, was quite popular among combat crews. Frank Finklang, a bombardier in the 301st Bomb Group, wondered why his navigator, who shared the plane's nose compartment with him, did not put on his flak helmet during a rough mission one day. After a piece of flak rocked the compartment, nearly killing both of them, he found the answer to the mystery: "I saw the yellow liquid running down his face. In an instant it was clear why he had not put on his flak helmet—he had used it as a urinal. When things got really rough, the instinct to survive outweighed any reluctance he might have had to wear it. My reaction was spontaneous laughter." Chuck Castle, a B-29 flight engineer in the 39th Bomb Group, witnessed a potentially dangerous situation turn humorous during a mission to Japan. The intense heat from fire bombings often caused thermal blasts that rocked the B-29s. Anyone not belted into his seat was thrown around the plane like a rag doll, and this happened to Castle's bombardier, knocking him unconscious. The bombardier received a shock when the urinal can in his compartment broke loose: "It dumped its contents on the unconscious form lying on the floor. There was no question that it revived him. He was not hurt, just madder than a wet hornet." When they returned to base, the man jumped into a puddle of muddy water to clean himself off, only adding to his stench and incurring more laughter from his crewmates. Castle laconically added: "We gave him plenty of room on the truck as we were driven back to the headquarters area for the customary briefing."

W. H. Nold, a copilot in the 449th Bomb Group, had an experience that can be viewed as either incredibly disgusting or morbidly funny. Naturally, his crew chose the latter attitude. Unbeknownst to his bombardier, Nold often used his canteen as a urinal and, when finished, stowed it under his seat. As their plane returned from a mission one day, the bombardier came up to the flight deck for a visit. A few minutes later, he tapped Nold on the shoulder: "I turned and it was Moose [the bombardier], with a strange look on his face. 'What do you have in that canteen?' 'You didn't drink from it, did you?' 'Yeah, I took a big slug and that was rough!'" Nold told him it was gasoline: "I didn't want to tell Moose the truth in fear that he might be sick on the spot." Nold told the rest of the squadron that Moose had "drunk deeply of urine," and the story was the object of much hilarity for a long time. As for Moose, he never knew the truth.

Besides humor, another morale booster for airmen was to keep pets. Being typical Americans, combat fliers loved animal companionship. Many fighter pilots and bomber crews befriended and took care of various animals during their combat tours of duty. Joseph Beswick, a top turret gunner/engineer, remembered that in his 483d Bomb Group, "Quite a few of the fellows had pets and if they got sick or injured the guys would take them on sick call and the medics would take care of them. I guess they figured they were good for morale. They were for a lot of the fellows." Beswick's crew kept a little dog they named "Peanuts." One day, they took her on a practice mission: "When we got to 10,000 feet, Peanuts fell over with her feet sticking straight up. We had to put an oxygen mask over her nose and put it on emergency oxygen to keep her from passing out." Another 483d man, Radio Operator Merle Perkins, kept a pet cat in his tent. He named the animal "Chocolate" because of her brown fur: "I would pick her up and hold her. Nuzzling into my left armpit, she would melt into my chest, start to purr softly, relax all over, soft, warm, a furry ball of affection."

Owning affectionate pets reminded men immersed in the deadly business of war that kindness, beauty, and unconditional love still existed in the world. As such, pets were treated with love as part of the family and took on great importance within each unit. During the difficult days of late 1943, waist gunner Jack Novey's 96th Bomb Group bartered for a small African donkey they named "Lady Moe." The crew that brought her home from Africa went head-to-head with British authorities, who wanted to quarantine the animal: "God knows what kind of diseases she could have brought into the airbase, but the crew and the base personnel threatened an armed battle with the British authorities, and finally Lady Moe was allowed in. She became everyone's pet and had total freedom of the base. She would come into the mess hall and eat cigarettes and food off the plates. I guess compared to North Africa, her life on the airbase in England was extremely tranquil."

Yank magazine correspondent Larry McManus flew with one crew that actually took their dog with them during a bombing raid on the Japanese-held Marshall Islands in early 1944: "Under the pilot's seat lay a rust-colored cocker spaniel, Pistolhead, whose name the crew members sometimes contract to two syllables when he misbehaves. The dog seemed to be asleep, but occasionally he would open his eye for a check-up on his master."

Such things as pets and humor kept men's spirits up in the midst of negotiating their way through what sometimes appeared to be a hopeless tour of duty. Most combat airmen, in stark contrast to ground-combat troops, had the mixed blessing of knowing that, at some fixed point, their combat days would reach an end. Unlike ground troops and ground crewmen, who were in the war for the duration, the vast majority of combat aviators flew a tour of duty, after which they would be rotated home. This rotation system offered airmen some hope for survival and allowed them to work toward the tangible goal of finishing their missions. At the same time, though, the tour of duty could be a distraction, causing some to focus more on the hope of survival rather than the task at hand. Even so, most airmen regarded the tour of duty positively, because it offered them the hope of exiting honorably from combat.

Tours of duty varied from theater to theater, unit to unit, and service to service. For example, the Navy often rotated its shipboard aviators on a roughly six-month schedule. By that time, airmen were more than ready for a rest, and some never returned to combat. Most did not serve any more than two tours of duty aboard a carrier. Jim Campbell, a fighter pilot in Air Group 5, breathed a huge sigh of relief the day he found out his group was rotating home. They had been in combat for nearly eighteen months: "We had been in any number of raids and three invasions. We had lost 13 pilots killed, two badly wounded, eight had ditched in the ocean but were rescued. I often wonder why I was one of the ones that survived." Naval airmen who flew from ground bases had a much more informal rotation system. After enough time in combat, they drew lots to see who got to go home. Pilot George Stevens and his crew came away winners one morning in 1945: "The skipper had a novel way of selecting a winner. Drawing out one slip [of paper] at a time, he announced the number and [said] that the LAST NUMBER in the hat would go home first. Talk about suspense! Crew Two prevailed! We were overjoyed."

In the Army Air Force, the length and parameters of a man's tour of duty depended on his unit and his circumstances. Those who flew early in the war, when missions could be highly dangerous and conditions difficult, generally flew fewer missions or combat hours to complete their tours. In the Eighth Air Force in England, bomber crews had to fly between twenty-five and thirty-five missions to complete a tour of duty. Ninth Air Force fighter pilots, based in England and France, generally flew between two hundred and three hundred hours of combat to finish their tours. In Italy, Fifteenth Air Force bomber crews flew fifty missions, while fighter pilots flew just over three hundred hours. The bomber crews in that theater, who often flew missions every bit as dangerous as those flown by the Eighth Air Force, sometimes were allowed to count difficult targets (such as Ruhland, Vienna, Berlin, Munich) twice in their mission tally. Charles Cope, a top turret gunner/engineer based in Italy with the 464th Bomb Group, often received double credit for flying over the Alps: "Due to the severity of this, we were given credit for two missions every time we crossed the Alps. I was given credit for fifty missions but actually only flew thirty-three."

In the South and Central Pacific, heavy-bomber crews and fighter pilots rotated home after flying between four hundred and five hundred hours. Some units devised a point system based on combat hours and the level of danger men experienced on their missions. In the China-Burma-India (CBI) theater, units often operated with no standard tour of duty, making some aviators in that theater unique in not having the benefit of a fixed rotation system. By 1944, though, most units in that theater had developed some kind of unofficial policy of transferring home aviators who had flown the most missions or combat hours. David Hayward, a pilot in the 341st Bomb Group in the CBI theater, benefited from the newly instituted rotation policy, and, in his opinion, it came not a moment too soon: "In a relatively short period of time, the 22d Bomb Squadron had sustained major losses that seemed to claim our most experienced crews. If the Air Force had only come up with a crew rotation policy, we thought, many of those lost might have had enough missions to go home. The morale was pretty low. We wondered who would be next to 'get it.' Well, the Air Force finally did come up with a crew rotation policy. After 50 missions we would be grounded and sent home. I had 52 missions."

In the Twentieth Air Force, B-29 crews generally flew between twenty-five and thirty-five missions. Many never flew complete tours, though, because the war came to an end.

• • •

Men negotiating their way through their perilous combat tours of duty usually went through three different mindsets during those tours. This was especially true among bomber crews in Europe, where casualties were often prohibitive and where fliers knew exactly how many missions they needed to fly to go home. For example, in the first six months of 1944 alone, heavy-bomber groups suffered a casualty rate of more than 88 percent; most had been killed in action or had become prisoners of war. In stage one of the tour of duty, combat fliers looked at missions almost as something unreal, a lark. The war went on outside the plane, never threatening to invade the supposedly secure interior of the aircraft. After a few missions, though, the combat airman began to realize, after seeing enough planes going down and perhaps dodging some near-misses himself, that the war was all too real and that, sooner or later, he would go down too. At that point, he began to focus on how many missions he needed to fly to get home. During the second stage, an airman sometimes succumbed to depression. By that point, probably ten to fifteen missions into his tour, he had lost many friends and yet had only made it halfway through his missions. Many fliers in stage two felt that their chances of surviving were slim, but they nonetheless clung to the completion of their tour of duty as a dim hope, a faraway and almost impossible-to-imagine goal. By stage three, when a combat airman had somehow managed to survive most of his tour of duty and had only a few more missions to go, increased hopes of survival sometimes led to extreme nervousness and anxiety as the man realized he had to make it through only a few more missions. At the same time, he knew from experience the multitude of dangers that could befall him. He could not escape the nagging feeling, after watching so many go down around him, that he was simply a fugitive from the law of averages, and that those immutable laws would eventually catch up with him on one of his remaining missions.

Keith Lamb described his personal mindset throughout his tour of duty: "For the first 10 missions or so I . . . considered it a lark— nothing but a lot of fun. During the next 10, I gave up all hope of ever coming out alive. The odds were too much against me; we were losing too many planes. I was spending my money as fast as I got it and living from day to day. I would have bet ten-to-one that I would never see Sacramento again. The last 10 [missions] you were living on borrowed time."

Indeed, for those closing in on the end of their tours, the tension could be next to unbearable. One Eighth Air Force bomber crewman wrote to his sister in the final days of his tour in early 1944. He could think of little else besides his impending final missions: "When you get in as many raids as I have, you sort of sweat out your last few. The law of averages says that . . . I should be eating wieners and sauerkraut at least ten raids ago, so myself and the rest of the crew sort of cross our fingers every time we step into our 'Lady' for another try over the Third Reich. The crew that sleeps in our barracks . . . can't wait to see us finish up and get the hell out of the barracks because they are the fourth crew to sleep with us[;] the three crews before them all got shot down, so the boys have an idea we're bad luck to anyone who lives with us—could be."

David McCarthy, a navigator in the 381st Bomb Group, was a veritable basket case as he waited to fly his twenty-fifth and final mission: "Waiting for that last mission was an agonizing ordeal. Apprehension filled the mind and soul, and it was very difficult to maintain an outward appearance of composure. No mission was ever a sure thing. Doubt of returning to your base alive and uninjured was always buried in the back of your mind." Bob Ryerson, a pilot in the 96th Bomb Group, worried before his final mission that he might be asked to fly even more missions: "When I flew my 35th mission, if they would have come up to me and said, 'We need you to fly a 36th,' I would have told them to stick it in their ear and if they would have tried to do anything, I would have taken out my .45 and blown their head off. They were talking to somebody that was on the edge. That was the case with all of the fellows."

Perhaps even worse than worrying about your final mission was the prospect of having your tour extended. Group commanders tried to be fair in setting tour parameters, but sometimes they received orders to increase the number of missions or hours their crews had to fly in order to rotate home. Needless to say, this could and would mean a death sentence for some men. During his tenure as commander of the Eighth Air Force, Jimmy Doolittle twice raised the number of missions his crews had to fly in order to complete their tours—the first time from twenty-five to thirty, the second time from thirty to thirty-five. He did so in reaction to the availability of long-range escort fighters and the ensuing decline in casualty rates in his bomb groups. His edict did not sit well with his bomber crews, though. Quilla Reed, a top turret gunner/engineer in the 91st Bomb Group, never forgot the overwhelming sense of frustration, hopelessness, and grief that overtook his crew when they found out they had to fly five additional missions. Having previously thought they had only two left, they received a rude awakening: "We all went into the debriefing room and sat down and cried." On what would have been their final mission, they went down over Holland.

Sometimes experienced crews, such as Earl Benham's in the 100th Bomb Group, received the benefit of a prorated system when tours of duty were extended: "General Jimmy Doolittle had increased the combat tour to 30 missions instead of the original 25. We . . . were extended to 28 missions on a pro-rated basis because we had 17 missions completed and we were exempt from the 30 mission order. The newer crews were stuck with 30 missions." Commanders in the Twentieth Air Force also upped the combat tour of their crews from twenty-five to thirty to thirty-five. Kevin Herbert, a tail gunner in the 498th Bomb Group based on Saipan, remembered the bitter reaction among crewmen when commanding officers broke the bad news that everyone would have to fly extra missions: "Those of us who had started our tour when the number was thirty and who now had fifteen or more missions completed felt especially aggrieved at this statement. The specter of being knocked down on one of those added five . . . was unpleasant to contemplate. One lieutenant jumped to his feet and in a voice quavering with emotion charged the higher brass with bad faith, breach of contract, callous indifference to the morale of the men, and several other actionable matters. But this was not a civil court, it was the 498th Bombardment Group, and this was war." Like Herbert, most airmen realized they had little recourse against the brass, so they concentrated on what they could control—flying their missions and trying to make it home in one piece.

Those who achieved that lofty goal experienced a nearly bound-less joy. The commanding officer of William Shelley, a gunner in the 7th Bomb Group in the CBI theater, called him into his office one afternoon in October 1943: "The CO . . . said the new rotation system was starting and since I had more combat time than any other man in the squadron, I could go home if I wished! I recall babbling a quick, 'Yes, thank you!'" Wayne Rothgeb and two other fighter pilots in the 35th Fighter Group reached the ends of their respective tours on New Guinea late in 1944: "I had flown over one hundred thirty-five combat missions and had nearly four hundred combat hours. Then one day it happened. Our orders . . . were in. We had been taken off flying status; we were going home! We were three happy guys." Omar Ash completed his tour with the 43d Bomb Group in the spring of 1945 and immediately wrote to his family to exclaim the joy he felt in his heart: "I'm one of the happi-est persons in the world. Yesterday I finished all flying. Ended with 410:45 hours, which was more than I needed. I feel like a huge weight I've been carrying on my shoulders has suddenly been taken off. I feel very fortunate to have finished . . . without a scratch too."

In the European theater, where casualty rates were highest, those who had defied the odds felt just as much elation, if not more. Mau-rice Fitzgibbons, a top turret gunner/engineer in the 95th Bomb Group, successfully completed a tour of duty in late 1943 in the most dangerous theater of the war at a time when the Eighth Air Force was taking some of its worst casualties. That night, he wrote to his parents: "Four out of every five combat men that came over in our original group are down. I realize that I am lucky. I feel as tho [sic] I am ten years younger. When I stepped out of our plane on our last one I felt as tho I were dreaming. I was snapped out of it by the Colonel, who grabbed my hand and invited me to the Officer's Club as his personal guest."

Jack Novey was also one of the lucky few who managed to finish up in the fall of 1943. After his final mission, his outlook on life changed completely: "My life was transformed. I was alive, had just been reborn, this time as an adult. In all my life, I have never expe-rienced such a feeling of pure joy. I looked around, and everything took on a new meaning. The trees, the grass, the crops in the fields—everything was bathed in a new light. The colors were vivid. Mundane, everyday sights became interesting and significant. Everything troubling fell away. I was like a snake shedding his old skin. I had such a delight in being alive and being able to see and smell and hear that I couldn't contain myself. I ran out into the field and just ran and ran and ran until I dropped."

Jule Berndt, a navigator in the 490th Bomb Group, finished up in early 1945. He confided his reverent and grateful mood to his diary: "O, what a grave and glorious feeling—years of anxiety and care dropped from my shoulders. Before the ship had stopped rolling, I offered my thanks to God, who had so mercifully protected us during our months of flying. There were so many instances when I could have been, or rather our ship could have been, one of those mentioned in the daily communique. I recall the number of close calls we had and from which we emerged unscathed."

When crews completed their tours together, they often celebrated deep into the night. Months of tension evaporated seemingly in a matter of moments, and they could share the excitement of collective survival. George Meshko, a waist gunner in the 96th Bomb Group, had the pleasant experience of finishing his tour with his entire crew: "Over our base, we buzzed the field and shot off two boxes of flares—about 200 rounds—to celebrate the completion of our combat tour. Our tail gunner was firing a Very pistol out the waist window and lobbed one right into the control tower. We all got a big kick watching the brass scramble. What happy warriors we were in the B-17 that afternoon. There at our hardstand to congratulate us on our tour completion were all our buddies, ground crew, and even the brass. As we came tumbling out of our ship, we were greeted with laughter, tears, hugs, back slapping. In the wee hours of the morning, our gallant crew crawled in loose formation, leaving strange contrails across some muddy plowed fields from the combat club to our Nissen hut. Our tour completed, the only thing left was the hangover."

Jim Lynch, a radio operator in the 379th Bomb Group, also finished with his crew, and they partied together to celebrate the occasion. Lynch never forgot the scene he witnessed when his crew's plane landed after their thirty-fifth and final mission: "Pete was the first one out from his position in the waist. He leaped out, bent down, and kissed the concrete runway. Casey and Johnny piled out of the forward hatch with shouts of joy. Casey threw his hat and earphones into the air, whooping like a victorious Indian. We were all leaping around like schoolboys at recess. Big Don, never one to show much emotion, grabbed Russ in a bear hug and kissed him on the forehead."

Some Air Force units afforded the lucky crews who made it safely through a tour of duty with special "Lucky Bastard Club" certificates and an honorary dinner. This was a way of commemorating their accomplishment and recognizing their bravery. At the same time, the Lucky Bastard Club ritual buoyed morale among the men who still had missions to fly. They could look at the happy crew who had just finished and see for themselves that survival was possible. Ball Turret Gunner Bill Hefley of the 92d Bomb Group finished his tour in June 1944 and immediately received his Lucky Bastard Club commendation from the group's commanding officer: "It affords me great pleasure to commend you upon the successful completion of your operational tour in this Theatre. Your courage, coolness, and tenacity of purpose in the face of the most determined enemy opposition reflect great credit upon yourself and the Army Air Forces. The example you have set will always live as a goal for succeeding combat crew members of this command."

Recognition of the Lucky Bastard Club was unofficial and varied from unit to unit. Some group commanders did not like the idea of a prescribed tour of duty and further did not like the idea of exalting the accomplishments of those who had no further operational use to their command. Accordingly, these commanders ordered that crews who had completed their tours should receive no special treatment and must not engage in excessive celebrations. One such officer took command of Eugene Fletcher's 95th Bomb Group just as he and his crew were about to finish their missions. Fletcher noticed the hurt and disappointment in the eyes of his crew when they found out they would not receive their rightful Lucky Bastard Club recognition, and he felt annoyance and defiance within himself. On their last mission, as they approached their base, Fletcher debated about whether or not to violate the group commander's orders and fire celebratory flares: "The colonel's orders were still ringing in my ears: 'No more . . . Lucky Bastard Dinner, no more victory flyovers.' My conscience was fighting hard, and it appeared to be winning the battle. But my heart was revolting. What's a court martial compared to the dangers of what we had faced in flying thirty-five missions against the Third Reich? I thought about my crew and the disappointment we had to face when these rule changes were made known to us—the misty eyes, the choked voices. I owed these men something. I told the crew that anyone who wanted to fire a flare should come on up to the flight deck and start firing when we reached the runway. To this day, I have a hard time forgiving the Group CO who denied my men the decoration they risked their lives to earn and so richly deserved!" His perilous tour completed, Fletcher chose defiance rather than obedience to insensitive and somewhat inane orders. He and the other members of the Lucky Bastard Club, whether recognized as such or not, would always remember the feeling of joy and liberation that came with completion of their final mission.

What about all the other missions between the first and the last? How did airmen go about trying to survive their combat tours? Most men turned to anything that might offer some hope of survival—whether prayer, superstition, or fatalism. Day after day, they witnessed arbitrary death and wondered if there was a larger plan that dictated that some must die and others must live. They struggled for control over that which was largely uncontrollable—their ultimate survival or death. David McCarthy wrestled with these difficult issues many times during his combat tour. He watched his buddies die and wondered if it was due to fate or mere chance: "How does Fate decide which . . . of the crews on the mission shall be destroyed and which shall return to base? These were very heavy ponderables for . . . confused young men."

Make no mistake. The ultimate goal for nearly every American combat airman was not winning the war or even finishing his tour—it was survival. Fliers wanted to do their duty and live to tell about it. Men like Dick Marshall, a fighter-bomber pilot in the Fifth Air

Force, were highly unusual. In a letter to his sister, he indicated little fear of death. To Marshall, his own personal survival was a mere triviality compared to the great forces of history: "We fear death because we don't want to give up friends, fun, material effects. It is a purely selfish law. The point is, that death is a personal thing—and what of personal pain and happiness? You and I cannot feel the pain or the happiness of some person a generation ago. And no one centuries hence will feel ours, but they will feel the results of what we have believed in and fought for, in direct proportion to the strength of our convictions and the accuracy of the worth of the belief." Sadly, Marshall did sacrifice his life for his beliefs, going down in New Guinea.

Most Americans, though, did not fight for patriotism or the Allied cause, as much as they believed in those things. When truly plunged into danger, they fought for their comrades and their own survival. James Good Brown, the chaplain of the 381st Bomb Group, watched the men in his outfit face death on a daily basis and became an adept student of their mindset. He wrote in his diary: "There is not to be found in the hearts of the men of the 381st the German idea of 'dying for the Fatherland.' We in America have not raised up men in this mold or with this philosophy. Our patriotism does not run in this vein. If patriotism means the desire to die for one's country, it does not exist. The American men in this bomb group want to Live for their country. Our men do not want to die. They want to live. The conversation never runs into topics such as 'The supremacy of democracy over dictatorship,' therefore let's go out and kill the dictators. Nor do we have conversations such as: 'Now, fellows, when you take off for combat today, remember that there is something at stake in the world; we are fighting for an ideal.' And never have I heard from the lips of the men: 'By God, we'll go out and knock hell out of those Germans! What do I care for my life? This struggle is worth everything I can give. I'll get a Jerry today if it kills me!' Our men . . . are not like that. They are human. They love living."

With survival as their highest priority, combat airmen struggled mightily to find ways of achieving that frighteningly elusive goal in a world that dispensed death and imprisonment with seemingly no pattern or justice. Some turned to prayer—a natural American impulse, because religion has historically been ingrained into the fabric of America. Combat airmen prayed not for the destruction of their enemies or out of righteous affirmation of the goodness of their cause; perhaps not even out of devout religious beliefs but rather for personal survival. They turned to God to control what they themselves could not. As Brown put it, "They would do anything to reach out for security, and if prayer helps, they are willing to try it. Prayer is a desperate attempt to come back alive."

Under the extreme stress of combat, many figured it could not hurt to turn to God. Maybe He would hear their prayers and have mercy. Joseph Hallock, an Eighth Air Force bombardier who made it through a thirty-five mission tour, wrote a piece about his combat experiences in *The New Yorker* magazine in the summer of 1944. Hallock acknowledged that prayer helped him cope at times: "My best friend over there was an ardent Catholic. He used to pray and go to confession and Mass whenever he could. I kept telling him, 'What's the use? The whole business is written down in a book someplace. Praying won't make a difference.' But whenever I got caught in a tight spot in Germany, I'd find myself whispering, 'God, you gotta . . . get me back. God, listen, you gotta.' Some of the guys prayed harder than that. They promised God a lot about swearing off liquor and women, if He'd pull them through. I never tried to promise Him anything, because I figured that if God was really God, he'd be bound to understand how men feel about liquor and women."

Turning to prayer offered airmen some degree of hope (whether well founded or not) of survival. Prayer gave them peace of mind. Walter Springer, a fighter pilot in the 413th Fighter Group, shared these sentiments with his parents in a letter: "We've got to believe that anything that happens to us is God's will. If I didn't believe that, I don't think I could go into this combat with the peace of mind I have. I know it's foolish to ask you not to worry, but remember [that] worrying won't help. I pray every night that God will spare you worry. If I happen not to come through the war, I deem it God's will, so I'm not worrying and I hope you won't."

Even as Springer articulated the belief that his death in combat would be God's will, he probably could not conceive of God "betraying" him in such a fashion. Men placed their faith in God and their fate in His hands in the hope that God would return their devotion with the reward of survival. Kenneth Michel, a B-29 navigator in the 504th Bomb Group, turned to prayer after seeing some of his friends from training go down over Japan. In a letter to his parents, he wrote: "A fellow's only salvation and hope of getting thru [sic] is Faith in God. I pray with all my heart that . . . God will find it in his will to allow me to return safely." Harry Beightol, a nose gunner in the Fifteenth Air Force, wrote to his mother and spoke of his newfound religiosity: "I never fail to thank God for bringing us back after each mission. I carry my Testament with me on every mission and before we go into enemy territory I read the 91st psalm. That passage means to me that my fears must vanish as dew in the morning sun." Unfortunately, Beightol's devotion did not prevent him from being shot down and listed as missing in action.

Unquestionably, combat airmen tended to embellish their level of religious participation in letters to parents, most of whom had raised their sons to go to church and believe in God. The proliferation of prayer among combat aviators, though, was not simply a correspondence invention designed to quell the fears of anxious Stateside parents. Many fliers, desperate for some control over their ultimate fate, truly believed that turning to God could help. After a very difficult mission in the spring of 1944, William Harris, a radio operator in the 389th Bomb Group, wrote in his diary: "The Lord sure is taking care of us. Because we go through some very tough spots [and] I know we couldn't come out of them if he wasn't looking after us." Edward Schlesinger, a navigator/bombardier in the 379th Bomb Group, believed that God intervened to save his crew on one mission. Schlesinger awoke with a strong premonition that death awaited him that day. Other crew members had the same terrible feeling. Still, they took off and proceeded toward their target in normal fashion. As they did so, they prayed to God for deliverance. Just when it seemed they were doomed, a message came over the radio: "We learned that the mission was scrubbed, because suddenly over Europe a tremendous weather system had developed. The weather picture was totally unexpected and unexplainable to the meteorologist. I felt quite certain that the power of prayer really saved us that particular day." Edward Hearty, a bombardier in the 95th Bomb Group, prayed constantly throughout his tour of duty in the fall of 1943. After a rough twenty-fourth mission, he thanked God in his diary: "Thank you Lord for all of your help and protection without which I would never have been able to write this 24th mission in." After his final mission, he gushed even more gratitude—not only to God but also to his unit's chaplain: "Thank God for all of his help and to the Chaplin [sic] for all of his Prayers and confidence. He sure was a swell fellow and a damned good friend. This has been a pretty swell place and a damned interesting job. But let the other fellow get his crack at them."

Although in the distinct minority, some men rebelled against the notion of praying to God for survival. They saw such behavior as selfish and narcissistic. Bryce Evertson, a pilot in the 91st Bomb Group, strongly believed in God but could not bring himself to think that God helped some and not others. He wrote to his parents in early 1944: "We can't be selfish with our prayers and pray that no harm will come to those we love. The friends I've lost had every bit as much to live for as I have. Best we pray that they will not be found lacking when they do get in trouble. At least that is the faith—the only faith I can have over here. You can't ask God to see that you personally never will come to harm. Freedom wasn't founded that way. Jesus himself did not say that His people would not suffer. He said instead that He would be with them in their suffering. So you see a man has to be ready to die any day. Just face the fact squarely and your problems are solved."

Few airmen wished to face death so squarely, though. Most preferred to pray and hope that God would intercede on their behalf. In that sense, their faith was little more than an unconscious wish for life in a world of death. But prayer was also pragmatic. Fliers figured praying could not possibly hurt their chances of survival. Kevin Herbert observed this prayer-driven mindset take hold in his unit, one that went on in every outfit that sent its aviators into danger: "This sudden conversion was, of course, less a matter of persuasion than of caution, for everyone now welcomed the aid of the divine in the task of getting us back whole from every mission. If God could make an R-3350 engine keep pulling along when shot up, a man would be a fool to ignore the availability of such help."

Perhaps even more powerful was the allure of superstition. Rare indeed was the combat aviator who did not have some sort of lucky talisman or established ritual, presumably designed to ward off danger. From a dispassionate and objective standpoint, the prevalence of superstition among combat airmen was nothing more than another attempt by the individual's ego to exercise control over that which seemed uncontrollable—namely, life or death. Because there seemed to be no pattern to how the war inflicted death, airmen sought to establish such a pattern. Thus, rational men convinced themselves that if they simply wore their lucky socks, or carried a lucky silver dollar, or settled into their compartment the exact same way at the exact same time before every mission, they could prevent disaster. In that sense, superstition was rational. Airmen had been trained to be in complete control at all times in the air. Superstitious beliefs gave them some small measure of mental security that if they took proper precautions—in this case, carrying a talisman—they could exorcise the demons of war and take control of their fate.

Donald McClellan, a top turret gunner/engineer in the 491st Bomb Group, explained the psychology of superstition that took hold among combat airmen: "When a person is caught in such a dilemma, he begins to pray for an edge—a talisman, if you will—something to give him and his fellow players that much-needed edge against the fickleness of fate. In life, we all seek a talisman to counterbalance the threat of death. Sometimes the need to control our fate becomes so desperate we conceal within ourselves our deepest and most sincere prayers which we silently embrace in solitude. It is then that we gamble our lives on whatever is thought to be capable of protecting our immediacy, an immediacy nowhere [more] threatened than in the skies above enemy strongholds when men await you whose sole purpose for being there is to kill you."

Early in 1944, *Yank* magazine spoke informally with bomber crewmen in England and asked about their superstitions. Almost all had some sort of lucky charm they carried on missions. One man believed his leather flying jacket had saved him from a fatal flak hit, and he refused to fly without it. Another took a "lucky" sword with him on every mission. A radio operator in one unit had a "lucky" boot he had used since his first mission, when he couldn't find one of his flying boots: "Somebody tossed an English-type boot to me and I wore it. I have 15 missions in now. I figure if it was lucky on the first mission, it should be okay until my last." Another radio operator went as far as insisting that the pilot fit his Mae West life jacket on him before every mission. The pilot had done so on their first mission and they had come home safely so, from then, he "wouldn't leave unless the pilot tucked me into it." Keith Schuyler, a pilot in the 44th Bomb Group, noted that men around him usually denied being superstitious even as their superstitions practically ruled their lives: "To a man, we would vehemently deny any trace of superstition. Yet there were probably few who did not carry some symbol of religion, love, or pagan charm just to be on the safe side of sentimentality. As a 'just in case,' my Roman Catholic cousin in Philadelphia had impressed upon me a St. Christopher medal that had a special place in my wallet. Despite all this occult frivolity, these charms and amulets came to have a special meaning about as ethereal as their supposed powers."

David McCarthy did not carry lucky items. Instead, he went through a supposedly lucky ritual, never varying for each of his twenty-five missions: "I had to be the first to enter the plane through the nose hatch, and my maps, charts, and navigational instruments had to be laid out precisely upon my work table. Before we took off, I always entered the cockpit, stood between the Pilot and Copilot until we were safely airborne, and then I put an arm around their necks and hugged them. After that ceremony was completed, we could get down to the business of war." McCarthy also recounted an eerie incident in which a good friend insisted on giving him his lucky toy donkey before his final mission, as if to prove to himself that he had made it that far not on mysterious powers but on competence. Although McCarthy did not want to accept the donkey, his friend insisted. On that final mission, the man's plane crashed on takeoff. There were no survivors.

Tom Miller, a pilot in the 448th Bomb Group, had extremely superstitious men on his crew. Before leaving to go overseas, one of them visited his home and picked out a "special" rock, which he carried on every mission: "He would give us all a quick glimpse of his rock from his cupped hands before he stuck it snugly . . . back in his pocket. He wouldn't fly without it! My tail gunner . . . had a baseball cap that was his lucky charm. He was so attached to this cap he wouldn't fly without it either! One morning he nearly missed going on a raid with us because he had misplaced his cap and I had allowed him to go back for it. My navigator . . . was of French origin and at that time a Roman Catholic. His attachment was to his prayer beads. I also had my long-johns which I wore on every combat mission and which were never washed until I had completed my combat tour!"

Pete Riegel, a pilot in the 487th Bomb Group, even had a crew member beg him to abort a mission because he had forgotten his St. Christopher medal: "He insisted we turn back, for without that medal, we would all be lost. He was very persistent and threatened to bail out. This went on for about fifteen minutes and I knew that there was no way that we could abort because of a lack of a St. Christopher medal." Finally, the man found the medal, along with his peace of mind, and they continued to and from the target safely.

Fighter pilots also had their share of superstitions. They battled the same unfathomable forces of fate as bomber crewmen and often reacted the same way. Leslie Traughber, a fighter pilot in the 27th Fighter Group, noticed that he and the men around him prepared for missions the same way every time. It became an unspoken, but rigid, ritual for them: "There were certain habits that we formed such as putting on the same glove or the shoe first, etc., and these habits were repeated daily until they became so entrenched in our subconscious that we would not change our routine for anything. The only time I can remember changing my routine was the day I got shot down." Quentin Aanenson wrote to his wife in July 1944 and described the pervasiveness of superstition in his unit: "Almost every pilot I know over here has some sort of good luck charm, or ritual he goes through before a mission. Before every mission, as I'm climbing into the cockpit, I whistle the first bar of the Air Corps Song, and kiss the ring you gave me. It seems to do the trick, because I'm still flying. Johnny Bathurst carries one of his baby shoes with him. One of the other fellows recites a little poem. Crazy ideas all—but it helps to be a little crazy in this business."

Being rational and intelligent human beings, combat airmen knew intellectually that their lucky charms or rituals probably could not save them. But, at the same time, they knew that in a world filled with indiscriminate death, they also could not hurt. Such was the nature of superstition.

Some airmen actively disdained such hocus-pocus. They preferred to believe that they would survive because they were invulnerable. Few, if any, human beings can truly contemplate their own demise. Some combat aviators took that tendency to its ultimate extreme, especially after they continued to survive difficult missions. They came to believe that they would survive because they were special. John Wood, a gunner in the 381st Bomb Group, definitely had this sense of invulnerability: "If they had said, 'We expect only two people to come back from this raid,' I would have wondered, 'Who will the other guy be?'" Robert Ramer, a B-29 pilot in the Twentieth Air Force, believed during much of his tour of duty that nothing could harm him: "When we would go to briefing and see what they had planned . . . we'd say, 'Good God, they're crazy! They're going to lose a lot of men.' I'd think to myself, 'Hey, a lot of *those* guys are going to get it.' There was some kind of protection around me. It was as if I were enclosed in some sort of plastic container for the war." Wayne Livesay served two tours of duty with the Eighth Air Force. After surviving so many hazardous missions, he came to believe that nothing could happen to him: "I experienced attacks from German fighters, constant flak barrages . . . and a few narrow escapes due to mechanical problems, but, although I recognized the involved danger, I never really thought that any adverse action would befall me." Livesay eventually was shot down and became a prisoner.

Harold Rosser's 33d Fighter Group buddies practiced a drinking ritual in which they sang a song of mourning for those who had died and for whomever would be the next to die. Part of the toast entailed extending your glass and looking at each man in turn, as if wondering who the next unfortunate would be. But, as Rosser explained, no one could bring himself to believe that he would be next: "Being practical, each recognized his exposure to death, but his ego-optimism forbade him to consider the fact, forcing him to look with sadness and sympathy on each of his buddies, wondering when their time would come." Merle Perkins provided an excellent description of the psychology of invulnerability in a diary he kept during his combat tour. After surviving many difficult missions and seeing the rest of his crew die on a day he flew in another plane, he came to think of himself as indestructible: "Before, I had my old 'my luck is running out' fears, 'the odds may go against me,' 'how I would hate to lose with only a few sorties to go.' Now, I have a strange high, a sense of being invincible and invulnerable. I am more alert, efficient. I feel as if I am at the peak of training, above any obstacle, confident in my skills, and carefree of notions of good and bad luck. Call it a sort of peace, acceptance. Not fatalistic in the sense of 'what will be, will be,' it is a sense of oneness with self, environment, Nature."

Some men eschewed trying to control their fate. Far from looking at themselves as invulnerable or attempting to curry favor with God, they instead took a fatalistic or pragmatic approach. They concentrated on what they could control—doing their jobs. Whatever happened beyond that was immaterial, and they felt there was nothing they could do about it. By declining to struggle for some degree of control over their fate, they often found peace of mind. Frank Halm of the 94th Bomb Group "was of the feeling that if there was a bullet with my name on it, I would get it and there wasn't anything I could do about it. Of course, I didn't do anything stupid to tempt fate. Those of us who were fatalistic had it easier than the others." John Houk tried to put aside all the death and suffering he saw around him. He could not let it bother him or worry him: "Friends' deaths didn't affect my performance. I deliberately made myself a fatalist. I knew it could happen to me. I half expected it to happen to me. But I wasn't worried about it." Leroy Watson, a pilot in the 17th Bomb Group, believed the same thing. He wrote to his mother and urged her not to worry about him: "I've got this thing figured out. I'm not a 'Hot pilot' but I believe I can take care of the flying part and the rest is mostly luck, and luck along with your prayers will bring me thru [sic] and I'll see you again one of these days." John

Charlton, a pilot in the 465th Bomb Group who also took a fatalistic approach, found that it was best to compartmentalize his life during his combat tour: "You were looking at the strong possibility of death, violent and sudden. You had to mentally go through a change of attitude from a soldier enjoying the companionship of his family, the crews, and the other crews' games, jokes, checking the sights of a foreign country, all very positive, upbeat, daily surroundings to the understanding that death, wounds, or capture were an immediate probability. If the above happened, it would be OK, it was part of the flying commitment."

Long after the war, those who had survived often came to the sad but inescapable truth that death in combat held no rhyme or reason. From an objective standpoint, superstitions, prayers, or fatalism could not protect men against enemy flak and fighters. During their combat tours, airmen turned to such hopes in an effort to afford themselves some peace of mind and some chance of survival. As Bob Ryerson explained, though, ultimately it did not matter. Death came indiscriminately to the religious, the superstitious, and the indifferent: "It was strictly a matter of fate. There were people who were very religious, but they got killed so certainly there was nobody watching over them, even though they thought there was. They grasped at every straw there was to try and survive. Because death was so arbitrary they did everything they could to try and cover whatever . . . governing factor may have been there if there was any. But you see there wasn't any. It was all fate. Period. Guys carried rabbits' foots [sic] with them. There were guys that didn't change their underwear. Any kind of a superstition. You're desperate. I don't think there was a soul out there that wanted to die. They tried to cover themselves with . . . anything to try and survive."

Naturally this stark existence had serious effects on combat airmen. During their combat tours, most experienced great fear—a normal reaction for these men in view of the dangers involved in their jobs. Most Americans who saw ground combat in World War II had no reluctance about admitting their fears, and combat airmen were no different. In fact, combat men were likely to be very suspicious of those who claimed to have no fear. The general sentiment was that anyone who made such a claim was either "a liar or a lunatic." Combat airmen, then, usually had little reluctance to admit the stressful and deleterious effect that fear had on them. Jackson Futch, a gunner in the 30th Bomb Group, wrote candidly about his fears in a letter to his family. He had just returned from bombing a Japanese base and had a vivid recollection of his terror: "I can't say I wasn't scared, plenty scared, while we were over the target and until we were a long way from it. I don't believe there is a man alive who can truthfully say he was not scared at times and if there is, he's the damnedest liar I ever heard of! I just can't describe how I felt. I've never come even close to feeling that way before."

Elmer Bendiner, a B-17 navigator in the 379th Bomb Group, wrote of a pervasive sense of fear that permeated his unit's base at Kimbolton, England, a kind of unacknowledged but universally recognized group terror: "Fear was part of the furniture in every hut, in every pub, in every parlor, bedroom, and bath. It did not claw at one's guts. When the fear was light and transient it drove some of us to the palliative of sex. When it was more troubling it provoked a throbbing headache in the back of the neck or hives or flatulence." David Lustig, a radio operator in the 384th Bomb Group, described the kind of fear he and his buddies experienced during a typical mission over Europe: "You are awaiting the results of your physical and the doctor starts off with, 'I'm afraid that your - - - .' Speeding on an interstate, a siren shriek pierces the air and flashing red lights fill your rearview mirror. You steer your new Buick a bit too fast into a sharp icy turn and suddenly all four wheels lose traction! From briefing to debriefing, a bombing mission involved any or all of these emotions. It was the inexorable now of a planned crisis that culminated in a moment of truth."

Even though combat airmen readily acknowledged the universality and appropriateness of fear among their ranks, a few young men, like radio operator Ben Smith of the 303d Bomb Group, tried to hide their fears behind devil-may-care personas borrowed from Air Force recruiting posters: "I recall that I used to lie awake in bed dreading the time when I would have to lay it on the line or forever be lost in the infamy of disgrace (I learned later that I was not the only one). This was so real to me. Outwardly, I was lighthearted and jovial, well liked by my friends. They thought I was a pretty cool customer, but inside I was sick, sick, sick! My bravado was sort of a rallying point, though phony as a three-dollar bill. I wore a 'hot pilot's' cap, smoked big black cigars, and drank boilermakers. The only one who wasn't fooled was me."

Smith constructed this facade not in response to his comrades' expectations that he should be free of fear, but rather as a coping mechanism, perhaps to convince himself that, if he could suppress his fear, he could make it through the war alive. Other men, like Fighter Pilot Charlie Dryden of the 332d Fighter Group, feared cowardice within themselves rather than combat and its inherent dangers: "The thing I worried most about was being chicken, turning and running. I wasn't a hero, but I wasn't going to turn chicken and run from someone who was obviously trying to kill me."

Most airmen shared Dryden's aversion to being thought of as a coward or malingerer. Many preferred death to such a fate and had little compunction about admitting their fears. Airmen knew that a coward was someone whose fear robbed him of his willingness to do his job in combat, thus placing his buddies in danger, not someone who felt fear in the face of danger. This common distinction made it acceptable for combat airmen to discuss the emotion of fear. Tom Miller's crew had many frank discussions of fear and collectively decided that "true 'courage' . . . and belief is best demonstrated by some thoughtful one who is scared half to death but who presses on and does the job that has to be done in spite of his fear!!!! Therefore I consider myself *very* courageous!!" Most combat aviators would readily have agreed with that statement.

Men especially struggled with their fears as mission time approached. J. Fred Baumann, a fighter pilot in the 52d Fighter Group, often felt apprehension spread over him the night before a mission: "It was a very strange feeling to live with the realization that at some unknown hour on the following day I could cease to exist. It was like a wispy veil which would descend upon you when you were least suspecting it. I suppose that I accepted it, but I certainly didn't like the sensation it gave. Fortunately . . . it disappeared when I started rolling down the metal strip on takeoff. It was during times of mental inactivity, especially the night before, that the veil moved in closer . . . in the quiet still of the night . . . lying there, thinking."

Roger Armstrong, a radio operator in the 91st Bomb Group, often felt physically ill after seeing his crew's name on the alert list for the next day's mission: "I developed a sick feeling in my stomach whenever I saw our crew was flying. It ruined your evening, as you usually didn't care about going into town when you knew you would be awakened by the alert corporal possibly as early as 3:00 A.M. You were not normal unless you were concerned that it could be the last day of your life." For some, the creeping sense of fright began at briefing, when they found they were headed for a tough target. Joseph Beswick recalled, "When . . . you heard the target was Munich, Brux, Vienna, Bleehammer, Berlin, or others that were just as rough, your heart would sink and you would get a sick feeling in the pit of your stomach and you would feel like you wanted to throw up. Anybody that said they were not afraid were either crazy or . . . lying like hell." James Barison, a copilot in the 485th Bomb Group, spent a sleepless night on the eve of a mission dealing with a fearful premonition of what would happen to him the next day. As he sat through briefing, fear burdened him like a lead weight on his chest. It became even worse as he sat in the cockpit waiting for takeoff: "I did not want to go on this mission. I felt that something ominous was going to happen. My stomach was in a knot. I wanted to climb down from the cockpit and run away. But I didn't." As it turned out, Barison was grievously wounded that day. A hunk of flak severed his left foot, and he nearly bled to death before his plane returned home. It is interesting to speculate as to whether Barison's acute fear that morning afforded him near-psychic powers or whether his premonition was simply a coincidence.

Sometimes airmen ironically found a reprieve from their fears during combat, when their jobs required them to think of nothing else besides the next task at hand. In other words, they sometimes had little time to think about being afraid while they fought for their lives. Other times, though, fear stayed with them during combat. Philip Ardery, a pilot in the 389th Bomb Group, sometimes felt fear coming over him as flak bursts exploded near his plane. The sense of terror and dread became even worse if he saw enemy fighters whizzing through his formation, or if American bombers, some of them full of his friends, exploded before his eyes: "The icy fingers which I hated would reach right around my heart. I would shut my eyes for a brief instant, pray for a little more nerve, and then say to myself, "R-e-l-a-x, you jerk!'" Another pilot in the 389th, Kenneth Jones, came to hate the fear he felt during missions. In his combat diary, he described the intense emotions of terror that German flak sometimes brought out in him: "Scared and frustrated, bouncing around and letting them beat your brains out and not being able to fight back. Sweating it out. Everyone thinking, 'What the hell are we doing here in a shooting war anyway?' A hundred years ago, I stumbled over my feet in my haste to sign enlistment papers as an Aviation Cadet and raised my hand so I wouldn't miss the war. Now some square-heads are trying to blast us into oblivion. There was complete and utter frustration."

Jim Lynch described what such overriding fear felt like: "The initial shock makes your heart pound so hard that breathing is difficult. Your mouth goes dry, and throat muscles tighten. You start to sweat in your heated suit to the extent that when the crisis is over, you have to pull the plug. The survival instinct takes over, and you react to the situation and do what is necessary. You get an exhilarating feeling that gives you added strength and purpose. It all takes place in a couple of seconds." Some men, such as Charles Nickell, a fighter pilot in the 348th Fighter Group, began to feel the effects of fear after the danger had passed. In Nickell's case, he became very frightened while flying home after a dogfight with Japanese fighters: "On the way home from a fight is when most people get nervous, especially me. By the time I land after a fight, I am so nervous that my knees are shaking."

Not surprisingly, this constant state of fear took its toll on the psyches of combat airmen. Fear led to nervous tension, particularly among crews far along in their tours. Fred Price, a radio operator in an Eighth Air Force bomb group, wrote in his diary about a prevailing testiness that took hold among his crew as they approached the end of their tour: "The Skipper is quick to yell at any one of us over the interphone. He admits on the ground that he is quick to loose [sic] his temper in the air, for no really good reason at all. Todd, our copilot, is easy to loose [sic] his temper when we kid him, and immediately he apologizes for it. Pappy, the other day at altitude, jerked his oxygen mask off of his face without exactly realizing what he had done. He just couldn't stand the feel of it any longer. The rest of the crew is equally nervous. I've had trouble several times with real weird dreams . . . and they're always connected with flying. It seems as if the farther a person gets on a tour, the more nervous he becomes."

Such constant fear and nervousness challenged the collective sanity of combat aviators, but they persisted and prospered in spite of it all. Franklin Shires, a Navy fighter pilot, spoke for most combat airmen on the subject of fear when he said that everybody felt fear but the key was to make sure that it did not interfere with doing your job: "You went ahead and had a job to do. You were afraid but you did it. You get feeling like, 'When am I going to get it?' And you get shaky and combat will do things to you. You're scared but you go ahead and do your job."

The incredible mental, physical, and psychological energy required to fly combat missions led to a significant amount of exhaustion among the airmen. A typical bomber crew, for instance, awoke four or five hours before they even took off for the day's mission. After takeoff, they could expect to spend as many as six to fourteen hours aloft. Then, when and if they returned, they had to face debriefing. It made for a very long day, and, as the missions piled up, mental and physical fatigue set in. As fatigue crept over him one night in early 1945, Kenneth Jones wrote in his diary, "It takes an extraordinary effort to keep smiling when life is measured day by day. The weariness brings on a feeling of general fatigue produced by lack of normal sleep and long periods of anxiety."

Keith Schuyler visited his enlisted men in their quarters during an especially taxing period that saw them fly close to thirty hours out of a possible one hundred. Previously, they had all looked like young kids, but, as exhaustion set in, they began to age: "They looked like men, like tired, drawn men with pale, pinched faces. Their grins when they saw me were genuine, but they lacked luster. Something wrenched inside me when I looked at their faces." Chaplain James Good Brown routinely saw exhaustion in the faces of combat crewmen. He observed them many times after they debarked from their planes: "Some looked wild. Others looked weird.

Others looked haggard and worn out. Others looked disappointed. Others cried because of what they saw happening to our men. Others were almost hysterical and talked fast. Others were sick—physically sick. The strain was too much for them."

Harry Crim, a pilot in the 21st Fighter Group, often felt exhaustion envelop him on the way home from long escort missions to Japan. After flying away from the dangerous Japanese skies, adrenaline wore off and he would experience a major letdown: "You suddenly realize that you are extremely fatigued, thirsty, and almost unable to fly the plane. The parachute harness irritates your neck, the sun is too hot, and worst of all you discover that you are 'butt sprung.' There is no position in which you can get rid of the ache in your sitting apparatus for more than a minute or two. You revive yourself long enough to land and taxi your airplane in, wave to your crew chief, and resolve to jump out of the plane to show what a hardy fellow you are, but after releasing the harness, you can't raise yourself."

Combat missions required tremendous reserves of physical strength, mental energy, and adrenaline. As young as most airmen were, they still felt considerable exhaustion after enduring such stress for so many hours. Harry Crosby, a navigator in the 100th Bomb Group, wrote that combat missions took almost every last reserve of energy he had. After a mission, he usually felt completely spent: "To do my job, I almost tore myself in two. Missions drained everything out of me that was in me. When I got out of a plane after a mission, I was so exhausted I could hardly walk. I smelled so much of sweat I left my flying clothes outside my barracks to air."

Sometimes the fatigue that airmen suffered from missions was not just physical. It could be a mental kind of exhaustion that threatened to eat away at a flier's soul. R. H. Tays, a pilot in the 392d Bomb Group, remembered feeling like he had nothing left after a long mission to Germany. He became morose and withdrawn, wondering if he could even continue to function: "Long missions, eight hours or longer, were extremely tiring and mentally fatiguing. I recall a long deep mission into southern Germany, flak most of the way, some bad weather, and the loss of several aircraft and crews. This was somewhere between my twenty-fifth and thirtieth mission.

We came home exhausted, and something happened to me after landing. War, death, and destruction just didn't make any sense to me anymore. That evening, instead of singing and whopping [sic] it up at the bar as was my custom, I chose a table off in the corner to be by myself." The chaplain noticed the change in Tays and went over to talk to him. Before long, Tays confided his feelings of hopelessness and exhaustion to the priest: "He looked me squarely in the eye and said, 'Tays, all of the major religions of the world have as their primary mission to teach man to live in peace and harmony with his fellow man. When I do not do my job as a man of the cloth, then you will have to do your job as a soldier.' His wisdom shocked me into reality."

Tays was probably experiencing the first stages of depression brought on by fatigue, stress, and the hopelessness that combat airmen sometimes felt. Combat aviators were susceptible to succumbing to depression when survival seemed impossible, when friends began to die, or when exhaustion and irritability came over them. Day after day, they witnessed suffering and death among those they most cared about, and inevitably many came to think that they could never escape this world of death. As losses mounted, depression became more common. Philip Ardery witnessed this many times in his unit: "It was hard for the boys coming back to go to quarters that were practically vacant, quarters which had been full a few hours before. It wore on their nerves to go to the club and find the place more filled with ghosts of those who had gone than the presence of the few who remained." Kenneth Jones experienced depression during his combat tour and wrote about it in his diary: "The nervous, hopeless existence of combat and death is never very far away. The only glory most of us can hope for is the glory of being alive after tomorrow. There is an unspoken obsession with death."

One sign of depression was withdrawal. As he approached the end of his tour, G. W. Pederson of the 306th Bomb Group increasingly wanted nothing to do with anyone else. He had lost so many friends and seen so much tragedy that he felt like he had nothing left to give: "I became almost a recluse, as close as one can be to a recluse in the Army anyhow. I ate by myself, went into town by myself. All my old friends on the aircrews were gone." William Black-

thoughtful tribute to his fellow Americans who fought their war on the ground in World War II: "At times I stare out the radio room window at the frozen desolate, pock-marked ground below and imagine those guys huddled in dismal, wet foxholes, with mortar shells crashing around them. They probably don't have an inkling of when they will eat their next hot meal or if they will eat at all. When I think of men sleeping in a hole in the ground in two inches of frozen slush, I sometimes experience guilt. After a mission, I get a warm meal and a dry bed to sleep in. I can shower and shave daily and have a drink or a smoke when I so choose. I have profound respect for those guys on the ground. Our tactical sorties in support of the infantry are especially gratifying to us in the air force. We can see the immediate results of our efforts in support of the ground troops. Strategical support is not nearly as gratifying as tactical missions, where the results are immediately obvious. God bless the ground troops!"

Combat airmen had close to the same level of respect and affection for the ground crews—noncombatants—who worked on their planes. At most airbases, the separation between flying personnel and ground personnel was usually distinct, but this did not prevent fliers from experiencing great feelings of closeness, camaraderie, and admiration for their ground crewmen. Although the ground crewmen enjoyed a mostly safe existence while combat aviators put their lives on the line, most airmen did not resent ground crews. They knew how hard ground crewmen worked and marveled at their dedication to their duties.

In fighter outfits, each aircraft usually had a two- or three-man ground crew, and fighter pilots often formed deep bonds with them. The pilots knew that their lives could depend on how well those fellows did their jobs. Harrison Thyng, a fighter pilot and commanding officer of the 31st Fighter Group, formed a friendship with his ground-crew chief, a man named Buck who came from the coalfields of West Virginia. Buck was a veteran mechanic who took immense pride in his work: "Buck spoke laconically and only when the occasion demanded. He was faithful to duty and loyal. He spent hours sanding and polishing . . . tuning the engine to get its utmost power, and patching flak holes that he felt I had 'carelessly' acquired." When it came to their airplanes and pilots, many ground crewmen formed protective instincts that bordered on the maternal. Pilots such as Robert Goebel knew that the crewmen worked so hard because they wanted to make sure they gave pilots the best chance for survival: "It was a point of honor with them that the aircraft and pilot came first; no task was too hard, too long, or too insignificant if it affected the ability of the aircraft to function or the pilot to survive. Individuals felt personally disgraced if their work was found to be wanting, and they suffered the double indignity of peer disapproval. There were no screw-offs; they were simply not tolerated." Quite simply, combat units had no toleration for "screw-offs" because lives were at stake every day. Everyone seemed to appreciate and understand that.

Francis Gabreski, a fighter pilot in the 56th Fighter Group, fondly recalled the extra hours his ground crew logged to make his plane faster and safer: "They were really the key to the performance of the airplane because of the pride they put into their work. They were out there polishing the airplane so I could get a little more speed out of it, that little advantage over the enemy. They would . . . make sure it was running as smooth as a sewing machine." The pilots in J. Fred Baumann's unit appreciated this dedication and made sure to communicate their gratitude as much as possible: "All of our relationships on the flight line with the crew chiefs, armorers, and other maintenance personnel . . . were of a highly informal nature. And although we never 'socialized' (they had their club, and we had ours), nevertheless we always made certain that they got their share of 'medical' whiskey. Those boys had a tough job, at times working all night before a mission in order to make their assigned aircraft airworthy for the mission. Moreover, our lives depended upon how well (and thoroughly) they performed their jobs."

The same situation held true for Navy fighter pilots, who relied heavily on their "plane captains" and formed affectionate relationships with them. As Navy Fighter Pilot Jim Campbell explained, Navy ground crews, like their Army counterparts, did an outstanding job: "They were enlisted seamen who were assigned to a particular plane and most of them looked after that plane like they were going to fly in it themselves. They took a lot of pride in their job and worked hard to keep their plane in first class condition. They were loyal and dedicated and took it very hard if their plane and pilot was [sic] damaged or lost."

Bomber crews relied on even larger ground crews to keep their planes running properly. They too found their ground crews to be extremely dedicated to their work and extremely sensitive to the dangers that combat aviators faced. Frank Halm of the 94th Bomb Group described his plane's ground crew as "highly knowledgeable and experienced. They really looked after the aircrews. While the flyboys may have gotten the glory, they . . . worked so that you would have everything possible in your favor. They were our best friends." David Hayward, a B-25 pilot in the 341st Bomb Group, believed that ground crews were responsible for much of his unit's operational success against the Japanese in the CBI theater: "The excellence of the mechanics on the ground was one of the main reasons for our success. Never once did I have a mechanical failure on a B-25, and never once did I have to turn back from a mission. Those things don't happen just by chance. The maintenance was superb." Willis Marshall, a top turret gunner/engineer in the 389th Bomb Group, was touched when he noticed ground crewmen with tears in their eyes waiting to greet his crew after a very rough mission: "Those ground crews did a bang-up job. It was almost unbelievable what those men did and had to put up with. Working at times through the night and in all kinds of weather to get those birds ready to go on the next day's mission. They have never received proper credit for their endeavors." Like most bomber pilots, William Cubbins of the 450th Bomb Group (known as the "Cottontails") had a soft spot for his ground crewmen. He knew that they agonized over the fate of bomber crews and that casualties were almost as hard on them as they were on the fliers: "They didn't seem to be able to work hard enough or long enough to do their part. Perhaps it was their way of apologizing for not being in a position to be shot at. If so, it was a misguided sentiment. We knew and appreciated the difficult conditions under which they labored. Fine men, heroic in their own manner, they often worked to exhaustion to keep us flying. Without their selfless efforts and devotion to excellence, combat would have been even more dangerous. Seldom praised, their consolation was the certain knowledge that they, too, were Cottontails."

Combat airmen readily understood that, ultimately, the job of everyone else on their entire base was to support their combat missions. Even though they took immense pride in their "tip of the spear" jobs, combat aviators realized that, without the support of countless people on the ground, they could do nothing. Many years after the war, Ray Zuker, a pilot in the 486th Bomb Group, wrote a grateful tribute in a veterans' newsletter to all the ground-support people in his unit: "Our mess hall personnel who were aroused in early hours to prepare breakfast for flight crews deserve more than a little recognition. They did their best under stressful conditions and without complaint. The Flight Surgeons assigned to squadrons were always available, no office hours then. These doctors conducted themselves in an exemplary manner that upheld their profession. The entire Support Teams on all bases did an outstanding job. A point that must be remembered, support-team personnel were on station for the duration. The Chaplains were held in special reverence, no matter their respective religious affiliation. The line Crew Chiefs and their mechanics deserve a special mention. Many times they had to work under dismal working conditions— out of doors in the cold, rain and high winds. Yet when the airplanes were scheduled to fly they were ready to go."

Some combat airmen faced not simply the challenge of enemy opposition but also the challenge of fighting against the prevailing racial attitudes and mores of mid-twentieth-century America. The Army Air Force trained and sent to Italy an entire fighter group of African-American fighter pilots. These combat airmen, usually called "The Tuskegee Airmen" because most were trained in Tuskegee, Alabama, fought what they termed a "two-front war." In combat, they fought the Germans, but on the ground they fought against racial stereotypes. They knew that only intense lobbying on the part of the black community, as well as wartime necessity, had persuaded the Army brass to earmark them for combat, since the vast majority of African-American servicemen in World War II were deliberately used for support duties. Many white Americans and high-ranking officers felt blacks did not have the "instincts, courage, or reliability" to function well in combat.

Roscoe Brown, a fighter pilot in the 332d, outlined the barriers that faced black combat pilots: "We fought two wars, one against Fascism, one against segregation, and sometimes you couldn't tell which one you were fighting. Our aim was to convince white people that if we could do the job as well as or better than they, they wouldn't be prejudiced. The only way people learn not to be prejudiced is if they have a whole range of social experiences. But we neutralized an excuse for excluding us."

In saying that he and his fellow pilots "neutralized an excuse," Brown was referring to the excellent combat record his unit compiled in Italy. Black pilots proved themselves to be willing, able, and aggressive pilots in combat, but they had to fight an uphill battle to establish that reputation.

Some whites, including some combat airmen, viewed blacks as inferior. They wanted to import American racial customs abroad with them during the war—very ironic, considering the fact that America viewed itself as fighting for freedom against murderous and intensely racist regimes. Dick Marshall, a confirmed Southerner, did not particularly dislike blacks but neither did he view them as equals. Upon visiting Australia and meeting aborigines, he wrote to his family that they would cringe "to hear a negro conversing with a broad British accent. This would undoubtedly cause old Zachary Taylor and the good members of our family of Peachtree Street, Augusta, to turn over in their graves. I think it's pretty funny myself." John Clarkson, a top turret gunner/engineer in the 34th Bomb Group, had far more intense feelings on the subject of race. He did not like blacks, and he especially did not like the idea of them dating white women, a sentiment he shared with many other white GIs. Nothing seemingly offended the sensibilities of confirmed racists more than black men dating white women. Clarkson wrote to his wife about it: "Here's something which should really make you wonder: The English *think* that the American Negro soldier is an American Indian [and] although our American Headquarters in London has told the English different the English cannot believe it. It is a *very common sight* to see an American Negro soldier walking, dancing, eating & *etc.* with a white English girl. Very disgusting to us Yanks, but the niggers have a priority I guess. One of many rumors is that the limey gals like the way a nigger kisses because of the nice big lips. How about that?"

Most white combat airmen, though, were far more moderate on the subject of race. As products of a segregated society, most did not have much experience with black Americans, so they carried with them a mixture of racial stereotypes, benevolence, and understanding in their racial attitudes. A good example of this is the way J. Fred Baumann's fighter unit reacted when they sometimes had near-collisions in the air with pilots from the 332d. In an effort to provide the greatest protection possible for the bombers they escorted, the 332d flew very tight formations, and this tactic sometimes cut down on their visibility—a very dangerous situation if another fighter unit was in the area, as was the case at times with Baumann's 52d Fighter Group: "A typical warning from one of our flights would be: 'Look out!! Here come the damn jigs!!!' . . . and suddenly, baroommm . . . there they were—cruising right through the middle of our designated area. No, these remarks are not intended as being 'racist,' regardless of how they may be interpreted. I witnessed this type of irresponsible flying on several occasions, always by the Red-Tail 332d. However, they compiled a good record and the conditions under which they were forced to serve were reprehensible. Their pilots were unquestionably the elite."

If confronted with charges of "irresponsible flying," the Red Tails would most likely have responded that their tactics were necessary for effective protection of the bombers. The Tuskegee Airmen claimed never to have lost a bomber they escorted to enemy fighters, a remarkable achievement.

Louis Purnell, a black fighter pilot in the 332d, experienced several examples of the "reprehensible" conditions Baumann mentioned. One time, he drew censoring duty for the letters of enlisted crew members of a stranded bomber crew. As he read one man's letter, he was shocked to read complaints about being "stranded at a nigger base, eating nigger food, and sleeping in a nigger bed." Later he confronted the man as the bomber crew prepared to leave the 332d's base. Purnell asked him if he had forgotten anything: "He said, 'No.' I said, 'The word is 'No, Sir.' That just boiled him. I said, 'After all, it wasn't so bad sleeping in nigger beds and eating nigger food, especially when we protect you in flight. I'll see you up there.' I walked away." After his combat tour, Purnell experienced a case of overt racism. He and a group of white pilots returned to America and went out "carousing" together as they traveled to their ultimate destinations. He became particularly close with one of them, but, when they landed in Florida one night, the Army did not allow them to stay together. Nor would they even be allowed to ride the same truck to their quarters: "He kept looking down, kicking at an imaginary stone. He extended his hand to me but kept looking to the side. As the vehicle came up and the headlights swept across his face, I could see his lower eyelids full of tears. The vehicle took him and the other bomber pilots to the Bachelor Officers Quarters. When a jeep came for us, it deposited us in a boarding house. There was a brass bed and something I hadn't seen since I was a kid—a wash stand, bowl, and pitcher—and a bare light bulb hanging down from the ceiling. Next morning my friend told me, 'You know, Lou, here we are in the good old USA, the country we've defended, and you can't even go to the same places I can.' I was so astounded, I couldn't answer."

Bernard Knighten, a 332d pilot, usually found that, while on leave in Italy, he could drink in the same bars as everyone else, but one time in Capri he found himself excluded from a party because of his race: "They had a dance at the white hotel, and a captain stopped us at the door [and] said, 'There are white nurses here.' We just walked off. We weren't torn up about it, we assumed that was the way it was; we weren't the aggressive type at that time."

Clearly, attitudes did not change overnight. Even so, black pilots did succeed in winning over some of their white comrades. The shared experience of combat often works wonders in overcoming racial barriers and stereotypes, and some men in the 332d found that out. Ed Gleed, a black fighter pilot and squadron commander, remembered an instance in which a group of stricken bombers made emergency landings in the middle of a snowstorm at the 332d's base. Most of the white bomber crewmen blended in quite well with black airmen, but the pilot of one B-24 crew would not let his crewmen leave their aircraft, preferring to expose them to the elements and make them eat cold rations rather than accept the food and shelter of black men: "I went out and tried to convince the guy that he and the rest of his men were going to freeze to death. At last, about three A.M., he reluctantly said OK, his men could come in. He himself accepted one of our cots, but he didn't sleep in our office, where we were sitting, waiting for possible orders for the next day's mission. And he brought his own C-rations from the plane. We never got another mission off for six days. About the third day, this captain finally came around and found out that the color wasn't going to rub off. We weren't monsters. I'll be damned if before he left there he wasn't converted!"

Eventually some white combat airmen forged such deep bonds with their black counterparts that they willingly stood up against injustice and segregation in the wartime military. Charlie McGee, a black fighter pilot in the 332d, met up with a group of white bomber pilots while on leave in Bari, Italy. The white pilots invited McGee's group to have a few beers with them, but when they tried to go out together, they came face-to-face with segregation: "There were others who wanted to continue the segregation in Europe that existed in America, and they tried to put us out of eating or drinking establishments because we 'weren't supposed to be there.' Our friends just said, 'Well, either they stay or we tear this place up.'" Another black fighter pilot, Henry Borland, even claimed that most of the white aviators he befriended in off-duty hours were Southerners: "I never had a bomber guy stop me to shake my hand or buy me a drink who didn't have a southern drawl. They were damned glad to see our black faces up in that 'wild blue yonder.'"

Such things probably would not have occurred in peacetime America, but men in combat, no matter their race, came to depend on each other and forge deep bonds of brotherhood based on shared danger and common respect. In a sense, the two races had to "get to know each other" after years of segregation. Kenneth Drinnon, a white ball turret gunner in the 487th Bomb Group, remembered sharing a hospital room with a black soldier—a small event, but one that opened his eyes to a new world: "This was the first time in my whole life that I had any close association with a young black person. We became close friends and played cards together. This was a small incident, but a very important one in my life." Many white combat aviators came to understand Roscoe Brown's point that black airmen had many goals that transcended combat: "We . . . wanted to improve the quality of life for our people. We knew we were different, and everyone was watching us. We were human beings with all the anxieties, jealousies, fears, and all the rest. But we were also black. It was more than a bunch of young black pilots flying fighter planes in a war and trying to be heroes. It helped to make us the men we needed to be, to come back and do the many, many things that had to be done."

Eventually many combat airmen, white and black, came to agree with what Sidney Brooks, a black fighter pilot, said in a speech to a Stateside crowd after his combat tour of duty: "America is its people—you. We are finding that the color of a man's skin, the blood in his veins, or his religion make no difference in finding whether he is or is not a man. The privileges of America belong to those brave and strong enough to fight for them."

From the postwar viewpoint, it is ultimately very clear that the sentiments Brooks expressed are largely what the United States fought for in World War II. Combat airmen who endured depression, fatigue, fear, and all the other terrible symptoms of modern combat did so to serve a cause that, in spite of its vexing contradictions, promised a better way of life for the twentieth-century world and beyond. The young men who put their lives on the line and managed to negotiate their perilous and sometimes terrifying combat tours of duty could have hoped for nothing less.

10

Breaking In Replacements

The flying has been as rough as I've ever seen it. We broke in some
new men in the midst of it. Interesting to see a fellow's outlook
change about this flying racket from a lot of glamour and shapely
women to honest-to-God hard, down-to-earth business—it doesn't
take long.

> —John Marshall, fighter pilot, 404th Fighter Group,
> in a letter to his father

Replacements were the lifeblood of American combat air
groups in World War II. Any unit with even the most rudimentary contact with the enemy experienced casualties. For
every fighter pilot or bomber crew lost in combat or to accidents,
new ones had to arrive to take their place. European-theater combat groups took particularly high casualties. By early 1944, heavy-
bomber groups were incurring 88 percent casualty rates over a six-
month period. In the same time frame, medium-bomber groups
lost 35 percent of their airmen and fighter groups 52 percent of
their pilots. Under these harsh circumstances, indoctrinating and
readying replacements for combat took on a high degree of importance. New airmen had to be quickly and smoothly blended in with
surviving veterans so that units could continue to fly missions. Only
rarely did American combat air groups stand down to accept and
orient replacements. That meant that new men had to learn swiftly
how to function and survive under combat conditions.

Combat replacements in American air units were far better prepared for their duties than their ground-combat brothers. In
ground-combat units, replacements sometimes went to the front
lines with little or no orientation, not as part of a group but as lonely
outsiders. By contrast, the combat air replacement often entered

his unit as part of a bomber crew, which gave him a group identity and cohesiveness with which to adapt to the stresses and challenges of being new to war. In addition, combat airmen were highly and specially trained for their jobs, and this gave most newcomers a reasonable amount of confidence when they joined a combat outfit. Fighter pilots, for instance, often had great confidence in their flying abilities. Even though they sometimes joined their units as lone replacements, their long training and natural aggressiveness (some would say arrogance) provided them with the necessary mental armor to deal with a very difficult situation.

Like inexperienced men in most combat units, air replacements had to prove themselves in combat before winning the respect of their veteran comrades. The treatment of new men in air combat groups was mixed. Brand-new replacements were often scorned or demeaned while being indoctrinated into the brutal world of combat. James Good Brown, a chaplain in the 381st Bomb Group, saw hundreds of new men come through his unit in the two and a half years it saw combat. In December 1943, he wrote about one such group. At that point, the unit had been in combat for close to six months, and only a small hard core of the original members remained: "The replacements come into the group as strangers, and they feel distant. No matter what one does, they feel somewhat lost, perhaps greatly lost. There is no way of getting around this difficulty because they were not members of the 381st during the long months of training back in the States. The new crews know, too, that they are not part of the original Group. They know also that they may go down in combat. This was not true of the original Group. Not a single man expected to be shot down. We were innocent."

In Robert Goebel's outfit, veteran fighter pilots cared little for the insecurities and fears that replacement pilots might have had upon entering the combat zone. New men were fresh meat, unproven, and immediately were given slots at the bottom of the pecking order: "As each new group came in, it had to suffer through the new-guy treatment of pulling lousy administrative jobs, living in crowded quarters, and being socially ignored by the veteran pilots. To begin with, they were overawed at the prospect of flying combat, and everything they saw and heard was strange and different. With a couple of missions under their belts and another group of re-placements below them in the squadron pecking order, they were finally accepted."

According to Goebel, one type of replacement rarely was fully accepted—the senior ranking novice: "We first lieutenants who had forty to fifty missions under our belts and were doing all the combat leading resented a newcomer senior in rank to us. Of course, it wasn't a captain's fault that he had been promoted while doing Stateside duty. But, as far as we were concerned, a new guy was a new guy. They were ignored, socially."

Jim Campbell, a Navy fighter pilot in Air Group 5, flew two tours of duty, including one on the USS *Yorktown*. Long after the war, when he reflected on the new pilots who joined his outfit after his first tour, he realized how shabbily he and his buddies treated them: "I'm afraid that we were rather hard on them and not very considerate in a lot of ways, but we older members had been together for nearly a year and had been through a lot together and had become a rather close-knit group. It was hard for a new man, an outsider, to come to a group like this. Through no fault of theirs, they didn't know what it was like and what all we had been through. Time takes care of a lot of things, and in time we accepted them and they became part of the group, but I don't suppose we ever felt about them as we did [about] the original squadron." Campbell even apologized to some of the former replacements at a reunion years after the war: "I made a point of telling them that we probably didn't treat them too well when they came aboard, and that I wanted to apologize to them for it. They accepted my apology but said that I was right, we weren't very nice to them, but that now they understood."

Those who ignored or mistreated replacements usually did so not out of hatred or mean-spiritedness but rather to establish emotional distance. Veterans often clung fiercely to the buddies with whom they had fought and managed to survive. These veterans did not trust newcomers. More than that, though, they had little emotional energy or compassion left to get to know new people after seeing so much tragedy and death around them. By the time they became veterans, they had most likely lost many friends, and this often left them with deep emotional scars. They reasoned that, if they no longer got to know new people, then they would not experience feelings of loss when the newcomers were killed. So when new men walked through the door of the barracks, some veterans actively tried not to get to know them in order to spare themselves the pain that inevitably would come when the new men were shot down or killed. Quentin Aanenson, a fighter pilot in the 366th Fighter Group, reached this hard-bitten stage in the late fall of 1944 after seeing his original group of pilots come close to extinction: "To keep our sanity, Johnny and I decided we had to protect ourselves emotionally. We had come into the Group with 18 other pilots—most of them close friends. As they were killed off, a little of us died with each of them. It was becoming too painful, so we decided to quit making new friends. We refused to let any new people move into our tent. It was an emotional defense system. It was an emotional control that I put on myself, and it affected me for many years after the war was over."

Jack Novey, a waist gunner in the 96th Bomb Group, found himself on both sides of the replacement equation. When he and his crew joined their group in the summer of 1943, their barracks mates made them feel anything but welcome: "There were no fond hellos or fond anything. After all, we were replacing people—friends, probably—who'd been shot down. We put down our belongings and tried to make ourselves comfortable. One of the others came over and said, 'Don't get too comfortable because most guys aren't here too long.' I said, 'What do you mean by that?' 'People just don't hang around too long,' was his retort. I didn't particularly appreciate what he was telling me."

Later, when he became a veteran, he afforded similar treatment to others: "For my own protection, I . . . decided not to memorize faces, not to look at anyone directly, and to keep contact to brief hellos. I guess this attitude was part of being a veteran. That's how we had been greeted when we were new. I don't remember the faces of the new crews; they all became a blur. It seemed safer not to know about their girlfriends and their parents, or to hear their dreams of marriage, jobs they wanted, or the good food they would eat. We just didn't want to hear it any more. It would be too painful when they were shot down."

Countless men had negative experiences as replacements. Veterans ostracized or ridiculed them. E. T. Moriarity, a waist gunner in the 306th Bomb Group, remembered that he "tried to make friends with my barracks mates, but they were not having anything to do with me. I could not break into the comraderie [sic] these combat men had established amongst themselves. It would take time for them to acknowledge that I was in the same boat." John Charlton, a replacement pilot in the 465th Bomb Group, found it hard to break into the close fraternity of combat-experienced pilots when he and his crew joined their unit: "Those of us that arrived as replacement pilots in Sept. 44 joined a group of original pilots that were like a fraternity, having not any interest in passing on helpful information on combat flying, or being friendly." Even so, Charlton did not resent the poor treatment he received from the veterans: "I think most of us realized that they had flown rougher trips, and at a worse time than we would have to fly, and were entitled to [have] that attitude."

Veterans often established emotional distance with replacements by razzing them with tall tales about the severity of combat. Keith Lamb, a copilot, experienced this treatment when he and his crew joined the 100th Bomb Group in 1944. Lamb and the other three officers on his crew walked into their barracks and immediately the razzing began: "'Here come the new replacements!' they shouted. That was the start of what we considered a particularly cruel initiation, which lasted for the next couple of days. Their aim was to thoroughly frighten us, and they related a lot of wild bloody tales to achieve their purpose. I took most of it with a grain of salt; it couldn't possibly be that bad. Unfortunately, we four took over the beds of a crew who had just been shot down. Most of their things were still there—pictures of girlfriends, and wives with children."

Pacific-theater units tended to incur lower casualty rates, so replacements were not always needed as badly and as often as in European-theater units. In these circumstances, it was not unheard-of for new men to be hazed by veteran fliers. One anonymous bomber crewman in the 494th Bomb Group related a story of mistreatment and neglect: "As replacement crews, we were treated like bastards at a family reunion. First, they decided to let their copilots be the First Pilots on our crews and make our First Pilots copilots on the old crews. At least, we might have gotten our fair share of mission assignments that way. They also threatened to have us drill. Like in MARCHING. We raised HELL and even threatened to quit flying. They finally decided to let us be, but [they] never were equitable in giving mission assignments. From 12 January 1945 to 8 May 1945, we flew 14 missions. The older crews flew 25 during that same time frame."

The treatment of replacements was a mixed bag, though. For every man with bad experiences, there was one with good experiences. Some men encountered veterans who welcomed them into their midst and who did everything they could to prepare the new men for combat. Wayne Rothgeb, a fighter pilot in the 35th Fighter Group, remembered that the veterans in his unit "seemed to enjoy the celebrity status we gave them. In spirit they were a relaxed, cheerful, and carefree lot who answered our questions with a few well-chosen, straight-from-the-shoulder words." J. Fred Baumann, a fighter pilot in the 52d Fighter Group, received a warm welcome from the veterans when he and his replacement buddies walked into the officers' club for the first time: "When we walked in, most of them were in there singing dirty songs, ordering (or enjoying) drinks at the bar, playing poker, and listening to V-discs (78 rpm 12-inch records). Without exception, they all gave us a hearty greeting, introduced themselves individually, and invited us to have a drink . . . which we gratefully accepted. As I looked around at the various fellows in the squadron, they appeared to be so mature, so experienced, so 'different'—and I felt so green, so out of place in such a group. Nonetheless, it wouldn't take long before feeling you 'belonged.'"

In fighter groups, some veteran pilots took special interest and care in the welfare of replacement pilots because of the wingman system. American fighters operated in two-man teams in combat. The wingman, often a new pilot, followed his leader and covered his tail. This encouraged the leader to teach the wingman how best to function in combat. Dick Macon, a replacement pilot with the 332d Fighter Group, had fond memories of being a wingman for a veteran fighter pilot who helped him survive his early missions: "Campbell was a big-brother type to me, my idol as a pilot. He had a good seventh sense. He could look down, and when he saw gunfire on the ground, he could dodge the bullets. He saved my life a couple times. Campbell would suddenly say, 'Break right,' and . . . you look back and, boom, you see flak where you would have gone." Before rotating home, Robert Goebel, who became an ace, even took the time to meet with new pilots and answer any questions they had about combat: "I had survived and learned, and I wanted the new pilots to do the same—that was all."

Some bomber crewmen, like top turret gunner/engineer James Bunch of the 453d Bomb Group, received very good treatment from the veteran crews. Bunch fondly remembered entering his barracks for the first time: "We were warmly welcomed into our new station by the combat crew of our new barracks. The men told us very little of their combat experience and tried to assure us that we would do OK in the months to come. They showed little concern for the next day's mission, so we thought there was nothing to worry about." Navigator David McCarthy and his crew reported to the 381st Bomb Group in the late summer of 1943. One of the first people they encountered was an airman who had completed twenty-four missions, a real rarity in those perilous days: "Dex was a compassionate young man who never tried to impress us with 'horror' stories of combat. To the contrary, he would spend hours explaining the operation and the mechanics of: Finding our way around England; Formation flying; Tactics of the Luftwaffe; and the Personalities of our senior officers." The other veterans of the group treated McCarthy just as well: "I do not remember meeting one of the veteran fliers who was burdened with an ego problem or who displayed any arrogance. There was definitely a camaraderie between the few surviving veterans and the replacement crews. We, the replacements, had been accepted as members of the . . . 381st Bomb Group!!"

Merle Perkins, a radio operator in the 483d Bomb Group, knew a ball turret gunner who never tired of speaking to replacements about gunnery and how best to survive in combat: "He used to sit on his cot holding forth on the fine points of gunnery to a newly acquired friend from a newly arrived, inexperienced crew. The rest of us were writing letters, playing poker, reading, mending a sock. We paid no conscious attention. We had heard the spiel so many times before! It was as if he were a tape-recorder rehashing for a new audience the basic facts of gunnery."

When Pilot Keith Schuyler and his crew joined the 44th Bomb Group, they were not treated poorly, but, like many newcomers, they felt awkward and unschooled. Lacking experience, they sometimes felt like impediments or afterthoughts, but this changed after a few missions. Schuyler first recognized this change at group briefings: "As we listened to instructions, I for the first time began to feel a part of this group of grim-faced men who had been boys only a matter of days or weeks or months ago. I didn't feel quite so much a mere appendage to a war machine that moved on mysterious orders relayed at these briefings. Some of the faces were becoming more familiar, and an occasional nod gave an impression that my presence was of some importance to others than my squadron CO. I had been voted in."

Acceptance of new men happened for many reasons—not the least of which was the basic fact that combat units needed them so badly. For veterans, the worst damage to the psyche did not come from seeing their dead friends replaced. Morale actually suffered more when it took a long time for new men to join the unit and replace those who were gone. Philip Ardery, a pilot and squadron commander in the 389th Bomb Group, underscored this salient point: "Our sorest trial of morale came when replacements were not quickly forthcoming for the crews we lost, and the old guys had to face empty barracks for days on end. If new men came in quickly, the missing ones were less conspicuous." Clearly, replacements helped mend the psyches of reluctant veterans. Along the way, they brought a fresh outlook to their units and provided a crucial morale boost, even for those veterans most reluctant to get to know them. Provided they did their jobs in combat, it did not take long for most replacements to be accepted into the combat brotherhood of fighter and bomber groups.

Achieving such acceptance and surviving long enough to enjoy it were the main challenges for air-combat replacements. From the first day they joined their units, a difficult task lay ahead of them. They had to prove themselves in combat, survive their inexperienced initiation into battle, and negotiate their way through their tours of duty.

Simply making it through the first mission could be quite a challenge, because replacements had the extreme disadvantage of inexperience and did not know what to expect. Willie Green, a top turret gunner/engineer in the 34th Bomb Group, had the good fortune of going on an easy mission his first time out: "We were going to the Metz area, France, and were scared. We had heard so much about how rough these missions were, we were actually shaking in our shoes. We made the trip OK and it turned out to be a milk run. I thought to myself, if they are all like this, I will be sure to get back home." Paul Homan, a pilot in the 448th Bomb Group, had a much more difficult initiation to combat, a six-hour mission to the heavily defended German city of Magdeburg. The first time he came under fire, he had to struggle hard to control his deathly fear: "When I was exposed to the first 'flak' bursts as we were on the bomb run, it was a time filled with awe, fear, and prayer. One cannot fully explain that very first exposure to enemy fire, and to the need for calm to complete the mission!"

Surviving the initial mission was only the first of many hurdles for replacements. Charles Cope, a top turret gunner/engineer in the 464th Bomb Group, had a rude awakening during the brief orientation period he and his crew went through after joining their unit: "None of the training which I had finished prepared me for the stark reality of war. During a lecture one day on what to expect as to losses, I was sitting in the front row when the speaker told four of us to stand up. This represented those who had first started. He then told three of us to sit down. Only 1 of 4 would survive." As Eugene Fletcher, a pilot in the 95th Bomb Group, eventually learned, part of the reason for these long odds was that replacement crews were very vulnerable on their first mission or two. They did not have battle knowledge or experience yet, and they were flying in the most vulnerable areas of the bomber formation and in the most expendable planes: "It was a battle-hardened rule that a new crew would not be given a new airplane. Common knowledge had it that crews were more apt to be lost on their initial mission than at any other time, so it followed that you wouldn't risk a new airplane on a crew that lacked experience."

Aside from beating the odds over the deady skies of Europe or the Pacific, replacement crews also had to avoid being spooked by the inevitable nervousness and fatigue of veteran crews. Navigator Jule Berndt encountered this problem soon after he joined the 490th Bomb Group. He and the other three officers of his crew lived with the officers of a crew that had nearly completed its tour of thirty-five missions: "The navigator of this crew had himself a good case of nerves (flak happy). It appeared that the smallest disturbance would annoy him. The door of our hut, if not closed entirely, would swing open with a creaking sound. One evening, when this had occurred a number of times, he suddenly sprang up and slammed the door with such violence that it almost went through the side of the wall."

Keith Schuyler summed up quite well the perilous and unenviable existence of a replacement bomber crew: "A replacement crew was a lonely entity. It was accepted to take over a spot which might have belonged to one of the old gang who had earned a certain affection and respect. Either the old crew was on the way home, rotting in prison camps, or scattered in charred chunks of flesh and bone somewhere east."

Brand-new fighter pilots faced a similar situation. Robert Goebel wrote about the disorienting experience of being a replacement fighter pilot. Most of the replacements, in his opinion, were not fully prepared for combat: "A replacement pilot's first weeks in an operational unit were difficult for the individual, and they worked a hardship on the unit as well. The step up from routine, 'bore-a-hole-in-the-sky-type' flying to combat was truly a quantum jump. The step was magnified when the new pilot had to be checked out in an aircraft different from the one he had been flying. Front-line units just didn't have the aircraft, instructors, or the patience and time to handle transition training."

In fact, the Twelfth Air Force, of which Goebel's unit was a part, set up a special training facility for replacement pilots to transition them to combat flying and check them out in their new aircraft.

This leads to the question of how well prepared American combat air replacements were and how well they did their jobs upon entering combat. After all, the typical American combat airman had probably received anywhere from one to two years of training before he ever set foot in a combat outfit, and he should have been quite ready for the challenges that faced him. In spite of this, most veteran fliers felt that their replacements were not very well prepared for battle. Although the replacements had been well trained to handle their jobs (pilot, bombardier, waist gunner, and so on), they had not been properly prepared on how best to succeed in combat. For example, most bomber crews did not know enough about formation flying. Their Stateside training had not emphasized that type of flying, even though American strategic-bombing doctrine had been designed around it. New fighter pilots did not know nearly enough about formation flying either, and many had little notion of combat tactics.

Thus, the evaluation of American air-combat replacements is mixed. Most were eager, brave, proficient, and earnest, but their incomplete training left them vulnerable in their early days of combat. Joe Boyd, a fighter pilot in the Twelfth Air Force, had no idea how to fly proper combat formation when he flew his first mission: "Because I had never had formation flying, I was all over the sky. I was messing everybody up. I would fall behind and then shove everything forward trying to catch up, and I would overshoot the formation and then I'd cut everything off trying to get in formation and I'd get behind again. I used up my gasoline fast."

Part of Boyd's problem was that he had originally been a transport pilot and thus had received little schooling in how best to maneuver a fighter. For their part, a few bomber pilots also filtered into fighter outfits as replacements. These were men who had flown entire tours of duty in bombers and had volunteered to fly another tour as fighter pilots. Most of them were probably still smarting over the fact that they had been assigned to bombers after they had completed pilot training. They were experienced in combat, yet they usually did not fare well. When Hub Zemke's 56th Fighter Group ran low on replacement fighter pilots, he decided to recruit some ex–bomber pilots for his unit. He circulated recruiting notices at many bomber bases and had no shortage of volunteers. Before long, however, Zemke realized that his idea had been a mistake: "Interviewing and making the final selection was a time-consuming job, nor did I appreciate how much effort had to be devoted to training these men in fighter formations, tactics, and gunnery. Of those first six pilots received in May [1944], five were soon lost. Many other ex–bomber pilots transferred to fighters during the final year of hostilities, and their loss rate continued to be much higher than that of men trained in fighters from the outset. To hazard a guess why, I would say that it was the difficulty in taking the step from the comparatively slow sit-and-take-it philosophy of the bomber cockpit to the instant gut reaction necessary to survive in the world of fighters."

Robert Goebel remembered seeing one ex–bomber pilot replacement during his tour of duty. In Goebel's opinion, the man had courage but did not make much of a fighter pilot: "'Libby' was only a so-so fighter pilot, which was to be expected considering the different flying characteristics of fighters and bombers. But all of us respected his heart and his experience, and he was not given the usual new-guy treatment."

Most fighter-pilot replacements had been trained specifically to be fighter pilots, but that did not mean they all became effective combat pilots. Sometimes, new men could be disastrous failures. One such man joined Harold Rosser's 33d Fighter Group in the CBI theater. From the beginning, he displayed an arrogant, condescending attitude toward the group's veterans, hardly the best way to ingratiate yourself with combat pilots. This replacement continually implied that his Stateside training techniques superseded those that Rosser and the other veterans had learned in real combat. One day, on a mission to Mandalay, the man's attitude led to tragedy. One of Rosser's buddies told him the story: "'When we approached the target, Garbarini [a veteran] told the SOB to cross over to the other side to get out of the sun so it wouldn't be in his eyes when we began the strafing run. He dropped down to slide across, but he didn't drop low enough. His prop chewed Garbarini's plane all to smithereens. He sliced Garbarini with that prop! Garbarini didn't say a word. His plane just fell. It started spinning, crazy-like. He never had a chance. He spun right into the ground and exploded.'"

Most fighter replacements, however, were far more eager to learn about combat flying from the veterans. They simply needed experience and instruction in combat formation flying to become reliable members of their outfits. Francis Gabreski, an ace fighter pilot and squadron commander in the 56th Fighter Group, wrote that new pilots usually lacked the proper training and experience for combat. He took a special interest in helping them adapt: "In nearly every case . . . these pilots lacked the experience that our original pilots had. Some of our old hands were telling me they didn't think the newest pilots had received sufficient training in the States. In my role as squadron commander, I wanted to feel confident that every pilot I sent out was capable of flying well enough not only to take care of himself but also to provide protection for his fellow pilots. When new pilots joined the 61st [squadron], I would take them up for a practice mission."

Gabreski did what any effective and intelligent commander should do—familiarize himself with the strengths and weaknesses of every person under his command. In so doing, he effectively taught new pilots how best to survive in combat. Although initially unprepared, his new men quickly learned how to be good *fighter* pilots, not just good pilots.

Bomb groups also had their share of problems with new replacements. Most veteran bomber crewmen did not have very high opinions of their new crew's state of readiness for combat missions. The biggest complaint was lack of formation flying experience, but the twin evils of arrogance and incompetence could also be a problem. Jack Novey could not believe the stupidity of a replacement waist gunner who flew with his crew one day on a mission to destroy submarine pens in northern France. In spite of the fact that it was the waist gunner's first mission, he slept most of the way: "I kicked him awake over the target, and then he went to sleep again. This dumb jerk told me if this was combat, he would sleep his tour away. He had a lot to learn. He was one startled human when the JU-88s attacked. As angry at him as I was, I was not happy that he and his crew were shot down on their next mission." Quilla Reed, a top turret gunner/engineer in the 91st Bomb Group, had a low opinion of replacement crews in general, especially after he had the misfortune to fly with one on their first mission: "I remember the ball turret man just couldn't make it—he'd just cry—and he wanted his mama, he really did. The pilot had been an instructor in the U.S. for four or five years, but he couldn't fly formation. He was trained on a B-17 in the U.S. but not long enough. If you can't fly formation, you're in trouble." Kevin Herbert also saw many bomber-crew replacements who simply were not prepared for combat. They made rookie mistakes and generally did annoying and foolish things: "Apart from the shortage of [replacement] crews, there was also the matter of their quality, which seemed to decline in the final months [of the war]. One yahoo brought in a gleaming new [B-]29 from Wichita, but forgot to check the landing gear as fully down and locked. Needless to say, the plane was somewhat used when the gear collapsed and it finally skidded to a halt at the end of the runway. Another of the later pilots chewed tobacco, the juice of which occasionally was found sprayed over instruments, windows, and the like. But the absolute nadir was reached by the tail gunner of a crew which once took our ship on a mission during a rest break for us. Upon return of the plane to us, I checked the guns in preparation for our next time out. I was shocked to discover that this cretin had loaded 1,500 rounds of .50 calibre [sic] ammunition into the tail guns [causing them to jam]."

Clearly, the bulk of American combat air replacements had not been completely prepared for combat by their extensive Stateside training. In spite of this shortcoming, though, most of those who survived their initial encounter with the enemy became effective fliers. With the kinds of casualties suffered by operational combat air groups in World War II, units had little other choice but to throw new men into battle quickly. This "sink or swim" proposition proved too difficult for some but not for the majority. In spite of the daunting challenges presented to American combat air replacements in World War II, most adapted well enough (usually with experience).

John Marshall, who welcomed and oversaw many replacements during his days as a fighter-squadron commander, wrote in a letter to his parents a very fair and thoughtful assessment of one such group he had recently indoctrinated into the ways of combat. It is fair to say that the group Marshall described is largely representative of most American combat air replacements in World War II: "These devils look young now and darn few razors in the crowd. They do a fair job of flying, but it is too big a picture for them to grasp (me too). Just high school, off the farm, young, and it isn't often that much imagination or initiative shows up. It is easy to understand. You have to be careful about discipline or you defeat yourself. All of them eat up the flying and to hell with the rest of it. We never had lace on our pants, but still I never knew a bunch could be so immoral, as a lot of them are, yet, at the same time, when they have to, they all have a nice thoughtful manner about them which isn't polished but just earthy manners that I like. They'll tip their hats to an old lady and help her across the street, but if a shapely young one goes by, they aren't worth shooting. They stay pretty straight, for they know I don't have any patience with their goings on, though gawd, you've got to laugh. You can tell 'em until you are blue in the face, but if it doesn't tie in with flying, you may as well forget [it]. This bunch is the most respectful bunch I've been with in spite of combat and the daily living together."

So it was for most American replacement fliers. Young and inexperienced, they had to make their way through the dangerous world of combat flying. Although the challenges were immense, those who managed to survive their early missions usually became part of the respected brotherhood of combat fliers—a brotherhood that motivated them to risk their lives day after day in a world of death and violence.

a friend: "We got to know one another pretty well and began to operate as a team. All of the crew were conscientious and anxious to do a good job. I think we all realized that, if we didn't do our individual jobs well, we could be responsible for [ending] the lives of others." Kenneth Drinnon, a ball turret gunner in the 487th Bomb Group, froze up the first time he saw a German fighter attacking his plane. He was not sure if he could take another person's life. Then he thought of his fellow crewmen, the best friends he had ever made, and knew what he had to do: "As the German approached, I began to debate in my mind as to whether I should begin firing. Here I was, a barely twenty-year-old boy, who had never before fired a gun at another human being. I suddenly realized that I would be letting my crew and my buddies down if I didn't begin shooting. That is the moment when I pressed the thumb button that caused both of my '.50s' to commence firing." In that instant, Drinnon understood one fundamental reality of warfare. He had to kill those whom he had never met (the enemy) in order to protect those whom he knew (his buddies). The barbarism and inhumanity of war cause combatants to make this unpleasant choice routinely.

William Cubbins, a pilot in the 450th Bomb Group, provided perhaps the most thoughtful and penetrating analysis of the reasons that brotherhood motivated the combat fliers in his outfit to fight: "Another face of courage is the love and respect that one has for comrades in battle. It is an allegiance more to one's self [sic] and others than to the 'cause.' That men may rise above their fears and fight in a self-sacrificial manner is not only noble, it is often the margin of victory in battle. There is also the impulse to do a thing simply because it is the thing to do. If we do not emulate our peers, we become . . . outcasts from our closed society. The two notions seem to coalesce into the most prevalent force of all—that is, 'fear of being perceived to be less than one's peers.' Fear-of-being-less-than is not a form of competition in its usual sense. It is more like willingness to do what other men find necessary, an unspoken bond of shared responsibility. For many it is a sustaining force that bridges fear-filled moments between battles, and allows them to find comfort in 'shared' danger."

Cubbins's words help foster some degree of understanding of what the brotherhood was like for American combat airmen in World War II. It was a blend of peer pressure, love, respect, and shared responsibility that became a "sustaining force" in motivating men to overcome their fears and face combat, in spite of the fact that combat could, and often did, lead to their very extinction. Comradeship sprung mostly from unselfishness and a desire to band together to survive and do the job at hand. John Crowe, a copilot in the 491st Bomb Group, served on a crew that became very close even before combat. Their pilot had called them together even before they had officially been assigned to the same crew. As they met and talked, a brotherhood soon developed: "Strangers became friends and friendships evolved that have stood the test of time for nearly half a century. There is no stronger bond between men than the one cast of war, where you look death in the eye together, willing without hesitation to pay the price if necessary to assure the safety and survival of your comrades, no questions asked. That's the way it was."

The same held true for fighter pilots, who often went out of their way to protect each other in combat. Charles Cummins, a pilot in the 361st Fighter Group, witnessed numerous selfless acts during his days in combat in the skies over Europe. It sprung from the mutual caring and concern that fighter pilots had for their buddies: "It was interesting how pilots outdid themselves trying to look after someone with a problem, even if they had to break away from the safety of the group to bring them home. We were trying to protect each other. Genuine camaraderie." Upon reaching the conclusion of his tour of duty, fighter pilot Robert Goebel of the 31st Fighter Group found it extremely difficult to leave behind the best friends he had ever known, men with whom he shared feelings of tremendous trust and respect: "I would be adrift from my comrades, severed from companionship so intense it was practically an interpretation of each personality. With my friends and fellow pilots . . . understanding and trust had grown so intimate that verbal communication was hardly necessary. Our companionship had to do with outrageous living and dying—sudden, violent dying. What I most feared about going home was being alone among people."

Ben Snyder, a bombardier in the 494th Bomb Group, had some pangs of regret when he and his crew finished their tour of duty in the Pacific. He would miss the rest of the men in his unit who had not finished: "Despite all the longing for home . . . there is no little regret in the prospect of leaving. We will be separated from two-thirds of the men who have been together for the better part of a year, often under dangerous and difficult conditions. There is a sense of 'letting the team down.' We have been bonded to one another by this experience." Eugene Fletcher, a pilot in the 95th Bomb Group, wrote to his wife about an emotional scene that took place not long after he and his crew finished their tour of duty: "I bid them good-bye in London, a rather touching ordeal. After all we've done, it seemed kind of odd to see them with tears in their eyes—and in mine too. A finer bunch of fellows will never be found again on one crew."

Because they experienced such feelings of brotherhood and trust, combat men could often be inseparable, as with Phil Garey's 94th Bomb Group crew in England: "We went everywhere together—drank together, took our passes together. If one of us got into a fight, it was for all of us, no exceptions." This closeness led to a great deal of unselfish sharing among combat fliers. Ben Smith, a radio operator in the 303d Bomb Group, looked back on this fellowship as one of the few silver linings of a violent and dangerous existence: "Our tenuous existence had the effect of ridding us of the twin sins of covetousness and avarice. The men on the combat crews were completely unselfish. They shared everything—nothing else would have made sense. When someone got a box from home, it was opened right on the spot and shared by all. Nothing was hoarded except whiskey. The flight crews were also generous with their English friends, sharing an endless booty of chewing gum, chocolates, silk hose, and cigarettes with them."

The same held true for Ray Zuker's B-17 crew. They flew together so often and established such a deep relationship that communication was often nonverbal. In combat, they worked together as an efficient team: "We lived, worked, and flew with such a high degree of concentration and awareness, each man giving his complete and undivided attention to the job at hand. We could anticipate a course of action just by a quick look, or a hand signal. When one gets that close to another individual, thoughts become orders that are executed quickly without hesitation. Certain facts emerged. The most important being the feeling of complete trust in the ability, and I must add the stability, of every man on the crew. As soon as this feeling became mutual, the bond was forged between us; it will continue for as long as we live."

James Good Brown, a chaplain in the 381st Bomb Group, witnessed this phenomenon in the combat aviators around him and even in himself, a noncombatant: "These men hung together like bananas on a bunch. They were closer than brothers. I am closer to these fliers than I ever was to my own two brothers. We . . . trembled together. We sorrowed together. We wept together."

There are, of course, countless examples of this unique brotherhood of the skies that developed among American combat airmen in World War II. Lee Archer, a fighter pilot in the 332d Fighter Group, rarely flew without his friend Wendell Pruitt at his side: "If there was any way we could fly together, we did. I flew 169 missions over there, and Pruitt and I flew close to 100 together. We were the two 'Hip Cats,' because we were both from big cities. We each had a little guy painted under our horizontal stabilizers, a guy with a zoot suit and a funny-looking hat." Jack Conger, a Marine fighter pilot on Guadalcanal, got into an intense dogfight with Japanese fighters one day and became separated from his wingman. When Conger finally returned to base, he found his wingman in a state of extreme agitation. Even though he had been wounded, the wingman could think of little else besides Conger's safety: "They tried to get him to a doctor. But he knocked them out of the way and ran around calling for me. He kept saying, 'Where's Jack? He's got to be here.' So pretty soon I came down out of the sky, and that was that. We were both mighty relieved."

Feelings of brotherhood could even surface when airmen were angry at each other. Harold Rosser, a fighter pilot in the 33d Fighter Group, witnessed just such an occurrence between his two closest friends, one named Reaves and the other nicknamed "Big Boy." After a long layoff from flying, Rosser's buddies grew tense and bored. One afternoon, their feelings of frustration nearly led to a fight:

"Big Boy thrust me aside. Without a word, he charged after Reaves. They squared off, leering at each other. Suddenly, Big Boy's eyes twinkled; Reaves grinned. The chemistry of combat friendship reacted and boiled over, subduing the flames of anger. Their grins widened. 'I don't want to fight you, Tommy.' Big Boy's voice was childish and tender. 'I don't want to fight you either, Big Boy!' Reaves's voice was just as tender, just as sincere. They threw their arms around each other and laughed. Arm in arm, they went back into the tent."

Brotherly feelings often extended to members of the ground crew, especially crew chiefs in fighter units. Harrison Thyng, a fighter pilot in the 31st Fighter Group and a future general, forged a very close relationship with Sergeant Buck, his crew chief. One time Thyng returned from a mission and greeted Buck, who responded by painting a tiny pink cradle on Thyng's plane. It was his way of informing Thyng that his wife had just given birth. Another time, Thyng was shot down and suffered various injuries, including a fractured ankle: "It was nearly midnight when I finally reached my squadron and hobbled into the operations shack. There stood Sergeant Buck. His dark eyes suddenly flooded with tears. He grasped my hand firmly. He picked me up bodily and carried me out to our parking area, and there was a Spitfire complete with my number and personal markings." Thyng flew so early in the war that his unit was equipped with British Spitfire fighters. After close to two hundred missions, he was shipped home, but not before an emotional good-bye with Buck: "'Thanks, Buck.' I said. He wheeled around and the trace of a smile flickered over his face. But the only farewell act was a quick salute and a terse, 'Sergeant Buck, Sir. Your friend, if it pleases the Colonel.' 'It pleases the Colonel,' I said. I never saw him again. We knew each other better than most men. Mutual trust, respect, and shared experiences were the bonds between us."

Robert Powell, a fighter pilot in the 352d Fighter Group, summed up the relationship that typically existed among men in fighter outfits: "There was brotherly love. We knew our lives depended on each other. Pilots developed some fantastic camaraderie that still exists today. The same was true between pilots and crew chiefs."

Merle Perkins, a radio operator in the 483d Bomb Group, wrote in his diary about the fellowship that existed among his crew. Frequently they would get together, ostensibly to discuss their jobs but mostly to hang around and talk about whatever came to mind, just a group of friends enjoying a "bull session": "The discussion is an airing of beefs, if there are any, but mostly we are there in a spirit of solidarity. All sense of rank disappears. It's just a good time, and the talk is free and easy." David McCarthy's crew spent Thanksgiving Day together in 1943. They were far away from home fighting for their lives in a war that had no end in sight, but they had each other: "We sat together at the same table and gradually the images of home and our families began to fade. That Thanksgiving Day, the ten of us *were* family, probably the closest family we were ever to have. With thanks in our hearts and love for each other, we celebrated one of the most memorable Thanksgiving holidays of our lives."

A major aspect of the brotherhood was the constant give-and-take among crewmen. They loved to tease each other. Like ballplayers, combat aviators had to have thick skins because one of the favorite pastimes of combat men was to give each other a hard time. Sam Ross, a ball turret gunner in the 384th Bomb Group, used to complain frequently to his buddies that he had the coldest position during missions—a valid point, because his ball turret was the only part of the plane without any kind of heating system. Even so, his buddies loved to razz him during missions: "For my benefit, the crew members used to talk together on the intercom: 'Too warm in the Radioroom. Just right back here in the Tail. Nice and warm here in the Nose. Turn it down, a little too warm here in the Cockpit.' While I sat by the hours in my cramped turret out in the slipstream, flexing my fingers and toes to keep circulation going. Buddies!"

In more serious circumstances, fliers did whatever they could to comfort and help one another. Richard Asbury, a pilot in the 449th Bomb Group, never forgot what his top turret gunner did for him during a mission when Asbury's heated suit went out. He immediately began to feel the effects of the outside temperature, which was fifty-seven degrees below zero: "I continued to fly the bomb run as my legs from the knees down became frozen stumps on the rudder pedals. After 'Bombs away,' I told my copilot to take control while I climbed out of my seat and onto the flight deck. James Carr [the top turret gunner] . . . took off my lower fittings and exposed my frozen feet. Then he opened his flight suit and quickly placed my feet inside and against the warmth of his bare skin. We rode this cuddly way for the entire four hours required to reach our base. This son of a West Virginia blacksmith saved my feet and I shall be forever grateful. This was typical of my crew, always willing to give of themselves."

Often as not, stories like this did not have a happy ending. The realities of combat meant that many fliers would inevitably lose buddies in action. This was the down side to the brotherhood. As men developed deep feelings for one another, it hurt that much more when someone did not return from a mission. Robert Vandegriff, a tail gunner in the 379th Bomb Group, wrote in his diary about the depressing effect of the loss of buddies on him and his comrades: "You live together, eat together, and fly together. Many times when you come back from a mission, there will be six, twelve, or more empty beds in your barracks. In the newspaper there will be a report, so many of our bombers failed to return in today's raid, but on the base, ground crews and air crews sweat out the return of their buddies, until all hope of a return is lost. That night is a sad one and most of the men are quiet. The empty beds testify to the thought in the back of everyone's mind, 'I may be next.'"

Indeed, the pain of such losses could endure for years, as in the case of one 448th Bomb Group veteran who exclaimed, "Losing friends was the hardest part. A crew was close—maybe even closer than brothers. And I just can't bring myself to think about it, okay?"

Harry Crosby of the 100th Bomb Group flew an entire tour of duty and then additional missions as a group navigator. Along the way, many of his friends died off, one by one, and it wore on Crosby: "When I thought of my friends . . . I had to sort them out, KIA, MIA, POW, stateside hospital, interned in Switzerland, or rotated. It got to me. I found myself rather numb to it all." Quentin Aanenson, a fighter pilot in the 366th Fighter Group, had to deal with the anguish of losing tentmates, some of the best friends he had ever had. One day, several pilots in his group were killed, including two of his tentmates: "It's the only time I remember breaking down and crying. Johnny Bathurst and I packed the footlockers for our dead tentmates."

There was no greater nightmare, though, than a bomber crewman losing his entire crew. Sometimes one or two men on a crew did not fly a mission with the rest of their crew. Maybe they were sick or maybe they were assigned to the lead plane of the group or squadron because of their proficiency. This happened to Oran Stover, a Fifteenth Air Force bomber crewmen. One day, the rest of his crew went on a mission, but for some reason, he was ordered to stand down. Stover never saw them again: "They were hit and exploded in midair. I lost my airplane and crew. I loved them. We were a team and worked together. I missed them. I still do, and will always miss them." This disaster also befell Merle Perkins, and it took him a long time to get over it. On a mission to Memmingen, Germany, he flew as the radio operator in the lead plane. That day, his group was hit very hard, losing half their planes, including the one flown by his crew. There were no survivors. Thereafter, Perkins repeatedly explored in his personal diary his acute grief and his guilt over not being with them. "They are gone! Gone! All gone! Alone in the tent tonight. Lost, all lost, gone, gone. My friends, all good soldiers, are dead. Headquarters says we had a great victory today. Headquarters is mad! Headquarters is lunatic!" A few days later, he wrote: "I have survived. My crew has not. Hot-pilot Link, story-telling Wil, beer-guzzling Adam, gentlemanly Lew, crazy, mustached Buck, somersaulting Genial, rock-throwing Jim, undertaker Jeff, and our boxing master, John, best friend, all gone, all nine gone. I am empty. I was there with my buddies, but in the lead ship, safe, while they were burning. For all the good I was to them, I in the lead ship, I with the big shots, I might as well have been on pass in Rome and wallowing in good times. I keep asking how I can be living and all my friends dead. That rips and tears me. They seem real and near."

Perkins raged at God in his diary. He could not understand why good people died: "How can You let them die! Why do You let them die? What is Your dark, mastering sense? Are we to laugh at all disaster?" Even months later, he thought about his buddies frequently and often relived conversations in his mind. In his thoughts, he could hear them talking as they once had, many days earlier: "I hear their cliches, the verbal tics that have come to individualize their persons . . . always accelerating, growing dimmer until I find myself straining to hear this cacophony that in real terms is not there. Then there is silence. I am alone again with a vague sense of uneasiness, the returning question: for what reason am I alive, when they are all gone? It's so hard to accept their death, I usually do not think of them as dead."

Perkins continued to wrestle with these uncomfortable questions, along with a mixture of guilt and exhilaration at survival, for the rest of his life. The death of his crew was truly a turning point in his life. Part of the problem is that Perkins had difficulty establishing what would later be termed "closure." His buddies remained real and alive to him long after they were gone. Milton Many, a gunner in the 464th Bomb Group, lost a buddy on a mission to bomb an oil refinery in Germany. One of the ways Many dealt with the tragedy was to write to his buddy's sister and fiancee. He then read to his crew the letters he wrote: "As I read it to . . . the crew, I read it with tears in my eyes and a lump in my throat. I know how they felt and when I had finished reading it with all my truest emotions, I felt like an actor receiving his ovation for something superbly done, in their silence." The act of writing the letters and reading them to his remaining crew members gave Many and the others a certain amount of closure on their friend's death. They could then come to accept it, even though the pain of losing such a good friend would always be with them.

In spite of the pain of loss, most airmen agreed that the brotherhood was worth it. Caring deeply for others presented the risk of grief if those others died, but mostly the brotherhood was a positive motivator for men in combat and one of the few beautiful sides within the ugliness of war. It is endlessly ironic that one of the ultimate evils, war, can often produce in human beings their finest qualities—love, selflessness, sacrifice, sharing, and kinship. All of these qualities made up the brotherhood of the skies, and those who experienced this brotherhood never forgot it. Every time he reflected on the war, Lowell Smestad, a radio operator in the 459th Bomb Group, thought mostly of the camaraderie of his crew: "As I look back, memories flood in of early morning flights into unknown territory, of living in a tent in Italy in the cold and dampness of winter, of the harsh conditions we faced daily. But what is strongest is the camaraderie—we relied on one another."

Edward Schlesinger, a navigator/bombardier in the 379th Bomb Group, felt gratitude toward his fellow crew members because he felt that their efforts had contributed to his survival: "I owe a great deal to the men that I flew with during the War and each one contributed greatly to the others' survival." In a postwar memoir, David McCarthy described his feelings about the men on his crew, who shared a brotherhood that endured for decades after the war ended: "These were the men with whom I ate, bunked, flew, and suffered during our time at Ridgewell [their base in England]. No finer group of men has ever been mustered. Our association, born in the spirit of adventure and nurtured in the horrors of combat, matured into mutual respect and enduring friendship. I love and respect them, each and every one!"

Many years after the war, as part of an interview for a Public Broadcasting special on one B-24 crew and its experiences during the war, the ball turret gunner of the crew told an interviewer his true and deepest feelings about his buddies: "I love all of you guys. You're different and your politics are different and your backgrounds are different, but I love you guys. You're a very important part of my life."

The brotherhood, then, never really faded. Once established, it helped young combat airmen motivate themselves to face death and, for those who survived, it provided wonderful memories of an otherwise terrible time. The words of Donald McClellan, a top turret gunner/engineer in the 491st Bomb Group, ring true for countless American combat airmen and the feelings of kinship and brotherhood they experienced with their comrades in World War II: "We were a cross section of American youth . . . but we blended well and encountered few personality problems. Our homes . . . crisscrossed the country from California to Alabama to Brooklyn and a few points in between. None of us were noticeably religious, but each of us appeared to observe God in some way. What we shared was mostly what every heavy bomber crew who flew combat . . . shared. We were the glue in the togetherness of a bomber combat crew, a bonding that by its nature is perhaps unparalleled. No stakes in teamwork are higher than the challenge facing those who ante up with death, and no man who experiences the gamble can tell you why one crew wins and another crew loses."

Such was the nature of the brotherhood of the skies among American combat airmen in World War II. It was probably the most uplifting aspect to the otherwise odious and monumental tragedy that was World War II—humankind's most destructive war.

Epilogue

The three years and four months I spent in the navy will always be with me. Those who were not with us would never understand. I remember the boys I served with and the things we did better than I recall what I did or whom I met last week. It was the greatest forty months of my life, but I would not want to do it again.
— Eugene Pargh, fighter pilot, Navy Composite Squadron 13

Not long after finishing his tour of duty, Radio Operator Merle Perkins of the 483d Bomb Group took a walk on a lovely day, the war seemingly far behind him and forgotten. Birds sang and the air smelled of spring. Yet even though his surroundings teemed with new life, he found he could not leave behind the days of the past, when death nipped at his heels: "In memory at times I still rejoin lost air crew friends. We walk down tent alley and into the old squadron mess hall alive with greetings and shouts. I hear our voices and laughter in discussions over coffee. Only a few seconds! Then silence, and the shadows fade." Like Perkins, many of those Americans who survived aerial combat could never really leave the war behind them. It affected them and shaped the way they lived the rest of their lives.

When the war finally ended in August 1945, most of those combat airmen fortunate enough to have survived breathed a fatigued sigh of relief. William Luther, a B-29 crewman who was in the middle of his tour of duty at the time hostilities ended, wrote to his grandmother about the joy he felt: "You can't know what a relief it was when the war ended. No more long grueling missions, no more fear and nervous tension and cold sweat, no more wondering when your number was going to be up or who was going to be next, but most of all the knowledge that sometime in the next few months we'd get to go home, to go back to the things and people we've been thinking about so long."

Rather than pausing to reflect on the past, most focused on what they hoped would be a brighter future. Quentin Aanenson wrote to his wife that he had fought "because my hope for happiness lies beyond this horror. I've gambled my life a hundred times so that my sons won't have to go through the same thing." Milton Many, a gunner in the 464th Bomb Group, wrote to his family and pondered the larger questions: "After this war, questions we ask of ourselves, 'What is this world to be like when we return?' 'How soon before another War?' Yes, we have our problems too, but life, no matter what hue it takes on, shall continue regardless."

When veterans returned home immediately after the war, they usually found that, for the rest of America, life went on, so they proceeded to focus their energies on adapting to the postwar world. Joseph Beswick, a top turret gunner/engineer in the 483d Bomb Group, had a homecoming experience that is often assumed in the popular imagination for returning World War II veterans: "When we pulled into the dock in the States, there was a little old lady on the dock waving an American flag and shouting, 'Welcome home, boys.' I get a lump in my throat every time I think of her. I will never forget her." For every veteran who received a welcome like Beswick's, there were many others who returned in virtual anonymity, wondering if those who had stayed at home appreciated their sacrifices. Without question, the rest of America did appreciate those sacrifices, but, while combat airmen had gone overseas to fight the war, life had moved on for the people at home. After the war, it was up to veterans to adapt themselves to fit back into society, not the other way around. Jack Novey, a waist gunner in the 96th Bomb Group, found this out when he returned to his Chicago neighborhood: "I was in uniform, wearing my wings, my sergeant's stripes, my Purple Heart, my Distinguished Flying Cross . . . but nobody gave me a second look. I don't know what I expected. I guess I wanted people to acknowledge me in some way, even to come up and shake my hand and thank me. But they looked right through me. In World War II, most of us returning soldiers weren't greeted with parades. Life in America was just going on."

Upon returning to his old training haunts in San Diego after the war, Marine Pilot Samuel Hynes found himself shaking his head at how little had really changed. Still, he noted a prevailing sense of exhaustion: "The same San Diego tramps were there, in the same low-cut dresses, drinking and talking in low voices to strangers. But it was profoundly different, too. There was no excitement now, no one waiting for orders to the war, no eager young men hanging around some veteran while he told them how it had been at Rabaul. We had all been there, somewhere, and we were through with it. It was like a locker room after a game, a game that you've lost. Or like the morning after a party, when you wake up and realize what you did last night, and how much of it can't be undone, ever."

Returning combat airmen had little other choice but to adjust to the America that awaited them. Initially, some wanted little more than to enjoy life again after so many years of sacrifice and stress. Joseph Hallock, a bombardier in the Eighth Air Force, told an interviewer from *The New Yorker* magazine his plans for the short-term future: "We feel as if we've been cheated out of a good big chunk of our lives, and we want to make it up. I want to go back to college. Damn it, I want to play drums in a band again. I want to feel that maybe I can look two days ahead without getting scared. I want to feel *good* about things. It seems to me that sooner or later I'm going to be entitled to say to myself, 'O.K., kid, relax. Take it easy. You . . . got a lifetime in front of you. Do what you damn please with it.'"

Gerrit Roelofs, a Navy pilot, decided to pursue an advanced degree and an academic career after the war, but he found the adjustment from years of military life back to civilian life very challenging: "I didn't anticipate what a shock it would be coming back to school. I would be sitting eight hours a day in a chair in the library, whereas for four years I'd been leading this violent, nonintellectual life aboard a carrier. I guess what I missed was that excitement and frenzy. I lost a lot of weight and couldn't sleep. I felt as if I didn't know anything and was starting all over again."

J. Fred Baumann, a fighter pilot in the 52d Fighter Group, had to think very hard about what he wanted to do with the rest of his life. He had worked so long and so hard to become a fighter pilot that the rest of his life threatened to be a terrific letdown: "I was twenty-two years old and had already achieved my 'life's ambition.' It would require time and willful adaptations in order for me to establish meaningful new goals for myself. Probably the greatest army-induced problem which I would have to overcome was that of pure laziness. As a pilot, when you were not flying, there was seldom very much that you had to do. Did I miss flying? Does a fish miss water?" Baumann ended up finishing his degree at the University of Tennessee and pursued a career in business.

Try as they might to focus on postwar goals, some combat air veterans had difficulty leaving their terrifying experiences behind. Upon returning home, some battled nervousness that came directly from their combat experiences. Harold Rosser, a fighter pilot in the 33d Fighter Group, had a very difficult time for the first few months after his return to America: "A yell, a car backfire, a plane overhead—these and a thousand other less obvious reminders of the recent past would set off a chain reaction that reverberated in my soul and kept me on edge for hours." Rosser credited his fiancee (later his wife) with healing the mental wounds he brought home with him from the war zone. Quentin Aanenson found himself profoundly grateful to have returned home safely to his wife and baby, but, for a long time, he could not seem to shake the war from his mind: "Every day I had to deal with the demons within me. I couldn't sit still very long. I had to get up and move around. While I didn't shake or have tremors, I could only read a newspaper for about 10 minutes at a time. Then I'd have to put it down. I couldn't stay inside very long. I felt restless—and nervous." As time passed, the nervousness gradually went away, even if the terrible memories never did. Upon returning home to Chicago after the war, pilot Bob Ryerson of the 96th Bomb Group turned to alcohol in a vain attempt to drive away the recurring nightmares of combat he experienced night after night: "I would get up at noon and then go to the corner tavern. I'd come home at four o'clock in the morning. I did that for thirty days. I was also bailing out of bed every night. My airplane was on fire. I'd fall eighteen inches to the floor and feel like a damned fool in the middle of the night. At least once a night, sometimes more. I was having terrible nightmares about the war. That kept up for . . . probably the first year." Gradually the nightmares faded and Ryerson's life came together. He eventually married and had a family and a successful career.

Some returning airmen experienced an altogether different sort of nightmare that had nothing to do with their combat experiences. Some of the veteran pilots of the all-black 332d Fighter Group found themselves confronted with the ugly face of racism in a country for which they had just finished risking their lives. Like many other returning black veterans, the Tuskegee Airmen were determined to strive for racial justice in America. After he returned to the United States, Spann Watson was appalled to discover that the base on which he was stationed had a segregated officers' club. Even though he had distinguished himself in combat as an officer and as a fighter pilot, he could not legally go to the club. He and some other black officers decided to take matters into their own hands. They would go to the club and desegregate it themselves: "Three or four people had already gotten arrested, but I had a pretty good reputation. I wouldn't take any bullshit from white folks." Rather than desegregate the club, the commanding officer of the base chose to close it down. Another pilot, Bill Melton, had several negative experiences after coming home: "We came back to an ungrateful country, just like the Vietnam veterans did. I was married to a very light-skinned young woman who appeared to be Caucasian. Charles Hall, Willie Fuller, myself, and our wives went to the bus station in Tuskegee [Alabama] to go to Montgomery to do some Christmas shopping, and when the bus driver used some nasty language, I saw red and went after him. Willie grabbed me and knocked the hell out of me. He said, 'Don't you know you can get killed?' But I just forgot where I was. Another time when I went into the train station to buy a ticket for my wife, I was wearing the uniform of my country, with my decorations and wings. There was no one behind the colored ticket window, so I went over to the white side. A little twelve-year-old kid was very insulting. A kid! This kind of treatment left scars. Those scars will never disappear."

Other African-American combat airmen experienced signs of progress, hints that perhaps the racial mores of America would change in the postwar world. Bob Deiz found that discrimination had no consistency, and that gave him some hope for the future: "It was strange, this prejudice we ran into; some places it was awful and some places there wasn't any at all." Former Fighter Pilot Howard Baugh came home from the war zone and found himself assigned to an airbase in Lubbock, Texas, the very heart of segregated America. Even so, he and his friends were treated well, perhaps because the base commander was a West Point classmate of Benjamin Davis, the commander of the 332d Fighter Group and the first African-American general to come out of World War II: "A staff car came out and the driver took us right to base headquarters; the base commander, Colonel Estes, wanted to see us. He said, 'I want to welcome you to the base. This base is open for your use.' He . . . gave us his office phone and home phone. 'If you have any trouble at all, call me up, day and night.' Everyone had been briefed and warned that we were to be treated like everyone else, and we were. We didn't have a bit of trouble."

Undoubtedly, no former combat airmen had quite as many challenges to overcome as did black veterans, but nearly all, white or black, had to deal with the tremendous effects, both positive and negative, that the war undeniably had on the rest of their lives. Bad memories of combat experiences generally marked those who experienced negative effects from their wartime service, but some, such as B-29 Pilot Robert Ramer, gave way to cynicism, especially in light of some of the bitter disappointments of the postwar era: "If I were nineteen or twenty, knowing what I know now, I would not do it. Just go down and enlist in the Air Force and climb in a bomber and kill Japanese just like that without a lot more thinking. I don't believe the president like I used to. Everybody rips off everybody else. I put my ass on the line for America and what do we have today? Was it worth it? Kent State, Watergate, Vietnam? What did it really mean? Today they are building Toyota plants in the United States and I drive a Datsun."

Many others, though, felt that the war had been responsible for many positive developments in their lives. After weathering all the flak and fighters the Germans could possibly throw at him, Gilbert Falck of the 94th Bomb Group felt prepared for any problem that arose in his postwar life: "I felt that in the future no person or situation could be as unnerving or threatening to me as what I went through on those . . . bombing missions." G. W. Pederson, who saw combat with the 306th Bomb Group, felt that facing death made him appreciate life: "I've always appreciated doing the ordinary things that people do in life. And having been so close to death, I live on a higher plane than I would have otherwise. Nearly half the people I flew with died, so each day I appreciate being here." Another 306th man, navigator Jim Talley, also found that the experience of combat made him cognizant of the truly important things in life: "My whole attitude towards my fellow man has changed. I'm so content and happy to be alive I don't worry about anyone having more money or more fun than I have. I'm happy, I'm alive, and I've got some friends. I'm warm, I'm dry. I think that war taught me to appreciate the simple good things about this life. A lot of people don't know that. Love is the greatest thing that I learned, loving your fellow man and trying to be helpful. My experience in service and my brush with death made a lasting impression on me that life is so fragile. To survive that has just meant all the world to me."

The experience of war also prepared some to succeed in postwar careers. Louis Purnell, a fighter pilot in the 332d Fighter Group, marveled at the fact that his fellow black pilots accomplished much more than racial justice in the years since their return from World War II service. Many of them also became quite successful in their chosen careers: "To look back at the accomplishments of the guys who were Tuskegee Airmen, a lot rose to heights—judges, doctors, millionaires, civic leaders—you name it, we've got it, enough to gag a maggot. I'm not a sentimental person, but by God, just to see the old guys, you get choked up and can't talk." Earl Wilburn, who spent the war as a B-29 bombardier in the 331st Bomb Group, became a prosperous labor attorney after the war. He felt that his war experiences gave him an advantage over others: "I always felt that I had a big edge because I had done something as a kid that was much tougher than whatever I was doing now. It gave me an edge."

If the effects of war were indelible on those who experienced it, so were the memories. Each combat veteran had to struggle with his cache of wartime recollections even as he went on with the business of living the rest of his life. George Russell, a top turret gunner/engineer in the 466th Bomb Group, noted: "There are two types of guys. Those who like to remember the times and those who just want to forget them." Many chose the latter category for three or four decades after the war. To them, the war represented nothing but pain, misery, and death. They chose to forget about it and enjoy their peaceful civilian lives, almost as if the war had never happened. Many years after the war, when these men reached middle age or old age, this form of denial often gave way to a desire to revisit what they had experienced. The war had left them with memories that had lain dormant for decades but never really went away. Jack Ilfrey, a fighter pilot in the 20th Fighter Group, went through this process: "For thirty years I had pretty much forgotten about it. When we got older, and many of us started retiring, we got together again. We talk about the days. And we miss the people who were lost, but we stay on the humorous side, because there were some very humorous things that happened, though we didn't think of them that way at the time. But we want to keep the memory alive, to pass along the message to the younger generations about the bad side of war, in hopes that they'll learn and that it won't happen to them or future generations."

For years, Jack Novey shut the war out of his mind almost completely: "After the war I closed the door on the past. For decades I was occupied with making a living, marriage, fatherhood, and all the other problems and joys of civilian life. I thought little about the war, except for the occasional flashback during a movie or while reading a book. I had almost forgotten about my involvement with the Eighth Air Force and the 96th Bomb Group. At times I would talk to my wife about it when we were first married, but that was more than three decades ago. By the early 1980s, we hadn't discussed it for many years." Then one day Novey and his wife visited the Smithsonian Air and Space Museum in Washington, D.C., and saw a large mural of a B-17 under attack. Suddenly a flood of memories came back to him. The memories inspired him to get back in touch with many of his wartime buddies and write a memoir about his experiences.

Men like Novey and Ilfrey eventually revisited their wartime experiences not just to educate future generations or reminisce with buddies about youthful days. They eventually revisited these experiences because their recollections never really faded. Unconsciously or consciously, many former airmen put their memories of war in the backs of their minds, but the remembrances were always there, waiting for the day when veterans wanted to deal with them again. In fact, the recollections, once revisited, were usually quite vivid. Keith Jones, a pilot in the 389th Bomb Group, wrote many decades after the war about the clarity of his war memories: "Four decades later, the memories are as vivid as yesterday. Notes scribbled on cheap paper with now fading ink create a stirring in the dust of years. The mind takes you back. Someone said it best for all of us. 'It was easy to die in bright sunshine, too easy for men who were young and unwilling to trade life for a few hours of glory.'"

In his elderly years, with the war many decades in the past, Donald McClellan, a top turret gunner/engineer in the 491st Bomb Group, could still close his eyes and almost taste and smell the past: "Today, I can still sense and smell and feel those moments. I can see the priest as he lifts his palm to bless our chances of returning safely. I can also feel the bomber vibrating up and into the dripping canopy of clouds hovering over the Channel cost [sic] of Great Britain, a checkered landscape far below from where the lumbering Liberators of the 491st Heavy Bomb Group soared skyward."

In fact, even years later, memories could be so vivid, so real, that the old emotions of terror and nervousness came back. Bob Ryerson found that whenever he talked about his wartime experiences, he would break down: "I would be nervous and I would be shaking . . . physically shaking, crying maybe. Then I thought . . . there must be something wrong with me that this bothers me so much. Within the last five years or so, I've seen videotapes. Guys would be trying to talk to people . . . and they would start to cry. That made me feel better." Indeed, Ryerson need not have worried about himself. Experiencing such emotions, even many years later, was quite normal and quite common, as he eventually found out. Ben Snyder, a bombardier in the 494th Bomb Group, found that thinking about the war produced frightening dreams: "I would awaken at night, trembling, seeking a target through ragged cloud cover from the nose of a B-29, the plane shaking in a field of black antiaircraft bursts, the danger and uncertainties of flying over enemy territory as vivid as

one's subconscious could make them." Instead of fearing these recollections, many came to embrace them later in life.

Probably the biggest reason men had wanted to forget the war
upon returning home was so that they could go on unhindered with
the rest of their lives. Decades later, their lives nearing a finish, they
realized that the painful memories of years past could no longer
hurt them. True to the cliché, time had undoubtedly healed some
of the wounds. In their twilight years, most, like William Binnebose,
a waist gunner in the 95th Bomb Group, came to realize that human nature ultimately hangs onto the good memories rather than
the bad: "It doesn't matter how bad an experience you may have
had, or how bad you want to forget it . . . there are always some
things that will bring a smile to your face and the thought of them
will help you to forget the bad times."

American combat airmen came to realize that the only thing left
of the war—and by extension their collective youth—was memory.
Harry Crosby's memories of his days as a B-17 navigator in the 100th
Bomb Group usually brought on a rush of ambivalent feelings: "I remember the cities we destroyed, and the German poets and inventors we stilled, but I remember the time when we went to the edge,
when we put our lives on the line, for a cause that we believed was
just. I remember my friends, those who made it and those who did
not. I remember the tragedies, and the horror, but I remember the
laughter." He often pondered why he had survived while others, no
better or worse, had not—a question for which there really is no answer: "I wonder what poets, what statesmen, what inventors, what
husbands, what fathers, never were permitted to play their part in a
contribution toward human well-being."

Many others also wondered why they had survived. Quentin Aanenson wrote fifty years after the war: "I see the faces of my buddies
who were killed. I see them as they were—while those of us who survived grow old—they will be forever young. I will always remember
them, and I will always wonder how it was that I escaped their fate."
Ray Zuker, a pilot in the 486th Bomb Group, visited the American
cemetery in Cambridge, England, and found the grave of a friend
of his from training days. The man had been killed when his plane
crashed on takeoff one morning. Zuker found himself hoping that

someday, perhaps after his own death, he would know why he had lived while people like his friend had died: "I recalled the last time I spoke with him. It was at briefing that fateful morning. He had no future, along with so many others who deserved better. We who survived, even after all these intervening years, have tried to answer the question—Why? Perhaps it will be answered all too soon."

Kevin Herbert, a tail gunner in the 498th Bomb Group, found himself coming back to this slippery question many times in his postwar life. Why had he lived while others had died? "I often think of . . . boyhood chums, school mates, and college friends who died in World War II. Always the reflections are in terms of the question, 'Why did they fall and the rest of us survive?' It is a query for which there is no answer. What contribution might they have made, had they lived, and what achievement can we the survivors point to that justifies the difference?"

The contributions or failures of the dead will, of course, never be known, so ultimately those combat airmen who survived had to focus on the worth of their own lives. In so doing, they found pride not just in their postwar achievements but also in what they had done so many years earlier as young air warriors. One bombardier who served in the 376th Bomb Group still beamed with pride at the thought of what he and so many others did during the war years: "I still marvel that every day thousands of young guys like me . . . would walk out and get on a B-24, a B-17, voluntarily, and go fly over enemy territory, where they die. Five miles up, no pressurized cabin, no heated cabins, little oxygen masks. I don't know if you could do that today." Robert Fesmire, who spent his war years as a pilot flying covert missions in the 492d Bomb Group, had nothing but the highest opinion of the men with whom he fought the war: "I will say this about all of them: if future generations have the characteristics these men possessed, our country will continue to be the best place in the world in which to live."

Beyond the obvious pride they exhibited in looking back at their service, many combat airmen also became wistful as they thought of days past. In so doing, they articulated the essence of what they as combat airmen had been all about—pride, sacrifice, fear, humor, teamwork, anguish—and what they had become as old men. At the very end of his postwar memoir, Jim Lynch, a radio operator in the 379th Bomb Group, provided some particularly moving prose to describe this essence: "Germany's devastated cities have long since been replaced by modern architectural wonders. The abandoned airfields are grown over by weeds. The sagging, moss-covered buildings of our former home base are quiet. The friendly banter of the laughing young crewmen and the staccato roar of the starting engines are long since silenced. We . . . are no longer the flat-tummied kids who rode the skies with romantic notions that we could save the world from self-destruction. We're older and wiser. We're tired senior citizens who have sent our sons off to war twice after fighting the war to end all wars. We have . . . raised families and lived a very normal American way of life, for which we were grateful."

Another combat airman, writing five decades after the war in a veterans' publication, perhaps expressed best the experiences of American combat airmen in World War II—and, in so doing, the kind of people these men were: "All air combat crewmen in World War II were the same. We all groaned when the curtain in our briefing room was pulled aside, and the long red ribbon stretching from our bases . . . to the target . . . was revealed. We all grabbed our mikes and our masks and our Mae Wests and heaved ourselves into the throbbing, shaking aluminum tubes of death, which smelled of high-octane gas, cordite, and urine. We all prayed a bit when the flak . . . whomped around us. We all cursed a lot when the fighters slashed in, wings aglow with our death candles. We all grieved for our buddies who didn't make it."

Truly, no greater and more appropriate epitaph to the American combat airman in World War II could ever be written.

Notes

Introduction

Everyone on a crew, p. 3. Wesley Wells, unpublished memoir, p. 4, Record Group 403, Box 50, Folder 3, Mighty Eighth Air Force Heritage Museum (hereafter referred to as Mighty Eighth).

That other larger, pp. 3–4. Elmer Bendiner, *The Fall of Fortresses* (New York: Putnam, 1980), p. 183.

Things that, p. 4. Stuart Leutnner and Oliver Jensen, *High Honor: Recollections by Men and Women of World War II Aviation* (Washington, DC: Smithsonian Institution Press, 1989), p. 188.

Make the truth, p. 4. Merle Perkins, unpublished memoir, p. 59, World War II Veterans Project, Special Collections, University of Tennessee, Knoxville, MS1892, Box 7, Folder 13 (hereafter referred to as SCUTK).

It means another, p. 5. Jule Berndt, "An 8th Air Force Diary," pp. 45–46, Mighty Eighth, RG 403, Box 9.3, Folder 11.

What glory, p. 5. Willis Marshall, unpublished memoir, p. 35, Mighty Eighth, RG 403, Box 9.4, Folder 12.

Perhaps the mission, p. 5. Gerald Rose, *Memories* (May 1997), p. 100, and (December 1997) p. 243.

When I read, p. 5. Wells, unpublished memoir, p. 14.

We here merely, pp. 5–6. John Marshall to father, 17 October 1944, MS1881, Box 16, Folder 15, SCUTK.

Their [the Germans'] job, p. 6. Tom Prior to brother, 2 December 1944, Collection Number 68, Western Historical Manuscript Collection, University of Missouri—Columbia (hereafter referred to as WHMC).

You returned, p. 6. Kenneth Jones, unpublished memoir, p. 134, Mighty Eighth, RG 403, Box 9.4, Folder 13.

It was for, p. 6. Terrence McArron, unpublished memoir, p. 6, Mighty Eighth, RG 403, Box 9.3, Folder 10.

When one of our, p. 7. Ray Zuker, self-published memoir, p. 49.

The towns, p. 7. Vince Cahill, *The Ringmasters: The 491st Bomb Group,* unpublished unit history, p. 129.

Today I would, p. 7. D. A. Lande, *From Somewhere in England* (Osceola, WI: Motorbooks International, 1990), p. 168.

Flying, fighting, pp. 7–8. Wayne Rothgeb, *New Guinea Skies* (Ames, IA: Iowa State University Press, 1992), p. 253.

Unfortunately, p. 8. Charles L. Brown, unpublished memoir, p. 5, Mighty Eighth, RG 403, Box 50, Folder 2.

So long as I live, p. 8. R. H. Tays, unpublished memoir, p. 30, Mighty Eighth, RG 403, Box 9.2, Folder 3.

It was the thing, p. 8. Lande, *From Somewhere in England,* p. 19.

I suppose there are, p. 8. Robert Goebel, *Mustang Ace* (Pacifica, CA: Pacifica Press, 1991), p. xiii.

War experiences, p. 9. Zuker, self-published memoir, p. 48.

The most surprising, p. 9. J. Fred Baumann, unpublished memoir, p. 428.

But perhaps, p. 9. Quentin Aanenson, unpublished memoir, p. 1, Mighty Eighth, RG 403, Box 9, Folder 7.

They were shared, p. 9. David McCarthy, *Fear No More: A B-17 Navigator's Journey* (Pittsburgh: Cottage Wordsmiths, 1991), p. xi.

For some, p. 10. John Crowe, unpublished memoir, p. 1, MS1427, Box 1, Folder 9, SCUTK.

Future generations, p. 10. Luther Smith, *Chronicles of War* (Winter 1998).

Chapter 1

In the case of, p. 12. Wesley Frank Craven and James Lea Cate, eds., *The Army Air Forces in World War II: Services Around the World,* Vol. VII (Washington, DC: Office of Air Force History, 1983), p. 402.

Some had even, p. 12. Samuel A. Stouffer, *The American Soldier, Studies in Social Psychology in World War II: Combat and Its Aftermath,* No. 2 (New York: John Wiley & Sons, 1949), pp. 325–26.

The numbers were, p. 13. John C. McManus, *The Deadly Brotherhood: The American Combat Soldier in World War II* (Novato, CA: Presidio Press, 1998), p. 10.

Seventy-two percent, p. 14. Stouffer, *Combat and Its Aftermath,* pp. 340, 328.

The Air Force created, p. 14. Craven and Cate, eds., *The Army Air Forces in World War II: Men and Planes,* Vol. VI, pp. 523–24.

I guess we were, p. 15. Lande, *From Somewhere in England,* pp. 21–22.

The fact is, p. 15. Chester Bennett to John, 8 April 1945, WHMC.

I don't think, p. 16. Samuel Hynes, *Flights of Passage* (Annapolis: Naval Institute Press, 1988), p. 112.

Understandably, p. 16. Craven and Cate, *The Army Air Forces in World War II,* Vol. VII, p. 386.

Scoring high, pp. 16–17. Craven and Cate, *The Army Air Forces in World War II,* Vol. VI, pp. 549–53.

To this day, p. 17. Goebel, *Mustang Ace,* p. 16.

No one knew, p. 17. Eugene Fletcher, *Fletcher's Gang: A B-17 Crew in Europe, 1944–45* (Seattle: University of Washington Press, 1988), p. 31.

I answered, p. 17. Crowe, unpublished memoir, p. 23, SCUTK.

I was amazed, p. 18. Robert Fesmire, *Flight of a Maverick* (Nashville: Eggman Publishers, 1995), pp. 15–16.

The service channeled, p. 19. Craven and Cate, *The Army Air Forces in World War II,* Vol. VI, p. 553.

To say that it was, p. 19. Clyde Bradley, unpublished memoir, p. 1, MS2012, Box 3, Folder 17, SCUTK.

I lived to see, p. 19. Philip Ardery, *Bomber Pilot* (Lexington: University of Kentucky Press, 1978), p. 20.

And navigation, p. 19. Bendiner, *Fall of Fortresses,* p. 34.

Just when, p. 20. Goebel, *Mustang Ace,* p. 26.

I'd be all right, p. 21. Keith Schuyler, *Elusive Horizons* (South Brunswick, NJ: A.S. Barnes, 1969), p. 3.

Nearly 40 percent, p. 22. Craven and Cate, *The Army Air Forces in World War II,* Vol. VI, p. 578. Much of the training information on the previous few pages is derived from pp. 566–78 of this excellent volume.

In some, p. 22. Hynes, *Flights of Passage,* p. 26.

I had two, p. 22. Robert Nelson, *Buzzard Brigade Bulletin* (December 1994), p. 12.

They were hard, p. 23. Jim Campbell, unpublished memoir, pp. 1–2, MS2012, Box 5, Folder 14, SCUTK.

All through the training, p. 23. Karl Smith, interview with author, 28 November 1997.

One member of the crew, p. 23. Fletcher, *Fletcher's Gang,* p. 219.

Like new bombardiers, p. 24. Craven and Cate, *The Army Air Forces in World War II,* Vol. VI, pp. 579–89.

I was . . . sent, p. 25. Elmer Zeidman, unpublished memoir, p. 1, MS1764, Box 7, Folder 21, SCUTK.

It gets tough, p. 26. Bruce Holloway, *Air Force: The Official Service Journal of the Army Air Forces* (January 1944), pp. 7, 64.

We selected fighter pilots, p. 26. Rothgeb, *New Guinea Skies,* p. ix.

It wasn't anybody else, p. 26. Smith, interview with author.

You have to have, p. 27. Francis Gabreski, *Gabby: A Fighter Pilot's Life* (New York: Orion Books, 1991), p. 35.

But if a strafing, p. 27. Baumann, unpublished memoir.

They would then, p. 27. John K. Breast, ed., *Missions Remembered: Recollections of the World War II Air War* (Brentwood, TN: J.M. Productions, 1995), p. 107.

In the final analysis, p. 28. Hugh Dow, *The Memory Is Still Fresh,* self-published unit history, p. 128.

He is probably, p. 28. Harry Crosby, *A Wing and a Prayer* (New York: HarperCollins, 1993), p. 46.

In this position, p. 29. Fletcher, *Fletcher's Gang,* p. 318.

We were the, p. 29. Leutnner and Jensen, *High Honor,* p. 193.

During the course, p. 29. Hank Koenig, unpublished memoir, p. 3, MS1764, Box 12, Folder 15, SCUTK.

He would also, pp. 29–30. Fletcher, *Fletcher's Gang,* p. 316.

I . . . saw that, p. 30. Keith Lamb, unpublished memoir, p. 34, Mighty Eighth, RG 403, Box 9.3, Folder 4.

I know how, p. 30. Crowe, unpublished memoir, p. 59, SCUTK.

Besides, I enjoyed, p. 30. McCarthy, *Fear No More,* p. 41.

They were content, p. 30. Crosby, *Wing and a Prayer,* p. 121.

I guess this is, p. 31. Berndt, unpublished diary, pp. 57, 59–60, Mighty Eighth.

When the plane, p. 32. Curtis LeMay, *Ex-CBI Roundup* (February 1990), p. 17.

This is a very, p. 32. James Campbell, *The Radical Rebel,* self-published memoir, p. 84.

Normally on a bomb run, p. 32. Edward Schlesinger, unpublished memoir, p. 39, Mighty Eighth, RG 403, Box 9.4, Folder 1.

During the mission, p. 32. Fletcher, *Fletcher's Gang,* p. 316.

But I'd practically, p. 33. John Patterson, *Ex-CBI Roundup* (January 1993), p. 8.

Little things, p. 33. Chester Marshall and Warren Thompson, *Final Assault on the Rising Sun: Combat Diaries of B-29 Air Crews Over Japan* (Hong Kong: Specialty Press Publishers, 1995), pp. 134–35.

There were many, p. 33. Lloyd Haefs, unpublished memoir, pp. 11–12, Files of the Center for the Study of War and Society, University of Tennessee—Knoxville (hereafter referred to as CSWS).

Things obey, p. 34. Perkins, unpublished memoir, p. 95, SCUTK.

He was quietly, p. 34. Schuyler, *Elusive Horizons,* p. 88.

His knowledge, p. 34. Fletcher, *Fletcher's Gang,* p. 317.

He also worked, p. 34. Koenig, unpublished memoir, p. 3, SCUTK.

I had all, p. 34. Crawford Weaver, *The Standard* (30 August 1995).

A photo reconnaissance, p. 35. Earl Benham, unpublished memoir, p. 21, Mighty Eighth, RG 403, Box 9.4, Folder 6.

He had a number, p. 35. Sam Ross, unpublished memoir, p. 24, Mighty Eighth, RG 403, Box 9, Folder 2.

Your thumbs were, p. 35. *Doing Our Job: Obion Countians in World War II,* self-published, p. 209.

If this sounds, p. 36. Wells, unpublished memoir, p. 2, Mighty Eighth.

I was much, p. 36. Donald Askerman, unpublished memoir, p. 97, MS2012, Box 1, Folder 9, SCUTK.

I can still recall, p. 36. Kenneth Drinnon, unpublished memoir, p. 3, MS1764, Box 7, Folder 22, SCUTK.

Whenever that happened, p. 37. Jack Novey, *The Cold Blue Sky: A B-17 Gunner in World War II* (Charlottesville, VA: Howell Press, 1997), p. 52.

But I set myself, p. 37. Kevin Herbert, *Maximum Effort: The B-29s Against Japan* (Manhattan, KS: Sunflower University Press, 1983), p. 61.

If I relaxed, p. 37. Novey, *Cold Blue Sky,* p. 1.

I was the left, p. 38. Bill Winchell, interview with Dr. Charles Griffith, MS1608, Box 13, Folder 30, SCUTK.

It was my job, p. 38. William Binnebose, unpublished memoir, p. 7, Mighty Eighth, RG 403, Box 9.4, Folder 7.

The right waist, p. 38. Fletcher, *Fletcher's Gang,* p. 318.

He was turret gunner, p. 38. Hynes, *Flights of Passage,* p. 176.

Older people realize, p. 39. Earl Wilburn, conversation with author, 29 September 1998.

Meanwhile, only 32 percent, p. 39. Stouffer, *Combat and Its Aftermath,* p. 343.

We left much, p. 39. Aanenson, unpublished memoir, pp. 1, 10, Mighty Eighth.

They are the very best, p. 39. James Good Brown, *The Mighty Men of the 381st, Heroes All* (Salt Lake City: Publishers Press, 1994), p. 287.

I was . . . nineteen, p. 39. James Talley, interview with Dr. Charles W. Johnson, 5 June 1990, MS1764, Box 17, Folder 47, SCUTK.

We had one guy, p. 39. Bob Ferrell, interview with author, 9 May 1998.

He was 23!, p. 40. Patterson, *Ex-CBI Roundup* (January 1993), p. 9.

I was 19, p. 40. Ross, unpublished memoir, p. 19, Mighty Eighth.

One cannot ask, p. 40. Julian Rebeles, unpublished memoir, p. 10, MS1892, Box 7, Folder 18, SCUTK.

Now that I look, p. 40. Joseph Beswick, unpublished memoir, p. 13, MS1892, Box 2, Folder 10, SCUTK.

Between missions, p. 40. Perkins, unpublished memoir, p. 5, SCUTK.

We all got along, p. 41. Tom Miller, unpublished memoir, p. 5, CSWS.

The economically poor, p. 41. Crowe, unpublished memoir, p. 56, SCUTK.

The pilot was, p. 41. Talley interview, SCUTK.

One is a former, p. 41. John Bernstein to family, 2 July 1944, WHMC.

He told about, p. 42. Bennett to colleague, WHMC.

The Airmen, p. 42. Ray Zuker, *The Fly Over* (Christmas 1994), p. 7.

After all, p. 42. Berndt, unpublished memoir, p. 74, Mighty Eighth.

Chapter 2

Conversely, if airmen, p. 44. Stouffer, *Combat and Its Aftermath,* p. 399. Army researchers studied heavy-bomber crews and found a direct correlation between aircraft satisfaction and willingness to go into combat.

With its low, p. 44. I. C. B. Dear and M. R. D. Foot, eds., *The Oxford*

Companion to World War II (Oxford: Oxford University Press, 1995), p. 360.

But pilots were, p. 45. Kreglogh et al., *The Memory Is Still Fresh,* pp. 64–65.

There were a lot, p. 45. John B. Holway, *Red Tails, Black Wings: The Men of America's Black Air Force* (Las Cruces, NM: Yucca Tree Press, 1997), p. 144.

In the case of, p. 45. Kreglogh et al., *The Memory Is Still Fresh,* pp. 59–60.

At 25,000 feet, p. 45. Chris Chant, *World War II Aircraft: The Allies* (London: Marshall Cavendish, 1979), pp. 52–53.

Rather, like a refined, p. 46. Rothgeb, *New Guinea Skies,* p. 142.

With so many instruments, p. 46. Harold Rosser, *No Hurrahs for Me* (Sevierville, TN: Covenant House Books, 1994), pp. 181–82.

Later models, p. 46. Lande, *From Somewhere in England,* p. 45.

A P-38 mechanic's, p. 47. Hubert Zemke and Roger Freeman, *Zemke's Wolfpack* (New York: Orion Books, 1989), pp. 138, 192–93.

It could just do, p. 47. Smith, interview with author.

They were just tops, p. 47. Franklin Shires, oral history, March 1996, SCUTK.

We found that we, p. 48. Campbell, unpublished memoir, pp. 5–6, SCUTK.

It proved to be, p. 48. Dear and Foot, *Oxford Companion,* p. 361.

To compensate for, p. 49. Rosser, *No Hurrahs,* p. 182.

It would only let us, p. 49. Holway, *Red Tails, Black Wings,* pp. 162–63.

We never realized, p. 49. Will Burgsteiner, unpublished diary, p. 6, Mighty Eighth, RG 403, Box 9, Folder 16.

I ducked behind, p. 49. Rothgeb, *New Guinea Skies,* p. 231.

He claimed, for instance, p. 50. Gabreski, *Fighter Pilot's Life,* pp. 83–84, 105.

Its range and speed, p. 51. Chant, *World War II Aircraft,* pp. 58–59.

And those who haven't, p. 51. Holway, *Red Tails, Black Wings,* pp. 184–85.

Best of all, p. 51. Zemke and Freeman, *Zemke's Wolfpack,* pp. 199–200.

I didn't want, p. 52. Goebel, *Mustang Ace,* pp. 145, 159.

For the most part, p. 52. Edward Popek, *Combat Evaluation Report,* MS2012, Box 11, Folder 25, SCUTK.

If that happened, p. 52. Breast, *Missions Remembered,* p. 114.

It was ideal, p. 53. Dear and Foot, *Oxford Companion,* p. 146, and Chant, *World War II Aircraft,* pp. 56–57.

What we sacrificed, p. 53. David Hayward, *Ex-CBI Roundup* (January 1989), p. 8.

Two had been, p. 53. R. W. Blake, *Ex-CBI Roundup* (April 1991), p. 22.

Thus, like most, p. 54. Dear and Foot, *Oxford Companion,* p. 146, and Chant, *World War II Aircraft,* pp. 54–55.

He conceded, p. 54. Jeff Ethell, *Bomber Command* (Osceola, WI: Motorbooks International, 1994), p. 61.

We consider it, p. 54. Donald Mrozek and Robin Higham, eds., *The Martin Marauder and the Franklin Allens: A Wartime Love Story* (Manhattan, KS: Sunflower University Press, 1980), pp. 522–24.

This was true, p. 56. Dear and Foot, *Oxford Companion,* p. 146, and Chant, *World War II Aircraft,* pp. 42–43.

More than once, p. 56. Guyon Phillips, *Briefing: The Official Publication of the B-24 Liberator Club* (Winter 1997), p. 15.

You could only tell, p. 56. John Charlton, unpublished memoir, p. 6, CSWS.

I wanted no part, p. 57. Schuyler, *Elusive Horizons,* p. 4.

I clutch those, p. 57. Kenneth Jones, unpublished memoir, p. 32, Mighty Eighth.

For us in the Tenth, p. 57. William Shelley, *Ex-CBI Roundup* (May 1986), p. 23.

We did operate, pp. 57–58. Breast, *Missions Remembered,* p. 119.

Such was the satisfaction, p. 58. Stouffer, *Combat and Its Aftermath,* p. 397.

In the minds, p. 58. Dear and Foot, *Oxford Companion,* p. 146.

The fore and aft, p. 59. Patterson, *Ex-CBI Roundup* (January 1993), p. 8.

It could carry, p. 59. Ethell, *Bomber Command,* pp. 126–27.

You don't give, p. 60. Patterson, *Ex-CBI Roundup* (January 1993), pp. 22–23.

Like I said, p. 60. Leutnner and Jensen, *High Honor,* pp. 189–90.

The chin turret, p. 61. Chant, *World War II Aircraft*, pp. 40–41.

When the Army, p. 61. Stouffer, *Combat and Its Aftermath*, p. 397.

She took us, p. 61. Ray Zuker, *The Fly Over* (Winter 1991), p. 10.

The sound of a B–17, p. 61. Crosby, *Wing and a Prayer*, p. 161.

To us, they were, p. 61. McCarthy, *Fear No More*, p. 172.

. . . *you can shoot*, p. 62. John Clarkson to wife, 13 May 1945, Mighty Eighth, RG 403, Box 9.2, Folder 8.

It was a miracle, p. 62. Barwick Barfield, unpublished memoir, pp. 6–7, MS2012, Box 1, Folder 22, SCUTK.

But still it came back, p. 62. Lamb, unpublished memoir, p. 56, Mighty Eighth.

The incredibly tough, p. 62. Ethell, *Bomber Command*, pp. 154–55.

The Army Air Force, p. 63. C. G. Sweeting, *Combat Flying Clothing* (Washington, DC: Smithsonian Institution Press, 1984). This book gives a fine overview of the various stages in American combat flight gear in World War II.

On top of that, p. 63. Gabreski, *Fighter Pilot's Life*, p. 64.

It was only, p. 63. Binnebose, unpublished memoir, p. 1, Mighty Eighth.

I always kept, p. 63. Kenneth Williams, unpublished memoir, p. 2, Mighty Eighth, RG 403, Box 51, Folder 1.

We are ready, p. 64. Perkins, unpublished diary, p. 72, SCUTK.

Ear flaps, p. 64. Roger Armstrong and Ken Stone, eds., *USA the Hard Way* (Orange County, CA: Quail House Publishing, 1997), p. 52.

I would set, p. 64. Marshall, unpublished memoir, p. 22, Mighty Eighth.

In addition we wore, p. 64. Edward Schlesinger, unpublished memoir, p. 30, Mighty Eighth, RG 403, Box 9.4, Folder 1.

But it had to be, p. 65. William McCormick, *Sortie* (Vol. XI, No. 3), p. 12.

Next we wore, Ross, p. 65. unpublished memoir, pp. 21, 24, Mighty Eighth.

This suit not only, p. 66. Berndt, unpublished diary, p. 48, Mighty Eighth.

I continued to wear, p. 66. Lande, *From Somewhere in England*, pp. 35–36.

Those suits did that, p. 66. Askerman, unpublished memoir, pp. 96, 121, SCUTK.

Gunner's gloves, p. 67. John Bradford, *Briefing* (Spring 1992), p. 14.

Here one dressed, p. 67. Herbert, *Maximum Effort,* pp. 41, 62.

Chapter 3

If one waited, p. 69. Haefs, unpublished memoir, pp. 22–23, CSWS.

We are off, p. 69. Leroy Watson to mother, 17 July 1944, Box 37, Folder 3155, WHMC.

The stark interiors, p. 69. Goebel, *Mustang Ace,* p. 71.

No doubt, pp. 69. Baumann, unpublished memoir, p. 360, CSWS.

We have electric, p. 70. Arthur Carpenter to family, 25 May 1944, Box 5, Folder 440, WHMC.

We were quite, p. 70. Aanenson, unpublished memoir, p. 11, Mighty Eighth.

Wood floor in the tent, p. 71. Marshall to family, 10 September 1944, 4 November 1944, and 8 April 1945, SCUTK.

The few they do provide, p. 71. Mrozek and Higham, *The Martin Marauder,* p. 423.

If I ever, p. 71. Clarkson, unpublished diary, Mighty Eighth.

Turning the water off, p. 71. McCarthy, *Fear No More,* pp. 164–65.

But we were lucky, p. 72. Lande, *From Somewhere in England,* p. 24.

Twelve fellows slept, p. 72. Lamb, unpublished memoir, p. 31, Mighty Eighth.

We had electricity, p. 72. John White interview with Winfried Moncrief, 28 March 1996, SCUTK.

It was punishing, p. 73. Novey, *Cold Blue Sky,* pp. 64–65.

In addition all streets, p. 73. Armstrong and Stone, *USA the Hard Way,* pp. 42–43.

The trains and 'bobbies,' p. 74. John Duke Eberhart to Carol, 17 August 1944, Box 8, Folder 788, WHMC.

This was followed, p. 74. Tays, unpublished memoir, p. 41, Mighty Eighth.

There were Free French, p. 74. Jones, unpublished memoir, p. 102, Mighty Eighth.

The higher rank, p. 75. Earl Benham, unpublished memoir, p. 38, Mighty Eighth, RG 403, Box 9.4, Folder 6.

This was the big time, p. 75. Jim Lynch, unpublished memoir, p. 18, Mighty Eighth, RG 403, Box 9.3, Folder 9.

Business was brisk, p. 76. Crosby, *Wing and a Prayer,* p. 178.

In the morning, p. 76. Benham, unpublished memoir, p. 27, Mighty Eighth.

It was bad enough, p. 77. Schlesinger, unpublished memoir, p. 29, Mighty Eighth.

Twice I watched, p. 77. Ardery, *Bomber Pilot,* p. 214.

If one fell, p. 77. Brown, *Mighty Men of the 381st,* p. 361.

They were too low, p. 78. Lamb, unpublished memoir, p. 35, Mighty Eighth.

Periodically one of us, p. 78. Askerman, unpublished memoir, p. 107, SCUTK.

In the North Atlantic, p. 78. Lande, *From Somewhere in England,* p. 28.

It meant I had, p. 79. Ethell, *Bomber Command,* p. 89.

It certainly seems, p. 79. Brown, *Mighty Men of the 381st,* pp. 474–75.

But fighting the clammy mists, p. 79. Schuyler, *Elusive Horizons,* p. 31.

The English weather, p. 79. Fletcher, *Fletcher's Gang,* p. 466.

There were instances, p. 80. Dale Smith, *Screaming Eagle* (Chapel Hill, NC: Algonquin Books of Chapel Hill, 1990), p. 72.

With temperatures frequently, p. 80. Ben O'Dell, unpublished memoir, p. 6, CSWS.

I told the mess hall, p. 81. Mrozek and Higham, *The Martin Marauder,* p. 515.

All I could get down, p. 81. Novey, *Cold Blue Sky,* p. 66.

On the whole, p. 81. Holway, *Red Tails, Black Wings,* p. 201.

We all eventually concluded, p. 81. Tom Miller, unpublished memoir, p. 56, CSWS.

The coffee tasted, p. 81. Cubbins, *War of the Cottontails,* p. 81.

Word traveled fast, pp. 81–82. Baumann, unpublished memoir, pp. 305, 356, CSWS.

Finally they were done, p. 82. Kreglogh et al., unit history, p. 52, CSWS.

That night, p. 82. O'Dell, unpublished memoir, pp. 11–12, CSWS.

Fish and chips shops, p. 82. Armstrong and Stone, *USA the Hard Way,* p. 87.

I didn't envy, p. 82. Crowe, *The Ringmasters,* unit history, p. 263.

For supper we had, pp. 82–83. Edwin Anderson to mother, nd, Box 1, Folder 50, WHMC.

I eat something, p. 83. Crosby, *Wing and a Prayer,* p. 43.

While going through, p. 83. Fesmire, *Flight of a Maverick,* p. 61.

And when I asked, p. 83. Smith, *Screaming Eagle,* pp. 82–83.

We had wine, p. 83. Richard Anderson to family, 23 November 1944, Box 1, Folder 61, WHMC.

We at least, p. 84. William Stafford to family, 26 December 1944, MS1881, Box 28, Folder 10, SCUTK.

A ship load, p. 84. Haefs, unpublished memoir, pp. 36–37, CSWS.

As a result, p. 85. Lamb, unpublished memoir, p. 58, Mighty Eighth.

I was asked, p. 85. Crosby, *Wing and a Prayer,* p. 288.

Nevertheless it was done, p. 85. Brown, *Mighty Men of the 381st,* p. 316.

McCarthy felt, p. 86. McCarthy, *Fear No More,* pp. 178–79.

Most people, p. 86. Perkins, unpublished memoir, p. 112, SCUTK.

It was kind of scary, p. 87. Askerman, unpublished memoir, pp. 88, 111, 117, SCUTK.

Moreover, their personal, p. 87. Baumann, unpublished memoir, pp. 365–66, CSWS.

When we went, p. 88. Beswick, unpublished memoir, p. 11, SCUTK.

You heard about, p. 88. Francis Mooney, interview transcript, pp. 88–89, MS1427, Box 6, Folder 17, SCUTK.

Have never had, p. 88. Marshall to family, 17 July and 2 August 1944, SCUTK.

He wrote to his family, p. 88. Lonzo Hetherington to family, 1 April 1945, Box 15, Folder 1309, WHMC.

The French people, p. 89. Robert Bagley to family, 18 September 1944, Box 2, Folder 114, WHMC.

The limeys will cut, p. 89. Clarkson to wife, Mighty Eighth.

Why can't they, p. 89. Novey, *Cold Blue Sky,* pp. 3–4.

I was an American, p. 90. Lande, *From Somewhere in England,* p. 86.

It was an elegant approach, p. 90. Bendiner, *Fall of Fortresses,* p. 84.

If they're going, p. 90. Mrozek and Higham, *The Martin Marauder,* p. 475.

We donated chocolates, p. 91. Drinnon, unpublished memoir, p. 10, SCUTK.

Looking back, p. 91. Lande, *From Somewhere in England,* pp. 16, 84.

It was not unusual, p. 91. Koenig, unpublished memoir, p. 2, SCUTK.

Some talk like, p. 92. Lande, *From Somewhere in England,* p. 120.

As the expression went, p. 92. Crosby, *Wing and a Prayer,* p. 177.

I turned a blind eye, p. 92. Smith, *Screaming Eagle,* p. 197.

It was not good, p. 92. Bendiner, *Fall of Fortresses,* p. 117.

It was reported, p. 92. Richard Baynes, unpublished memoir, p. 70, RG 403, Box 9.2, Folder 4, Mighty Eighth.

Somewhat amused, p. 93. Fesmire, *Flight of a Maverick,* pp. 59–60.

After surviving, p. 94. Novey, *Cold Blue Sky,* pp. 49–50, 96, 99–101, 124.

We were married, p. 94. Marshall, unpublished memoir, pp. 25, 38, Mighty Eighth.

The Army movies, p. 94. Miller, unpublished memoir, p. 69, CSWS.

In Goebel's view, p. 95. Goebel, *Mustang Ace,* p. 152.

Those who tested, p. 95. Lamb, unpublished memoir, p. 59, Mighty Eighth.

They are cultured, p. 95. Marshall to parents, 13 March 1945, SCUTK.

They would promise, p. 95. Mooney, interview transcript, p. 90, SCUTK.

I think I marry him, Sortie p. 96. (May 1998), p. 11.

They had found, p. 96. Perkins, unpublished memoir, pp. 82–83, SCUTK.

Chapter 4

Also toss in, p. 97. George Sheafor to sister, 5 October 1944, Box 32, Folder 2698, WHMC.

Burmese natives, p. 98. Charles Bond, *A Flying Tiger's Diary* (College Station, TX: Texas A & M University Press, 1984), p. 42.

At night we watched, p. 98. David Hayward, *Ex-CBI Roundup* (February 1989), p. 6.

Even in washing, p. 98. Rosser, *No Hurrahs,* p. 63.

We put it up, p. 99. Charles Nickell to sister, 21 February and 29 April 1944, SCUTK.

In their bomb bays, p. 99. Rothgeb, *New Guinea Skies,* pp. 232–33.

There are a few, p. 99. Dan Sasser to mother, 6 September 1944, Box 31, Folder 2608, WHMC.

Most of the seats, p. 99. Edward Harris to mother, 8 November 1944, MS1259, Box 5, Folder 1, SCUTK.

The food is good, p. 100. Walter Springer to parents, 19 June 1945, Box 33, Folder 2839, WHMC.

We were between, p. 100. Marshall and Thompson, *Final Assault,* pp. 152–53.

When the ship, p. 101. Campbell, unpublished memoir, p. 10, SCUTK.

We had linen, p. 101. Smith, interview with author, SCUTK.

Robert Nelson, p. 101. Robert Nelson, *Buzzard Brigade Bulletin* (March 1995), p. 20.

It boasted, p. 101. Stevens, unpublished memoir, p. 284, CSWS.

Seventeen men, p. 102. Marshall and Thompson, *Final Assault,* pp. 152–55.

We were under, p. 102. Gabreski, *Fighter Pilot's Life,* pp. 39–40.

One very pitiful, p. 103. Bond, *Flying Tiger's Diary,* p. 168.

We usually get out, p. 103. Gene Ryan, *Colonel Randy's Flying Circus* (September—October 1983), p. 3.

We all dived, p. 103. Harris, unpublished memoir, p. 8, SCUTK.

I was very lucky, p. 104. Howard Skidmore, *Clarion: USS Cabot Association* (March 1996), p. 9.

It killed something, p. 104. Shires, oral history, SCUTK.

I looked upon it, p. 104. Rothgeb, *New Guinea Skies,* pp. 123, 205.

It's been raining, pp. 104–105. Omar Ash to mother, 22 November 1944, MS1314, Box 1, Folder 4, SCUTK.

The climate can be described, p. 105. Harris to mother, 10 January 1945, SCUTK.

Rain became, p. 105. Hynes, *Flights of Passage,* p. 235.

By mid-morning, p. 105. Patterson, *Ex-CBI Roundup,* p. 21.

You realize, p. 105. Leutnner and Jensen, *High Honor,* p. 48.

Once I was picked up, p. 106. Joe John Bond to family, 20 April 1945, Box 3, Folder 271, WHMC.

He would say, p. 106. Leutnner and Jensen, *High Honor,* p. 233.

Earl Wilburn, p. 106. Wilburn, conversation with author.

About the only decent, p. 106. Kenneth Michel to parents, 27 May 1945, Box 23, Folder 1950, WHMC.

As for the chicken, p. 106. Hayward, *Ex-CBI Roundup,* p. 6.

Had roast beef, p. 107. Sasser to mother, WHMC.

We also get, p. 107. Harris to mother, 27 November 1944, SCUTK.

About 99.9 percent, p. 107. Stevens, unpublished memoir, pp. 206–7, CSWS.

So they were, p. 107. Hayward, *Ex-CBI Roundup,* p. 6.

We had everything, p. 108. Everett Geer to family, 13 May 1944, Box 11, Folder 1019, WHMC.

His warning, p. 108. Rosser, *No Hurrahs,* p. 113.

Now I don't know, p. 108. V. F. Cozad to June, 23 July 1945, Box 6, Folder 591, WHMC.

They . . . took a picture, p. 108. Nelson, *Buzzard Brigade Bulletin* (March 1995), p. 20.

For the next six hours, p. 109. Herbert, *Maximum Effort,* p. 44.

They paddled, p. 110. Stevens, unpublished memoir, pp. 79–80, CSWS.

Leadership, p. 110. Rothgeb, *New Guinea Skies,* p. 124.

When we ran out, p. 110. Max Brand, *Fighter Squadron at Guadalcanal* (Annapolis: Naval Institute Press, 1996), p. 188.

Some of them, p. 111. Nickell to family, 10 December and 21 December 1944, SCUTK.

It looks like, p. 111. Harris to mother, 10 January 1945, SCUTK.

Right along with these, p. 111. Dwight King, *Ex-CBI Roundup* (March 1983), p. 12.

And the clothes, p. 112. Howard Longhead to parents, 5 April 1945, Box 21, Folder 1797, WHMC.

And how!, p. 112. Cozad to sister, WHMC.

It was a bad deal, p. 112. Patterson, *Ex-CBI Roundup,* p. 22.

Their lack of regard, p. 114. Rosser, *No Hurrahs,* pp. 81, 72–73, 122.

My blue-eyed date, p. 115. Rothgeb, *New Guinea Skies,* p. 179.

Chapter 5

There is no feeling, p. 117. Lande, *From Somewhere in England,* p. 46.

They get closer, p. 117. William Monroe, self-published unit history, 1976, p. 167, CSWS.

Back to the Ready room, p. 117. Gene Moxley, self-published unit history, 1996, p. IV, CSWS.

I relax and light, p. 118. Charles Murrell to aunt and uncle, 9 March 1945, Box 24, Folder 2062, WHMC.

We're wondering, p. 119. Novey, *Cold Blue Sky,* p. 2.

The City of Bologna, p. 119. Haefs, unpublished memoir, p. 25, CSWS.

We would then, p. 120. James Campbell, *The Radical Rebel,* self-published memoir, pp. 78–79, CSWS.

I felt a mixture, p. 120. Wilbur Morrison, *Ex-CBI Roundup* (July 1994), p. 14.

Let us say, p. 120. Ardery, *Bomber Pilot,* p. 101.

Intelligence would tell you, p. 121. *Doing Our Job,* pp. 224–25.

His devious habit, p. 121. Armstrong and Stone, *USA the Hard Way,* pp. 49–50.

The "flimsy," p. 122. Baumann, unpublished memoir, pp. 303, 307, CSWS.

I guess we all, p. 122. Aanenson, unpublished memoir, p. 10, Mighty Eighth.

You'd burn up, p. 122. Lande, *From Somewhere in England,* p. 30.

You're getting up, p. 122. Talley, interview with Dr. Charles W. Johnson, SCUTK.

This would always, p. 123. Askerman, unpublished memoir, p. 110, SCUTK.

It also meant, p. 123. William McCormick, *Sortie* (Vol. XI, No. 3), p. 13.

Also, all the gunners, p. 124. Campbell, self-published memoir, pp. 82–83, CSWS.

There was no margin, p. 124. Fletcher, *Fletcher's Gang,* pp. 462–63.

If not, each air division, p. 125. Miller, unpublished memoir, pp. 54–55, CSWS.

I tell him, p. 125. Crosby, *Wing and a Prayer,* pp. 284–85.

In bombers, p. 126. Lande, *From Somewhere in England,* p. 45.

Even so, until pulling, p. 126. Zemke and Freeman, *Zemke's Wolfpack,* p. 142.

He listened politely, p. 127. Schuyler, *Elusive Horizons,* p. 53.

You can't fly, p. 128. John White, diary, CSWS.

The crew thought, p. 128. Tays, unpublished memoir, pp. 43–44, Mighty Eighth.

They were calling, p. 129. Bill Chamberlain, oral history, SCUTK.

But if you have, p. 129. Ardery, *Bomber Pilot,* p. 87.

His nose turret, p. 130. Tom Young, *Ex-CBI Roundup* (April 1988), pp. 18–19.

Suddenly he rolled, p. 130. Maxon Wotring, unpublished memoir, pp. 3–4, MS2012, Box 15, Folder 24, SCUTK.

We assumed, p. 131. David Rogers, ed., self-published unit history, 1994, pp. 235–36, CSWS.

Then they all, p. 131. Stevens, unpublished memoir, p. 150, CSWS.

I flinched, p. 132. Ken Bragg, *Sortie* (May 1998), p. 14.

Low and to my right, p. 132. Cubbins, *War of the Cottontails,* pp. 39–40.

I must have said, p. 133. Perkins, unpublished memoir, pp. 80–81, SCUTK.

I am sure, p. 133. Beswick, unpublished memoir, p. 7, SCUTK.

I can only hope, p. 134. Novey, *Cold Blue Sky,* p. 88.

It looked like, p. 134. Ethell, *Bomber Command,* p. 150.

I used 1,700 rounds, p. 134. Edward Hearty, diary, RG 403, Box 9.4, Folder 19, Mighty Eighth.

His crewmen, Larry p. 135. Wallerstein, unpublished memoir, pp. 2–3, RG 403, Box 48, Folder 2, Mighty Eighth.

From the moment, p. 135. Lloyd Martin to parents, 5 May 1944, Box 22, Folder 1899, WHMC.

When you started, p. 136. Lande, *From Somewhere in England,* p. 39.

Low-velocity flak, p. 136. Bob Ryerson interview with author, 10 August 1995, SCUTK.

There was really, p. 136. Ardery, *Bomber Pilot,* p. 125.

You feel just like, p. 136. Carpenter letter to family, WHMC.

Every time, p. 137. Lon Lilley to parents, 11 May 1944, Box 21, Folder 1771, WHMC.

It seems as tho, p. 137. White diary, CSWS.

When an antiaircraft shell, p. 138. David Hayward, *Ex-CBI Roundup* (January 1989), p. 8.

We had one, p. 138. Tom Young, *Ex-CBI Roundup* (January 1990), p. 14.

Paisley [one of the gunners], p. 138. Rogers, ed., self-published unit history, p. 106, CSWS.

I didn't think, p. 138. Steve Birdsall, *Saga of the Superfortress: The Dramatic Story of the B-29 and the Twentieth Air Force* (Garden City, NY: Doubleday, 1980), p. 120.

After what seemed, p. 139. Morrison, *Ex-CBI Roundup,* pp. 15–17.

I could have, p. 139. Richard Fisher to parents, 5 July 1945, Box 9, Folder 912, WHMC.

But the minute, p. 140. Bagley to parents, WHMC.

There were many, p. 140. Joe Kenney, *Briefing* (Spring 1988), p. 19.

During those moments, p. 140. Ardery, *Bomber Pilot,* pp. 104–105.

We were so low, p. 141. Ray Hubbard, *Sortie* (Vol. XII, No. 2), p. 14.

You could hear, p. 141. Clarkson to wife, Mighty Eighth.

The busier, p. 141. Armstrong and Stone, *USA the Hard Way,* pp. 63–64.

Will it always, p. 142. E. T. Moriarity, self-published memoir, 1992, p. 44, CSWS.

Lynch had the, p. 142. Lynch, unpublished memoir, p. 60, Mighty Eighth.

It didn't make sense, p. 142. Smith, *Screaming Eagle,* p. 119.

The smoke and noise, p. 143. Lonnie Osborne, combat diary, p. 17, MS1881, Box 19, Folder 4, SCUTK.

Our bombs, p. 143. William Redmond, combat diary, p. 12, MS2012, Box 11, Folder 73, SCUTK.

The dense flak, p. 143. Fesmire, *Flight of a Maverick,* p. 76.

At that time, p. 144. John Brown to girlfriend, 16 June 1945, Box 4, Folder 354, WHMC.

I know I hit him, p. 145. Holway, *Red Tails, Black Wings,* p. 110.

This whole action, p. 145. Aanenson, unpublished memoir, p. 13, Mighty Eighth.

We must have, p. 145. Breast, *Missions Remembered,* pp. 91–92.

A lot depended, p. 146. Goebel, *Mustang Ace,* p. 82.

Another sure kill, p. 146. Gabreski, *Fighter Pilot's Life,* pp. 71–72, 127–28.

I never fired, p. 147. Zemke and Freeman, *Zemke's Wolfpack,* p. 177.

A few seconds later, p. 148. Kreglogh et al., self-published unit history, p. 54, CSWS.

The shroud lines, p. 148. Brand, *Fighter Squadron at Guadalcanal,* pp. 137, 164.

The plane went, p. 149. Charles Francis, *The Tuskegee Airmen* (Boston: Brandon Publishing Company, 1993), pp. 119, 185.

He was probably, p. 149. Holway, *Red Tails, Black Wings,* pp. 228–29.

Bishop and I, p. 149. Breast, *Missions Remembered,* p. 83.

I squealed, p. 150. Bond, *Flying Tiger's Diary,* pp. 86–87.

Black smoke billowed, p. 150. Rothgeb, *New Guinea Skies,* p. 206.

Moutenot saw, p. 150. Leutnner and Jensen, *High Honor,* p. 58.

I was aiming, p. 151. Breast, *Missions Remembered,* pp. 2, 22.

I can't describe, p. 152. Campbell, unpublished memoir, pp. 35–36, SCUTK.

Yet to my way, p. 153. Frank Harrington, *The Fly Over* (Summer 1997), p. 7.

He disguised, p. 153. Lande, *From Somewhere in England,* p. 51.

I saw the other, p. 153. Breast, *Missions Remembered,* pp. 32–33.

The .50-caliber shells, p. 154. Holway, *Red Tails, Black Wings,* p. 236.

When he hit it, p. 154. Kreglogh et al., self-published unit history, p. 90, CSWS.

As we discussed, p. 155. Aanenson, unpublished memoir, p. 13, Mighty Eighth.

Never enjoyed, p. 156. John Marshall to parents, 1 July and 18 July 1944, SCUTK.

We just laid, p. 156. Boyce Holleman, interview with Winfried Moncrief and Douglas Mansfield, April 1997, SCUTK.

It was a sickening, p. 156. Bond, *Flying Tiger's Diary,* p. 109.

It left, p. 157. Rosser, *No Hurrahs,* pp. 13–14.

The only protection, p. 157. Franklin Shires, interview with Stan Tinsley, 16 August 1995, SCUTK.

We would pull, p. 157. Campbell, unpublished memoir, p. 20, SCUTK.

In fact, p. 158. Brand, *Fighter Squadron at Guadalcanal,* p. 115.

You keep low, p. 158. Robert Quinn, *The Sky Lancer,* unit publication, MS1881, Box 30, Folder 12, SCUTK.

This maneuver, p. 158. Stevens, unpublished memoir, p. 122, CSWS.

Just shooting, p. 159. Hynes, *Flights of Passage,* p. 177.

They were the boys, p. 160. Baumann, unpublished memoir, p. 346, CSWS.

I'll never forget, p. 161. Warren Johnson, *The Fly Over* (Fall 1991), p. 4.

His canopy, p. 161. Goebel, *Mustang Ace,* p. 111.

He then easily, p. 162. Robert Woody, *Memories* (June 1998), pp. 121–22.

I had to follow, p. 162. Holway, *Red Tails, Black Wings,* p. 217.

I then climbed, p. 163. Marshall and Thompson, *Final Assault,* pp. 157–58.

Who knows?, p. 163. Fletcher, *Fletcher's Gang,* p. 447.

'This is all . . . ,' p. 164. Bendiner, *Fall of Fortresses,* pp. 138–39.

If he had not, p. 164. Richard Asbury, *Sortie* (Vol. XI, No. 2), p. 10.

Praying comes, p. 165. Crowe, self-published unit history, p. 164, CSWS.

I got the feeling, p. 165. Lande, *From Somewhere in England,* p. 137.

But it was, p. 165. Herbert, *Maximum Effort,* p. 41.

It was a very, p. 166. Breast, *Missions Remembered,* p. 23.

That is what generates, p. 166. Dick Lincoln, *486th Bomb Group Association Newsletter* (Winter 1994), p. 14.

The bomb-bay doors, p. 167. Lynch, unpublished memoir, pp. 28–30, Mighty Eighth.

Even now, p. 167. Novey, *Cold Blue Sky,* p. 121.

They . . . kept flying, p. 168. James Shea to aunt, 27 January 1944, Box 32, Folder 2696, WHMC.

A few hours later, p. 168. Holway, *Red Tails, Black Wings,* pp. 229–31.

The PBY, Prentiss Burkett, *The Unofficial History of the 499th Bomb Group* (Temple, CA: Historical Aviation Album Publication, 1981), p. 25.

With proper rest, p. 169. Henry Sakaida, *Pacific Air Combat in World War II: Voices from the Past* (St. Paul, MN: Phalanx Publishing Co., 1993), p. 14.

They spent, p. 169. Robert Nelson, *Buzzard Brigade Bulletin* (March 1995), pp. 22–25.

Wilson rode, p. 170. Charles Wilson, *Challenge Specials* (Vol. 4, 1994), p. 37.

'These Italian babes . . . ,' p. 70. Jesse Bradley, *The Retired Officer* (September 1983), p. 27.

They treated us, p. 171. White diary, CSWS.

A person suffering, p. 171. Berndt, unpublished diary, p. 56, Mighty Eighth.

It was a very, p. 171. Cozad to sister, WHMC.

To our happy, p. 172. Benham, unpublished memoir, p. 38h, Mighty Eighth.

I gave him hell, p. 172. Beswick, unpublished memoir, p. 5, SCUTK.

After reviving, p. 172. O'Dell, unpublished memoir, pp. 1–2, CSWS.

They made it, p. 173. Crosby, *Wing and a Prayer,* pp. 158–59.

He saved my life, p. 173. Crowe, self-published unit history, p. 126, CSWS.

Hansell was shouting, p. 174. Philip Abbott, *Briefing* (Spring 1988), p. 12.

A savage burst, p. 174. John Williamson, *The Toretta Flyer: The 461st and 484th Bomb Group Association Publication* (Winter 1989–90), p. 22.

A lot of people, p. 174. Joe Boyd, interview with author, 4 August 1995, SCUTK.

Luckily Purnell, p. 174. Holway, *Red Tails, Black Wings,* p. 206.

51 degrees below, p. 175. Hearty diary, p. 14, Mighty Eighth.

After an hour, p. 175. Crowe, unpublished memoir, pp. 96, 98, SCUTK.

'Let me in . . . ,' p. 175. Novey, *Cold Blue Sky,* pp. 6, 130–31.

My feet were, p. 176. Robert Geraghty, *Ex-POW Bulletin* (September 1989), p. 25.

There, the greenhouse, p. 176. John Bradford, *Briefing* (Spring 1992), p. 14.

Therefore, I always, p. 176. Baumann, unpublished memoir, p. 319, CSWS.

Still, I had to, p. 176. Gabreski, *Fighter Pilot's Life,* p. 125.

If it spilled, p. 177. Lande, *From Somewhere in England,* p. 119.

No one writes, p. 177. Novey, *Cold Blue Sky,* pp. 127–29.

This item became, p. 178. Tays, unpublished memoir, pp. 35–36, Mighty Eighth.

I had to do, p. 178. Ethell, *Bomber Command,* pp. 58–59.

Most of the crew, p. 178. Herbert, *Maximum Effort,* p. 56.

I didn't even try, p. 179. Goebel, *Mustang Ace,* p. 101.

Those were, p. 179. Boyd, interview with author, SCUTK.

I informed, p. 179. Jones, unpublished memoir, p. 103, Mighty Eighth.

Needless to say, p. 179. Ron Bereman, *486th Bomb Group Association Newsletter* (Winter 1994), p. 14.

Fighter Command, p. 180. O'Dell, unpublished memoir, p. 8, CSWS.

If you had strafed, p. 180. Lande, *From Somewhere in England,* p. 65.

They wanted to get, p. 180. Campbell, unpublished memoir, p. 23, SCUTK.

Those six have been, p. 181. Brown, *Mighty Men of the 381st,* pp. 101–102.

Here any person, p. 181. Berndt, unpublished diary, p. 69, Mighty Eighth.

At interrogation, p. 182. Armstrong and Stone, *USA the Hard Way,* p. 54.

Chapter 6

The vast majority, p. 183. John Ellis, *World War II: A Statistical Survey* (London: Facts on File, 1993), p. 254. Also see Norman Polmar and Thomas Allen, *World War II: America at War, 1941–1945* (New York: Random House, 1991), p. 193, for corroboration of these numbers. The Army Air Force's official history records a slightly higher number of overall casualties—121,000.

In a few minutes, p. 184. Armstrong and Stone, *USA the Hard Way,* pp. 66–67.

'Well, he's a bombardier,' p. 185. H. C. White, *The Fly Over* (Winter 1991–92), p. 1.

We gave him, p. 185. Elmer Vogel, *Briefing* (Winter 1995), pp. 24–25.

In spite of the fact, p. 186. Burkett, *History of the 499th Bomb Group,* pp. 24–25.

Enemy fighters, flak, p. 186. Herbert, *Maximum Effort,* p. 76.

He never said, p. 187. Baumann, unpublished memoir, p. 389, CSWS.

She gave me, p. 187. Rothgeb, *New Guinea Skies,* pp. 169–71.

I had thirty-six, p. 188. Holleman interview, SCUTK.

He eventually recovered, p. 188. Bond, *Flying Tiger's Diary,* pp. 165–67.

After a short, p. 189. Monroe, self-published unit history, pp. 171–73, CSWS.

There was only, p. 189. James Barison, *Sortie* (Vol. XII, No. 2), pp. 12–13.

After two months, p. 190. Roger Sandstedt, *Ex-CBI Roundup* (November 1995), pp. 7–8.

They have my, p. 190. Reuben Martin to friend, 24 September 1944, Box 22, Folder 1900, WHMC.

For example, p. 190. Ellis, *Statistical Survey,* p. 254.

Have you any idea, p. 191. Holway, *Red Tails, Black Wings,* p. 198.

Show me the glory, p. 191. Hearty diary, pp. 11–12, Mighty Eighth.

We know what, p. 191. Blaine Briggs to parents, 30 July 1944, Box 4, Folder 324, WHMC.

Let's hope we can, p. 191. Nolan Ducote letter, WHMC.

However, this is, p. 192. Joe Stalder to sister, 22 November 1944, Box 34, Folder 2851, WHMC.

My heartfelt sympathy, p. 192. Nickell collection, SCUTK.

I truly believe, p. 193. Marshall collection, pp. 314, 25–26, SCUTK.

We watched closely, p. 193. Marshall and Thompson, *Final Assault,* p. 91.

Like a bird, Schuyler, p. 194. *Elusive Horizons,* p. 45.

I've never been, p. 194. Milton Many to family, 10 February 1945, Box 22, Folder 1872, WHMC.

I swore mightily, p. 194. John Abney, *Leatherneck: The Magazine of the Marines* (September 1945), pp. 42–43.

Enemy 20mm rounds, p. 195. Lande, *From Somewhere in England,* p. 37.

It was the face, p. 195. Brown, *Mighty Men of the 381st,* pp. 152–53.

I was stunned, p. 195. McCarthy, *Fear No More,* p. 27.

We stood dumb, p. 196. Perkins, unpublished memoir, pp. 10–11, SCUTK.

It was a terrible day, p. 196. Aanenson, unpublished memoir, p. 6, Mighty Eighth.

Experience has shown, p. 197. Charles Sewell collection, MS1892, Box 11, Folder 3, SCUTK.

The absence of remains, p. 198. Crowe, unpublished memoir, p. 18, SCUTK.

Since then, p. 198. Francis, *Tuskegee Airmen,* p. 124.

T and Joe and I, p. 198. Hynes, *Flights of Passage,* p. 206.

We knew our buddies, p. 199. Novey, *Cold Blue Sky,* p. 67.

Ready for the next crew, p. 199. Crosby, *Wing and a Prayer,* p. 141.

More than 40,000, p. 199. Ellis, *Statistical Survey,* p. 254.

My flight coveralls, p. 199. Kenneth Williams, unpublished memoir, p. 2, RG 403, Box 51, Folder 1, Mighty Eighth.

It isn't noisy, p. 200. Ethell, *Bomber Command,* pp. 105–6.

Within a few, p. 200. Barwick Barfield, unpublished memoir, pp. 9–10, MS2012, Box 1, Folder 22, SCUTK.

It made me, p. 200. Milton Abernathy, unpublished memoir, p. 8, RG 403, Box 50, Folder 1, Mighty Eighth.

The Arabs had, p. 201. Kreglogh et al., self-published unit history, p. 59, CSWS.

Clearly someone had, p. 202. John Moulton, unpublished memoir, pp. 4–8, MS1314, Box 3, Folder 2, SCUTK.

I was rewarded, p. 202. "The Gentlemen from Hell," unpublished memoir compendium, p. 9, RG 403, Box 9.5, Folder 2, Mighty Eighth.

About twenty minutes, p. 203. Wayne Livesay, *Ex-POW Bulletin* (November 1992), p. 16.

Each man performed, p. 204. Holway, *Red Tails, Black Wings,* pp. 256–57, 222.

However, a group, p. 204. Francis, *Tuskegee Airmen,* p. 288.

But the soldiers, p. 205. John Boisseau, *Ex-POW Bulletin* (October 1991), p. 23.

After that, p. 205. George Collar, unpublished memoir, pp. 24–26, RG 403, Box 9, Folder 6, Mighty Eighth.

At riflepoint, p. 205. Ferrell, interview with author, SCUTK.

The following day, p. 206. Leon Berkovsky, *Ex-POW Bulletin* (May 1996), pp. 26–27.

He even fed him, p. 207. Cubbins, *War of the Cottontails,* pp. 98–106.

My immediate thoughts, p. 207. George Fitzgibbon, *Memories* (October 1996), pp. 229–30.

A German dentist, p. 208. Haefs, unpublished memoir, pp. 38–39, CSWS.

Just thank God, p. 209. William Stafford, unpublished memoirs and POW letter, MS1881, Box 28, Folders 9, 11, SCUTK.

Real nice people, p. 209. Kreglogh et al., self-published unit history, p. 197, CSWS.

My plan, p. 210. Campbell, self-published memoir, p. 8, CSWS.

Suffice to say, p. 211. Milton Woodside, unpublished memoir, pp. 2, 3, 4, 5, 7, MS2012, Box 15, Folder 23, SCUTK.

They took pictures, p. 212. Lou Zamperini, *Ex-POW Bulletin* (January 1985), pp. 24–25.

In December of 1943, p. 212. Francis Sawyer, *Ex-POW Bulletin* (October 1982), p. 25.

Govednik endured weeks, p. 212. Martin Govednik, *Ex-CBI Roundup* (December 1994), pp. 24–26.

According to him, p. 213. Burkett, *History of the 499th Bomb Group,* p. 34.

Because of her, p. 213. Sakaida, *Pacific Air Combat,* p. 58.

What efforts, p. 215. Moriarity, self-published memoir, pp. 76, 115, 157, CSWS.

After saying 'so long,' p. 216. Howard Turlington, *Memories* (June 1997), pp. 115–18.

Within an hour, p. 217. Dick Arrowsmith, *1st Fighter News* (Spring 1995), pp. 3–4.

Kelley was debriefed p. 218. Bob Kelley, unpublished memoir, pp. 4–9, MS1892, Box 6, Folder 4, SCUTK.

They brought up wine, p. 218. Holway, *Red Tails, Black Wings,* pp. 219–20.

Finally, after about, p. 219. Richard Willis, *Sortie* (Vol. VIII, No. 2), p. 13.

I felt deeply, p. 219. Breast, *Missions Remembered,* pp. 12–15.

And we hugged, p. 220. Quilla Reed, interview with Mrs. Lin Folk, 23 January and 13 February 1993, transcript, pp. 6, 7, 10, 11, 13, MS1892, Box 7, Folder 20, SCUTK.

This was my Christmas, p. 221. Hohn, unpublished memoir compendium, Mighty Eighth.

In the village, p. 221. Wayne Adler, *Ex-CBI Roundup* (February 1986), pp. 6–7.

The four Kachins, p. 221. Otto Snapp, *Ex-CBI Roundup* (May 1995), pp. 20–21.

They treated us, p. 222. Rogers, ed., self-published unit history, pp. 124–29, CSWS.

They arranged, p. 222. William Martin, *Buzzard Brigade Bulletin* (December 1988), pp. 10–13.

They administered first aid, p. 223. Marshall and Thompson, *Final Assault,* pp. 80–82.

But they should, p. 223. Smith, *Screaming Eagle,* p. 137.

There was no heat, p. 224. R. J. Hammer, *Sortie* (Vol. VIII, No. 3), p. 15.

Other fellows, p. 224. Joseph Krajewski, *Memories* (April 1998), p. 79.

Like many Americans, p. 225. Virgil Broyhill, *Memories* (June 1998), p. 115.

I hitchhiked, p. 225. Crowe, unpublished unit history, p. 46, CSWS.

Combat is a fluid, p. 226. Fletcher, *Fletcher's Gang,* pp. 336, 479.

Since these gunners, p. 226. Miller, unpublished memoir, p. 72, CSWS.

After Snapp's crew, p. 226. Snapp, *Ex-CBI Roundup,* p. 21.

Moments later, p. 227. Harrison Thyng, *Memories* (August 1996), p. 184.

It seems the British, p. 227. Kreglogh et al., unit history, p. 72, CSWS.

If I had fired, p. 227. Aanenson, unpublished memoir, pp. 8–9, Mighty Eighth.

It wouldn't have, p. 228. Goebel, *Mustang Ace,* p. 149.

To say it was, p. 228. Fletcher, *Fletcher's Gang,* p. 462.

Here were twenty, p. 229. Ardery, *Bomber Pilot,* pp. 2–3.

They operated on him, p. 229. Ethell, *Bomber Command,* p. 156.

Most were crying, p. 229. Rosser, *No Hurrahs,* p. 90.

And—they deserved, p. 230. Brown, *Mighty Men of the 381st,* pp. 281–83, 376–77.

The other theaters, p. 231. Craven and Cate, *Army Air Forces in World War II,* Vol. VII, p. 404.

It grinds away, p. 231. Jones diary, p. 74, Mighty Eighth.

While he was gone, p. 231. Crosby, *Wing and a Prayer,* p. 140.

Upon reading, p. 232. Armstrong and Stone, *USA the Hard Way,* p. 93.

This poor soul, p. 232. Herbert, *Maximum Effort,* pp. 86–87.

George was, p. 233. Goebel, *Mustang Ace,* pp. 157–58.

The man was, p. 233. Wilburn, conversation with author.

'It took a lot . . . ,' p. 234. Bendiner, *Fall of Fortresses,* p. 114–15.

So I relented, p. 234. Zemke and Freeman, *Zemke's Wolfpack,* pp. 183–84.

I felt that the group, p. 235. Cubbins, *War of the Cottontails,* p. 68.

The real benefits, p. 235. Craven and Cate, *Army Air Forces in World War II,* Vol. VII, pp. 418–19.

The stronger their desire, p. 236. Lande, *From Somewhere in England,* p. 125.

A discouraged Sally, p. 236. Arthur Heiden, *The Fly Over* (Winter 1997–98), p. 10.

It was a 'rough' life, p. 236. William McSween to parents, 10 October 1943, Box 25, Folder 2153, WHMC.

This is about, p. 237. Lewis Smith to family, 25 January 1945, Box 33, Folder 2788, WHMC.

Served buffet style, p. 237. McCarthy, *Fear No More,* pp. 159–60.

After two fun-filled, p. 237. Cope, unpublished memoir, p. 6, SCUTK.

I unwound, p. 238. Marshall and Thompson, *Final Assault,* pp. 172–73.

Pine woods always, p. 238. Hynes, *Flights of Passage,* p. 232.

Chapter 7
The Jap is a foe, p. 241. Mrozek and Higham, *The Martin Marauder,* p. 353.

With a vengeance, p. 241. Rosser, *No Hurrahs,* p. 248.

The Japanese are, p. 242. Wilburn, conversation with author.

I've seen too many, p. 242. Smith, interview with author, SCUTK.

Very few people, p. 242. Breast, *Missions Remembered,* p. 88.

That bothers me, p. 242. Leutnner and Jensen, *High Honor,* p. 58.

I could not, p. 243. Bond, *Flying Tiger's Diary,* pp. 106, 88.

In a way, p. 243. Brand, *Fighter Squadron at Guadalcanal,* p. 174.

These 'fifties' leave, p. 243. John Filbrick to parents, 5 March 1944, Box 9, Folder 896, WHMC.

Where ground-combat troops, p. 243. McManus, *Deadly Brotherhood,* pp. 171–77.

And if anyone, p. 244. Bennett to friend, WHMC.

I find the Jap, p. 244. Dick Marshall to parents, 9 April 1943, Marshall collection, SCUTK.

You try to knock, p. 244. Shires, oral history, SCUTK.

You have to kill, p. 244. Sheafor letter, WHMC.

I never let one, p. 245. Holloway, *Air Force,* pp. 7–8.

Numerous times, p. 245. Breast, *Missions Remembered,* p. 5.

You ought to hear, p. 246. Clarkson letter, Mighty Eighth.

After 'Bombs away,' p. 246. Richard Baynes, unpublished memoir, p. 60, RG 403, Box 9.2, Folder 4, Mighty Eighth.

Throwing rocks was, p. 247. Perkins, unpublished memoir and diary, p. 53, SCUTK.

When I salvoed, p. 247. Crosby, *Wing and a Prayer,* p. 309.

The majority, p. 247. Hohn, unpublished memoir compendium, p. 10, Mighty Eighth.

By December of 1944, p. 248. Marshall, letters to family, 10 September 1944, 12 October 1944, 26 November 1944, 9 December 1944, Marshall collection, SCUTK.

But as we saw it, p. 248. Zemke and Freeman, *Zemke's Wolfpack,* p. 130.

I had difficulty, p. 249. Lande, *From Somewhere in England,* p. 90.

I felt no hatred, p. 249. Benham, unpublished memoir, p. 37, Mighty Eighth.

In the article, p. 249. Editors, *Reporting World War II: Part One* (New York: Library of America, 1995), p. 627.

This is not to say, p. 249. Wells, unpublished memoir, p. 13, Mighty Eighth.

The Japanese were the ones, p. 250. Ryerson, interview with author, SCUTK.

But they had guns, p. 250. Kreglogh et al., unpublished unit history, p. 178.

One must admire, p. 250. Brown, *Mighty Men of the 381st,* pp. 536–37.

They risked all, p. 251. McCarthy, *Fear No More,* p. 43.

The pilots, p. 251. Winchell, interview with Griffith, transcript, p. 5, SCUTK.

All of a sudden, p. 251. Moriarity, self-published memoir, pp. 48–49, CSWS.

Their best were . . . superior, p. 252. Lande, *From Somewhere in England,* p. 49.

They were never, p. 252. Boyd, interview with author, SCUTK.

They were sitting ducks, p. 252. Holway, *Red Tails, Black Wings,* p. 112.

This was in marked contrast, p. 252. Zemke and Freeman, *Zemke's Wolfpack,* p. 188.

If there was disputed, p. 253. Leutnner and Jensen, *High Honor,* p. 236.

That sort of thing, p. 254. Brand, *Fighter Squadron at Guadalcanal,* p. 170.

I hope the P-51s, p. 254. Charles Olson diary, 14 May 1944, RG 403, Box 9.4, Folder 3, Mighty Eighth.

I don't think, p. 254. Goebel, *Mustang Ace,* p. 137.

It was a humane thing, p. 255. Peg Magness, *Sortie* (Vol. XI, No. 2), p. 11.

I had never seen, p. 255. Goebel, *Mustang Ace,* p. 188.

But I never felt, p. 256. Aanenson, unpublished memoir, pp. 5, 14, 9, Mighty Eighth.

I thought about him, p. 256. Lande, *From Somewhere in England,* p. 169.

And you wonder, p. 257. Holway, *Red Tails, Black Wings,* p. 237.

We were both, p. 257. Campbell, unpublished memoir, p. 36, SCUTK.

The why of the last two, p. 257. Perkins, unpublished memoir, pp. 93, 134, SCUTK.

It's foolish to ask, p. 258. Brand, *Fighter Squadron at Guadalcanal,* p. 73.

Today I had succeeded, p. 258. Gabreski, *Fighter Pilot's Life,* p. 113.

Williams, however, p. 260. Williams, unpublished memoir, pp. 1–12, Mighty Eighth.

I would have been, p. 261. Leutnner and Jensen, *High Honor,* p. 187.

But it was, p. 261. Lande, *From Somewhere in England,* p. 150.

If I visualized, p. 261. Baumann, unpublished memoir, p. 325, CSWS.

The bombardier replied, p. 262. Fletcher, *Fletcher's Gang,* p. 339.

Not when one thinks, p. 262. Editors, *Reporting World War II: Part Two* (New York: Library of America, 1995), p. 769.

May the future, p. 262. Miller Anderson to parents, 2 September 1945, Box 1, Folder 59, WHMC.

I pray for the ending, p. 262. Fisher letter, WHMC.

My part carried, p. 263. Schuyler, *Elusive Horizons,* p. 61.

We may try, p. 263. Lynch, unpublished memoir, p. 45, Mighty Eighth.

Dresden was known, p. 263. Mission compendium, RG 403, Box 48, Folder 2, Mighty Eighth.

I have to live, p. 263. John White, interview with Winfried Moncrief, 28 March 1996, SCUTK.

So after 40 years, p. 264. George McGovern, *Toretta Flyer* (Winter 1989–90), p. 22.

I would much rather, p. 264. Ken Tichener to parents, 25 March 1945, Box 35, Folder 3007, WHMC.

With that rationale, p. 265. Cubbins, *War of the Cottontails,* p. 69.

Our radio operator, p. 265. Dan James, interview with Dr. Charles W. Johnson, 2 December 1987, MS1427, Box 4, Folder 3, SCUTK.

And I am all, p. 265. "Bill" to parents, 27 May 1945, Box 39, Folder 3335, WHMC.

If I had known, p. 266. Novey, *Cold Blue Sky,* pp. 48, 109.

For many of us, p. 267. Bendiner, *Fall of Fortresses,* pp. 154–55, 238.

Chapter 8

In fact, they were, p. 268. James McPherson, *Battle Cry of Freedom: The Civil War Era* (New York: Ballantine Books, 1988), p. 330.

Rated pilots, p. 270. Herbert, *Maximum Effort,* pp. 84–85.

Only 16 percent, p. 270. Stouffer, *Combat and Its Aftermath,* pp. 348–50.

His skill, p. 271. Novey, *Cold Blue Sky,* p. 55.

He was a task maker, p. 271. Claude Basler, *Briefing* (Summer 1995), p. 22.

When I think of Link, p. 271. Perkins, unpublished memoir, p. 167, SCUTK.

He was an excellent, p. 272. Fesmire, *Flight of a Maverick,* p. 77.

Years later, p. 272. Abe Wilen, *Ex-POW Bulletin* (March 1996), pp. 31–32.

The longer I live, p. 273. Fletcher, *Fletcher's Gang,* p. 503.

He had been, p. 273. Baumann, unpublished memoir, pp. 367–68, CSWS.

He was my flight, p. 274. Nickell to family, 9 March 1945; G. W. Greever to Nickell family, 25 June 1945, Nickell collection, SCUTK.

We tried to give, p. 274. Goebel, *Mustang Ace,* p. 158.

We always made, p. 275. Harris, unpublished memoir, pp. 14–15, SCUTK.

How fortunate, p. 275. Brown, *Mighty Men of the 381st,* p. 95.

When he was introduced, p. 276. Goebel, *Mustang Ace,* pp. 156–57.

I gave an exaggerated, p. 277. Rosser, *No Hurrahs,* pp. 216, 248, 251, 259.

He is full of life, p. 278. Bernstein letter, WHMC.

His opinion meant, p. 278. Brand, *Fighter Squadron at Guadalcanal,* pp. 111, 148.

Your flying, p. 279. Leutnner and Jensen, *High Honor,* p. 54.

None of us, p. 279. Breast, *Missions Remembered,* p. 38.

These two intrepid, p. 280. DeWayne Bennett, *Memories* (June 1998), p. 119.

For the lives, p. 281. Crosby, *Wing and a Prayer,* pp. 205, 209–10.

Under the pressure, p. 281. Ardery, *Bomber Pilot,* p. 191.

He's the commanding, p. 282. Novey, *Cold Blue Sky,* pp. 116–17.

Looks as though, p. 282. Marshall to family, 11 June 1944 and 9 February 1945, SCUTK.

We tried our best, p. 283. Zemke and Freeman, *Zemke's Wolfpack,* pp. 76–77, 200–201.

There was not much, pp. 283–284. Ethell, *Bomber Command,* p. 83.

My crew members, p. 284. Campbell, self-published memoir, p. 94, CSWS.

Finally Chuck saw, p. 284. Askerman, unpublished memoir, pp. 1, 106–7, SCUTK.

The matter of rank, p. 285. Crowe, unpublished memoir, p. 55, SCUTK.

But after facing, p. 285. Novey, *Cold Blue Sky,* pp. 86–87.

The CO . . . told him, p. 286. Lynch diary, Mighty Eighth.

I never stayed long, p. 287. Goebel, *Mustang Ace,* p. 104.

We never discussed, p. 287. Hynes, *Flights of Passage,* p. 176.

Another colonel turned, p. 288. Herbert, *Maximum Effort,* pp. 87–88.

In London there were, p. 288. Crosby, *Wing and a Prayer,* p. 261.

So, we started, p. 288. Askerman, unpublished memoir, p. 119, SCUTK.

They soon learned, p. 288. Tays, unpublished memoir, p. 36, Mighty Eighth.

Although this sounded, p. 289. Goebel, *Mustang Ace,* pp. 106–7.

Later, when married, p. 289. Crosby, *Wing and a Prayer,* pp. 105–6.

It was funny, p. 289. Hynes, *Flights of Passage,* pp. 212–13.

I don't think, p. 290. White, interview with Moncrief, SCUTK.

The pilot was, p. 290. Leutnner and Jensen, *High Honor,* pp. 189, 191.

Our lives could, p. 291. Ray Hann diary, p. 5, RG 403, Box 9.3, Folder 6, Mighty Eighth.

Every combat man, p. 291. Boyd, interview with author, SCUTK.

My only acceptable, p. 291. Cubbins, *War of the Cottontails,* pp. 59–60.

This is a terrible, p. 292. Fletcher, *Fletcher's Gang,* p. 407.

They have to see, p. 292. Gabreski, *Fighter Pilot's Life,* p. 250.

Signs of nervousness, p. 292. Ardery, *Bomber Pilot,* p. 137.

Eventually Smith became, p. 294. Smith, *Screaming Eagle,* pp. 95–96, 127.

Human nature being, p. 294. Zemke and Freeman, *Zemke's Wolf-pack,* p. 49.

Chapter 9

The vast majority, p. 295. Stouffer, *Combat and Its Aftermath,* pp. 333–34. Among medium-bomber crewmen, 79 percent answered yes; among light-bomber crewmen, it was 82 percent.

Discovering, remembering, p. 296. Lamb, unpublished memoir, p. 1, Mighty Eighth.

You laugh at things, p. 296. Lande, *From Somewhere in England,* p. 117.

Humor in an operational, p. 296. Goebel, *Mustang Ace,* p. 161.

My reaction was, p. 297. Frank Finklang, *Sortie* (Vol. X, No. 2), p. 12.

Castle laconically, p. 297. Marshall and Thompson, *Final Assault,* pp. 137–38.

As for Moose, p. 297. W. H. Nold, *Sortie* (Vol. V, No. 2), p. 14.

We had to put, p. 298. Beswick, unpublished memoir, p. 6, SCUTK.

Nuzzling into my, p. 298. Perkins, unpublished memoir, p. 112, SCUTK.

I guess compared, p. 298. Novey, *Cold Blue Sky,* p. 79.

The dog seemed to be, p. 298. Larry McManus, *Yank* (18 February 1944), p. 1.

I often wonder, p. 299. Campbell, unpublished memoir, p. 45, SCUTK.

We were overjoyed, p. 299. Stevens, unpublished memoir, p. 280, CSWS.

I was given credit, p. 300. Cope, unpublished memoir, p. 6, SCUTK.

I had 52 missions, p. 300. David Hayward, *Ex-CBI Roundup* (February 1989), p. 11.

Many never flew, p. 301. Craven and Cate, *Army Air Forces in World War II,* Vol. VII, p. 421–22.

At the same time, p. 301. Stouffer, *Combat and Its Aftermath,* pp. 385–87, 407.

The last 10, p. 302. Lamb, unpublished memoir, pp. 48–49, Mighty Eighth.

The crew that sleeps, p. 302. Anonymous letter, 8 January 1944, Box 36, Folders 3129–30, WHMC.

Doubt of returning, p. 302. McCarthy, *Fear No More,* pp. 202, 211.

That was the case, p. 302. Ryerson, interview with author, SCUTK.

On what would have been, p. 303. Reed, interview with Mrs. Lin Folk, SCUTK.

The newer crews, p. 303. Benham, unpublished memoir, p. 50a, Mighty Eighth.

But this was not, p. 303. Herbert, *Maximum Effort,* p. 60.

I recall babbling, p. 304. William Shelley, *Ex-CBI Roundup* (May 1986), p. 23.

We were three, p. 304. Rothgeb, *New Guinea Skies,* p. 251.

I feel very fortunate, p. 304. Omar Ash to family, 8 April 1945, MS1314, Box 1, Folder 4, SCUTK.

I was snapped, p. 304. Maurice Fitzgibbons to parents, 6 December 1943, Box 9, Folder 916, WHMC.

I ran out, p. 305. Novey, *Cold Blue Sky,* pp. 143–44.

I recall the number, p. 305. Berndt, unpublished diary, p. 43, Mighty Eighth.

Our tour completed, p. 305. Ethell, *Bomber Command,* pp. 129–30.

Big Don, p. 306. Lynch, unpublished memoir, pp. 133–34, Mighty Eighth.

The example you have set, p. 306. Bill Hefley papers, MS1892, Box 3, Folder 18, SCUTK.

To this day, p. 307. Fletcher, *Fletcher's Gang,* pp. 481–83.

These were very heavy, p. 307. McCarthy, *Fear No More,* p. 32.

And no one, p. 308. Dick Marshall to sister, ca. 1943, Marshall collection, SCUTK.

They love living, p. 308. Brown, *Mighty Men of the 381st,* pp. 161–62.

I never tried, p. 309. Editors, *Reporting World War II, Part Two,* p. 484.

If I happen, p. 309. Springer, letter to parents, WHMC.

I pray with all, p. 310. Kenneth Michel to parents, 27 May 1945, Box 23, Folder 1950, WHMC.

That passage means, p. 310. Harry Beightol to mother, 7 May 1944, Box 2, Folder 183, WHMC.

Because we go through, p. 310. William Harris diary, RG 403, Box 9.4, Folder 16, Mighty Eighth.

I felt quite certain, p. 311. Schlesinger, unpublished memoir, pp. 37–38, Mighty Eighth.

But let the other, p. 311. Hearty diary, Mighty Eighth.

Just face the fact, p. 311. Bryce Evertson to parents, 28 February 1944, Box 8, Folder 852, WHMC.

If God could make, p. 312. Herbert, *Maximum Effort,* pp. 44–45.

It is then, p. 312. Crowe, self-published unit history, p. 245, CSWS.

The pilot had done so, p. 313. *Yank* (10 March 1944).

Despite all this, p. 313. Schuyler, *Elusive Horizons,* p. 127.

There were no survivors, p. 313. McCarthy, *Fear No More,* pp. 145–46, 149.

I also had, p. 314. Miller, unpublished memoir, pp. 61–62, CSWS.

Finally, the man, p. 314. Hohn, memoir compendium, p. 2, Mighty Eighth.

The only time, p. 314. Breast, *Missions Remembered,* p. 132.

Crazy ideas all, p. 315. Aanenson, unpublished memoir, p. 5, Mighty Eighth.

If they had said, p. 315. Lande, *From Somewhere in England,* p. 31.

It was as if, p. 315. Leutnner and Jensen, *High Honor,* p. 187.

Livesay eventually, p. 315. Livesay, *Ex-POW Bulletin* (November 1992), p. 16.

Being practical, p. 316. Rosser, *No Hurrahs,* p. 205.

Not fatalistic, p. 316. Perkins, unpublished memoir, p. 180, SCUTK.

But I wasn't, p. 316. Lande, *From Somewhere in England,* pp. 136, 141.

I'm not a 'Hot pilot,' p. 316. Watson, letter to mother, WHMC.

If the above happened, p. 317. John Charlton, unpublished memoir, p. 12, CSWS.

They tried to cover, p. 317. Ryerson, interview with author, SCUTK.

I've never come, p. 318. Jackson Futch to family, 19 August 1943, Box 10, Folder 979, WHMC.

When it was more, p. 318. Bendiner, *Fall of Fortresses,* p. 116.

It was the inexorable, p. 318. David Lustig, *Memories* (January 1998), p. 10.

The only one, p. 319. Ethell, *Bomber Command,* p. 115.

I wasn't a hero, p. 319. Holway, *Red Tails, Black Wings,* p. 86.

Therefore I consider, p. 319. Miller, unpublished memoir, p. 68, CSWS.

It was during, pp. 319–320. Baumann, unpublished memoir, p. 322, CSWS.

You were not normal, p. 320. Armstrong and Stone, *USA the Hard Way,* p. 48.

Anybody that said, p. 320. Beswick, unpublished memoir, p. 13, SCUTK.

A hunk of flak, p. 320. Barison, *Sortie* (Vol. XII, No. 2), p. 11.

I would shut, p. 321. Ardery, *Bomber Pilot,* p. 90.

There was complete, p. 321. Jones diary, Mighty Eighth.

It all takes place, p. 321. Lynch diary, Mighty Eighth.

By the time I land, p. 321. Charles Nickell to sister, 12 November 1944, Nickell collection, SCUTK.

It seems as if, p. 322. Fred Price, unpublished memoir, p. 28, RG 403, Box 9.5, Folder 7, Mighty Eighth.

You're scared, p. 322. Shires oral history, SCUTK.

The weariness, p. 322. Jones diary, Mighty Eighth.

Something wrenched, p. 322. Schuyler, *Elusive Horizons,* p. 88.

The strain was too much, p. 323. Brown, *Mighty Men of the 381st,* p. 330.

You revive yourself, p. 323. Marshall and Thompson, *Final Assault,* pp. 158–59.

I smelled so much, p. 323. Crosby, *Wing and a Prayer,* p. 256.

His wisdom shocked, p. 324. Tays, unpublished memoir, p. 44, Mighty Eighth.

It wore on their nerves, p. 324. Ardery, *Bomber Pilot,* p. 166.

There is an unspoken, p. 324. Jones diary, Mighty Eighth.

By the time, p. 325. Lande, *From Somewhere in England,* pp. 63, 130.

He had completed, p. 325. Marshall and Thompson, *Final Assault,* pp. 69–70.

Like many who suffered, p. 325. Rosser, *No Hurrahs,* pp. 250–54.

I . . .maintain, p. 326. Warren Johnson, *The Fly Over* (Fall 1991), p. 4.

They were coming down, p. 326. Leutnner and Jensen, *High Honor,* p. 193.

A greater . . . miracle, p. 327. Basler, *Briefing* (Summer 1995), p. 23.

If it was possible, Holway, *Red Tails, Black Wings,* pp. 252–54.

They'll call up, p. 327. Reid Sprague to wife, 3 April 1945, RG 403, Box 9.4, Folder 9, Mighty Eighth.

We thought of them, p. 328. Tays, unpublished memoir, p. 52, Mighty Eighth.

They warm my heart, p. 328. Marshall to mother, 4 January 1945, Marshall collection, SCUTK.

Our life is practically, p. 328. Bagley letter, WHMC.

At least, this morning, p. 328. Perkins, unpublished memoir, p. 121, SCUTK.

God bless, p. 329. Lynch diary, Mighty Eighth.

He spent hours, p. 330. Thyng, *Memories* (August 1996), pp. 183–84.

There were no, p. 330. Goebel, *Mustang Ace,* p. 104.

They would . . . make sure, p. 330. Gabreski, *Fighter Pilot's Life,* p. 100.

Moreover, our lives, p. 330. Baumann, unpublished memoir, p. 319, CSWS.

They were loyal, p. 331. Campbell, unpublished memoir, p. 15, SCUTK.

They were our, p. 331. Lande, *From Somewhere in England,* p. 61.

The maintenance, p. 331. Hayward, *Ex-CBI Roundup* (January 1989), p. 11.

They have never, p. 331. Marshall, unpublished memoir, pp. 28, 22, Mighty Eighth.

Seldom praised, p. 332. Cubbins, *War of the Cottontails,* pp. 34–35.

Yet when the airplanes, p. 332. Ray Zuker, *The Fly Over* (Summer 1997), p. 6.

But we neutralized, p. 333. Holway, *Red Tails, Black Wings,* p. 315.

I think it's pretty, p. 333. Marshall collection, SCUTK.

How about that?, p. 334. Clarkson letter, Mighty Eighth.

Their pilots were, p. 334. Baumann, unpublished memoir, p. 340, CSWS.

They were damned glad, p. 336. Holway, *Red Tails, Black Wings,* pp. 99–100, 151–52, 251–53.

This was a small, p. 337. Drinnon, unpublished memoir, p. 1, SCUTK.

It helped to make, p. 337. Leutnner and Jensen, *High Honor,* pp. 246–47.

The privileges of America, p. 337. Francis, *Tuskegee Airmen,* p. 74.

Chapter 10

In the same, p. 338. Stouffer, *Combat and Its Aftermath,* p. 407.

We were innocent, p. 339. Brown, *Mighty Men of the 381st,* p. 239.

They were ignored, p. 340. Goebel, *Mustang Ace,* pp. 155, 201.

They accepted, p. 340. Campbell, unpublished memoir, pp. 33, 47, SCUTK.

It was an emotional, p. 341. Aanenson, unpublished memoir, p. 12, Mighty Eighth.

It would be too painful, p. 341. Novey, *Cold Blue Sky,* pp. 39, 67.

It would take time, p. 342. Moriarity, self-published memoir, p. 32, CSWS.

I think most of us, p. 342. Charlton, unpublished memoir, p. 3, CSWS.

Most of their things, p. 342. Lamb, unpublished memoir, p. 31, Mighty Eighth.

The older crews, p. 343. Rogers, ed., self-published unit history, p. 101, CSWS.

In spirit they were, p. 343. Rothgeb, *New Guinea Skies,* p. 136.

Nonetheless, it wouldn't, p. 343. Baumann, unpublished memoir, p. 283, CSWS.

Campbell would suddenly, p. 344. Holway, *Red Tails, Black Wings,* p. 207.

I had survived, p. 344. Goebel, *Mustang Ace,* p. 212.

They showed little, p. 344. Bunch, unpublished memoir, p. 55, SCUTK.

We, the replacements, p. 344. McCarthy, *Fear No More,* pp. 16–17.

It was as if, p. 345. Perkins, unpublished memoir, p. 84, SCUTK.

I had been voted in, p. 345. Schuyler, *Elusive Horizons,* p. 39.

If new men, p. 345. Ardery, *Bomber Pilot,* p. 154.

I thought to myself, p. 346. Willie Green diary, p. 3, SCUTK.

One cannot fully, p. 346. Paul Homan, unpublished memoir, p. 12, Box 9.5, Folder 8, Mighty Eighth.

Only 1 of 4 would survive, p. 346. Cope, unpublished memoir, p. 19, SCUTK.

Common knowledge had it, p. 347. Fletcher, *Fletcher's Gang,* p. 12.

One evening, p. 347. Berndt, unpublished diary, p. 72, Mighty Eighth.

Either the old, p. 347. Schuyler, *Elusive Horizons,* p. 13.

Front-line units, p. 347. Goebel, *Mustang Ace,* p. 62.

I used up, p. 348. Boyd, interview with author, SCUTK.

To hazard, p. 349. Zemke and Freeman, *Zemke's Wolfpack,* pp. 170–71.

But all of us, p. 349. Goebel, *Mustang Ace,* p. 142.

He spun right, p. 350. Rosser, *No Hurrahs,* pp. 178–79.

When new pilots, p. 350. Gabreski, *Fighter Pilot's Life,* p. 117.

As angry at him, p. 350. Novey, *Cold Blue Sky,* p. 90.

If you can't fly, p. 351. Reed, interview with Mrs. Lin Folk, transcript, p. 2, SCUTK.

I was shocked, p. 351. Herbert, *Maximum Effort,* p. 62.

This bunch is, p. 352. Marshall to parents, 11 February 1945, Marshall collection, SCUTK.

Chapter 11

In most cases, p. 354. Stouffer, *Combat and Its Aftermath,* pp. 348–50.

All the men, p. 354. Barfield, unpublished memoir, p. 4, SCUTK.

We worked, played, p. 354. McCarthy, *Fear No More,* p. 88.

No one wanted, p. 354. Moriarity, self-published memoir, p. 34, CSWS.

One of those things, p. 354. Lamb, unpublished memoir, p. 51, Mighty Eighth.

This acceptance, p. 355. Herbert, *Maximum Effort,* pp. 42–43.

Our crew worked, p. 355. Novey, *Cold Blue Sky,* p. 55.

The fear of failing, p. 355. Herbert, *Maximum Effort,* p. 84.

That's the . . . way, p. 356. Baumann, unpublished memoir, p. 347, CSWS.

But more important, p. 356. Kreglogh et al., self-published unit history, p. 128, CSWS.

You get to lean, p. 356. Wilburn, conversation with author.

I mean, that's why, p. 356. Winchell, interview with Dr. Charles Griffith, transcript, p. 4, SCUTK.

You feel like, p. 356. Ducote letter, WHMC.

I think we all, p. 357. Baynes, unpublished memoir, p. 39, Mighty Eighth.

That is the moment, p. 357. Drinnon, unpublished memoir, p. 16, SCUTK.

For many, p. 357. Cubbins, *War of the Cottontails,* pp. xi–xii.

That's the way, p. 358. Crowe, unpublished memoir, p. 53, SCUTK.

Genuine camaraderie, p. 358. Lande, *From Somewhere in England,* p. 169.

What I most feared, p. 358. Goebel, *Mustang Ace,* p. 214.

We have been bonded, p. 359. Rogers, ed., self-published unit history, p. 161, CSWS.

A finer bunch, p. 359. Fletcher, *Fletcher's Gang,* p. 489.

If one of us, p. 359. Lande, *From Somewhere in England,* p. 60.

The flight crews, p. 359. Ethell, *Bomber Command,* p. 85.

As soon as, p. 360. Zuker, self-published memoir, p. 18, CSWS.

We wept together, p. 360. Brown, *Mighty Men of the 381st,* p. 221.

We each had, p. 360. Holway, *Red Tails, Black Wings,* p. 209.

We were both, p. 360. Brand, *Fighter Squadron at Guadalcanal,* p. 159.

Arm in arm, p. 361. Rosser, *No Hurrahs,* p. 223.

Mutual trust, respect, p. 361. Thyng, *Memories* (August 1996), pp. 184–85.

The same was true, p. 361. Lande, *From Somewhere in England,* p. 14.

It's just a good time, p. 362. Perkins, unpublished memoir, p. 70, SCUTK.

With thanks in our hearts, p. 362. McCarthy, *Fear No More,* p. 93.

Buddies!, p. 362. Ross, unpublished memoir, p. 22, SCUTK.

This was typical, p. 363. Asbury, *Sortie* (Vol. XI, No. 2), p. 10.

The empty beds, p. 363. Robert Vandegriff diary, RG 403, Box 9.3, Folder 3, Mighty Eighth.

And I just can't, p. 363. Lande, *From Somewhere in England,* p. 15.

I found myself, p. 363. Crosby, *Wing and a Prayer,* p. 174.

Johnny Bathurst and I, p. 364. Aanenson, unpublished memoir, p. 12, Mighty Eighth.

I still do, p. 364. *Doing Our Job,* p. 199.

It's so hard, p. 365. Perkins, unpublished memoir, pp. 77–78, 81, 89, 91, 107, SCUTK.

I know how, p. 365. Many letter, WHMC.

But what is strongest, p. 366. Lowell Smestad, *Briefing* (Spring 1991), p. 9.

I owe a great deal, p. 366. Schlesinger, unpublished memoir, p. 48, Mighty Eighth.

I love and respect, p. 366. McCarthy, *Fear No More,* p. xiii.

You're a very important, p. 366. PBS documentary, *A B-24 Crew,* 1994.

No stakes in teamwork, p. 367. Crowe, self-published unit history, p. 245, CSWS.

Epilogue

Then silence, p. 368. Perkins, unpublished memoir, p. 189, SCUTK.

No more long, p. 368. William Luther to grandmother, 23 August 1945, Box 21, Folder 1828, WHMC.

I've gambled my life, p. 369. Aanenson, unpublished memoir, p. 16, Mighty Eighth.

Yes, we have, p. 369. Many letter, WHMC.

I will never, p. 369. Beswick, unpublished memoir, p. 8, SCUTK.

Life in America, p. 369. Novey, *Cold Blue Sky,* p. 158.

Or like the morning, p. 370. Hynes, *Flights of Passage,* p. 266.

Do what you, p. 370. Editors, *Reporting World War II: Part Two,* p. 488.

I felt as if, p. 370. Leutnner and Jensen, *High Honor,* p. 47.

Does a fish, p. 371. Baumann, unpublished memoir, p. 419, CSWS.

A yell, a car backfire, p. 371. Rosser, *No Hurrahs,* p. 260.

I felt restless, p. 371. Aanenson, unpublished memoir, p. 18, Mighty Eighth.

That kept up for, p. 371. Ryerson, interview with author, SCUTK.

We didn't have, p. 373. Holway, *Red Tails, Black Wings,* pp. 272, 277–79.

Today they are, p. 373. Leutnner and Jensen, *High Honor,* p. 187.

Nearly half, p. 374. Lande, *From Somewhere in England,* p. 169.

To survive that, p. 374. Talley, interview with Dr. Charles Johnson, SCUTK.

I'm not a sentimental, p. 374. Holway, *Red Tails, Black Wings,* p. 314.

It gave me, p. 374. Wilburn, conversation with author.

Those who like, p. 375. George Russell, *Briefing* (Spring 1984), p. 5.

But we want, p. 375. Ilfrey, *From Somewhere in England,* p. 170.

The memories inspired, p. 375. Novey, *Cold Blue Sky,* p. 171.

'It was easy . . . ,' p. 376. Jones, unpublished memoir, p. 131, Mighty Eighth.

I can also feel, p. 376. Crowe, self-published unit history, p. 245, CSWS.

That made me feel, p. 376. Ryerson, interview with author, SCUTK.

I would awaken, p. 376. Rogers, ed., self-published unit history, p. 162, CSWS.

It doesn't matter, p. 377. Binnebose, unpublished memoir, p. 14, Mighty Eighth.

I wonder what poets, p. 377. Crosby, *Wing and a Prayer,* pp. 326, 328.

I will always, p. 377. Aanenson, unpublished memoir, p. 19, Mighty Eighth.

Perhaps it will be, p. 378. Zuker, *The Fly Over* (Christmas 1994), p. 7.

What contribution, p. 378. Herbert, *Maximum Effort,* p. 78.

I don't know, p. 378. *Briefing* (Spring 1997), p. 24.

I will say this, p. 378. Fesmire, *Flight of a Maverick,* p. 127.

We have . . . raised, p. 379. Lynch, unpublished memoir, p. 136, Mighty Eighth.

We all grieved, p. 379. Bob Geraghty, *Ex-POW Bulletin* (December 1994), p. 17.

Selected Bibliography

Ardery, Philip. *Bomber Pilot.* Lexington: University of Kentucky Press, 1978.

Armstrong, Roger, and Stone, Ken, eds. *USA the Hard Way.* Orange County, CA: Quail House Publishing, 1997.

Astor, Gerald. *The Mighty Eighth: The Air War in Europe as Told by the Men Who Fought It.* New York: Dell Publishing, 1997.

Bendiner, Elmer. *The Fall of Fortresses.* New York: Putnam, 1980.

Birdsall, Steve. *Saga of the Superfortress: The Dramatic Story of the B-29 and the Twentieth Air Force.* Garden City, NY: Doubleday, 1980.

Blum, John Morton. *V Was for Victory: Politics and American Culture in World War II.* New York: Harcourt Brace Jovanovich, 1976.

Bond, Charles. *A Flying Tiger's Diary.* College Station, TX: Texas A & M University Press, 1984.

Brand, Max. *Fighter Squadron at Guadalcanal.* Annapolis: Naval Institute Press, 1996.

Breast, John, ed. *Missions Remembered: Recollections of the World War II Air War.* Brentwood, TN: J. M. Productions, 1995.

Brown, James Good. *The Mighty Men of the 381st, Heroes All.* Salt Lake City: Publishers Press, 1994.

Burkett, Prentiss. *The Unofficial History of the 499th Bomb Group.* Temple, CA: Historical Aviation Album Publication, 1981.

Chant, Chris. *World War II Aircraft: The Allies.* London: Marshall Cavendish, 1979.

Childers, Thomas. *Wings of Morning: The Story of the Last American Bomber Shot Down Over Germany in World War II.* New York: Addison Wesley, 1995.

Colgan, Bill. *Fighter-Bomber Pilot.* Blue Ridge Summit, PA: Tab Books, 1985.

Comer, John. *Combat Crew.* New York: William Morrow, 1988.

Craven, Wesley, and Cate, James, eds. *The Army Air Forces in World War II: Men and Planes. Vol. VI.* Washington, DC: Office of Air Force History, 1983.

———. *The Army Air Forces in World War II: Services Around the World.* *Vol. VII.* Washington, DC: Office of Air Force History, 1983.

Crosby, Harry. *A Wing and a Prayer.* New York: HarperCollins, 1993.

Cubbins, William. *The War of the Cottontails.* Chapel Hill, NC: Al gonquin Books of Chapel Hill, 1989.

Dear, I. C. B., and Foot, M. R. D., eds. *The Oxford Companion to World War II.* Oxford: Oxford University Press, 1995.

Dower, John. *War Without Mercy.* New York: Pantheon Books, 1986.

Editors. *Reporting World War II: Part One.* New York: Library of America, 1995.

———. *Reporting World War II: Part Two.* New York: Library of America, 1995.

Ellis, John. *World War II: A Statistical Survey.* London: Facts on File, 1993.

Ethell, Jeffrey. *Bomber Command.* Osceola, WI: Motorbooks International, 1994.

Fesmire, Robert. *Flight of a Maverick.* Nashville: Eggman Publishers, 1995.

Fletcher, Eugene. *Fletcher's Gang: A B-17 Crew in Europe, 1944–45.* Seattle: University of Washington Press, 1988.

Francis, Charles. *The Tuskegee Airmen.* Boston: Brandon Publishing Company, 1993.

Freeman, Roger. *The Mighty Eighth.* London: MacDonald & Co., 1970.

———. *Mighty Eighth War Diary.* New York: Jane's, 1981.

Gabreski, Francis. *Gabby: A Fighter Pilot's Life.* New York: Orion Books, 1991.

Goebel, Robert. *Mustang Ace.* Pacifica, CA: Pacifica Press, 1991.

Herbert, Kevin. *Maximum Effort: The B-29s Against Japan.* Manhattan, KS: Sunflower University Press, 1983.

Holway, John. *Red Tails, Black Wings: The Men of America's Black Air Force.* Las Cruces, NM: Yucca Tree Press, 1997.

Hynes, Samuel. *Flights of Passage.* Annapolis: Naval Institute Press, 1988.

Keegan, John. *The Second World War.* London: Hutchinson Publishers, 1989.

Kluger, Steve. *Yank, the Army Weekly.* New York: St. Martin's Press, 1991.

Lande, D. A. *From Somewhere in England.* Osceola, WI: Motorbooks International, 1990.

Leckie, Robert. *Delivered from Evil: The Saga of World War II.* New York: Harper & Row, 1987.

Leutnner, Stuart, and Jensen, Oliver. *High Honor: Recollections by Men and Women of World War II Aviation.* Washington, DC: Smithsonian Institution Press, 1989.

Marshall, Chester, and Thompson, Warren. *Final Assault on the Rising Sun: Combat Diaries of B-29 Crews over Japan.* Hong Kong: Specialty Press Publishers, 1995.

Maurer, Maurer, ed. *Air Force Combat Units of World War II.* Washington, DC: Office of Air Force History, 1983.

McCarthy, David. *Fear No More: A B-17 Navigator's Journey.* Pittsburgh: Cottage Wordsmiths, 1991.

McManus, John. *The Deadly Brotherhood: The American Combat Soldier in World War II.* Novato CA: Presidio Press, 1998.

McPherson, James. *Battle Cry of Freedom: The Civil War Era.* New York: Ballantine Books, 1988.

Mrozek, Donald, and Higham, Robin, eds. *The Martin Marauder and the Franklin Allens: A Wartime Love Story.* Manhattan, KS: Sunflower University Press, 1980.

Novey, Jack. *The Cold Blue Sky: A B-17 Gunner in World War II.* Charlottesville, VA: Howell Press, 1997.

Osur, Alan. *Blacks in the Army Air Forces in World War II.* Washington, DC: Office of Air Force History, 1977.

Overy, Richard. *Why the Allies Won.* New York: W.W. Norton, 1995.

Perret, Geoffrey. *Winged Victory: The Army Air Forces in World War II.* New York: Random House, 1993.

Polenberg, Richard. *War and Society.* New York: J.B. Lippincott Co., 1972.

Polmar, Norman, and Allen, Thomas. *World War II: America at War, 1941-1945.* New York: Random House, 1991.

Rosser, Harold. *No Hurrahs for Me.* Sevierville, TN: Covenant House Books, 1994.

Rothgeb, Wayne. *New Guinea Skies.* Ames, IA: Iowa State University Press, 1992.

Sakaida, Henry. *Pacific Air Combat in World War II: Voices from the Past.* St. Paul, MN: Phalanx Publishing Co., 1993.

Sandler, Stanley. *Segregated Skies.* Washington, DC: Smithsonian Institution Press, 1992.

Schaffer, Ronald. *Wings of Judgement: American Bombing in World War II.* Oxford: Oxford University Press, 1995.

Schuyler, Keith. *Elusive Horizons.* South Brunswick, NJ: A.S. Barnes, 1969.

Smith, Dale O. *Screaming Eagle.* Chapel Hill, NC: Algonquin Books of Chapel Hill, 1990.

Spector, Ronald. *Eagle Against the Sun.* New York: Vintage Books, 1985.

Stouffer, Samuel A. *The American Soldier, Studies in Social Psychology in World War II: Combat and Its Aftermath.* Vol. 2. New York: John Wiley & Sons, 1949.

Sweeting, C. Glen. *Combat Flying Clothing.* Washington, DC: Smithsonian Institution Press, 1984.

———. *Combat Flying Equipment.* Washington, DC: Smithsonian Institution Press, 1989.

Weinberg, Gerhard. *A World at Arms.* New York: Cambridge University Press, 1994.

Wells, Mark. *Courage and Air Warfare.* Portland, OR: Frank Cass, 1995.

Zemke, Hubert, and Freeman, Roger. *Zemke's Wolfpack.* New York: Orion Books, 1989.

Zuker, Ray. *Remember.* Johnson City, TN: Tennessee Valley Publishing, 1993.

Manuscript Collections

Columbia, MO. Western Historical Manuscript Collection, University of Missouri—Columbia, Collection Number 68, World War II Letters, Files 1–3466.

Knoxville, TN. University of Tennessee Special Collections Library, Collection Numbers 1230–2012, World War II Collection.

Knoxville, TN. Center for the Study of War and Society, University of Tennessee, World War II Files.

Montgomery, AL. Air Force Historical Research Archives, World War II collections.

Savannah, GA. The Mighty Eighth Air Force Heritage Museum Archives, Record Group 403, World War II memoirs, letters, diaries.

Index